LOST IN T

SYD BARRETT
AND THE PINK FLOYD

LOST IN THE WOODS

SYD BARRETT
AND THE PINK FLOYD

JULIAN PALACIOS

BOXTREE

First published in 1998 by Boxtree, an imprint of Macmillan Publishers Ltd, 25 Eccleston Place, London, SW1W 9NF and Basingstoke

Associated companies throuhout the world

ISBN 0 7522 2328 3

9 8 7 6 5 4 3 2 1

A CIP catalogue record for this book is available from the British Library

Cover photographs courtesy of Pictorial Press
All other photographs courtesy of Strange Things Archive
Designed by Nigel Davies
All lyrics reproduced by kind permission of Lupus Music

Typeset by SX Composing DTP, Rayleigh, Essex

Printed by Mackays of Chatham plc, Chatham, Kent

Contents

Acknowledgements

I would like to thank all the people whom I interviewed for their time, memories and insights. I found them all to be most intriguing, witty and wise. Miles, Hoppy, Duggie Fields, Dave Gale, Nigela and Jenny Gordon, Peter Wynne-Wilson, Pete Brown, Mike Leonard, Keith Rowe, Jenny Fabian, Peter Whitehead, Kevin Ayers, Seamus O'Connell, Jack Monck and Joe Boyd.

For tea, sympathy, conversation and encouragement in the darkest hours: Nigel Thompson (who took me to Cambridge for the first time), Michael Horovitz, Carolyne Pim, Michiko Hirohata, Molly McAdams, Lila McDonald, Nick and Andrew Beaumont, Sophia, Jason Creed, Gary, Simon Lamb, Emanuelle, Pete and Nadege, Riccardo Olocco, Maggie White, Bob and Mike Jacoby, Susan, Janos, Anja, Magdi, and Rob Peets. Thanks to everyone in Jakarta, Madrid, London, Paris, San Clemente, Boston and Austin whom I haven't mentioned and who helped me.

Many thanks to all at the National Sound Archives, and also to the Scott Frank for invaluable research materials and discussions. Thanks to Vernon Fitch of the Pink Floyd Archives, and to the many others who provided informaton and comments on the Echoes mailing list. Thanks to Andrew and all at Dillons for your courtesy and free Internet time. Thank you Sean at Helter Skelter. Many thanks to Meriel Talbot (where ever you are) for putting me in touch with the best agent in the world, Sarah Hanningan, and all at Darley Anderson. Thanks also to Jake for seeing merit in this work, and Jenny Olivier at Boxtree for your extreme patience and help. I am particularly indebted to Jonathan Green, author of the definitive history of the 1960s English Underground, *Days in the Life: Voices from the Underground, 1961-1971*. Green provided me with full access to his unedited interviews and unedited text, for which I am thankful. I urge you to buy the book, it truly altered the way I thought.

Thanks for my aunt Kasha Swiatkowski for sanctuary at the eleventh hour, and to my dear parents, Hugo and Barbara Palacios for complete support. I love you Rachel. And lest we forget, Roger Keith Barrett.

LOST IN THE WOODS

JULIAN PALACIOS

In 1997, several musicians contributed original artwork to the War Child relief organisation. Among them was Graham Coxon, guitarist of Blur, who made a polystyrene lightening bolt, measuring 96 x 36 cm, entitled 'Scream Thy Last Scream'. It was in tribute to a retired English musician once known as Syd Barrett. The yellow thunderbolt, emblazoned with the title of one of Barrett's most notorious (and still unreleased) songs, hurtles into the earth, an apt metaphor for Barrett himself.

In his very brief time as master musician of the sixties psychedelic Underground, Barrett lit up the entire sky with a tremendous roar of noise and a blinding flashing of light; anyone who saw that celestial flash would be hard pressed to forget it, even thirty years on. So unexpected were the sounds that sprang from his nimble mind, pen, mouth and Telecaster that it must have seemed like he did indeed come from the sky. Coxon attached a short poem:

SYD BARRETT.........Conjurer, Wizard
(non hippy)

Bigger than the space POP could ever
hope to offer.
Jailed within boundaries......districts
so silent.
A wall, save for eyes.
SYD, mummified within the realm of
POP, in which this elegy is entrapped.

A CALL TO CREATIVITY............
'SCREAM THY LAST SCREAM, MR.........

a) Sonic painter
b) Auto Soundsmith
c) Expressionable Non cynic
d) True Believer
E) Emotional innocent

WHO KNEW THE IMPORTANCE OF TANTRUM...................'

Stage One:
The River Bank (1946-1965)

'All movement is accomplished in six stages, and the seventh brings return.'

The I-Ching, or Book Of Changes

'"So beautiful and strange and new! Since it was to end all too soon, I almost wish I had never heard it. Nothing seems worthwhile but just to hear that sound once more and go on listening to forever. No! There it is again!" he cried, alert once more. Entranced, he was silent for a long space, spellbound.'

The Wind In The Willows, Kenneth Grahame

And so it must have been, turning the dials of a small radio set in the early days of 1967. The distant crackle of Radio Caroline, one of the pirate radio stations broadcasting from off the English shore, spilled forth an exotic, mysterious sound. 'Arnold Layne' by the Pink Floyd. Its author was Roger Keith Barrett, better known as Syd.

Who was Syd Barrett? Barrett himself said, 'I don't think I'm easy to talk about. I've got a very irregular head. And I'm not anything that you think I am anyway.'[1] Syd Barrett was the lead singer, songwriter and guitarist for the Pink Floyd during 1965-1968, which became London's premier Underground band. In a meteoric rise, Barrett became the figurehead of the nascent psychedelic Underground by the time he was twenty-one. Along with John Lennon, he created English psychedelic music, and defined its parameters.

The English version of psychedelia, as opposed to the strain found in San Francisco, was a melange of indigenous folk music, traces of 1930s dancehall and vestiges of the blues and R&B boom of the preceding years, informed by the anarchic wail of free jazz, plus a strong dose of the peculiarly English fantastical storytelling of Lewis Carroll's *Alice's Adventures In Wonderland*, Edward Lear, J.R.R. Tolkien's *The Hobbit* and Kenneth Grahame's *The Wind In The Willows*. No one captured the ethos of this mood better than Syd Barrett.

In all its various mutations over the years, many of the tributaries of psychedelia point back to the sylvan banks of the River Cam in Cambridge, where Syd as a teenager first began channelling the alternately discordant and peaceful Spirit of Nature into music, playing his songs for his friends on idyllic spring afternoons after classes. That riverbank at Mill Pond is as much a touchstone for the dream-like evocation of childhood that lies at the core of psychedelia, as is Strawberry Fields, the spacious wooded grounds of the girls' reform school where John Lennon played as a child with his friends. One of the unconscious aims of the psychedelic music they pioneered was to map their inner world, their dreams and childhood, and by extension, their subconscious. The conduit to this was often marijuana and LSD.

The inner world Barrett sought to explore was paradoxically surrealistic and vague, or literal and pin-point precise in its descriptions. The songs were peopled with the archetypes of his subconscious, called forth in various guises, such as the 'Scarecrow'. The duality extends to the very quality of the sounds used to evoke this world: plaintive acoustic guitars, piano, dissonant sound effects, string instruments, garbled voices floating in the background. Mirroring the disorienting effects of LSD, Barrett's songs called forth images of both the infinite reaches of space, with its multiplicity of unknown worlds, or the immediately familiar surroundings of his childhood home.

In a very few years, Barrett traversed a vast expanse of territory in a relentless quest for musical and lyrical exploration. The combined pressures of sudden fame, excessive ingestion of mind-altering chemicals, and the onset of a nervous breakdown led to Barrett's dismissal from the band in early 1968. With his replacement, Barrett's teenage friend David Gilmour, Pink Floyd achieved world renown, selling countless millions of albums and playing live in stadia the world over. After two erratic yet brilliant solo albums, *The Madcap Laughs* in 1969 and the eponymous *Barrett* in 1970, Syd Barrett renounced music and retired back to Cambridge. Since 1974, he has lived in seclusion, shedding his nickname 'Syd' along with all the trappings of pop fame.

Following the abrupt end of his career, the myths and misinformation surrounding his activities and whereabouts have abounded. Barrett is sometimes dismissed as an acid casualty; one who indulged too freely in the excesses of his time. He is also often labelled one of music's madmen. That Syd Barrett lost his way is undeniable, and some would charcterise it as an unfortunate descent into the silent seas of schizophrenia. Others would say Barrett had a stomachful of the various indignities of fame and wisely turned his back on its mad fanfare for the quietude of home.

Roger Waters, the bassist for Pink Floyd and teenage friend of Syd, says, 'Syd was a visionary, an extraordinary musician, he started Pink Floyd . . . Syd was the key that unlocked the door to rock'n'roll for me.[2] I still consider Syd a great primary inspiration; there was a wonderful human tenderness to all his unique musical flights.'[3] Waters pointedly stated, 'Syd was a genius,'[4] and acknowledged him as 'one of the three best songwriters in the world'.[5]

'Syd was a beautiful person, a lovely guy. He had a creative brain, a way of looking at things that was really genuinely revolutionary and different,' says John Marsh, who engineered Pink Floyd's light-show.[6] The Pink Floyd's first manager, Peter Jenner, says, 'Syd Barrett was the most creative person I've ever known.'[7]

Why is it precisely that the minds that reach furthest, which strive to test the perimeters of their world or even edge beyond it, are especially susceptible to all manner of corrosive and withering indulgences? For the short time he was fully in the here and now, Syd left in his wake a trail of true magic.

The rise and fall of the Underground movement in London during the late sixties is mirrored by the annual cycle of the seasons; a long thaw after the harsh winter of the 1950s brought forth an exquisite spring, and one of those all too rare majestic summers, followed by a long Indian summer, before descending inevitably into a doubly bleak and unforgiving winter. Barrett was one of the English Underground's most brilliant blossoms, which made his sudden withering doubly dramatic. His withdrawal from the excessive demands of his day-to-day reality should come as no surprise after reading this book, which seeks to illustrate why someone with exceptional talent and personal charisma was destroyed by forces greater than him, both from within and without. Wittingly or not, he helped in his own downfall, but Syd is dismissed all too easily by those who don't want to take the time to understand why. His nephew Ian says, 'I don't think people are prepared to understand the true extent of his breakdown or the pressures he was put under.'[8]

Syd, like Icarus in Greek mythology, flew too close to the sun, striving for an ephemeral musical ideal, and fell from the sky, the terrifying sight of his singed wings scorched into our minds. This is not a story of a late-sixties burnt-out rock star, but rather about Icarus in flight, and in fall.

Lost In The Woods is also an exploration of the myriad musical and literary influences which Barrett utilised in creating his unique work. In the popular music of the latter half of the twentieth century, where adherence to formula and rampant trainspotting have been the norm, Barrett was that rarest of all blooms, a true original. And like Brian Wilson of the Beach Boys, he had the gift of making the complex appear simple. An examination of the circumstances leading to Barrett's mental breakdown, this book considers why Syd Barrett vanished into an internal exile so profound he never returned and seeks to present a portrait of an exceptional person and an unsung innovator who remains largely misunderstood, his accomplishments obscured by the aura of madness connected to his name.

What makes Barrett such a compelling songwriter lies in his accurate portrayal of childhood, alternately turbulent and exhilarating, fearful and promising. Syd's songs were tinged with a hint of foreboding, as childhood truly is; the idealised vision of childhood comes with hindsight. They are also unique in that they document his own incipient breakdown and descent into mental illness, with songs such as 'Jugband Blues' showing that he was quite aware of what was happening to him. Peter Jenner, described 'Jugband Blues' as 'the ultimate self-diagnosis on a state of schizophrenia.[9] A really sad song, the portrait of a nervous breakdown.'[10] Co-manager Andrew King says, 'Syd knew exactly what was happening to him, but was powerless to stop it. He knew he was going wrong inside.'[11]

Barrett's music is intriguing because of a duality between songs of almost unearthly, transcendental, beautiful melodicism alternating with a turbulent cacophony of noise. From his earliest experiments in music to his final attempt, this would be the defining motion in Barrett's creative genius. A song like the Pink Floyd's 'Interstellar Overdrive' is a case in point; what on an initial listen sounds like a mess of ideas and a barrage of noise can prove full of surprises and twists, unheard subtleties and nuances . . . and reveal order under its illusory chaos.

Syd's music, especially his solo works, can come as a bit of a shock to those more accustomed to Pink Floyd's later work, with its perfect transitions, skilful musicianship and superb production. But a knowledge of his work does much to shed light on the intricacies of later post-Barrett Floyd, which is coloured with his spirit of grasping for the ungraspable. Barrett's songs can be abrasive, out of tune, skewed in timing, or dogged by fluffed notes and erratic singing. That they also comprise one of the most compelling oeuvres in popular music of the last forty years is made more poignant by the fact that there is precious little of it extant. His slim book of songs, carried in a small black folder, was open for only a short time. Barrett's elaborate wordplay rife with double meaning, his exquisite sense of humour, superb sense of irony and unerring eye for capturing the essence of an image with a few words is always striking.

Syd's near mystical connection with nature was drawn from his youth in Cambridge and his avid reading of books like Kenneth Grahame's *The Wind In The Willows*. His work is illuminated by lyrics and sound collages evoking the woods, fenlands and rivers of his childhood, with its menagerie of croaking frogs, scarecrows standing in fields, mythic gnomes, field mice, silently ambling cows and grazing horses. In the words of one unknown writer, Barrett had the gift of making the ordinary magical. And Barrett himself alluded to a mystical experience he'd claimed to have had, whereby the full complexity of Nature was opened and laid bare for him.

If Dame Edith Sitwell were alive today, she would surely profile Barrett as one of the great English eccentrics. His peculiar songs about scarecrows, gnomes, cats, bikes, chapter 24 of the *I-Ching* and 'interstellar overdrive' endure, while so much of the cod-psychedelic songs of that era are forgotten. What can explain his continuing appeal? His twenty-three-year-old nephew, Ian, professes amazement that so many people should express such keen interest in someone who hasn't recorded a note since 1974. But there is something in those songs which never ceases to amaze. This is his story.

Several miles outside the English town of Cambridge, the Gog Magog hills rise above the otherwise remarkably flat landscape of Cambridgeshire. The towns below all spring from a landscape of drained marshlands, known in Old English as *fenns*, that today form flat pastureland of dark, rich silt earth. Here, the sparse woods are devoid of human presence, and nature reigns unfettered. Weeping willows are framed against the slow swirling clouds of spring, their gnarled roots twisted around outcroppings of rock. Deserted green roads are hemmed in by copses of bramble bushes and small trees, with scattered patches of heather and daisy, bedstraw and blackberry, saxifrage, and snapdragon blossoming in the undergrowth. The sun shines in intervals through skies partly obscured by a drifting canopy of clouds. These clouds, holding a thousand tons of rain in weightless suspension, cloak the land.

Edging through the thicket, wooden fenceposts strung with ancient wire rein in pastures of impeccable green. The ubiquitous cows carry their mute secrets as they plod in herds, their hooves marking serpentine trails in the grass. In spring dandelions thread the air with dander, borne by winds from the sea forty miles distant. A battle between land and water has been waged since the beginning of Cambridgeshire's recorded history, and a pumping station nearby bears the inscription: *'These fens have oft times been by Water drowned/Science a remedy in Water found/The power of steam she says shall be employ'd/And the destroyer by itself destroyed'*.

The River Granta cuts a narrow meandering swathe through the fens. In the Fen Causeway, approaching Coe Fen, the river becomes the Cam. Here there is a small iron bridge, painted dull ochre red, spanning the River Cam where the *elixir vitae* of Nature courses below. Marsh grass undulates underwater with the strong currents of the river, each tendril trying to break the surface but never succeeding. It's becalming but eerie; deserted but for the odd, errant cow nibbling grass at the river's edge or a college don wheeling his bicycle along the bridge's metal track in absent thought.

All these are signposts on the hidden map of one Roger 'Syd' Barrett, who used to tread the back paths outside the medieval and scholastic town. Cambridge lies on a particularly flat stretch of land where the River Cam snakes its way around the perimeter of the town, bordered by trees that stand in vast silhouette against the sun, casting spectral shadows on the lawns, gravel paths and bicycle lanes which lead into a town of cobblestones and narrow sidewalks, with small squat buildings, hundreds of years old, arranged willy-nilly along winding roads and narrow, closeted alleys, with impassive garrets of hewn stone. A carved granite arch, 800 years old, opens on to the town centre's eyesore shopping centres. A glimpse into a courtyard behind a locked gate reveals a green lawn of luminescent hue struck by the half-hidden sun. Lead-framed windows reveal rooms stacked with old books where students prepare for their gruelling exams. Traditionally a centre of learning since the thirteenth century, Cambridge itself evokes a slightly other-worldly feel, with its medieval spires, turrets and bridges, ancient stone archways and cobbled stone streets. It was in this atmosphere that Barrett grew up.

Wrought-iron gates stand guard at the ivy covered halls of academe. The chill of the River Cam as it swirls under the numerous bridges of the various different colleges that span the Backs, like the wooden bridge built without a single nail, until engineering students took it apart to learn its secrets, and failing, had to rebuild it with nails. One bridge, as every true Cantabrigian knows, has thirteen complete stone balls lining its span, the fourteenth ball having a small piece chipped off it. In Market Square, vendors line up their stalls around a fountain, selling bric à brac, trinkets, curios, vegetables and fruit, books and music. There is a high, curved brick wall on Sydney Street, where faded white paint daubed by middle-class radical teenagers a generation ago reads 'Ban the Bomb'. The wide grass lawns ringing the perimeter of the town centre are known either as commons or pieces. One of them, Parker's Piece, is close to the house where Syd grew up, and there is a single lamp-post halfway across, where someone has scratched the words 'Reality Checkpoint'. Behind are the college buildings and the town centre; ahead are the housing estates of Romsey Town. This is the no man's land, so to speak, of Cambridge. If you are a student you know damn well not to cross the checkpoint after dark on a Saturday lest you want to become acquainted with the fist of a 'Townie'. For in Cambridge, in addition to the rowing races, the sport of 'grad-bashing' is also something of a tradition.

The flow of the River Cam, the Grantchester Meadows later immortalised in song by Pink Floyd, the bucolic fens and the expanses of green fields all hint at an essential untamable wildness which hides under the immaculate gardens, walkways, arches and spires of the town. The waters of Hobson's Conduit run underground beneath Cambridge, their currents swirling in the darkness. Cambridge lends itself easily to the imagination. The Fens, once a swampy marshland, was rumoured to be the home of strange creatures. It wasn't so long ago that packs of wild dogs roamed the banks of the river, or at least that's what parents told their children to dissuade them from exploring at night and risking falling into the strong currents. Seemingly every college in the town has a ghost who roams its halls, though usually it's a grumbling charwoman rather than Sir Isaac Newton.

But during the daytime nothing seems amiss, as punters glide across the water in flat punts powered by barge poles. The swirling currents push the punts further down the river; green grow the rushes past Grantchester, swelling at the riverbank, anchored in ancient mud. And past Cambridge, toward the drained marshlands of Ely, the massive spires of Ely Cathedral stand. The cathedral once stood on an island, its turrets reflected in the grey still water, a sight none living has ever seen. The breezes billow from the north, with bees and birds carried along on the thermal swells rising from the pasturelands which run all the way to the sea.

Cambridge was home to three members of Pink Floyd: Roger Waters, David Gilmour and Roger Barrett all grew up there in relative middle-class comfort. Cambridge, as a seat of academic learning, was a bit of an anomaly in East Anglia. 'East Anglia is a very odd area,' says Syd's childhood friend David Gale, 'because the towns sit on this great flat expanse and can be seen from quite a distance. The university is slightly misleading because it brings tremendous vitality, crowds and bustle and multi-faceted cultural activity to the city, and it tends to obscure the fact that Cambridge would only be a one-horse market-town were it not for the university. Cambridge in the early sixties was a bit of a hick town, and London seemed very exotic, despite its geographic proximity an hour away by rail.'

The vitality of the university-dominated town was significant when Waters, Barrett and Gilmour were growing up, as it was an oasis in a rather provincial landscape. Seamus O'Connell, a teenage friend of Waters and Barrett, says, 'Around Cambridge it's dead flat, except for the Gog Magog hills just nearby. In winter, we used to get these ghastly cold winds. The university was there, there were new students around at the beginning of term and the centre of town was dominated by the university. But we didn't have much to do with the university; there was a town-and-gown divide. On Guy Fawkes Night, there was a tradition that the town and gown would have a punch-up.'

Social tensions aside, as with any large college town, new ideas in music, art, politics, culture and religion circulated from the ivory citadel of Cambridge University into the town. What the youths, including Syd, shared in the early sixties was a near-scholarly interest in the world, both physical and internal. The direct and emotional appeal of rock'n'roll was blended with the more sartorial trends in jazz and rhythm and blues. Avant-garde composers and theorists such as Stockhausen and Cage were discussed in Cambridge long before their influence, second- and third-hand, seeped into British popular culture. The native folk music of Cambridgeshire flowed like a current through the music of the town's aspirant musicians. American Beat poets and authors, such as Jack Kerouac, Allen Ginsberg and (by association) William S. Burroughs, found an immensely receptive audience. Other influences were the visionary ramblings of William Blake, the satirical witticisms of Hilaire Belloc, and the French symbolist poets Arthur Rimbaud and Charles Baudelaire. All the seeds for the alternative culture of the sixties were in place when spring came after the long winter of the 1950s – and the flowers were colourful indeed.

Roger Keith Barrett was born on 6 January 1946 in a small semi-detached house which bears the name 'Jesmond' on a chiselled stone over the door, at 60

Glisson Road, the youngest of a family of five. Glisson Road is set a mile or two from the town centre, but could be a hundred miles from the turreted spires of the various colleges, being very much town rather than gown. In 1950, the Barrett family moved closer to the centre of Cambridge, to 183 Hills Road, Cherry Hinton, a quiet, comfortable street, where their large, detached ivy-clad house stood back from the road with well-attended hedges edging the front lawn.

The family valued literature, music and painting. Barrett's father, Max, was a pathologist, cultured and formal in manner, if a bit eccentric. His hobbies were studying fungi and painting watercolours, as well as playing in the local philharmonic orchestra. Barrett's mother, Winifred, was a remarkable woman, energetic and jolly by nature. His four brothers and sisters – Alan, Donald, Ruth, and Rosemary – all indulged Roger. David Gale recalls, 'Cambridge was full of eccentric men on bicycles in those days, who looked slightly out of time, but it was a community that could support that eccentricity rather comfortably. And so Syd's father was a familiar figure cycling on a very upright bicycle, up and down the Hills Road. His mother was a jolly white-haired figure. One of his sisters, Rosemary, was extremely jolly; the older one, Ruth, less so, more contained. And he had a curious elder brother who seemed to be pale, withdrawn, quiet and moody. Possibly he just didn't like us, but that was the impression that I got.'

This marked difference in temperament within the Barrett family is noteworthy. While his father and elder siblings were quieter and reserved, his mother and Rosemary and Syd himself were more ebullient. In adulthood, Syd would slowly but steadily gravitate towards the 'withdrawn, quiet and moody' personality of his father and elder brother.

Schoolfriend Nigel Gordon says, 'Syd came from a middle-class background; they were well off. They were all big houses on Hills Road. I never met the other siblings, beside Rosemary. They must have been out getting jobs.' Syd himself recalled childhood birthdays fondly, with their 'parties and games that you play in the dark, when someone hides and hits you with a cushion. We also used to dress up and go into the street and throw stones at passing cars.' Syd's parties were a smash with his two elder brothers laughing as their little monster of a brother dashed through the house with sparklers.[12]

Piano lessons began at seven, but Syd was driven around the bend by the boring repetition and endless practicing of scales. Two weeks after commencing lessons he staged a rebellion, and that was the end of that.

'Syd was very much a product of the English middle- to upper-middle-class university or cathedral town background,' says [Barry] Miles, one of the intellectual leading lights of the sixties. 'Very well grounded in English fairy stories. Children's stories and the imagery of childhood were very strong for him – nursery stories, *Wind In The Willows*, Rupert the Bear, Winnie the Pooh – all the classic children's stories which tend to be middle-class. He was a very British product in that sense. Oddly enough, [jazz psychedelic band] the Soft Machine were similar as their background was in Canterbury, and Canterbury and Cambridge weren't that different. And in those towns everyone was very nice. Nice, nice, nice. And a nice way to grow up. Syd was very much like that, a very highly developed sense of wit, and also of English eccentricity. Nothing too strange, just whimsical. And I imagine he wasn't that different than quite a few other people around at the time.'

Syd Barrett mused on the influence of fairy-tales in his music: 'Fairy-tales are nice. I think a lot of it has to do with living in Cambridge, with nature and everything.'[13]

Among Barrett's other favourite childhood books were *Cautionary Verses* by Hilaire Belloc, Lewis Carroll's *Alice's Adventures In Wonderland* and *Through The Looking Glass And What Alice Found There*, J.R.R. Tolkien's *Lord Of The Rings* trilogy and *The Hobbit,* C.S. Lewis's *Narnia Chronicles* and Edward Lear's *Absolute Nonsense.* All were traditional English whimsical authors of prose and verse whose works could have been viewed as children's stories, although their erudite and highly imaginative wit, fantasy and sly surrealism endeared them to old and young alike. They were tales of gnomes, goblins, hobbits, unicorns, Cheshire cats, hooka-pipe-smoking caterpillars, and moles and toads who talked and walked as humans would, and these creatures were also quintessentially English in their eccentricities and mannerisms. They wore waistcoats, carried pocket-watches, smoked pipes, and were irritable and witty by turns.

Barrett's childhood was, by all accounts, ordinary. It was his mind and personality that were exceptional. He absorbed his manifold influences readily but it was his remarkable insight, springing from a seemingly inexhaustible fount deep within, that illuminated and put a mischievous sparkle in his green eyes. Chaucer, Shakespeare and Joyce all vied for Barrett's attention and he took the best from each and allowed these to germinate in his mind. His mind was fired by the improbable tales and flights of fantastical fancy of Belloc, Carroll and Lear, and the division between fantasy and reality might have been rendered somewhat transparent. His natural imagination was remarkable, as was his ability to absorb and re-combine whatever influences were at hand. A stray image captured on one of his walks would be duly sketched in charcoals into his sketchbook; later, whatever caught his often fleeting fancy would find its way into his music or lyrics.

The beguiling abstractions of fantasy must have been preferable at times to the dull rigours of the Morley Memorial Junior School on Hills Road, which Barrett and Roger Waters attended in the early 1950s. Two years older than Barrett, Roger Waters, for one, was miserable in school. This was compounded no doubt because Waters grew up fatherless, his father having been killed when Roger was three months old by a dive-bombing German Stuka at the beachhead at Anzio in 1944. Waters says, 'I was brought up in Cambridge by my mother, who's a schoolteacher. She didn't encourage my creativity. She claims to be tone deaf, whatever that means, and has no interest in music and art or anything like that. She's only interested in politics. I didn't really have a happy childhood.'[14] Seamus O'Connell, a childhood friend of both Waters and Barrett, notes, 'Her attitudes were progressive, she was very big in local politics, a very energetic and remarkable woman. The house Roger Waters lived in on Rock Road wasn't all that big and Mary had to bring up these two boys on her own.'

Roger Waters, along with future Pink Floyd album cover designer Storm Thorgerson, and Tim Renwick, who thirty years later would play guitar with Pink Floyd, attended the Cambridge High School, known to all and sundry as 'the County', also on Hills Road. Waters says, 'I loathed school, particularly after I went to grammar school. Apart from games, which I loved, I loathed every single second of it. The grammar-school mentality at that time had very much lagged behind the way young people's minds were working in the late 1950s, and it took them a long time to catch up. Grammar schools were still being run on pre-War lines, where you bloody well did as you were told and kept your mouth shut, and we weren't prepared for any of that. Maybe toward the end when I was a teenager, going to school was just an us-and-them confrontation between me and a few friends who formed a rather violent and revolutionary clique. That was all right, and I enjoyed the violence of smashing up the school property . . . It erupted into a very organised clandestine property violence against the school, with bombs, though nobody ever got hurt.'[15]

In 1957, Roger Barrett started at the County. He seemed to enjoy school, where he was popular and acknowledged as an intelligent, if slightly lackadaisical student, particularly in the very same art classes that young Waters so loathed. Barrett had an offhand brilliance, and wherever he chose to indulge his formidable mind, he was met with success. Tim Renwick told *Guitar World*, 'I went to school with Roger Waters and Syd Barrett. They were older than me, but I remember them quite clearly, they were very cool. Roger made history by refusing to join the cadet force; he was a bit of a rebel. And Syd, believe it or not, was my patrol leader in the Scouts! He was a very impressive and charismatic bloke, as was Roger.'

Roger Barrett's natural talents in art soon expanded to a growing interest in music, which his parents encouraged. 1957 was the year of the skiffle craze that took Britain by storm. The skiffle anthem 'Rock Island Line' by Lonnie Donegan, was followed soon after by Bill Haley's 'Rock Around The Clock' and its impact was immediate. Rock'n'roll, an American import, was an odd symbiosis of African-American blues and white country and western music, and it started a worldwide craze. Dismissed upon arrival as another curious fad, rock'n'roll would prove to have lasting power beyond all expectations. Adults regarded the swivelling hips of Elvis Presley, the gospel derived shout of Little Richard and the backwoods twang of Chuck Berry with marked bemusement.

The boys were at an age where rock'n'roll made a tremendous impact on their lives. Radio at that time was of huge importance, and its influence on young musicians such as Lennon and McCartney, Pete Townshend, Eric Clapton, and Barrett, Gilmour and Waters can't be overestimated, nor on the entire post-War generation around the world. Youngsters from every strata of society would huddle under the covers in bed, turning the dials to catch a stray fragment of rhythm and blues, jazz or rock'n'roll.

Rock'n'roll was transmitted through the radio, turning what had once been dismissed as a fad into a global phenomenon. David Gale says, 'These were people who had grown up with Elvis and the weird austerity of the 1950s, and had ridden that rock'n'roll strand. Rock'n'roll had been tremendously comforting and reassuring, a solidarity-creating thing which had run through our lives. I was twelve when I first bought "Rock Around the Clock" by Bill Haley, it had just come out.' Nigel Gordon says, 'Before the pirate radio ships, which came later, we heard Radio Luxembourg, which used to come and go, fade in and out. One just got used to the weak signal. The first records which made an impact were "Heartbreak Hotel" by Elvis Presley and "Rock Around The Clock", which my mother had a copy of, "Shake, Rattle And Roll", "Wandering Eyes" by Charlie Gracie, and Vince Taylor, Chuck Berry, and the Everly Brothers. There were just a lot of silly pop songs in England, so it was mostly American rock'n'roll we listened to.'

The tinny blare of transistor radios would very occasionally carry the raucous songs of Elvis Presley, Chuck Berry, Eddie Cochran or such home-grown rockers as Cliff Richard and the Shadows. The Shadows' guitarist, Hank Marvin, with his echo-laden Stratocaster, was to prove a strong influence on an entire generation of budding English rockers. The Shadows were much emulated, with Peter Green, Eric Clapton and Pete Townshend all listening to the Shadows and learning Marvin's echo-drenched solos note by note. Hank Marvin would also prove a vital primary inspiration for Roger Barrett and David Gilmour, who would spend hours listening to Shadows' instrumentals like 'Apache'. Another influence was the Ventures, with their surf instrumentals heavy on the echo-delay, notably 'Walk Don't Run', which later provided the basis for Barrett's own 'Matilda Mother'. The ragged quasi-Middle Eastern scales of surf rock, particularly those of Dick Dale, who as a child lived in Beirut, also show up in Barrett's music.

'My first instrument, at a very tender age,' said Barrett, 'was a ukulele, then, when I was eleven years old, my parents bought me a banjo.[16] I'm not quite sure why, it just seemed a good idea at the time. I picked it up in a second-hand shop and plunked away quite happily for about six months.' In 1958, Barrett talked his parents into buying him a guitar. 'The first one was a £12 Hofner acoustic which I kept for a year.[17] I learned to play it from tutor books and from friends who could play a little.'[18] Barrett would strum his guitar for hours on end, and a family photograph from that time shows him playing in the garden behind the house on Hills Road, eyes intent, hunched over the guitar. 'I picked up playing guitar quite quickly,' he said.[19]

Clive Welham, a childhood friend of Roger's, attended the Perse, a nearby school, along with two other lads, David Gilmour and David Gale. Gale says, 'From the age of about thirteen or fourteen, I became aware of Syd, though I didn't actually meet him at that point. I met him as a result of knowing Storm, who went to the same school as Syd, the County.'

The two schools were only three-quarters of a mile apart on the Hills Road. Welham and Barrett, with various others, formed an amateur band known as Geoff Mott and the Mottoes. Together they played on Sunday afternoons, often at Barrett's house, as his mother indulged the youths' attempts at music. Welham says, 'There was Geoff Mott, Roger Barrett, me and Nobby Clarke, who was another Perse boy. I met them at a party in Cambridge near the river. They'd got acoustic guitars and were just strumming and I started picking up sticks and making noise. We were in the kitchen, away from the main party. They asked me if I played drums and I says, "Not really, but I'd love to." It just started like that.'[20]

David Gale says, 'Syd was slightly younger, and I knew him by virtue of the people he knew at school, who were slightly older. Two years made a big difference at that age, and it wasn't until later that the two groups merged. Syd, Roger, and Storm were all at the same school. And they were all deeply into guitars and rock. I was a very amateur guitarist. I had a Spanish guitar and Syd used to teach me chords, and somewhere I have a piece of cardboard on which he'd written the chords out to "Oxford Town", which Bob Dylan used to sing as a protest song. Syd was very much into Bo Diddley, and Roger Waters also, I think. Roger lived a few hundred yards from Syd and we would go round his house as well.'

At the front-room jam sessions, the out-of-tune banshee howl of the lads shouting out the words to Buddy Holly's 'That'll Be The Day' must have been amusing. 'They weren't a gigging band, more a rehearsal band, a fun band, people learning to play pop music,' said Clive Welham. 'I can't remember if the Mottoes recorded anything. There may have been odd tape recordings done at Roger's home; but if we did, it was nothing of significance. Roger Waters used to come to the Mottoes do's on a Sunday afternoon. He was very friendly with Roger Barrett, and used to come round on a beat-up old Matchless motorbike. He was very keen on motorcycles then. I don't think he actually played a guitar, he was just a mate.'[21]

Waters says, 'I had made one or two feeble attempts to learn to play the guitar when I was around fourteen but gave up because it was too difficult. It hurt my finger, and I found it much too hard. I couldn't handle it.'[22]

'I liked Roger Barrett,' says Welham, 'he had a nice, offbeat sense of humour. He was a talented painter, a better painter than a musician. The fact that he was a painter, his artistic make-up, made him an interesting musician; a creative musician, not a good guitarist. It was just ideas, he was flowing with ideas. There were no signs of the problems that were to come.'[23]

In 1960, another important figure in Barrett's life entered the picture. David Gilmour, who was a student at the Perse along with David Gale, recalls, 'We became friends when I was about fourteen.[24] Syd was a strange guy even back in Cambridge. He was a very respected figure in his own way.[25] A truly magnetic personality. When he was very young . . . people would look at him in the street and say, "There's Syd Barrett", and he would be only fourteen years old.'[26] David would drop in and join the Mottoes for their front-room jam sessions.*

Another friend of Syd's was Paul Charrier. Cambridge friend Jenny Gordon says, 'Paul Charrier was a huge influence on Syd and was at school with him. I do think that Syd was deeply influenced by Paul, because Paul was such a wild person; he had this long, curly blond hair that just stood up, and these little glasses, and he'd ride a bicycle singing at the top of his voice around Cambridge. They were good friends. Paul was a little bit younger but a very strong character.' David Gales notes, 'Paul Charrier was a remarkable young man, in many ways a Dean Moriarty/Neal Casady [from Jack Kerouac's *On The Road*] figure, being a person of tremendous energy and exuberance. Paul lived, as it happened, between me and Syd. The three of us would often hang out and have an uproarious time. Paul was absolutely outrageous, and very amusing, very kindly, ultimately quite serious and spiritually inclined.'

Sadly, on 11 December 1961, young Barrett's happiness was shattered by the death of his beloved father from a heart attack. In Storm Thorgeson's view, this was the first catalyst in Barrett's eventual breakdown. David Gilmour also shares this view: 'In my opinion, it's a family situation that's at the root of it all. Syd's father's death affected him very heavily and his mother always pampered him, made him out to be a genius of sorts.'[27] Syd's sister Rosemary says, 'His father's death affected him a lot. You would never think they were close but they had a sort of unique closeness. If Roger says anything witty, our father would always be the first to laugh.'[28] Rosemary, ever the inquisitive little sister, snuck up to her brother's room one day to leaf through his journal. She recalls, in an interview with Mike Watkinson and Pete Anderson, that his scrawl filled every page save for the one dated 11 December 1961, when he left the page completely bare. It was Syd's first blank brought on by emotional shock, and later on, in times of overwhelming distress, these blanks, literal and metaphorical, would serve to shield him.

Although Syd suffered deeply from the death of his father he kept his sorrow private. David Gale says, 'I was around at the time but I don't recall Syd ever talking about his father's death.' Barrett began to draw inward, his personality

*Gilmour noted, 'I knew Syd but I didn't know Roger Waters.' (MTV interviews with Pink Floyd, 1992)

taking on a tinge of deep introspection. At night he would listen in his room, alone, to popular radio science fiction shows like *Journey Into Space* and *Quartermass*, which he later acknowledged as the source for the outer-space metaphors woven into his songs. Science fiction, in the guise of Eagle comics hero Dan Dare was a firm favourite.

There was a certain solace to be derived from being alone outdoors. Biographers Mike Watkinson and Pete Anderson noted that Barrett was prone to go to the Botanical Gardens a stone's throw from his house, and wander for hours after classes let out for the day. The vast gardens were bordered on one side by Hills Road, and Barrett would walk over through the Cherry Hinton Gate. Passing the scented garden planted with aromatic flowers for the blind, he would roam down the path to the fountain in the centre of the gardens and make his way across to the glasshouses, where a most incredible series of rooms led one into the other. Each room housed plants, vines and small trees from the four corners of the world, divided by temperature; starting with a winter room where alpine lichens are buried in unforgiving soil, to the tropical room, where cocoa plants and liana vines flourished in the intense heat. Barrett would wander from room to room, opening and closing the various doors, his imagination drifting from the sadness of his father's death. The first stirrings of an essentially solitary nature were slowly making themselves manifest. 'Syd had a very secret side, there was a part of him that you could never reach,' says Tim Francis, another friend.[29]

Around more or less the same time, in Liverpool, two young lads called John Lennon and Paul McCartney were also swept up by the skiffle fad. The polite and well mannered McCartney became friends with the rebellious Lennon via their shared interest in music, as well as through the fact that both of their mothers had recently died. This common bond cemented their friendship in a way that simple musical camaraderie could never have done. Likewise, the two Rogers were brought closer together by the shared tragedy of their father's deaths as well as their growing interest in music. Cambridge friend Nigel Gordon says, 'Syd and Roger bonded over the deaths of their respective fathers.'

'Syd and I went through our most formative years together,' remembered Waters in 1988, 'riding on my motorbike, getting drunk, doing a little dope, flirting with girls, all that basic stuff.[30] Syd, who was a couple of years younger, and I had similar interests, rock'n'roll, danger and sex and drugs, probably in that order. I had a motorbike before I left home, and we used to go on mad rides out into the country. We would have races at night, incredibly dangerous, which we survived somehow. Those days, 1959 to 1960, were heady times.'[31]

Concurrent with the death of his father, Barrett began to play guitar in earnest. He said, 'At fifteen, I took a dramatic step forward, becoming the proud possessor of an electric guitar, with a small amplifier that I made myself. And with this kit, which I fitted into a cabinet, I joined my first group, a local

Cambridge group called Geoff Mott and the Mottoes, playing at parties and the like around my home town of Cambridge.[32] When I joined them I splashed out on a Futurama 2. At the time I thought it was the end in guitars. Fantastic design and all that.* We did a lot of work at private parties. And some of our material was original, but mostly we stuck to Shadows' instrumentals and a few American songs. Eventually the group dissolved and I moved into the blues field, this time playing bass. It was another Hofner, and I played that for a couple of years.'[33]

Barrett played rhythm guitar, Nobby Clarke played lead, Tony Sainty played bass, Clive Welham played drums, and Geoff Mott sang. 'Syd wasn't a bad rhythm guitarist,' says Geoff Mott. 'It was nice to hear someone who could play as opposed to thumping around.'[34]

Eventually the Mottoes played a 1962 benefit gig at Cambridge's Union Cellars for the Campaign for Nuclear Disarmament (CND). This was Barrett's first appearance on stage, and to be front of an audience, no matter how small, must have made a strong impression. CND was another ingredient in the development of what came to be known as the English Underground. CND's various Aldermaston marches, protesting over the presence of US nuclear weapons on British soil, were a focal point for activism among the young. Waters in particular, was passionate about CND. Peter Wynne-Wilson, later Pink Floyd's lighting engineer, recalls, 'I did a lot of political stuff for CND, which was a strong influence at that time. I was completely absorbed with the pacifist ethic and was completely surprised when I went on the Aldermaston march in 1962. I met extremely aggressive political factions under that banner. Interesting and exciting, but strange.'

Another marked influence to the nascent Cambridge Underground was jazz; 'Modern jazz was our thing,' says Nigel Gordon. Charlie Parker, Charlie Mingus and Theolonious Monk formed a holy triumvirate for the hip. LPs like Miles Davis's *Seven Steps To Heaven*, Mingus's *The Black Saint And The Sinner Lady* and Monk's *Criss Cross* all found their way on to Cambridge teens' record players. There was also the influence of the emerging free jazz splinter movement. Hip undergraduates listened to Ornette Coleman, Eric Dolphy and Albert Ayler.

Poet Pete Brown says, 'People were just beginning to be exposed to jazz and blues. It caused a really strange response, people didn't really know how to respond, they wore funny clothes. The beginnings of fashion started to happen around music, and which of course at first was very self-conscious and weird. People wore duffel coats, there were even a group of women wearing sack dresses called "ooblies", which lasted for about five minutes. This stuff was even happening in the 1950s, it was the strangeness we came out of.'

*Syd added, 'Incidentally, Geoff Mott was a great singer . . . wonder what happened to him?' Mott is now a teacher in London.

Despite their warm response from their performance at the CND rally, the Mottoes drifted apart. 'For a couple of years, from the age of sixteen,' said Syd Barrett, 'I wasn't with any regular group, and during this time I acquired a twelve-string guitar and then a bass guitar which I played with another group, the Hollering Blues.'[35] During 1962, Barrett seemed to have been influenced as much by literature as rock'n'roll, and perhaps his earliest attempt at songwriting was putting music to a poem by James Joyce called 'Golden Hair'. Soon after, he wrote a silly song, 'Effervescing Elephant', which shines with the strength of what was to become his characteristic wit, derived from Lear and Belloc. Another early song, 'Matilda Mother', Cliff Jones noted, used the opening lines of Belloc's *Cautionary Verses* as its lyrics. At sixteen, Barrett was already demonstrating a strong understanding of the written word and of the humour permeating his favourite books. A good sense of humour requires not only intelligence but a deft juggling of elaborate wordplay and timing. Barrett, even at this young age, displayed both. 'I did tend to take lines from other things,' said Syd, 'lines I liked, and then wrote around them . . . It was just writing good songs that mattered, really.'[36]

Syd loved *The Goon Show* – Harry Secombe, Peter Sellers and Spike Milligan's brilliant comedy radio routines, where they would improvise wildly on the most disparate themes. The Goons were a strong influence on Syd, not only for their improvisation, but also in their use of sound effects, nonsense syllables and vocal tricks . He would listen to their shows with rapt attention. Friends recall Syd in paroxysms of laughter upon hearing certain favourite lines. It slotted in nicely with his natural ebullience. 'From the time I came to know him until he "turned", Syd was fantastic,' says Gilmour. 'There wasn't a single person who didn't like him, think he was brilliant, or wasn't certain he was going to be a success at something. He was good looking and fantastically talented at anything he cared to put his hand to. He was also one of the funniest people I've ever come across. When he wanted to, he could be really witty and surreal.'[37]

In 1962 Syd won a scholarship and began a two-year programme at the Cambridge College of Arts & Technology. 'Syd was often misunderstood,' says childhood friend John Gordon. 'People thought he was rebellious . . . If we had a lecturer who was particularly boring he would become so disruptive that he would be thrown out of the class, if he hadn't walked out already . . . He was always mature for his age and hated being treated like a child.'[38] Syd also had a short attention span save for the things he was passionate about, namely music and painting. When his attention was focused it was powerful, but his focus was often fleeting and he lost interest quickly if things weren't moving along as quickly as he wanted them to. He had to achieve spectacular results first time out or it wasn't worth it. But in music and painting he found something that captured his scattershot interest and allowed him to refine his ideas through persistent effort.

After classes ended, Barrett used to meet Paul Charrier, Nigel Gordon, Storm Thorgerson and David Gilmour. David Gale says, 'Through knowing Storm, I got to know Syd, who was a year or two junior to Storm. Mill Pond, the place at which we met, was down by the River Cam, near the Silver Street bridge, close to a pub called the Anchor, where there was a mill. And we used to go down to the mill where there was grassland on the banks of the river, and sit there and talk. These were the earliest days of am emerging beatnikism in Cambridge. In all the warm months of the years, all these boys and girls used to hang out down by the mill and gradually coalesced into various interest groups. The common interest was between boys and girls, but there were subgroups becoming interested in beatnik matters.'

Storm Thorgerson recalls that during 1962 the group of friends would go to each others' houses and listen to LPs of jazz organist Jimmy Smith. 'Then 1963 brought dope and rock. Syd was one of the first to get into the Beatles and the Stones. Syd started playing guitar around then, used to take it to parties or play down at this club called the Mill at Mill Lane.'[39] The Beatles immediately affected Barrett, who would play 'Love Me Do' to absolutely anyone who would listen, carrying the single around to his friends' houses. On 26 November 1963, the Beatles played in Cambridge but Syd couldn't attend due to entrance examinations for art school. He was very disappointed, as he had been not only the first to catch on to them but had been one of the first to queue up for tickets.

The Anchor, next to the bridge at Silver Street, had a coffee shop in its cellar, where a wide verandah opened out on to the river. David Gale says, 'It was a crucial adolescent territory where boys and girls could stalk around, form little groups and look at each other.'

The Anchor remains virtually the same today as when Roger, Syd and Dave were teenagers. Rough, oaken pillars support the low-slung beams hanging over wooden tables with generations of students' names carved into the wood. Framed pictures of prize-winning sows are hung on the walls, incongruously placed next to portraits of genteel willowy women. Empty wine barrels are perched behind the high-backed seats and small upholstered stools. In spring and summer, sunshine streams in through the broad windows with faded green drapes overlooking the Silver Street bridge and the River Cam where punters embark on their jaunts on the river, pushing their barge poles into the turgid muddy water. Rows of bicycles are parked on the flagstones outside, and small crowds mill around the bridge, talking or watching the punters.

'Syd was extremely handsome, well built and had a very sunny, jolly, jovial disposition. Very well liked, women found him immensely attractive. He was witty and interested in art and rock'n'roll,' explains Gale. 'He was extremely striking, in so far as the clothes that he wore when not in school uniform were very extreme within the beatnik/bohemian iconography that was evolving. In that period Syd had wrap-around shades and extremely tight blue jeans that you couldn't imagine it was possible to get a foot into, flecked with paint; *authentic* paint flakes. He also had a pair of pale grey suede moccasins, and I thought these were fantastic objects. Even when we were young teenagers growing up close to each other, in terms of getting the look, or at least our interpretation of the "look", he got it absolutely right.' Barrett was the embodiment of teenage bohemianism, roaming through town with his LPs under his arm, sketchbooks and cigarettes, clad in black leather, black jeans and woolly jumper. Gale adds, 'It made him look very interesting to adolescents who were completely intoxicated by having read Jack Kerouac's *On The Road*, and who were possibly about to read William S. Burroughs' *Naked Lunch*, and who were beginning to take an interest in certain drugs that they had read about through American Beat literature. In my late teens, as I was nearing the end of my school days, I had already read Kerouac, discussed it with Nigel, Storm and Syd.'

Jenny Gordon recalls, 'Bob Dylan, Davey Graham [British folk guitarist] and Dave Van Ronk [American folk singer and associate of Dylan] was what we listened to, and later came the Rolling Stones and the Beatles. But also a lot of modern jazz and going to the local jazz clubs. Fist it started with the coffee bars, but there was one pub that we went to called the Criterion, which was the in pub to go to. But really, everyone went to coffee bars. I loved the jazz and the jazz clubs. We would listen to Ornette Coleman, Dizzy Gillespie and Miles Davis. The Anchor was the coffee house. There was the Riverside Jazz Club, and also the Rex, where all the students went and where they had modern jazz. The Riverside Jazz Club was trad jazz, which we frowned a bit upon. Modern jazz was more our scene.'

The Riverside Jazz Club was another weekly event at a nearby coffee house (whose name no one can seem to remember), where the teenagers climbed up the narrow steps to get a taste of that hideous variant of jazz called 'trad'. It was here that Roger Barrett received his nickname. One of the regular performers was an ancient bass player called Sid 'The Beat' Barrett, who upon finding out that he shared a surname with the schoolboy, dubbed him Syd. 'Syd was just a nickname,' says Clive Welham, 'we knew him as Roger Barrett at school.'[40]

Poet Pete Brown notes, 'We all came out of the trad jazz revival, or most did, because we went to the jazz clubs and they played trad. These were people recreating stuff from the 1920s, which made for an antique sort of atmosphere. It actually got in the way of creativity because people got sidetracked into recreating something they had no part in creating. The trad jazz revival was very conventional and static, and based on certain misapprehensions. You got people trying to play like Bunk Johnson, one of the leading figures of the trad jazz revival, an old New Orleans musician who they found. When they found him, he had no teeth, so they bought him teeth. The trad jazz revival, they say, was invented by the American jazz writers as a counterbalance to bebop, and to bebop's more political subtext. Bebop was black and militant although it had white people involved in it. But it was black intellectual musicians asserting themselves and saying, "This is our art, you stole it from us before, you're not going to steal this." So they created these caricature figures like Bunk Johnson, who couldn't really play. People like Ken Collier, in Britain, who used to actually copy a seventy-year-old with no teeth playing badly. I exaggerate a bit, but it struck me as being a strange thing, even if it did create a good atmosphere.'

Nigel Gordon says, 'Beat literature was a trickle, and no one knew it was coming until it arrived. I read *On the Road* when I was sixteen and at school. I knew I was in the Underground when I was sixteen, reading Kerouac. From Kerouac onward, I had always felt it was there. But it wasn't until *International Times* came along later that I realised I was part of it, and that it was already there. We used to have regular readings. Kerouac, Ginsberg, Ferlinghetti, Henry Miller, Samuel Beckett, James Joyce. They influenced us when we wrote poetry. We got involved with the *New Departures* group: Mike Horovitz, Pete Brown, William Pryor. They used to do readings in Cambridge.' It was at these readings that Barrett discovered the French Symbolist Arthur Rimbaud and Cambridge poet Rupert Brooke. Brown remembers those readings vividly, 'One of the problems of trying to do gigs in those days, was the amplification was so terrible that no one could hear what you were doing. If you were trying to work with music, even if it was quiet jazz, it would drown you out.'

New Departures, a poetry and literature journal, was *de rigeur* reading for aspiring young English bohemians and a breakthrough in British alternative publishing. Its creator, poet Michael Horovitz, was to prove an inspiration to many. Miles, later an Underground luminary and then a young art school student from Cheltenham, recalls, 'I met Michael Horovitz in Oxford in 1960, when he was still at college. The first issue of *New Departures* magazine was published in 1959. Shortly after I met him the second issue came out, and I was very impressed with it. It was an English equivalent to the American *Evergreen Review*. It had the same focus, with material by William Burroughs and John Cage, and an article on the Living Theatre. That whole new avant-garde scene was very very new then. That was what I really wanted to find out about. Michael Horovitz was the first person to publish Burroughs in Britain; the first two episodes of Burroughs' *Naked Lunch* was in the first issue.'

Miles adds, 'I was in art college in Cheltenham, and I used to hitchhike down the A-40 to Oxford, not every weekend but most weekends. I would sleep on people's floors. There used to be a big building there called 4A St Clement's. Nigel "Fred" Young lived there, and he had come from Cheltenham, where he had run the local chapter of CND. He'd locked into the whole Oxford scene. Paul Jones, later of Manfred Mann, was very interested in Beat Generation literature and had quite a good collection of it. Pete Brown was there and he would hitchhike from London. He and Michael Horovitz had already met up. I was very impressed that Pete had a couple of poems in *Evergreen Review*, which was regarded as such an avant-garde, distant thing, so to meet someone who was published in it was fantastic. Through Michael I got involved in the whole poetry thing in Britain and met Spike Hawkins and Johnny Byrne and Bryan

Patten, who they worked with whenever they were in Liverpool. It was mainly poetry readings, but whenever they could afford it, they would put on jazz. In 1962 I put on a *New Departures* event at Cheltenham when I was still at art college. It was a mixed media event, and a lot of people from the art college, myself included, put on an exhibition there, and a painter called Paul Francis did a huge abstract expressionist painting while Mike and Pete read their poetry. There were jazz musicians there, Mal Dean played trumpet. A lot of the people who were associated with *New Departures* were also kind of associated with early line-ups of the Soft Machine, and they used to jam with them quite a bit.'

Miles fondly remembers American Beat poet Allen Ginsberg's epic 1956 poem 'Howl': 'It absolutely knocked me out, I sent away for it just because of the title. I sent away for a City Lights catalogue, and they sent back a tiny postcard with eight books on it, because that was all they had published at that time. And there were a few others typed on to the card. I ordered *On the Road* and that was 75 cents, and *Howl* was quite a lot, it was a dollar. I'd never heard of Ginsberg, but the titles sounded so great, different than anything I'd ever heard about. They arrived and were astonishing.'

The group of friends that developed, this loose Cambridge set, with its myriad subsets, was remarkable for its diversity, relaxed intermingling and intellectual ambitions, mixed with a common interest in experimentation and adventure. Nigel Gordon says, 'Those who went to the Perse and those who went to the County just merged together, effortlessly. Even the university undergraduates mixed in. It got a bit fragmented for a while because a lot of us were sent to public schools away from Cambridge. Syd, David Gale, Andrew and Storm remained at day school in Cambridge.'

Jenny Gordon remembers when the set began to coalesce, 'When I was sixteen I met Nigel, Storm, David Henderson and David Gale. There was also Ian 'Imo' Moore, Pip Carter, Russell Page and Dave Gilmour. Dave, like Syd, was a bit younger, so he didn't come along till later. Somehow, it all came together. Bill Barlow had two houses in Clarendon Street where everyone lived, and Nigel had a room, and Seamus, Chris Case and Bryannie Payne. That was where everyone would come round. There was also Eden Street where Pete Downing and Anthony Stern lived. It was a special group of people, like-minded and rebellious, and also a bit lost. Yet creative and different. There were a lot of drugs. There was always speed, it was always around. But there was also a new understanding that everyone had. I didn't actually have a clue what was going on, but I assumed everyone else did. But I don't think they did, because they were all like me, stumbling in the dark. I just liked their minds, they had a nice way of looking at and questioning things.'

Nigel Gordon says, 'We were so affected by Kerouac and post-War liberation, you can imagine how we felt about our elders. We thought they were completely hopeless.'

Explains Pete Brown, 'People didn't really know how to fight the huge, monolithic "You can't do anything artistic; get a job and work for ever" mentality, which people now feel very nostalgic about because there aren't permanent jobs any more. In those days, Britain was very much like Japan, you got a job and you were in it for life, which was security because everybody remembered the 1930s. Your parents were very worried on your behalf and would do strange things in order to make you do what they felt was secure.'

'Although some of us did go to Cambridge University,' says David Gale, 'we were entirely town reared and not all of us came from academic families. There was quite a good class mix in our particular group, which Syd moved in and out of. And although it was largely middle-class youths on a consciousness expanding quest, there were significant numbers of people from working-class backgrounds and some US servicemen, now and again, although they weren't a major factor. There would have been a sprinkling of undergraduates as well, and they brought their big-city culture with them.'

Meanwhile, Peter Jenner, Pink Floyd's future manager, was an undergraduate at Cambridge. Sam Hutt, a fellow undergraduate, recalls, 'Pete Jenner was my oldest mate; we smoked our first joint together in Cambridge in 1960.' That year, before starting his studies, Jenner and Pink Floyd co-manager Andrew King went to America. They travelled to Chicago and saw a lot of American blues music and jazz music. Returning to England, Jenner started at Cambridge and was active in the jazz and poetry circles there. Late-night studying sessions with friends were conducted to a constant backdrop of LPs by John Coltrane, Muddy Waters and Charlie Mingus. 'Pete Brown was often there. There was a very good jazz society. Ian Somerville and William Burroughs were around. Burroughs was a slightly mysterious force who floated around Cambridge at the time. Somerville, who was his boyfriend, was a link with all those American poets and Brian Gysin. Cut-ups were a big thing in that period.'[41] It's ironic that the young quasi-bohemians of Cambridge, roaming through the streets, chattering away about *Naked Lunch*, may very well have passed Burroughs in the street without knowing.

'Some boys at the Perse were getting access to speed,' says David Gale. The fad for amphetamines presumably had trickled down from the university undergraduates, who would take vast quantities of amphetamines to help themselves through their gruelling exams. Sam Hutt, recalls, 'In Cambridge there was quite a lot of amphetamine; there was the university pharmacy where you'd just walk in and say I'll have 150 Drinamyl please", and they'd say "Yes, that's 6/6d".'[42]

'And there was an interesting axis here,' says Gale, 'because fifteen miles to the north-east of Cambridge were Mildenhall and Lakenheath, two US Air Force bases from where American servicemen used to come in from. Cambridge for the servicemen was the most interesting town in a rather bleak landscape. They would drive past Newmarket, which was the nearest town, and into Cambridge. They would come to a pub called the Criterion, which was a very heavy pub. I used to find it very intimidating, being a nice middle-class boy. The Criterion was where a strange collection of marginal types, and those who wished to be perceived as marginal, such as us middle-class kids, would hang out. You'd have heavy guys from the town, who had emerged from the teddy boy culture, would-be beatniks who still lived at home with their parents, some genuine bohemians, and servicemen from the USAF in their civilian clothes, who were black and white. It took me several months to realise that my black and white servicemen friends never spoke to each other. We didn't notice that racism at first. What that community of servicemen did, as well as bringing in cheap booze and cigarettes which we would swap records and money for, they also brought drugs with them.

'They were one of the roots whereby people like myself and Syd were exposed to drugs in the early sixties. Dope smoking became very fashionable and desirable, and it completely supplanted the alcohol culture. It was considered uncool to drink. People who drank were known as "beer heads" and we were "tea heads".

'Because of the prevailing propaganda surrounding cannabis, it was seen as a consciousness expanding drug that would lead you to inner depths of yourself and reconnect you to a spirituality which you'd become divorced from, put you in touch with psychological insight, enhance your perception of the everyday world, including sights, sounds, smells, taste, music, sex, etc. This was all very popular, and was indulged in on a nightly basis at Storm's house, who had a permissive, bohemian mother, unlike most of our parents who were conventionally strict.'

Another popular hangout for the Cambridge set was the home of Seamus O'Connell, whose mother was quasi-bohemian and also tolerant of youngsters running amok in her house. 'Although a progressive woman,' says O'Connell, 'people like Roger Waters' mother Mary would have regarded my mother as a bit of a disgrace. People were told that they shouldn't come out to my house at all.' Seamus's mother was deeply interested in the occult, and had amassed countless books on tarot cards, astrology and esoteric books on Chinese oracles such as the *I-Ching*. There was a part of Syd's nature that erred towards the mystic, and he would often leaf through the books on visits, always keen to find something new, asking Mrs O'Connell endless questions.

David Gale says, 'There was an occasion where we went into the cellar of Syd's house, because we were all interested in hypnosis. William Pryor, who was a member of this Cambridge set and also went down to London, was swinging a watch in front of Anne McBey, who was Nigel's then girlfriend, and she went into a trance and we couldn't get her out. We had to carry her upstairs through Syd's house, to an upstairs bedroom where she lay down and eventually came out of it. These anecdotes reinforce the idea that people at that time were keen to examine the nature of consciousness from any angle, because there was also Ouija board stuff going on. Ultimately, though, drugs were far more interesting.'

Not every moment was an existential quest though; the intellectual curiosity was balanced with the light-hearted levity of youth. 'Syd and I had become quite firm friends,' says David Gale, 'and at Christmas every year for two or three years, we used to go and work at the post office as part-time Christmas postmen. Because we lived so close together, we would cycle to the post office at six in the morning and then do our letter routes, skive off home, hang about drinking tea in each other's homes and then go back to the post office as if it had been a long and busy morning. We used to call it going up the "Royal". This was Syd's term, because we were going to work for the Royal Mail.'

Summer afternoons were filled with exhilarating bicycle races, where friends were chased with deft steering, storming down the commons in a madcap chase. Breathless, the bicycle chase would end at the water's edge to watch the punts go by. 'Syd was always very good company, he was always a laugh, very jolly. I keep stressing that because he changed so much,' said Gale. Jenny Gordon says. 'At a party Syd picked up a plant and says, "Is this a rubber plant?" and bounced it! He was just a freewheeling guy.'

The many literary influences that Syd had absorbed were starting to bear fruit. His songwriting was free even then from the inane boy-meets-girl themes which dominated pop music at the time. Even the Beatles' lyrics focused on the banal intrigues of romance. It was Dylan's and Kerouac's influence that led songwriters to tentatively branch out into personal narrative. The Beatles' 1964 'I'm A Loser' was Lennon's first stab at autobiographical lyrics, paving the way for 'Norwegian Wood' and 'Help!' in 1965, both of which were fiercely personal breakthroughs in songwriting. Barrett didn't like to use overtly autobiographical narrative, preferring to assume the guise of a storyteller. Dylan's primary influence on Barrett was in pointing the way to densely poetic images, often abstract, freed from the rhyming verse of his childhood's books.

In 1963, David Gilmour joined Syd at the Cambridge College of Arts & Technology to take his A-levels in modern languages. This was when he and Syd Barrett strengthened their friendship. 'We would hang around in the art department, playing guitars every lunch-time,' said Gilmour. 'Teaching each other, basically. The thing with Syd was that his guitar wasn't his strongest feature. His style was very stiff. I always thought I was the better guitar player. But he was very clever, very intelligent, an artist in every way. And he was a frightening talent when it came to words, and lyrics. They just used to pour out.'[43] Roger Waters also affirmed that Syd displayed 'an incredible way with words'.[44]

In later years, there would be much debate as to who taught who during those halcyon lunch-hours in the art department. Syd and Gilmour would sit and play Rolling Stones' songs together with guitars and harmonica. 'We spent a lot of time together as teenagers listening to the same music. Our influences are probably pretty much the same, and I was probably a couple of streets ahead of him at the time and was teaching him to play Stones' riffs every lunch-time for a year at technical college,'[45] says Gilmour. 'We learnt them together,' he adds. 'I was better at learning other people's stuff parrot-fashion than he was.'[46] Clive Welham recalls, 'Dave and Syd used to compare ideas when they were at the Tech together. Dave was always ahead of Syd. Syd may have started playing at around the same time as Dave, and at one time they would have been very much at the same level, but Dave really stepped far ahead.'[47] Gilmour began playing in a local band, the Newcomers, and was recognised for his natural talent on the guitar.

Syd played in various amateur groups from sixteen on, such as the Hollering Blues, playing Bo Diddley and Jimmy Reed numbers like 'Bright Lights, Big City'. 'I didn't play much in Cambridge because I was from the art school, you know. But I was soon playing on the professional scene and began to write from there.'[48]

In 1963, Syd and Dave Gilmour took their acoustic guitars down to the Mill on Mill Lane. where they played some acoustic sessions. At the tail end of that year Gilmour formed his own band, Joker's Wild, who would perform in local pubs, playing rhythm and blues covers. Clive Welham recalls that Syd used to come and see Joker's Wild at the Victoria Ballroom in Market Square for their regular Wednesday night gigs.[49] Mick Rock, a friend of theirs, remembers Joker's Wild playing R&B songs like Wilson Pickett's 'In the Midnight Hour': 'Syd would go and watch Dave play because I think Dave had got his chords down a bit better than Syd in the early days. Syd was always a bit weird about Dave.'[50]

Syd was always a bit weird, period, according to Nigel Gordon, 'Syd was always a little odd, he was never an ordinary person.' His sense of humour masked a flippant view of social conventions, coupled with a true streak of anarchy. Channelled into his music, it would prove consistently interesting and often ground-breaking. But in his personal life, the death of his father at an important juncture in a teenage boy's life was to perhaps exacerbate Syd's contention that rules were there only to be broken. And perhaps with an indulgent mother, there was little direction. With his father dead and his elder siblings gone, there was no one to check Barrett's teenage excesses or tell him 'no'. And a firm 'no' is useful, even if only to provide a framework against which to rebel.

But generally these were idyllic times, and Storm Thorgerson remembers Syd as a 'bright, extrovert kid. Smoked dope, pulled chicks, the usual thing. He had no problems on the surface. He was no introvert as far as I could see then.'[51] Gale says, 'Syd's girlfriend then was called Libby Gausden, and she was very sexy with a great figure and a lot of fun to be with. I always imagined Syd and Libby having dynamite sex at a time when the rest of us were more hard pressed.' Syd's girlfriend Libby Gausden remembers his deep absorption with music, 'He'd find a new chord and concentrate on that for the rest of the evening.'[52] In the summer of 1963, Syd and Libby went on a summer holiday to Butlins. A modish Syd, in coat and slim tie, and Libby, with a PVC raincoat and bobbed hair, were photographed smiling broadly. Gausden also snapped Syd wearing a black leather coat, dark glasses and black jeans, aiming for that existentialist Parisian Left-bank look. Sartre and Camus were also hot reads in the Cambridge set, although 700 pages of Sartre droning on about being and nothingness held less immediate appeal than the Beats.

The folk and traditional music boom was happening around Britain, concurrent with the CND movement. The annual Cambridge Folk Festival began in 1963 and the young aspirant Cambridge rockers received a strong dose of traditional music. The stereotypical image of that time was of bearded, Shetland-sweater-wearing protest singers armed with acoustic instruments. Across the Atlantic, the civil rights movement was gathering steam, also fed by an upsurge in acoustic-guitar-playing folk singers, one of whom was Bob Dylan, who played in the bars of Greenwich Village in New York and had just released his album *The Freewheelin' Bob Dylan*. Dylan was one of the first to capture people's interest in both the US and Britain. Peter, Paul and Mary, an America folk trio, charted in November 1963 with a cover of Dylan's 'Blowing in the Wind', the words of the song seeming to have universal meaning for teenagers everywhere. Gilmour and Barrett were both keen Dylan enthusiasts, perhaps having seen him appear on the BBC in 1962 warbling some unreleased, semi-mythic song whose words went 'The swan on the river went gliding by'.

Barrett and Libby Gausden attended Dylan's first major show in London in March 1963. Gausden remembers that at the Dylan concert, 'My first reaction was seeing all these people like Syd, it was almost as if each town had sent one Syd Barrett there. It was the first time I'd seen people who were like him.'[53]

David Gale notes, 'Folk and pop music created a sensibility that predisposed some people to want to read *On the Road*. Some people would probably have read Steinbeck before Kerouac, but Kerouac was an explosion! We were all just schoolboys and girls, but it seemed to crystallise something that we wanted. We all wanted to hitchhike and take drugs and be promiscuous.'

On Easter Sunday 1964, the pirate radio station Radio Caroline began transmission. Radio Luxembourg had been available for a while, but Radio Caroline, and its rival, Radio London, would soon be jockeying with Radio Luxembourg for a share of the emerging youth market. Radio Caroline's DJ Simon Dee inaugurated a new era with the simple introduction, 'Good morning, ladies and gentlemen. This is Radio Caroline broadcasting 199, your all-day music station'. Radio Caroline was the first of what were to be many pirate stations broadcasting from just beyond the twelve-mile territorial waters of the UK, flouting the BBC's dull monopoly on broadcasting. Their vibrant DJs presented a panoply of music unavailable on government bandwidths; a potent antidote to the bland fare of the BBC's *Light Show*. Now there would be a new medium to propel the coming explosion of British and American bands throughout the UK, and later the Pink Floyd would be a direct beneficiary of the growing influence of the pirate stations. In little more than a year, Radio Caroline and

Radio London would reach over 13 million listeners every day.

Peter Whitehead, a future film-maker and falconer, lived in Cambridge in the early sixties, having taken a year off school before leaving for London's Slade school of art.[54] He found lodgings at the home of a local scientist, Peter Mitchell, where he lived for a year, painting. Whitehead told *Record Collector*, 'I've joked that I really invented the Pink Floyd sound. I was living in this house where the band used to practice their music in the hall. And their music got louder and louder, and my music, lots of Janacek and Bartok, got louder too. Poor old Syd was doing his Chuck Berry and Little Richard and having to compete with my copy of *Das Rheingold*.

'They probably thought I was a bit crazy, but would drop into talk occasionally. Syd was just one of a bunch of younger guys who came around, mainly because there were pretty girls in the house.' Barrett had begun seeing Mitchell's daughter, Juliet. When her parents left for their holidays, the band set up in the basement to pound out their repertoire of R&B standards. 'It sounded awful to me,' remembers Whitehead, 'like listening to bad Schoenberg.[55] Syd was a weird experimenter on the guitar.' Even in the early stages of his playing, this was what set Barrett apart from the pack. He was edging away from the cliché R&B riffs (probably because he couldn't play them with the fluidity and technical skill that others like Gilmour could) for the beginnings of discordant soundscapes. This was during an era when duplicating Stones and Chuck Berry riffs note for note was seen as the apogee of guitar playing. Gale recalls, 'I remember being in Syd's big front-room in Hills Road and Syd first drew his Zippo lighter along the strings of the guitar, thereby ushering in the psychedelic music era. I was there, and clearly it was something that he had discovered on his own, because he said, "Listen to this!" and he picked up his Zippo and dragged it along his amplified guitar. This was to become a key ingredient in the Pink Floyd sound.' This glissando technique was one of Syd's inventions, an electronic update of the blues slide riffs he loved to listen to.

Anthony Stern was one of Syd's friends who would attend the jam sessions, and in time Whitehead and Stern became fast friends. Whitehead put on an exhibition of his paintings in Cambridge, and soon after, Anthony Stern had a two-man exhibition with Syd at a local hall. Eventually Stern would become Whitehead's assistant on all the films he made throughout the sixties. 'I remember Syd as the most beautiful and feminine of the guys around,' says Whitehead. Though not effeminate, Barrett was ahead of his time, with longish hair and a stylish black leather coat.

Whitehead enjoyed his time in Cambridge spent painting, reading imported copies of the American *Evergreen Review*, with its references to the barely-known Ginsberg and Kerouac, and smoking the very occasional joint of dope that passed his way. Whitehead was influenced by the grotesqueries of Francis Bacon, while the flash Pop Art of Lichtenstein was just beginning to be known about, along with homegrown talent like David Hockney and Peter Blake.

Abstract expressionists such as Jackson Pollock were also influential, their revolutionary techniques acutely felt by young aspirant painters, including Roger Barrett. Duggie Fields, now a well-known painter, remembers that at the time, 'English television had a segment or two on Jackson Pollock dripping paint on to the canvas, and insinuating it was rubbish, but I thought it was brilliant. I always liked Pop Art, because of my interest in comic books. Lichtenstein wasn't even as interesting as his sources. Though I did like his technique. I was happy looking at the comic books, and thought they were great, I didn't differentiate. When I came to London, I got into David Hockney and Peter Blake.' Barrett, even then skilled at painting, would talk to Whitehead and showed him some of his early work, the style of which Whitehead characterised as 'loose, dreamy and not very striking, but memory is vague'. 'Syd's painting would have been in the Pop Art tradition,' says David Gale, 'and would be rather good. I remember thinking it was a bit like the work of Jim Dine. I remember him applying crumpled fabric to the surface of the canvas and working it in.'

Winifred Barrett, widowed and still raising Syd and Rosemary, her three elder children having left Hills Road, decided to follow Mary Waters' example and take in student boarders, a common practice in Cambridge. The house was much too large for just her and the two teenagers, and the extra money would come in handy. Roger Waters says, 'Both my mother and Syd's mother had students as lodgers because there was a girls' college up the road so there was constantly great lines of bras and knickers on our washing lines.'[56] In one curious incident, the bras and knickers that hung on the washing lines in the Barrett's garden proved irresistible to a local underwear fetishist. This character, whom Barrett would later immortalise in song as Arnold Layne, made off with many of the poor nursing students' undergarments, presumably to indulge his fantasies. 'Arnold or whoever he was, had bits and pieces off our washing lines. They never caught him. He stopped doing it after a bit, when things got too hot for him.'[57] 'I was in Cambridge at the time I started to write the song,' Syd Barrett told *Melody Maker*. 'I pinched the line about "moonshine washing line" from Roger because he had an enormous washing line in the back garden of his house. Then I thought "Arnold must have a hobby" and it went on from there. Arnold Layne just happened to dig dressing up in women's clothing.'

At the end of the summer of 1964, Syd prepared to move to London to begin studying at the Camberwell School of the Arts.

That summer another milestone occurred in Syd's life, when he was one of the earliest in his circle to try a new drug, then legal, that was touted as mind-expanding. 'Towards the end of my teens,' says David Gale, 'having left school and hanging out with Syd, there arose on the horizon the spectre of LSD.'

Swiss chemist Dr Albert Hoffman synthesized LSD at the Sandoz laboratories in Switzerland in 1938. Searching for an asthma medicine, the doctor was investigating lysergic acid derived from ergot, a mould that grows on wheat. Though initial tests showed LSD to have no unusual qualities, Hoffman wrote 'A peculiar presentiment that this substance could possess properties other than those established in the first investigations, induced me to produce LSD-25 once again.' LSD-25 was the 25th derivative of the original substance Hoffman had discovered.

On 16 April Dr Hoffman synthesised more LSD-25 and was struck with odd symptoms. He had absorbed infinitesimal quantities of the substance through his skin. Slight hallucinations followed for the next two hours. The doctor noted, 'This was, altogether, a remarkable experience.' Indeed, some eighteen years before cosmonaut Yuri Gagarin, Hoffman was about to become the first man in space. His interest piqued by the preceding events, Dr Hoffman decided on a self-experiment. On 19 April 1943, he administered himself a dose of the substance and, to use the parlance of the sixties, tripped. Within forty minutes, the doctor found he could no longer string together two sentences and asked that his assistant accompany him home. They rode their bicycles. 'Everything in my field of vision wavered and was distorted as if seen in a curved mirror. I also had the sensation of being unable to move from the spot. Nevertheless, my assistant later told me that we had travelled very rapidly. . .

'In spite of my delirious, bewildered condition, I had brief periods of clear and effective thinking . . . The dizziness and sensation of fainting became so strong at times that I could no longer hold myself erect, and had to lie down on a sofa. My surroundings had now transformed themselves in more terrifying ways. Everything in the room spun around, and the familiar objects and pieces of furniture assumed grotesque, threatening forms . . . Every exertion of my will, every attempt to put an end to the disintegration of the outer world and the dissolution of my ego, seemed to be wasted effort. A demon had invaded me, had taken possession of my body, mind, and soul . . . I was taken to another world, another place, another time. My body seemed to be without sensation, lifeless, strange. Was I dying? Was this the transition? At times I believed myself to be outside my body, and then perceived clearly, as an outside observer, the complete tragedy of my situation.'

After the arrival of a hastily summoned doctor, who pronounced Hoffman physically sound, he began to relax, his fear of going insane diminishing. Seemingly, the doctor's diagnosis had eased his mind a bit. 'Now, little by little I could begin to enjoy the unprecedented colours and plays of shapes . . . Kaleidoscopic, fantastic images surged in on me, alternating, variegated, opening and then closing themselves in circles and spirals, exploding in coloured fountains, rearranging and hybridizing themselves in constant flux. It was particularly remarkable how every acoustic perception, such as the sound of a door handle or a passing automobile, became transformed into optical perceptions.'

Eventually Hoffman fell asleep and woke the next morning tired, but oddly refreshed. 'A sensation of well-being and renewed life flowed through me. When

I later walked out into the garden, in which the sun shone now after a spring rain, everything glistened and sparkled in a fresh light. The world was as if newly created. All my senses vibrated in a condition of highest sensitivity, which persisted for the entire day.'

The events of those days in 1943 were difficult to keep secret. Word spread through medical journals to psychologists, and soon to writers, musicians and hipsters eager for the newest 'kick'. Large quantities of the stuff found their way around the world, circulating mainly from research facilities, some more credible than others. The CIA's repugnant MK-Ultra experiments during the fifties had made much use of Sandoz's own, testing the drug on unsuspecting victims, sometimes driving them out of their minds with fear, as they didn't know what was happening to them. But others, through experiments conducted at universities by psychology departments, had wonderful experiences and spread the word. News of the 'wonder drug', spread quickly.

By 1963, Aldous Huxley, Cary Grant, George Clinton of Parliament-Funkadelic, Harvard psychologist Dr Timothy Leary, jazz players Thelonious Monk, Charlie Mingus and Maynard Ferguson, John Coltrane, and allegedly, John F. Kennedy had all had the LSD experience. Englishman Michael Hollingshead, a British cultural attaché in New York, managed to get hold of a large quantity, and his Manhattan flat became the scene of many 'acid' (as it became known) parties. Hollingshead was the man who had first turned on Timothy Leary to LSD, giving him a generous dose from the near mythical batch of pharmaceutical Sandoz acid known as 'Lot. no. H-00047'. Hollingshead had been dispensing doses from this batch since the very early sixties, carrying his acid in a tightly sealed mayonnaise jar. Jazz players Monk, Mingus and Ferguson were all dosed by Hollingshead.

Nigel Gordon, the first of the Cambridge set to move to London, to be a student at a film school, packed his clothes and belongings at the end of term for a holiday back home. In his bag were the 8mm camera from his film course, and carefully wrapped, a glass vial of pure pharmaceutical LSD. Gordon and Ian 'Imo' Moore began the task of placing one drop into cubes of sugar. They prepared hundreds, but as the day wore on, they absorbed the LSD transdermally, as Hoffman had, through their skin, and soon were quite high.[58] 'The acid we took in the sixties was incredibly powerful,' says Gordon, 'The dosage was upwards of 250 mcg, and it would have been inconceivable to have gone dancing in a club like people do today.'

David Gale says, 'LSD came to Cambridge, and it was absolutely imperative that you take it; you had to, whether you wanted to or not. In those days the dosage was very high compared to what's considered normal now. We had been led to believe by Timothy Leary and his followers that 500 micrograms was the average dose, whereas these days 250 or less is quite adequate. At 500 mcg there is an irresistible and powerful surge dropping away from the ego and leading you back into the unconscious and the world of hallucinations. We had read about this great excitement, and Syd and I would have been fully conversant with the whole panoply of LSD values.

'There was an occasion when my parents went to Australia for six months, leaving me their well-appointed, middle-class house to live in, all on my own. In fact, a number of people moved in, and people started to come around the house on a regular basis, much to the alarm of the neighbours, who were quiet, academic middle-class Cambridge types. A certain amount of consciousness expanding experimentation was held. These days, LSD seems a recreational drug; in those days the aura around it was quite different. That's not to say that people weren't hedonistic about it, because they were, but it was dignified by saying that you were involved in a consciousness expanding quest for the inner self.'

Jenny Gordon says, 'When David Gale's parents went to Australia, everybody moved in. Nigel did, Johnny Johnson and Paul Charrier. There was this wild time in Gale's house which just turned to chaos. And Dave didn't seem to mind, but his parents did when they got back.'

Syd Barrett's great friend Paul Charrier, being the most adventurous of the Cambridge set, was the first to try acid. Gale remembers, 'Paul took to cannabis and anything else he could lay his hands on with great enthusiasm, and when LSD came along, he was the first person in our group to take it. When he came back, he was a kind of a space pilot stepping out of the capsule to be clapped and greeted as a hero by the assembled bohemians. He says that you saw God and went to territories that were absolutely unbelievable. In quick succession, all of us, including Storm, myself, Syd, and lots of other people all took it. And we all thought it was great, although in my case it was hard to conceal the fact that it was profoundly terrifying. Syd, however, found it amazing. It was around this time that all these people from Cambridge decided to move to London.

'The evidence of strangeness that I saw in Syd prior to our moving to London, took place in the garden of my parent's house. Syd and Paul took acid together on a summer's day, and Paul was ebullient and explosively energetic, he would dash around and laugh when he was on acid, as would Syd. But I think this was a key transitional point for Syd. It became apparent during the course of the afternoon that he had been holding a plum, orange and matchbox. Syd had them in his hands, and his attention gradually devolved from the world around him to studying these objects. That's common enough on LSD, which after all gives you that distorted sense of time and space, and microscopic vision that makes it seem very wonderful. But he became more and more engrossed in these three objects, and Paul started to tease him, saying, "What are you doing with the orange, the plum and the matchbox?" and Syd would go, "Leave me alone", quite amiably. In the end Paul seized them and jumped up and down on them. He then chased Syd into the bathroom and turned the shower on him, and they played like six-year-olds, showering each other with bath water. Syd seemed to have been jerked out of that solipsistic episode. Looking with the benefit of hindsight, you might argue that this was an augury of things to come.'

Indeed, the utter absorption that Barrett had demonstrated in these three innocuous objects, seeing as them planets in a vast acid-induced solar system, would resurface in later years. This absorption in this world of his own imaginings would lead others to see him as locked in some sort of catatonic stupor. The plum, orange and matchbox incident was to be engraved in the minds of the friend who had been there that odd afternoon. For Storm Thorgerson, it was to remain a potent symbol linked in his mind with Syd, as the plum, organ and matchbox would show up years later on a Barrett LP set designed by him, and also in Thorgerson's film clip for 'Shine On You Crazy Diamond', which accompanies live Pink Floyd renditions of that song.

Syd, Storm, Ian Moore and David Gale were all duly turned on that summer. It was a logical progression from their cannabis-fuelled antics of the past two years, but it was a very great bound forward indeed. The literature was scant, the long-term effects unknown, and even the side effects were a matter of conjecture and inarticulate murmurings about 'bad trips'. As for dosages? Who really knew; even Leary and Alpert were virtual neophytes. 'We were all seeking higher elevation and wanted everyone to experience this incredible drug,' says Nigel Gordon. 'Syd was very self-obsessed and uptight in many ways so we thought it was a good idea. In retrospect I don't think he was equipped to deal with the experience because he was unstable to begin with. Syd was a very simple person who was having very profound experiences that he found it hard to deal with.'[59]

That autumn was the beginning of what would be Syd's intense infatuation with psychedelic drugs. Literally hundreds of trips would occur in the space of the next six or so years, ultimately wreaking a devastating toll. For Syd at least, LSD was a Pandora's box of delights. However with such a powerful substance as LSD, the heights one reached on acid would surely be matched by equally spectacular lows. LSD truly was, to paraphrase Aldous Huxley, the 'heaven and hell drug'. But none of this was apparent at the time, and the long-term effects of acid were unknown. The strength of the LSD experience is hard to gauge or even illustrate in words. A flurry of incredible revelations, the dimensions of which are so vast it's well nigh impossible to capture them. A disorienting rupture in day-to-day reality, for better or for worse.

Thus began a lengthy summer of experimentation with acid. Gilmour, Barrett, Gordon, Gale, Thorgerson, Charrier, Imo, Russell Page, Johnny Johnson – everyone took it eventually, and the Cambridge set had some unusual experiences during this feverish time. David Gale recalls one such incident, 'There is a place called the Roman Roads outside Cambridge, where an old Roman road runs through the countryside, and it's only a mile beyond where Syd lived, on the edge of town. We drove out to the Roman Roads one night, four or five of us in a car, including Syd. We were driving in the middle of the night on a bumpy country track and we suddenly came across what we thought looked like the site of some strange black magic ritual. There seemed to be crosses driven into the earth with curious things on them. I had a vague impression of a cloaked figure standing there, so we just screamed and drove very fast away back to Cambridge and the warmth of our own households. I don't know what we saw out on the road that night, whether it was more than a bush with an old coat hanging off it, I'll never know, but you have to look at an era where people were doing massively powerful things to their personality structures with mind-altering drugs . . . Nobody really knew the implications; the strongest information available came from Timothy Leary, which was entirely positive. The psychoanalytic implication rather than the consciousness expansion implication was never talked about. The idea that you would have a bad trip which would lead to more bad trips which would unhinge you wasn't a popular idea, it was considered uncool. It was a test of psychedelic manhood or personhood to take trips and to survive and have had a great time. And of course, most people did have a great time, 98 per cent of the time. Psychologist R.D. Laing was writing about schizophrenics who had become schizophrenic for reasons other than drugs, Laing didn't talk about LSD causing schizophrenia, although there was the term "psychotomimetic", which was current then, so it was a thought in the minds of the psychoanalytic establishment, but not in the minds of the ravers.'

John 'Hoppy' Hopkins, a primary catalyst in the emerging English underground, first took acid in spring 1964, a few weeks before the annual CND-sponsored Aldermaston march. He was working as a freelance photographer at the time, having dropped out from his 'proper' job with the Atomic Energy Commission after a brouhaha with M15 and a canary yellow hearse.* Hoppy had set up house in Westbourne Terrace, in the Notting Hill Gate district of London. He also had a profitable sideline in dope, which was slowly but surely turning on ever larger numbers of the new intelligentsia. Hoppy was brilliant at connecting people and acting as a catalyst, and was hip to whatever was new and interesting. 'A friend whom I'd known from Cambridge,' says Hoppy, 'a very bright guy who had been at Stanford University doing research, phoned up and says, "Hullo, I'm back in London and I've got something interesting, come and see me." So I went to see him and he says, "Look, there's this stuff, LSD-25, a new drug." He told me about it and I guess I'd heard about it. Five of us took our first trip together, there was Peter Jenner, Andrew King, my girlfriend Allison and me. We went down to St Ives, to a flat with a great glass picture window and we took this stuff. As I recall, it was on sugar cubes wrapped in tinfoil. The guy who provided the acid also gave us a copy of Huxley's *Doors Of Perception/Heaven And Hell*, and it was done with seriousness, not as a sacrament but with due attention to Leary's "set and setting". And I'm very pleased looking back that the guy took so much trouble. It's very important how you

*Jonathan Greene's *Days In The Life* covers this and a great many other classic sixties stories. A must-read.

take your first trip, things are never the same afterwards. I was pleased that I'd been set up with a framework so that I could understand and relate to it.

'Various people brought it from the States, I know of about two, and one was my friend from Stanford and the other was Michael Hollingshead. Hollingshead arrived in England bringing some acid with him, and he was dealing it out in sugar cubes as well. And when the Aldermaston march actually happened, instead of carrying a banner, me and some other people ran up and down by the side of the march in Whitehall with signs that had things like question marks on them. Things were never the same after acid. That was the great turnover point.'

'Hoppy was working as a freelance photographer,' says Joe Boyd. 'I'd been in Britain in 1964 as the tour manager of the Blues and Gospel Caravan, with Muddy Waters and Sister Rosetta Thorpe among others. Hoppy was assigned to take pictures and I got him tickets to one of the concerts and we became friends.' Boyd, an American, was overwhelmed by the strength of English audiences' reactions. Where many of the stars of the Caravan were criminally ignored in their own country, in England they were raised to a status of near deity. Hoppy told him, 'If you need a place to stay, you can stay here,' which Boyd duly did. Boyd decided to stay in the UK, and except for a year or two in L.A., he's never been back.

'Through Nigel Young and Michael Horovitz,' says Miles, 'I met up with a similar scene in London, which was John Hopkins and his merry men. And Hoppy had this communal flat at Westbourne Terrace where Oxford people used to stay. So I met Hoppy. John Howe was there, sharing one of the rooms. In 1960, he was featured in a scare story about beatniks, and he was quoted as saying, "Why should I wash?" The same article had a picture of these beatniks at Liverpool's Gambia Terrace flat with John Lennon, Johnny Byrne and Stu Sutcliffe lying around on the floor.'

Miles recalls London as being terribly dull but peppered with small vibrant scenes, ranging from the late-night caffs in Notting Hill to bizarre Primrose Hill parties where people dropped mescaline and went looning about in the nearby park. But for the most part, the city effectively shut down at midnight, and food, dancing, booze and other essentials of life were nowhere to be found. The city was still seized by a sort of paralytic limbo brought on by the War, the end of the Empire and its riches, and the boredom of the fifties. 'I was living in Gilbert Place across from the British Museum, and the whole street was lit by gas lamps. There was no electricity in the house, so you had no phones or televisions or light bulbs. You're talking about London just creeping out of the post-War period, huge numbers of bomb sites everywhere. A tremendous number of streets had never had electricity. A phone was such a luxury.'

Slowly, though, things were coming around. Horovitz and Brown had ongoing *New Departures* events at the ICA in Dover Street starting in 1964. The Profumo scandal and subsequent resignation of the Conservative government the previous year, growing economic prosperity, the rescinding of the ban on

D.H. Lawrence's *Lady Chatterley's Lover* and the advent of the Beatles all amounted to a loosening of the Victorian corset of society. There were large numbers of young people born after the War, and they were the first young generation to have loot for records, clothes and hair-dos. The Teds of the 1950s, with their swinging chains and drape coats, had given way to the Mods and Rockers. The mods looked to Europe for inspiration, largely France and Italy, and favoured clean, tailored clothes and pop music. The rockers were stalwarts by comparison, clinging to BSA motorcycles, American rock'n'roll and black leather. The riots at Brighton and Margate on Bank Holiday weekend 1964 sparked off by confrontations between rival gangs of mods and rockers signified if nothing else a new restlessness in youth. All dressed up and nowhere to go!

Miles found a job working at Better Books bookstore soon after. 'Better Books was full of the young poetry scene people. An American guy called Tom Clarke who was studying at the University of Essex, but was also the poetry editor for the *Paris Review*, which was the most prestigious literary/poetry magazine, slightly straighter than the *Evergreen Review*. He did a tremendous interview with Ginsberg in 1965, probably the best one ever. Tom was around a lot, Stuart Montgomery from the Falcon Press, all these little editors. They were hanging out at the shop, also the poets. There a lot of mimeograph poetry books, limited editions. They were called "Night Train" and "Beat Express". Lee Harwood did one in the East End, and they and all their friends were there. And there was the *New Departures* crowd. And also the beatnik scene, people like Donovan, who used to hang out anywhere there was a free drink. You'd have visiting Americans, like Andy Warhol, Edie Sedgwick and Baby Jane Holzer for the poetry reading that Allen Ginsberg did. I was privileged to meet everyone I wanted to meet. I first met Burroughs in 1964.'

Nigel Gordon often stopped in at Better Books, 'Poet Adrian Haggart was there a lot, he now lives as a hermit in New Zealand. Also, Burroughs was in London and accessible.'

Miles says, 'When I was managing Better Books during 1965, we had a great deal. We used to swap Penguin Books for City Lights Books publications, box after box. I used to bring in Grove Press editions from America of *Sexus*, *Nexus* and *Plexus* by Henry Miller and sell them at 10 shillings each. I would take a whole box of them into Soho and sell them for £2 10 shillings each to the pornographers, and they would sell them for £5 each. So people could chose if they wanted to buy them from a dirty book shop or buy them at a literary book shop. We never kept them under the counter, and no one busted us. We used to bring 200 at a time of each title. Tony Godwin owned the shop and was the publisher and chief managing director at Penguin. He changed the orange covers and brought in Alan Aldrige, the Scottish designer, to make full colour covers. We did limited edition records of Ginsberg and Ferlinghetti doing readings at Better Books. Alan Aldrige did the sleeves for those as well, which were some of the earliest quasi-psychedelic design work.'

*

In the summer of 1964, Barrett had moved down to London to study painting at Camberwell Art School in Peckham, sharing a flat with David Gale in a building owned by Seamus O'Connell's mother. Others in the Cambridge set would drift in and out, including Mick Clark. 'Syd was staying with us in Tottenham Court Road,' says Seamus O'Connell. 'He had a bedsit there. My mother had set up house in this place, and various friends had gotten bedsits there. An appalling place, but it had an atmosphere to it. And Syd was getting interested in the occult, which my mother was also into. She would do tarot card readings for him.' Indeed, Barrett was very keen on the occult and many a night would sit up talking to Seamus's mother about astrology, tarot cards and the like. She introduced him to the *I-Ching*, the Chinese oracle based on readings drawn from random numbers thrown with coins, probably the most interesting of occult fortune telling devices, as it has as much to do with probability and mathematics as divination and mysticism. Syd was suitably intrigued.

'When we moved from Cambridge,' says David Gale. 'Syd and I shared a flat in Tottenham Street, off the Tottenham Court Road. Seamus O'Connell was at school with Syd, and his mother was a strange bohemian lady who read palms. And she used to read our palms in her flat in Tottenham Street. Syd and I got a room in this hideous block full of deranged people, and the rent tribunal practically insisting the landlord give it to us for free, it was so dreadful. Syd and I lived in the same room for a number of months before I moved down to nearby Earlham Street, near Cambridge Circus.

'And we had a very good time there. We were very impressed by London, small-town boys coming to London. We used to get back at the end of our separate days and discuss the famous people we'd seen in the street. We'd award points depending on how famous they were. I saw Petula Clark in a white sports car and was awarded six points. And then Syd would see Sandie Shaw and then we'd tot up the points for the day. That was very entertaining. We went to the London Zoo and watched a baboon picking shit out of its arse and eating it, which we found rather compelling. Syd did a marvellous cartoon drawing of a baboon's arse with this hand picking shit out, which he pinned to the wall of our hideous room. He made up a very good experimental magazine which he called "Fart And Joy", which was just a collection of bits of writing and drawing and painting. He was, visually, very competent indeed, and an excellent draftsman. He bound this book, just a few pages of cardboard with strange artwork. He was still very jolly in those times.'

'One time when Syd came back from a visit to Cambridge, something weird had happened with his eyes,' recalls O'Connell. 'One eye actually looked deader than the other. So we asked him about it, and though he didn't go into detail, he says he'd had some strange experience in Cambridge which was psychic in some way. For a few days, this one eye looked dead.' This incident suggests that Barrett had a mild brain trauma, the first physiological sign of impending trouble. The nature of Barrett's strange experience is unknown, but later he told Pink Floyd co-manager Andrew King that he'd had a mystic encounter with Nature during a visit back home.

Barrett would take the tube down to Camberwell School of Arts, in Peckham, south London. He was enthusiastic and showed promise, but wasn't terribly committed to his studies. Roger Waters opined, 'People who go to art schools are people who don't want to indulge in a career with a big C. Also, art school is one of those situations where you have got time if you want it, and can get away with it. There's not so much to learn. You have to do more and learn less.'[60] Barrett said, 'I came up to London. It was painting that brought me here to art school. I always enjoyed that much more than school.'[61]

Art school was of tremendous importance in the development of what we know as the sixties. A tremendous number of gifted painters, fashion designers, writers and multi-media artists came from the various schools: Hornsey, St Martins, Camberwell and others. It was also a laboratory of crucial importance to the generation of young English rock musicians about to emerge. Peter Townshend, Eric Clapton, Syd Barrett, John Lennon and others all attended art schools in the early sixties, where government grants enabled a young musician to form bands, be exposed to a wealth of new influences, and generally have time to develop their own ideas.

'One of the only sectors of society that resisted the phoniness in society were the people in the art schools,' says Pete Brown. 'Although I never attended art school, which was my regret, I always hung around people from the art schools because I knew that that was where it was at. That was where most of the creativity came from. I got turned on to the Beats because the art school people were always looking for, and open to, outside influences. Most of my friends, even people who I worked with a lot, or have remained friends with to this day, like Roger Chapman and Viv Stanshall, all went to art school. There was a freedom in the art schools that was totally missing in the universities and in other forms of education from the late fifties to the mid sixties. They were the best cultural breeding grounds for the more creative white musicians, writers and artists.'

'Some fantastic things were done at art schools,' says Pete Townshend in an interview with *International Times*. 'People were doing things which are now recognised as psychedelic images, and slides with liquid in them and things like that. Some great things were being produced.' Joe Boyd, who would produce Pink Floyd's début single, says, 'An awful lot of the British bands in the sixties were art school students, so there already was an attitude of theatricality, being very conscious of the way things looked. I think that was a natural extension into psychedelic light shows and theatricality. And that was a British tradition, one thing that British brought to rock music.'[62]

Roger Waters had been studying architecture at London's Regent Street Polytechnic since September 1962. During 1963 he met fellow architecture students Nick Mason and Rick Wright. Wright lasted a year at the school before switching to Trinity College of Music. Roger Waters says, 'The encouragement to play my guitar came from a man who was head of my first year. He encouraged me to bring the guitar into the classroom. If I wanted to sit in the corner and play guitar during periods that were set aside for design work and architecture, he thought that was perfectly all right. It was my first feeling of encouragement. At the Polytechnic I got involved with people who played in bands, although I couldn't play very well. I sang a little and played the harmonica and guitar a bit.[63] I'd had a guitar in Cambridge, but I never really played it much. Nick and Rick were both there doing the same course and we had a kind of blues group when we were in our second year.'[64]

Formed in 1963, the band, initially known as Sigma 6, counted among its members Waters, Wright, Mason and Keith Noble (vocals), Clive Metcalf (bass), and Juliet Gale (vocals). Juliet lasted but a few months in the band, marrying Rick Wright soon after. During the next three years, the band would be variously known as the T-Set (a pun on the ruler used in drafting classes), the Megadeaths (reflecting Waters' continuing interest in CND and disarmament), the Architectural Abdabs, the Screaming Abdabs, and simply the Abdabs.

'I went to architecture school at the Regent Poly in 1963,' says painter Duggie Fields. 'I met Roger Waters, who was in the same group. On Fridays there would be an afternoon dance, and I was Rick's wife Juliet's dancing partner. When I started architecture school I was living at home, at the end of the first term I got a flat in Queensway Terrace with two other architecture students and a fashion student.'

'We were all students together in the first year,' says Nick Mason, 'and there was a guy in the year who was writing songs and he wanted to play the songs to a publisher. So he asked various people if they played instruments and if they might be prepared to put a little band together to play his songs. So, Rick and Roger and myself all "admitted" that we did play instruments in some sort of fashion, and so we sort of put a band together. I remember we played the songs for the publisher and he says the songs were quite good but "forget the band". I think if we'd listened to anyone who had any taste at the time we'd have all folded up right then and there. But fortunately we were so egocentric and just carried on.'[65] Waters says, 'We like to think that we would have made it anyway, later on maybe. We definitely didn't believe in the myth of managers making bands.'[66]

Wright played piano and had grown up entranced by jazz and classical music, listening to Duke Ellington and Aaron Copeland. 'We had all the usual influences,' he says, 'the music I was into at the time was Miles Davis.'[67] Jazz trumpeter Davis's 1959 masterpiece, *Kind Of Blue*, featuring John Coltrane on saxophone and Bill Evans on piano, was a strong Wright influence. The modal structures of that album were to prove a strong influence of Wright's keyboard style. Wright told *Q* in a 1996 interview, 'When I was first in the Floyd I wasn't into pop music at all – I was listening to jazz and when the Beatles released 'Please Please Me' I didn't like it at all. In fact, I thought it was utterly puerile. The first music I ever heard was classical, because I was growing up in the days before rock'n'roll, but then I was exposed to jazz on radio stations and started listening to the more traditional players like Humphrey Lyttelton and Kenny Ball. Then I discovered Miles Davis's *Kind Of Blue* album and got very excited. *Porgy And Bess* is a brilliant record – the nearest thing to hearing a trumpet being made to sound like the human voice. The influences in the Floyd came from lots of different areas. Syd was more into Bo Diddley; I had the more classical approach.'

Hornsey College of Art lecturer Mike Leonard says, 'I first met Roger, Nick and Rick because I was teaching architecture and they were students at the Regent Poly. When I bought my house in 1963 I said, "Well, there's some space here," and they moved into the ground floor.' Nick and Rick were the first to move in, but both soon went back home. 'Then there was Bob Close, Dave Gelpin, another Camberwell bloke, Syd, and Roger Waters. While they were living in the house, I was starting to work with light projections. This was during the time they were starting the group up.'

Leonard owned a three-floor house on a quiet street in Highgate, north London. In his free time he made light machines. Descended from the lights used in stage craft, Leonard's light machines were entirely mechanical; bulky light projectors with various rotating discs attached to them. On each circular disk Leonard would hammer designs and shapes, such as stars or wavy lines and patterns, cover them in coloured cellophane, then project the light through crystals of varying shapes and sizes to create ever-shifting patterns. It was to prove a key influence on the new band.

Leonard says, 'I was doing most of my experiments at Hornsey, where I got a couple of days teaching. A guy called Clive Lattimore, who ran the Department of Interior Design was a friend of mine and one Christmas he invited me for a lunch. After lunch we had a projector out and started playing with it, I put some coloured cellophane toffee papers in it and combs and made wiry patterns. He was a bit of an opportunist, Clive, because all these art school people are always looking at a way to expand their empire. In 1962 or 1963 he set up a department and we used to play around with lights, building three-dimensional arrangements, shining spotlights and we acquired a fairly reasonable collection of lighting equipment. I gave Clive some ideas of what I wanted, rotating disks and things, and he built them in the workshop. So most of the lighting experiments were done there, during the time of Syd Barrett. Later on I left Hornsey and set up my own workshop in my house. Up in the attic I used to play around with music, and that was where we did the "Tomorrow's World" segment with Pink Floyd [in late 1967], with them playing music and me with the light machine.

'There was a big mutiny at Hornsey, when the students went on strike for a year because all the staff were hogging the workshops building light machines. The whole thing there was people building their empires. The workshop was always taken up by things like this, so the students went out and got stroppy. It was traumatic because the students ended up doing no work, and a couple of the staff had a breakdown because they wanted to help the students, yet keep their jobs. So there was a split.'

Light machines were something that sprung up spontaneously around the world in the early sixties. William Burroughs and Brian Gysin were experimenting with stroboscopic light machines in Paris's famous 'Beat Hotel' at 9 rue Git-le-Coeur. Leonard says, 'In San Francisco there was a group who did light shows in a planetarium with all electronic music and I got a record from them. But it was before they had the equipment to do electronic sound properly and it sounded like someone's vacuum cleaner being switched off and on.'

Artist Mark Boyle, who would become renowned for his own light work in the Underground, was involved with the Hornsey Light and Sound workshop as well. He claims to have staged the first public light show in Britain during 1963, a piece called 'Suddenly Last Supper' which he and fellow artist Joan Hills staged at their house. They also worked on light shows for Michael Horovitz's *New Departures* and several avant-garde musicians and composers.[68]

After six months, off and on, of playing together, the band were joined by Syd Barrett and guitarist Bob Close, another student at Regent Poly. Barrett joined in December 1964. Waters explains, 'Syd and I had always vowed that when he came up to art school, which he inevitably would do being a very good painter, he and I would start a band in London. I was already in a band, so he joined that.'[69]

'Syd breezed in,' says Leonard, 'He was a very sparkling, ebullient character. Buoyant and bouncy, full of energy. Later, he went strange in the head; you would never have realised it at the time. There wasn't any shadow hanging over him. The others could be a bit remote and standoffish, superior in some way. You would ask them a question and they wouldn't deign to reply. But Syd was always a very warm and happy guy.' Nick Mason says, 'Syd was absolutely delightful at a time when it was fashionable to be rather cool, and no one introduced anyone to anyone else, so you could spend whole parties addressing everyone as "man". And Syd was someone who would come up and say, "Hi, I'm Syd", a really easy and outgoing personality.'[70]

Syd Barrett at this stage, was still playing bass, as he had since his days with the Hollering Blues in Cambridge. He explained, 'I had to buy another guitar because Roger played bass, a Rickenbacker, and we didn't want a group with two bass players. So I changed guitars.'[71] Roger Waters says, 'With the advent of Bob Close we actually had someone who could play an instrument. It was really then we did the shuffle job of who played what. I was demoted from lead guitar to rhythm guitar and finally bass. There was always this frightful fear that I could land up as the drummer.'[72] Barrett claimed, 'Bo Diddley was definitely my greatest influence. Around that time one came across so many unheard of records that one felt one was really discovering something.'[73] Nick Mason remembers that they learned their repertoire off of a handful of *Authentic R&B, volumes 1 to 3* LPs, as well as Syd's collection of Bo Diddley.[74] Bo Diddley would provide the bulk of the early Pink Floyd's slim repertoire with his Gretsch guitar-driven songs like 'Roadrunner', 'I Can Tell', 'Bo Diddley' and others that would provide Barrett and co. with a firm R&B base from which Barrett would later launch his excursions.*

'Syd's great inspiration was Bo Diddley,' says Leonard. 'He was always doing Bo Diddley licks, the one that sounds like the South American clave beat. Syd was a great Bo Diddley fan. They did offbeat jazz standards, Lowell Fulson's "My Babe" and "Green Onions" by Booker T. and the MGs. Nothing experimental at that time. Syd's key thing was rhythm, which was quite strong. He was quite keen on syncopated Bo-Diddley-style cross rhythms, chopping in. That kind of attack really suited his temperament. I can remember him playing with that sort of grit, drive and enthusiasm. He was the internal dynamo of the band; a dynamic person.'

'The Floyd's music arose out of playing together,' said Barrett, 'We didn't set out to do anything new. We worked up to "See Emily Play" and so on quite naturally from the Rolling Stones numbers we used to play. None of us advocated doing anything more eccentric. We waited until we had got the lights together and then went out.'[75]**

The influence of Diddley in Barrett's later work isn't immediately apparent, but the trebly leads, twangy bass notes and hard-layered rhythm of Diddley's more outré material suffuse Barrett's work. He would also make great use of Diddley's bluesy leads played in sharp counterpoint to the rhythm section. Diddley's scratchy strums, like the ones on tracks like 'Bo's Bounce', approximating the sound of a train rolling full bore on its tracks, are also deeply ingrained in Barrett's playing. The distorted glissandi at the very end of 'Roadrunner' are worth noting as well.[76]

'During that period we kept changing the name until we ended up with the Pink Floyd,' said Barrett. 'I'm not sure who suggested it or why, but it stuck.'[77] Though Barrett offered many explanations for the origins of the band's name, most of them fanciful exaggerations or witty lies, even denying naming the band, he is generally acknowledged to have been the one to have picked up a Blind Boy Fuller LP and picked off at random two surnames of old Delta bluesmen from the liner notes. This fits with his creative style, drawing on whatever

*Diddley, an innovator in his own milieu, was considered such a misfit in 1950s Chicago that, according to *Mojo*, his peers wondered if he was from the West Indies. On his song 'Say Man' an incredulous voice asks Diddley, 'Say man, where you from?' to which Diddley replies, 'South America.' 'What part?' asks the voice. Diddley shouts, 'Texas!'

**The Rolling Stones were to be a lifelong favourite of Barrett's, and their influence suffused his music from the very beginning.

was at hand to make something uniquely his own. 'So the Pink Floyd was first formed,'said Rick Wright, 'although we changed the name and returned to it as we went along.'[78]

By now, Leonard and his Hornsey cronies' experimental lights and sound workshop at the college was in full swing, and their experiments with light were accompanied by records. 'We had a little lighting group and some esoteric Japanese koto music and jazz flutes from Yusef Lateef to accompany it. You could move to the music, you could control the lights. But my theory was always not to parallel the music but to provide a counterpoint, so if the music was very dynamic you would do something very gentle with the colours. Or the reverse.' Leonard recruited the band for the workshops. 'I said, "Do you want to come into Hornsey a few evenings and play your music and I'll do my images?" So we did four sessions. At Hornsey we did film and back projections, all sorts of things. They were doing a bluesy sort of thing, they hadn't gotten into their more esoteric music. I was trying to get them out of 4/4 rhythms into free rhythms so they relate to the coloured imagery, because they were still into a bluesy thing.'

These events formed the basis for the Floyd's use of light shows, an integrated part of their stage show throughout the past thirty years. Nick Mason acknowledged this in 1994, 'The most important starting point for the light show was Mike Leonard and the Hornsey College of Art. That was the idea that the music could be improvised and the lighting could be improvised to go with it.[79] And that definitely was an influence.'[80]

Waters says, 'We stopped doing twelve-bar three-minute numbers, i.e., we started doing one chord, going on and on and seeing how we could develop that . . .'[81] We were called the Pink Floyd pretty early on, and . . . we stopped adhering rigidly to the twelve-bar blues thing, and just started improvising around one simple root chord.'[82] Leonard smiles when he remembers, 'But Clive Lattimore said, "Oh, we don't want those sort of people in here." They weren't "cultured" enough for him. Later of course, he became sycophantic and says, "Oh, isn't it marvellous the Pink Floyd are doing so well after we let them use our hall and lights."

'The band was very ordinary, they weren't that good, some of the tapes made here that I listened to were fairly awful. Roger couldn't sing in tune properly, though he later developed his whispering style. There wasn't really a singer in the group. They used to fish around for people to sing when they had to do gigs. Long John Baldry, who was quite a personality, was one of the people they used to chase. One would never have thought they would get anywhere. They never got out of bed until one or two in the afternoon. They found a cat which Roger brought home wrapped in his coat, Syd named it Tunji, after a jazz tune.* They

*This is an interesting aside from Leonard, as it points to a seminal Barrett influence. Jazz saxophonist John Coltrane, with his classic quartet of McCoy Tyner (piano), Jimmy Garrison (bass) and Elvin Jones (drums) recorded 'Tunji' on 29 June 1962 for the album *Coltrane* on the Impulse! label.

used to rehearse here and the noise was so ferocious that the neighbours finally got a petition up, and one woman down the road says it was affecting her health, so they moved off to rehearse in the pub up the road, the Woodman, on Archway Road. When they were here I could the turn the road at the corner about a third of a mile away and still hear them practising. When I worked at my drawing board here I could feel the instruments jumping up and down, because you'd get the sound coming through.' Waters says, 'We played together occasionally. We'd go out and do £10 gigs and play at people's parties, and we bought some gear and gradually got a bit more involved.'[83]

The band performed at various local Highgate pubs, where the locals watched in dismay as the band hacked their way through Bo Diddley's 'Roadrunner' and Rolling Stones and R&B covers. Despite Close's prowess on lead guitar, the band was fairly indistinguishable from any of the hundreds of other bands around at the time. The only elements which set the band apart were Close's capable guitar playing, and the songs of Syd Barrett, which were increasingly inventive. No one in the band had the confidence to sing, so they recruited Chris Dennis, a blues singer from Cambridge.[84]

During the autumn of 1964 and the spring of 1965 the band played at the Woodman Pub, the Regent Street Poly, the Hornsey workshops and at the Beat City Club on Oxford Street. Dennis's singing was adequate, but his style didn't really seem to fit with the others, according to Leonard. Dennis left the band in January of 1965, joining the RAF.

Barrett, during his school holidays, returned to Cambridge. On 2 January, along with his mates Smudge and Stephen Pyle, in an inpromptu band called Those Without, played at a party where a photographer snapped a shot of Barrett, hair beginning to grow out, playing an acoustic guitar and singing.

Presumably the first Barrett original the band began to play was 'Lucy Leave', an R&B style rave-up. Though unclear, the band may have recorded 'Lucy Leave' and a cover of Slim Harpo's 'King Bee' at a studio as early as April 1965.

Leonard notes, 'Even in those day there would be a few groupie ladies, or potential ones, who used to gather outside because the group had long hair. They thought it must be a famous group. I used to go downstairs and eat with them on Sundays and each of them in turn was the Sunday cook. We had a big table, which was really just an old door which I'd put steel legs on. Syd was the cook one Sunday and came round and put half a cabbage on my plate! As we were eating there would be these girls looking in through the window from the street. They would creep round the side of the house.'

Leonard was very tolerant; he must have been to put up with the phenomenal barrage of noise from the early Floyd's primitive amplifiers. In acknowledgement of this, the band briefly billed themselves as Leonard's Lodgers. Leonard at one point was keen to join the band, and played organ with them a few times. Rick Wright says, 'It was quite funny, because we were living with Mike Leonard, our tutor, who wanted to be in the band, and there was no way we wanted him to be in it.'[85] Mike Leonard adds, 'I looked a bit like the way I am now, the same presence and short of wearing a wig, I don't see how anyone would have really accepted me. That's the way things go, if you're born fifteen years too late, you miss out.'[86] 'Mike thought of himself as one of the band,' says Nick Mason. 'But we didn't, because he was too old basically. We used to leave the house to play gigs secretly without telling him.'[87] This particular form of subterfuge would crop up again later, when Syd became a liability.

Leonard's studio, where he built his light machines, opened on to a most incredible living-room. Carpets from Central Asia ran wall to wall, a grand piano under wide front windows. Frozen in time, it's still the focal point of a hip lecturer's flat from the sixties. The clutter, dust and genteel poverty do nothing to detract from its charm. Hundreds of paperbacks line the handmade wooden shelves, alongside hundreds of odd-shaped books on every conceivable subject. A Brassai photo book, an engineering manual, a study of the Sufi mystics, books on science, volumes of poetry, psychological textbooks and a great many other tomes on esoteric subjects. Asian gongs, flutes, African percussion instruments, silver gamelan xylophones from Bali with wooden mallets, lutes, flutes are arrayed everywhere. Crystals and metal discs for the light machines, tools, scattered slides and mountains of accrued papers, newspaper clippings, ancient jazz 78s. Yusef Lateef's LPs mixing jazz with world music, Berlioz, Beethoven, Coltrane, the Radiophonic Workshop, the Goon Show.

Syd must have been thrilled. After the squalor of Tottenham Court Road, here was a fantastic room, an archive of ephemera. Reflecting the deeply English collector's mentality, Leonard had assembled a veritable treasure trove of base materials from which Syd refined his aesthetics. It was here that he sat at the slightly out of tune grand piano working out primitive versions of his new songs, the sun streaming in through the curtains in that far-off spring of 1965. Inventing and restlessly improvising as he went along, a sort of self-guided tutelage followed. The strength of the autodidact lies in unfettered originality, as the individual is forced to come up with new ways of tackling old problems simply because of a lack of previous patterns to follow. Creativity expended in this search, powered by focus and work, results in increased creativity. Barrett worked best in this sort of milieu, where funded by school grants and unpressured surroundings, he had time to think and develop his music. In Leonard's parlour, Syd was like the gifted child who has found mysterious antique instruments and picking each one up, instinctively learns to play each to its maximum potential. It was here and later on, at the Spontaneous Underground, the All Saints' Hall and UFO that Syd Barrett developed ideas he'd had germinating inside his curious head since back in Cambridge. The songs he'd written on sunny days, lazing at Mill Pond began to take form and alter slightly under the new influences he dug up in Leonard's big room. He'd take a few bars of melody tentatively explored on his guitar, surprising his new band mates with his novel melodic approaches.

Nick Mason says, 'Syd brought the ability to play the guitar, which was quite unusual at that time, and he also brought the ability to perform, and eventually, obviously not immediately, he brought songwriting.'[88] 'I remember when Syd joined the band,' recalls Rick Wright, 'he had all these incredible ideas, lyrically and musically. Very strange, and very childish in a way, some of his stuff, like fairy-tales but totally unique. I'd never heard anything like it.[89] It was great when Syd joined. Before him we'd play the R&B classics, because that's what groups were supposed to do then. But I never liked R&B very much. I was actually more of a jazz fan. With Syd the direction changed, it became more improvised around the guitar and keyboards. Roger started playing the bass as a lead instrument, and I started to introduce more of my classical feel.'[90] Leonard recalls, 'I remember him coming up with all sorts of strange poems about effervescing elephants and things, like Lewis Carroll or Edward Lear. He had a whimsical side, and that really was him, this word spinning that he did.'

Syd Barrett, in a 1971 interview, rather bitterly recalled his bandmates, 'Their choice of material was always very much to do with what they were thinking as architecture students. Rather unexciting people, I would've thought, primarily. I mean, anybody walking into [a] school like that would've been tricked, maybe they were working their entry into an art school. But the choice of material was restricted, I suppose, by the fact that both Roger and I wrote different things. We wrote our own songs, played our own music. They were older, by about two years, I think. I was eighteen or nineteen.'[91]

The age difference was to bother Syd. Like George Harrison in the Beatles, his relative youth led the others to take him less seriously, and it took time before he was on equal footing. He had to assert himself to compete with Waters' sharp tongue and bossy demeanour.

He bought a Fender Esquire Telecaster, which was to remain his mainstay throughout his time with the Floyd and his solo albums until he traded it. He played other guitars during this period, but 'I [always] seemed to use that first one,' said Barrett in 1967. 'It was painted several times, and once I even covered it in plastic sheeting and silver discs . . . I haven't changed anything on it, except that I occasionally adjust the pickups when I need a different sound.'[92] The change in pickups, sometimes out of phase, gave Syd's Esquire Telecaster a distinctive sound. Barrett was fascinated by the actual mechanics of the guitar, in much the same way as others such as avant-jazz guitarist Keith Rowe of AMM were. Barrett was forever trying out new combinations in pickups, tunings, picking, amplification.

His experimental and unorthodox approach to the guitar was something he shared in common with his sixties peers, who, especially under the influence of drugs, were seeking to explore the limits of the instrument. John Lennon alleged that his 'I Feel Fine', released on 18 October 1964, contained the first intentional use of feedback in the intro, though American black musicians had been playing with it for years, notably Buddy Guy, whom Hendrix often cited as an influence. The mortar attack riff of the Kinks' 'You Really Got Me' and 'All Day and All of the Night', big hits in late 1964, paved the way for more adventurous guitar styles.

In the small attic in Leonard's house, Syd had chanced upon a primitive echo box known as the Binson echo unit. Hank Marvin's use of echo had made a strong impression on him, and it was likely with Marvin's style in mind that he duly rigged it up between his guitar and amplifier. Leonard says, 'At that time, there was the Watkins Copycat and the Binson echo unit, which was a tape loop with a magnetic head. Anyone using echo was using one of those two because there wasn't anything else around. All the Binson did was give you five echoes of the original sound in a sequence, with little variation. Syd found it here, it was the only piece of machinery we had. It always used to squeak, and the squeak got picked up in the sound somehow. It was a bit of a nuisance. They borrowed it when they did the odd gig. They had no money so anything they could scrounge they used.'

'We always felt right from the beginning that there could be more to rock'n'roll than standing on stage playing Johnny B. Goode",' says Roger Waters.[93] Nick Mason says, 'To be honest there was no master plan, no perception of what we were, or would become. If we were going to play Bo Diddley covers, fine. We wanted to become famous Bo Diddley players. It was a gradual transition, [until] we began playing improvisations like "Interstellar Overdrive", basically free-form R&B, which we thought was intellectually OK.'[94] Leonard remembers, 'Roger was quite good, he was quite inventive with sound. We didn't have much in the way of sound when we did the workshops, so he made a one-string guitar that I could play around with and make weird bottleneck effects. I had a Farfisa organ and a Binson echo machine, and we used to take those into Hornsey as well. Roger was quite nimble in the mind and was good at seeing what we could get out of what we had. They got some quite good things going. The creativity was there, and I felt sympathetic to people who were moving into different territory, who are doing new things. It was quite a while back, but one can still feel time telescoping.'

Meanwhile, others in the Cambridge set had moved to London. Nigel and Jenny Gordon had been the first. Nigel Gordon says, 'John Dunbar [later the owner of the Indica Art Gallery] was also at Cambridge, and he was going out with pop star Marianne Faithful. I was washing up in Churchill College, where he was a student. I was literally scrubbing these pans clean and he was talking to me through the window saying, "You should go to my Dad's film school," and it seemed like a good idea! John Dunbar's father owned the London School of Film Technique. I actually got a grant to go and moved to London in January, and Jenny and I got married in March.' Jenny Gordon adds, 'He said, "Come and live with me," and I said, "No," because if I was going to be with someone I wanted to be married. So we married very quickly and came to London.'

In January 1965, Gordon joined Bill Barlow from Cambridge to set up house at 101 Cromwell Road, a two-storey flat in Kensington. The flat was to prove a crucial nexus during the coming years. From the start many of the Cambridge contingent would pass through when visiting London, and Cromwell Road became the epicentre of hip. Duggie Fields, who had studied architecture at the Regent Street Poly along with Waters, Wright and Mason, moved in too, 'I moved a few times before ending up in Cromwell Road in 1965. It was a big flat on two floors, with seven bedrooms. There were always at least nine people living there, some nights there would be fifteen people sleeping there. On weekends, there could be any number of people sleeping there. During the week when I came home from college, I can remember walking in and there would be twenty to thirty people sitting around. I didn't know any of them and none of them lived in the flat. Sometimes there would be some amazing people amongst them. Lots of people passed through the flat, lots of people lived there at different stages. Certainly the number of people was enormous. Also, in the building there was another flat full of people from Cambridge who obviously overlapped. They were slightly older, among them were Nigel and Jenny Gordon, who lived downstairs, this couple from Cambridge who I used to see in the street before I met them and think, "Wow, what a wonderful pair!" They were very beautiful, stylish and hip, very impressive.'

David Gale says, 'Nigel and Jenny were the beautiful people of the drugs scene, they were physically exquisite, beautiful and charming. They were admired by people of all sexual persuasions in Cambridge and London and had a constant stream of people coming through. Nigel had a curious, slightly vaporous charm, and was immensely interested in Beat culture. He wrote profusely and hung out with poets. He was visited by people like Ginsberg.'

'One day bled into the next at Cromwell Road,' says Nigel Gordon. 'I liked the atmosphere because I had my camera and would go and film things that were taking place. When Jenny and I got married, the party we had after our marriage was when all the people from Cambridge and all the people I'd met in London first got together.' For Barrett, Cromwell Road was to prove a fateful address, and he began to visit frequently.

In May 1965, at the end of the school term, Bob Close left the band. Leonard says, 'Bob Close's parents told him to stop messing about and he had to leave the group. He wasn't really Pink Floyd in a way.' Nick Mason says, 'When he left, that was another reason to get rid of the old material.' Roger Waters quipped, 'Because we couldn't play it any longer.[95] I think Bob Close leaving had a lot to do with us stopping playing blues; he was a man with a great wealth of blues runs in his head, and when he left we hadn't anyone who had any blues knowledge, so we had to start doing something.[96] We just got bored with rhythm and blues. As Syd wrote more songs, we dropped others from our repertoire. But we went on doing [Bo Diddley's] "I Can Tell", "Roadrunner" and "Gimme a Break".'[97]

Another change in direction came from hearing the Who, who had begun around the same time as the Floyd, with Townshend also enrolled in art school. The influences were similar, mostly R&B, plus the Shadows and Stax. The Who's brilliant guitarist, Pete Townshend, handling lead and rhythm roles simultaneously, as Barrett would, had an eclectic ear, and listened to Beach Boys records, Motown and contemporaries such as the Yardbirds or the Animals. Fuelled by the purple-heart amphetamine tablets prevalent in the Mod subculture they came out of, the Who began to pound their own compositions with great volume and force. A comparison of their 1964 'I'm the Face' (recorded as the High Numbers) and their February 1965 'I Can't Explain' shows a marked progression in clean, aggressive guitar lines, what artist Pearce Marchbank summed up as the very epitome of Pop Art injected into music. Townshend was literally trying to make pop singles into art, not in a pretentious way, but mirroring the audacious colours and size of a Rosenquist painting.

The formidable rhythm section of bassist John Entwistle and brilliant drummer Keith Moon provided Townshend with a firm base on which to take excursions on guitar. Their live set at clubs like the Marquee became legendary for their full-bore fifteen-minute covers of Motown songs. On-stage at the Marquee, the Who would use a heavy guitar attack, differing from the singles they had issued, and giving them a chance to work out ideas at length and high volume. Barrett was listening, and Townshend's long drawn-out distorted solos made a strong impression. Roger Waters affirmed, 'I'm sure it was the noises that Pete Townshend was making then, squeaks and feedback, that influenced Syd, so we started making strange noises instead of doing the blues.'[98]

The watershed was the Who's single 'Anyway, Anyhow, Anywhere', released on 21 May 1965. In his biography of the Who, *Before I Get Old*, Dave Marsh relates how Townshend, the band's guitarist, had been lying around at home, stoned, listening to Charlie Parker. The sheer freedom in Parker's solos stirred him to scribble the phrase 'anyway, anyhow, anywhere' on a piece of paper. In the morning, realising it was an apt summation of the freewheeling spirit of London, Townshend and singer Roger Daltrey penned lyrics which celebrated the new youth's defiantly energetic attitude. Within months it was the theme song for the TV pop show *Ready, Steady, Go!*, heralding the arrival of the weekend. The single was a major influence for Syd Barrett, not its lyrics but its astonishing barrage of guitar pyrotechnics. It's perhaps the single greatest forerunner of Barrett's emergent style. Townshend unleashes epic squalls of then-shocking feedback, doing distortion-laden glissandos and manic Morse-code blips to the accompaniment of drummer Keith Moon matching every note with crazed drum rolls. 'Anyway, Anyhow, Anywhere' provided the outline for Barrett's course over the next year, as he began to experiment, raising the volume and not worrying so much about playing tidy solos, listening instead to the sound of his own 'intuitive groove'.

Other things were stirring in London at large. On 8 May Beat poet *extra-*

ordinaire Allen Ginsberg arrived after a whirlwind tour of Czechoslovakia. No sooner had he been crowned king of the exuberant Czech students May Day festivities than he was deported by the equally suspicious Czechoslovakian government. The timing of Allen's arrival was fortuitous, as his presence in London can be seen in retrospect as one of the catalysts for much of what was to come. Allen showed up at Better Books, where an astonished Miles invited him to stay at his flat upon learning that he had nowhere to stay. Ginsberg used Better Books as his centre of operations during his stay, conversing with the poets, scenesters and intelligentsia. Miles notes, 'There was a room devoted entirely to readings, and had tables, chairs, a drinks dispensing machine and a little stage. Allen took it over as his headquarters, and would sit there most days.'

The following evening Ginsberg and Miles, along with several thousand others gathered for a pivotal Albert Hall concert for that other American Jewish bard, Bob Dylan. It was an epochal concert, with Dylan making a massive impact on those who witnessed the shows.

Ginsberg held a momentous poetry reading at Better Books. There were so many people that that those who couldn't squeeze into the room stood ten deep at the door to hear the *eminence grise* of Beat verse. Inspired by the turnout, a meeting was held at Better Books on 1 June to organise a poetry reading. Miles recalls, 'I was present at the initial meeting for the poetry reading where we were talking about the success of the reading Allen Ginsberg did at Better Books, which was very very successful, with no advertising at all, and the place was standing-room only. It was so crowded. Allen was saying that Ferlinghetti was in Paris, Gregory Corso was in Rome, and Vosnezensky was coming over from Moscow. And Allen says, "Why don't we do a big reading with all the poets?" We couldn't have it at Better Books because there wasn't enough room, so we were thinking of other places to have it. And Barbara Rubin, who was Allen's girlfriend from New York, said, "Where is the biggest place in town?"

'My wife, Sue, said, "The Albert Hall." So Barbara Rubin went to the phone, rang up the Albert Hall and booked it, for ten days' time. It cost £450, and Dan Richter, an American and publisher of *Residue* magazine, was sitting there too; he was married to an English girl called Jill, who came from a wealthy family. Dan called up Jill and she said she would guarantee the money, so we had the Albert Hall. I wasn't all that involved in the organisation of it, Allen was staying at my flat so there were plenty of meetings there. There were a couple more meetings in Better Books, and John Esam and Mike Horovitz got involved slightly later.' John Esam, an ebullient New Zealander, was a resident of 101 Cromwell Road with Nigel and Jenny, and put considerable energy into organising the Albert Hall poetry reading.

'There was this big pressure from the English Poets Co-op, who says they wanted to read too,' says Miles. 'Allen suggested Harry Fainlight read and Alex Trocchi compere the thing. We had meetings at Alex's place. There were lots of meetings in those days. All the people who were engaged in organising it also wanted to read. The list got to be about eighteen people, and I was thinking by then that it would be appalling. A lot of these poets had never read anywhere except outside a pub! To go and read in the Albert Hall was just a big ego trip. I remained involved in it though.'

Publicity was left in the formidable hands of Hoppy and Rubin, who generated an impressive media response. A lead-in on the BBC's evening news and a photo shoot with all the poets gathered in front of the Albert Memorial guaranteed a large turnout. Hoppy's photos appeared in all the Sunday papers, and a mass mailing for the 'Cosmic Poetry Visitation Accidentally Happening' was sent out through the post. The leaflets bore Hoppy's clever ad copy, 'Come in fancy dress, come with flowers, *come!*'

Miles recalls the entire lead up to the poetry reading in his superb biography of Ginsberg, a first-hand account well worth reading. On 3 June, Ginsberg celebrated his birthday at Miles's flat with a generous cross section of London's emerging Underground. John Lennon and George Harrison arrived with their wives, and were quite surprised to see the eminent poet deliriously drunk and completely naked. Everyone danced to Smokey Robinson, and marijuana joints were surreptitiously passed around. The sixties were now in full swing.

The event, formally dubbed 'Poets of the World/Poets of our time', began at 7 p.m. on Friday 11 June. Hoppy's girlfriend Kate Heleczer and a contingent of her friends had descended upon the Covent Garden Market the night before and collected the unsold flowers from the stalls. As the crowd filed into the hall, the girls stood at the door in fancy dress, greeting and handing out the flowers in generous bouquets, their faces painted in bright colours.

Peter Whitehead who, during his early sixties painting sabbatical in Cambridge had known Syd, had come to London to study fine arts at the Slade on a scholarship. He eventually veered towards film making, and filmed the momentous Albert Hall poetry reading. The film, *Wholly Communion*, captures that moment when the Underground began to gel. 'The sense of there actually being an Underground was there already, poetry readings at Better Books, then UFO later,' says Whitehead. 'The Underground became collectively conscious, though, after *Wholly Communion.*'

The turnout was impressive; the audience was 7,000 strong, and seated in the Albert Hall's circular tiers, listened as dozens of poets read. Ginsberg sat on the ground, awaiting his turn, nervous and a little drunk. Nigel and Jenny Gordon, attired in flamboyant garb, were seated in the front row. Nigel Gordon says, 'Ginsberg was at Wholly Communion. The hall was two-thirds full, quite a lot. It was timely, because all those American poets were beginning to have their work sold in Britain. 'It certainly couldn't have happened before.' Jenny Gordon says, 'I felt it was a special, special time. I didn't particularly like poetry at that time, but I liked the buzz, a great buzz of excitement and life.' Jenny Fabian, soon to be one of the bright young things in the Underground, recalls, 'I was at the Albert Hall, sitting there gawping, thinking, "Wow, I must go out with a poet!"' and so she did, soon seeing Liverpool poet Johnny Byrne.

Miles says, 'Psychologist Ronnie Laing brought all his schizophrenic patients, and Jeff Nuttall got glued into the bath. Ian Sommerville played a tape of William Burrough's 'Valentine's Day' reading during the intermission, which Bill had recorded in February of that year. Ginsberg was appalled by the reading, he was drunk and read badly. Harry Fainlight read badly and stopped halfway through his poem. Gregory Corso, who hadn't read for three years, chose a very personal, quiet poem to read for some reason, instead of something declamatory or one of his great public poems. It was a terrible reading, but brilliant in the way it put everybody together. Suddenly we recognised an enormous community, that had been living in London, but London being so big, we hadn't noticed each other, and there we were. Seven thousand people, not all of them part of that community, but a very large number of them seemed to be on the same wavelength. And there was clearly something happening, and it was to cater to that audience that Hoppy and I started Lovebooks, the company that eventually published *International Times*. We were so turned on by the audience.'

Cromwell Road was now the essence of hip. 'Nigel and Jenny were very influential,' says Duggie Fields. 'The architecture students from the Regent Poly who had moved into Cromwell Road before me had been very straight, they didn't take any drugs. I used to smoke dope, and had for a number of years. They disapproved. There was a social divide between those who smoked and those who didn't. You'd go to parties and people would whisper, "They're taking drugs! Disgusting!" One weekend, three of four of the guys who hadn't taken any drugs got tripped out by Nigel and Jenny. It changed their lives; suddenly they could not get enough of getting high. They found God, they had a major revelation with their first acid trip. That was still before Syd moved in, and the Cambridge connection came by chance from people also living in the same building.'

Others from the Cambridge set soon followed in a mass exodus to London. Among them Christopher Case, who moved into Cromwell and found work as hip gallery-owner Robert Fraser's assistant. 'This girl Sue Kingsford was living with Christopher Case,' says Duggie Fields, 'and they both came from Cambridge. And this fellow Jock was living with Hester. One night I remember going to bed, and it was Sue Kingsford and Christopher and Jock and Hester, and when I woke up the next day, it was Jock and Sue, and Christopher and Hester weren't terribly happy about that!' Jock and Sue would later live with Syd, and join him for a madcap hippie tour of Britain in 1968.

Nigel Gordon says, 'I was the first person to take acid in Cambridge and I was selling it in London before anyone else. I took my first trips with people like John Esam, Bill Barlow and David Larcher, who I'd meet in London. But I suppose we did bring people into the London scene, we used to bring people with us. But it seemed to be happening in Cambridge all the same. John Esam was the first person I knew of who had acid, though Michael Hollingshead was around as well. Esam might have gotten it from Hollingshead.'

A period of exuberant drug taking began at Cromwell, with blocks of hash being broken down on the kitchen table and sugar cubes being impregnated with LSD dispensed from a syringe, and widely distributed throughout London.

Hoppy recalls, 'John Esam had acid in liquid form, he would dispense it with a hypodermic. A gram of acid would make 4,000 250 mcg trips. Some of it came from Sandoz, and a medical source as well in Czechoslovakia. I never dealt in it myself. Soon people were coming over with it from Europe and the US all the time. By then it was being made in liquid, later in tablets. Later, acid dealers would deal it in crystalline powder, and you'd have to cut the powder into capsules. It was hard to handle; it was transdermal and absorbed through your skin, and before you knew what was happening, you were tripping. Anyone who came into the room would start tripping, the cat would start tripping.'

Whitehead remembers the time after Wholly Communion as a rapidly changing melting pot of new influences, including drugs. 'After the Albert Hall poetry reading, drugs were easy to get. Acid just turned up from America, and I took it, but it was mescaline that I thought was truly revelatory.'

In summer 1965, Jenny and Nigel returned to Cambridge for the summer. Nigel says, 'David Gale really didn't like LSD, wasn't very keen on it. I certainly tripped with Storm. I didn't feel like the Pied Piper bringing acid to Cambridge, nor was I particularly aware of spreading it around. It was something that was happening simultaneously in London and Cambridge.' Soon after, out in the Gog Magog hills outside Cambridge, Jenny, Nigel, Syd, Russell Page, and David Gale all took a magic mushroom trip. Nigel Gordon took along the 8mm film camera he'd brought from his film course in London and filmed a jumpy, abstract portrait of the trip. In a desolate, abandoned quarry Gordon filmed the nineteen-year-old Barrett, dressed in black and with close-cropped hair, scampering around. 'We did all take that trip,' remembers Jenny Gordon, 'and Syd had very short hair and his black raincoat. He looked very ordinary, and was still very down to earth before he started to grow his hair out. I remember that Syd and I were quite worried because Russell Page, David Gale and Nigel were all making a bonfire. We thought it was uncool and we were a bit scared.'*

The twelve-minute silent movie, commercially released in 1994 as *Syd's First Trip* (which it wasn't), is a strange documentary. Barrett is by turns restless and seemingly rapt in a world of his own imaginings, as if he had found another door in his house, leading through to strange rooms. Like the children in C.S. Lewis's *The Lion, The Witch And The Wardrobe*, he could hardly know what he was in for, but there was a subtle foreshadowing. He scans the hills, his face reflecting a mixture of wonderment and uncertainty. Nigel Gordon affirms, 'He looked a bit wide-eyed and slightly vulnerable in that film.'

*Barrett may have been alluding to this trip in 'It Is Obvious', on *The Madcap Laughs*, when he sings of a quarry on a wooded hill covered by 'a curtain of velvety grey'.

Gordon adds, 'When we went away that summer Paolo Leonni [Italian film-maker] took it over. A "legalise marijuana" meeting was held in our flat, organised by Steve Abrams, John Esam and Paolo, publicised all over London, so when we got back the police raided it.' Duggie Fields recalls, 'They had a meeting for the legalisation of marijuana which Nico [future Velvet Underground chanteuse] came to and the police also came to, resulting in pictures in the newspaper of people with their eyes blacked out. "Smoking marijuana after midnight!" was the headline.'

Russell Page, from the Cambridge set, was the first person in the UK to be prosecuted for acid, which his good friend Peter Wynne-Wilson, remembers, 'It was quite surprising because at the time it wasn't a listed drug, so they couldn't actually convict him.' John Esam was arrested soon after as well. Several policemen charged into Cromwell Road and turned the flat upside down searching for the acid that a visitor had tipped them off about. Someone was holding a quantity of acid cubes in a bag as the police raced up the stairs, and threw it out an open window. Peter Wynne-Wilson notes, 'For some reason the police never thought to look in the briefcase that they carried their stash in.' Unfortunately, a policeman waiting in the garden out back for just such a jettisoning caught it, and Esam was duly arrested. A court case similar to Page's resulted in a dismissal of the charges, largely due to the presence of Dr Albert Hoffman on the witness stand. Inevitably though, soon after, LSD was declared illegal.

In August, Syd and David Gilmour went on holiday together with some friends in the South of France. Gilmour and Barrett took their acoustic guitars with them, playing their slim repertoire of R&B, Beatles and Rolling Stones covers. The Beatles' stellar *Help!* had just been released, and the duo warbled hastily learned covers of the Dylan-inspired 'You've Got To Hide Your Love Away' and the confessional title track. When not searching for Brigitte Bardot or drinking excessively, they sat on street corners busking. 'We were busking in St Tropez once,' says Gilmour, 'and got arrested for our troubles.'[99] The arresting gendarmes could be seen as the Pink Floyd's very first critics. The would-be troubadours were released with a slap on the wrist.

Meanwhile Storm, Ponji, Po and David Gale took a flat in Egerton Court, South Kensington. Gale says, 'Around the time of the move to London, there was an extraordinary schism in our group. It split into two halves, and this split was caused by the community of people taking LSD – half of them got God. Paul Charrier had been on LSD, in the toilet, reading a book called *Yoga And The Bible*. He learned that there was a guru in India called the Maharaji Charan Singh Ji, who would guarantee if you were initiated into his movement, to get you off the wheel of incarnation in three lifetimes, something like that. I could never quite see why this was such a good thing myself, but there we are.' Sant Mat, or Path of the Enlightened Masters as it was known, was met by a great interest in Asian philosophy and religion as well as a hunger among the youth for spiritual direction.

Jenny Gordon remembers, 'A strange thing happened later on, half of us became Sat Sanghi's (as the followers of the Master were called) and the other half made it in the world or went to a psychiatrist.'

Gale says, 'If you followed his meditative technique, the Master would take you through levels like you got on LSD, and even further, but he would available at each level to guide you through the multiple temptations. LSD was seen to be simply as a rather crude substance which ripped the top of your head off and exposed you to a melange of confused signals from various levels. If you followed the Master, you could go on a pure, clean path by following the audible sound current which would lead you back to the centre of all being, and God. Paul Charrier thought all this was dynamite, so he promptly had all his hair cut off and went over to India, where he was initiated by the Master. He described it as a blinding bolt of pure white energy flashing through his body, stripping away all the pretension and fear that characterised his life before. He came back, shorn of hair, wearing neat clothes, got a job, stopped taking drugs, stopped drinking, stopped eating meat, persuaded a number of others to go to India, and would subsequently only consort with people who had been there. Later he married Bridget, who had also been there, retreated from the group and went to live in countryside, as did Nigel and Jenny.

Storm Thorgerson and Syd had gone together to a hotel in London where the Master Charan Singh Ji was holding an audience. Syd wanted to receive initiation into the Path of the Masters, but the smiling guru apparently thought Barrett was too young. Nigel Gordon offers an alternative view, 'Initiates had to forswear use of alcohol or drugs, and in the initial interview Syd might have, quite candidly, let on that he might have difficulty with this. That could have contributed to his being turned down. Or, if one prefers, the guru might have seen what was ahead for Syd,' says Nigel Gordon. Either way, the guru recommended Barrett instead concentrate on finishing his studies. Syd, his friends remember, was very disappointed by the implied rejection. He is said to have asked on two separate occasions, but the Master refused. Like the death of his father, he affected indifference, confining his disappointment inside. A veritable maelstrom of emotion was beginning to brew beneath Barrett's placid, easy-go-lucky exterior.

Thorgerson told Nicholas Schaffner that there were three catalysts in Syd's eventual breakdown; the first being the death of his father, the second being his rejection from Sant Mat, and the third was the continual attention he received from women.

Gale says, 'The Cambridge group split right in half; there were the followers of the Master and there were the followers of another path. Syd wavered between the spiritual group and the other group, which tended to be more interested in psychoanalysis and experimental art culture. They tended to want to hang out more, to continue to socialise, they were more hedonistic and definitely less spiritual. After wavering, Syd fairly firmly joined the latter group. Around the time of this schism there were instances of mental instability emerging, not with Syd, but others. There were one or two individuals, fairly jolly, ordinary people who took LSD – one in particular was a guy named Cred, who was ex-services, and when he came down he joined a fundamentalist Christian sect and was never seen again. So it was quite clear that LSD wasn't wholly straightforward in what it did to people. It didn't simply open up your mind and make life marvellous, there was evidence of strangeness.'

Meanwhile the Pink Floyd languished in amateur disarray. The band headed back to Cambridge in November for Storm Thorgerson's engagement party. David Gilmour's band Joker's Wild and the newly dubbed Pink Floyd Sound were both booked to play at the party in Shelford. Also on-stage that night was the then unknown Paul Simon.

'They were called the Pink Floyd Sound originally,' says David Gilmour, 'and we played gigs together, my band in Cambridge and then when we actually went up to London and played things on their sort of patch, schools. We were friends, I used to see them all the time, they just used to do Bo Diddley numbers and things.'[100] Clive Welham had joined Joker's Wild, and he recalls they 'did one big gig in 1965 at Shelford, three or four miles out of Cambridge. It was a big affair for some millionaire called Douglas January. The Pink Floyd Sound and Joker's Wild were the two pop bands and Paul Simon was the cabaret artist! He was singing songs criticising businessmen to all these wealthy estate agents and they hadn't a clue; they were applauding wildly. He actually came on and played a couple of numbers with us; jamming, you might call it.'[101] The evening ended in riotous drunkenness and general goodwill among all the musicians.

Barrett's style was becoming ever more pronounced. His music and lyrics began to develop in tandem, becoming more experimental. His deep-rooted interest in fairy-tales and poetry was grafted on to his R&B derived guitar riffs, and he seemed to be on a quest for a breakthrough; just as he had been during his teens, he was slightly ahead of everyone else. His acid forays and guitar experiments were pushing him in a new direction, albeit unclear as yet. Waters, also, was stimulated by Barrett's search, and was developing his own ideas. He said, 'There was a need to experiment in order to find another way of expressing ourselves that didn't involve practising at playing the guitar for ten years. At the time people were standing there in little suits, with those Gibson guitars held against their chests going [imitates rigid stance and strumming]. And even though it wasn't very complicated stuff, it wasn't something I was very interested in.'[102]

They began to harmonise on vocals occasionally, their voices complementing each other well. Roger Waters says, 'I had a Rickenbacker that I'd bought with my entire term's grant. I found that if you turned the bass up loud and used a plectrum and if you banged it hard, it made strange noises. I found that if you pushed the strings against the pickups, it made funny clicking noises.'[103]

Educational studies were going by the wayside, with Wright (who had switched to the Trinity College of Music) dropping out and Waters spending the bulk of his time baiting his witless teachers with politically charged remarks.

In November 1965 Joe Boyd returned to England from a stint working in the US for Elektra Records. He'd signed the remarkable Butterfield Blues Band, which pleased his boss, Jac Holzman, enough to offer him the post of Elektra representative in London. 'I rang up Hoppy the week I got back. He told me there was going to be that night a meeting which I ought to attend. So I attended the first meeting of the London Free School.' Boyd went over that night and joined Hoppy, Andrew King, Peter Jenner, Alan Beckett, Ron Atkins and Kate Heleczer for the meeting. 'The main thrust was that the people in the room were possessed of a number of skills which would be of benefit to the community if offered in a constructive way. It was an idea to start a community based on the idea of further education for the under-privileged of Notting Hill Gate. The main thing was that it ended up being a galvanization of certain forces and energy.'[104] (The two lasting contributions of the London Free School were to be the Notting Hill Carnival, which each year still draws up to two million people, and of course, the Pink Floyd.)

One cold Friday night in December, the Pink Floyd Sound packed their gear into the van for a gig at the Countdown Club, in Palace Gate, London. Though not the first time they had been billed as Pink Floyd, contrary to myth, from now on they would be known solely as the Pink Floyd or the Pink Floyd Sound. Typical of the gigs they were beginning to do, the Pink Floyd played from 8 p.m. to 1 a.m. with twenty minutes rest between their two sets. Waters recalls that they were paid £15, which meant they were working for less than 15 shillings each per hour, hardly glamorous work.

Revisiting their garage band days, Roger Waters says, 'I was quite happy standing there thundering about, playing whatever I could – that's *fun*. And I see young bands occasionally now doing the same thing. I think it's called thrash now. It's the same thing: it's just kids who can't play, pissing about. It's terrific, that's all we were doing.'[105] Syd Barrett said, 'All the equipment was battered and worn, all the stuff we started out with was our own, the guitars were our own property. The electronic noises were probably necessary. They were very exciting. That's all really. The whole thing at the time was playing on-stage.'

Soon-to-be manager Peter Jenner says, 'Syd was an exceptional figure. Far and away the most important in the band, he wrote the songs, he was the singer, he played most of the solos, he was the lead guitarist, it was his band.'[106]

Wright adds, 'The big influence when we formed the band was Syd's writing, but I'd also put a word in for my keyboards and Nick's drumming; he was fanatical about Ginger Baker and his style was nothing like today's heavy kick drum and tight snare, it was all very free and rolling, much more jazz influenced.

We did get better as musicians. If we hadn't gone through our experimental phase we wouldn't be here today, though. I'm so glad we did it.'[107] Rick Wright began to use his knowledge of jazz to introduce modal tonalities to the mix, extending the range of Barrett's soloing and giving him a crucial counterpoint.

'Lucy Leave' was the first Barrett song they ever recorded, with surprisingly paranoid lyrics masquerading as a standard R&B rave-up: 'You've got my heart, you've got my soul, oh no! You hold on so tight, so tight I just can't breathe, now Lucy leave, Lucy go!' A bootleg of the recording is fairly widely available, a valuable document of the band's progress. The sound is tentative and formulaic, sounding identical to the hundreds of other bands in England playing R&B covers badly, but Syd's idiosyncratic stamp is apparent from the first bars with a descending chromatic riff that bears that treble-laden Telecaster tone that is indubitably Syd's. Barrett tries too hard to get that raspy blues shout as he howls out the lyric. The B-Side is a perfunctory reading of Slim Harpo's 'King Bee' with little to distinguish it other than making one thankful the Pink Floyd didn't pursue their R&B direction any further.*

Syd was creating rather unique paintings using a palette of dazzling bright paints. Not with canvas though; he had exchanged his brush for a Telecaster and had plunged into music. Syd's proper artwork itself quickly went by the wayside, and he virtually dropped out of Camberwell, attending classes only sporadically as he became more involved in the band. Only once did he ever allude to his breakdown in later interviews, when he said, 'Maybe if I'd stayed at college, I would have become a teacher. Leaving school and suddenly being without that structure around you and nothing to relate to . . . maybe that's a part of it, too.'[108] He explained, 'I'm a painter [and] I was trained as a painter [but] the fine arts thing at college was always too much for me to think about. What I was more involved in was being successful at arts school.'[109] 'Syd was a great artist,' says Storm Thorgerson. 'I loved his work, but he just stopped. First it was the religion, then the painting. He was starting to shut himself off slowly even then.'[110]

Barrett was inspired by the rhythmic rigour of Bo Diddley and Steve Cropper [of Booker T. & the MGs], utilising their iron-clad sense of rhythm and the 'right note' to underlay his lead guitar flights. Clive Welham, who played with Barrett in his earliest aggregation, Geoff Mott and the Mottoes, recalled Barrett's rhythm skill even from his earliest days. Rhythm was close to Barrett's heart, and blues and R&B were key starting points for him; idioms that he felt comfortable in. In later years, he would seek succour from blues and R&B.

*There is considerable debate as to the correct recording date for the 'Lucy Leave/King Bee' acetate. Some sources date it to April 1965, though the fluidity of Barrett's lyric and guitar work would suggest it was recorded much later. Please refer to the discography for more information. The guitar on the acetate is very much in the Barrett style, strongly suggesting it was he, rather than Bob Close, playing guitar. Barrett scholar Scott Frank suggests October 1965 as the true date of the session.

Though having begun with rhythm and blues, Barrett's blues would become steadily more astral and whimsical, quickly changing direction under the aegis of the Stones, the Beatles, the Who and the Yardbirds.

Syd was only one of many to emerge from English art schools, all bringing fresh ideas to pop, a music then considered as disposable as 45s with grooves worn out from repeated playing. As his style developed, he was to become a veritable fountainhead for musical innovation, and many of the plants that flowered subsequently in the garden of English music sprang from seeds of Barrett's pods. His influence is undeniable, not only musically, but in terms of his stage presence. The theatrics of glam would take its cues from Barrett; it's hard to imagine David Bowie, Marc Bolan or Peter Gabriel developing their early 1970s live act and look without Barrett's example. Barrett's inventiveness would also soon inspire contemporaries such as the Move, the Soft Machine and Jimi Hendrix. The perpetual feedback loop among this generation of British guitarists extended to all aspects of life, including styles of dress, riffs, guitars and clubs.

Even the petrol stations they used while driving up and down the motorway going back and forth to gigs would be the same ones, enabling them to meet at odd places in the provinces in the dead of night as if it was the most normal thing.[111] The musical thread connecting the US and the UK was particularly strong, stronger than it has been before or since. The Byrds would listen to 'British Invasion' records endlessly, alternating with Ravi Shankar and John Coltrane. Guitarist Roger McGuinn notes that the anarchic keyboard coda on the Zombies 1964 UK hit 'She's Not There' inspired part of 'Eight Miles High', released in 1965. The Byrds would also pick up such cues as George Harrison using a twelve-string Rickenbacker in the film *Help!* and quickly adapt them to come up with their own unique variant.

Pop music was changing rapidly during the last few months of 1965. The Who's *My Generation*, the Rolling Stones' *Out Of Our Heads*, Bob Dylan's *Highway 61 Revisited* and the Beatles' *Help!* all pointed the way forward. Pop music also mirrored the changes in society at large, particularly among the young. A new attitude of acceptance and openness among the youth, not only in Britain and America, but virtually everywhere where the English language was understood, was to be one of the defining factors in the coming years. Drugs, in their initial entry into the lives of the young, were seen as a positive tool in the eradication of class and racial prejudice and those all-important 'hang-ups'. The young people that had gathered at the Albert Hall Dylan concerts or the poetry reading, or at the CND Trafalgar Square demonstrations and Aldermaston marches, began to look around and see themselves reflected a thousandfold. For the first time, youth became a power to reckon with, certainly in economic terms. They voted with their pockets, their tastes fuelling entire industries. Sociologists say hem-lines are a signifier of economic prosperity; in 1965 they rose to heights never imagined. A chain of boutiques sprung up along

Carnaby Street in London to cater to the new youth's celebration of the moment. If you had a job you didn't like, leave it, you could always find another. Why study for exams that would only lead you to a hard chair, a desk and a position as a trainee in a solicitor's firm? Military conscription was over with, your paypacket or grant money was in hand, and as Cathy McGowan announced every Friday at the beginning of TV's *Ready, Steady, Go!* – the weekend was here.

---

1 *Rolling Stone*, December 1971
2 *The Amazing Pudding*, # 57
3 *Penthouse*, September 1988
4 *Q*, November 1992
5 *ZigZag*, July 1973
6 Greene, Jonathan. *Days In The Life: Voices From The English Underground, 1961-1971*. Minerva, 1988
7 Schaffner, Nicholas. *Saucerful of Secrets*. Delta, 1991
8 Ian Barrett interview with Rob Peets
9 *NME*, 13 April 1974
10 *Mojo*, May 1994
11 Jones, Cliff. *Echoes: The Stories Behind Every Pink Floyd Song*. Omnibus Press, 1996, p. 39
12 *Fabulous*, 13 January 1968
13 Giovanni Dadomo interview with Syd Barrett
14 Roger Waters interview with Chris Salewicz, June 1987
15 *Musician*, May 1992
16 Miles & Mabbett, Andy. *Pink Floyd: The Visual Documentary*. Omnibus Press, London 1994
17 *Beat Instrumental*, October 1967
18 Miles & Mabbett, Andy. *Pink Floyd: The Visual Documentary*. Omnibus Press, London 1994
19 *Melody Maker*, 27 March 1971
20 *The Amazing Pudding*, # 50
21 *The Amazing Pudding*, # 56
22 *Musician*, May 1992
23 *The Amazing Pudding*, # 50
24 *Sounds*, May 1983
25 *NME*, 13 April 1974
26 *Musician*, December 1982
27 *NME*, 13 April 1974
28 Watkinson, Mike & Anderson, Pete. *Crazy Diamond: Syd Barrett & The Dawn of Pink Floyd*. Omnibus Press, 1993. p. 20
29 Ibid.
30 *Penthouse*, September 1988
31 *Mojo*, May 1994
32 Miles & Mabbett, Andy. *Pink Floyd: The Visual Documentary*. Omnibus Press, London 1994
33 *Beat Instrumental*, October 1967
34 *Q*, November 1992
35 Miles & Mabbett, Andy. *Pink Floyd: The Visual Documentary*. Omnibus Press, London 1994
36 Giovanni Dadomo interview with Syd Barrett
37 Watkinson, Mike & Anderson, Pete. *Crazy Diamond: Syd Barrett & The Dawn of Pink Floyd*. Omnibus Press, 1993. p. 19
38 Ibid.
39 *NME*, 13 April 1974

40 *The Amazing Pudding*, # 50
41 Jonathan Greene, *Days in the Life: Voices from the English Underground, 1961–71*, Minerva, 1988
42 Unedited transcripts of interviews with Sam Hutt by Jonathan Greene. *Days In The Life: Voices From The English Underground, 1961-1971*. Minerva, 1988
43 *Mojo,* May 1994
44 *Circus,* 1972
45 *The Amazing Pudding*, # 50
46 *NME*, 11 Jan 75
47 *Sounds,* May 1983
48 *Melody Maker*, 27 March 1971
49 *The Amazing Pudding*, # 50
50 'Syd Barrett Careening Through Life'. Kris DiLorenzo, Trouser Press, February 1978
51 *NME,* 13 April 1974
52 Watkinson, Mike & Anderson, Pete. *Crazy Diamond: Syd Barrett & The Dawn of Pink Floyd.* Omnibus Press, 1993. p. 26
53 Ibid.
54 *Harpers & Queen,* November 1996
55 Press release for 'Pink Floyd: London 1966/67' video
56 *ZigZag*, July 1973
57 Ibid.
58 Watkinson, Mike & Anderson, Pete. *Crazy Diamond: Syd Barrett & the Dawn of Pink Floyd*. Omnibus Press, 1993. p. 36
59 *Mojo,* June 1996
60 *Dark Side Of The Moon*. Japanese CD edition liner notes
61 *Terrapin* 7, 1975
62 *Dancing In The Streets*, BBC series, 1996
63 *Musician*, May 1992
64 *Disc & Music Echo*, 8 August 1970
65 *Shades of Pink*, interviews with Charlie Kendall, Source. 1984
66 *ZigZag*, July 1973
67 *The Amazing Pudding*, # 58
68 Jonathan Greene. *Days In The Life: Voices From The English Underground, 1961-1971*. Minerva, 1988
69 *Musician*, May 1992
70 *Omnibus* special on Pink Floyd, 1994
71 *Beat Instrumental*, October 1967
72 Wale, Michael. *Voxpop: Profiles Of The Pop Process*. Harrap, 1972
73 *Terrapin* 7, 1975
74 *ZigZag*, July 1973
75 Macdonald, Bruno, editor. *Pink Floyd: Through the Eyes of. . .* Sidgwick & Jackson, London, 1996
76 *Beat Instrumental*, October 1967
77 Ibid.
78 Miles & Mabbett, Andy. *Pink Floyd: The Visual Documentary*. Omnibus Press, London 1994
79 *Omnibus* special on Pink Floyd, 1994
80 Danish television interviews with Pink Floyd, 1992
81 Miles & Mabbett, Andy. *Pink Floyd: The Visual Documentary*. Omnibus Press, London 1994
82 *Disc & Music Echo*, 8 August 1970
83 Ibid.
84 Watkinson, Mike & Anderson, Pete *Crazy Diamond: Syd Barrett & The Dawn Of Pink Floyd.* Omnibus Press, 1993
85 *Omnibus* special on Pink Floyd, 1994
86 Ibid.
87 Miles & Mabbett, Andy. *Pink Floyd: The Visual Documentary.*
88 Omnibus special on Pink Floyd, 1994
89 Ibid.
90 *Mojo,* May 1994
91 *Melody Maker*, 27 March 1971
92 *Beat Instrumental*, October 1967
93 *Dark Side Of The Moon*. Japanese CD edition liner notes
94 *NME*, 9 July 1988

95 *ZigZag*, July 1973
96 *Disc & Music Echo*, 8 August 1970
97 *ZigZag*, July 1973
98 *Disc and Music Echo*, 8 August 1970
99 *Sounds,* May 1983
100 Ibid.
101 *The Amazing Pudding*, # 50
102 *Dancing In The Streets*, BBC series, 1996
103 Unedited transcripts of interviews with Joe Boyd by Jonathan Greene. *Days In The Life: Voices From The English Underground, 1961-1971.* Minerva, 1988
104 *Musician*, November 1992
105 Unedited transcripts of interviews with Peter Jenner by Jonathan Greene. *Days In The Life: Voices From The English Underground, 1961-1971.* Minerva, 1988
106 *Mojo*, July 1995
107 *Dancing In The Streets,* BBC series, 1996
108 Giovanni Dadomo interview with Syd Barrett
109 *Melody Maker*, 27 March 1971
110 *NME,* 13 April 1974
111 Jonathan Greene: *Days in the Life: Voices from the English Underground, 1961–71*, Minerva, 1988

Stage Two:
The Wild Wood (1966)

'Societies of people sharing the same views are formed. But since these groups come together in full public knowledge and are in harmony with the time, all selfish separatist tendencies are excluded and no mistake is made.'

Chapter 24: Fu/Return – The Turning Point,
The I-Ching or Book Of Changes

'It's a good feeling being in a territory where the limits aren't well defined, where there is some room for adventure.'

John 'Hoppy' Hopkins

It was now the height of 'Swinging London', a phenomenon that some say was a media invention. In was in part, but the 27 April 1966 issue of *Time* magazine that sparked it off acted as a catalyst, gelling the twenty-odd disparate scenes it described into a cultural tideshift. The *Time* issue also prompted a lot of interesting people to come to London, popularising the idea that it was the most exciting city in the world.

The hype, for once, was fact: there were the designers Mary Quant, Michael Rainey, and the Chelsea set of young aristocrats; the Beatles staring out from the fairground mirror of fame on the cover of *Rubber Soul;* the Rolling Stones being photographed by Michael Cooper as Regency dandies, or tramping along in a chemical daze by the Serpentine at dawn, on the way home from all-night revelry in Chelsea; models Twiggy and Jean Shrimpton; actresses Sarah Miles, Vanessa Redgrave and Julie Christie; painters David Hockney and Peter Blake; and photographer David Bailey. On television, hostess Cathy McGowan presided over the Op-Art black and white striped set of *Ready, Steady, Go!,* heralding the arrival of the weekend from the back of a Vespa, and presenting bands like the Animals, the Spencer Davis Group, and the Yardbirds, performing live for Michael Lindsay-Hogg's cameras. All seemed to be somehow part of the same scene, however disparate they might have actually been. The scene celebrated itself with David Bailey's box of pin-ups cataloguing the prime movers, from the owner of the hip Ad-Lib nightclub to the paragons of the underworld, the Krays. Some of these 'youthquakers', as *Vogue* dubbed them, had sprung up from the working-class or from the provinces, and 'classlessness' was the new vogue. The Beatles were perhaps the most prominent symbol of this new plurality, even though three of them were from solid middle-class backgrounds. Ten years earlier the marriage of an Ormsby-Gore to a East End lad like David Bailey would have been unthinkable. A seemingly effortless overthrow of the boring fifties had taken place.

Revisionist eulogisation aside, Hoppy says, 'Society was more class-ridden and uptight in those days but it was also far more prosperous, there wasn't much unemployment. Despite the rigidity of society, if you have overall prosperity it engenders an unconscious optimism. That's a difference between the sixties and the nineties. When you are born into and grow up in a culture, you don't know anything else, so you accept this is how it is. So people growing up in the nineties might have a historical perspective of the sixties as more interesting. Actually, on the whole, I don't think it's true. You just grow up in the culture and think this is the way it is. A lot of things about the nineties are pretty shitty but the same was true for the sixties. There were many people who still imagined that Britain was a first-class county, a world leader, and still had an Empire. We were just discovering the problems of post-industrial society, which nobody had a clue about.'

The bands of the time were the Beatles, Kinks, the Who and the Rolling Stones, along with the Byrds and Dylan across the ocean, who both made forays to Britain. 'I used to see the Stones before they had even released a record. There would be thirty people in the place,' says Duggie Fields. 'They suddenly were famous a few months later and you couldn't get into the place. I used to see the Who at the Marquee, again, just before they had a hit record and right after they first hit. Roger Daltrey used to sign me in. I was listening to Bob Dylan and a lot of black American R&B. I saw James Brown in Brixton in 1965. I knew the Floyd at the time but seeing James Brown was culturally more exciting. Swinging London didn't really exist, it was a media invention, but it brought about a whole tourist boom. I used to get tourists stopping me in the street to take my photograph. The media always got it wrong. Now, there are far more people in the media paying attention and maybe getting it right, whereas then the media was very much not aware of what was around, and when it did get into the media it was frequently wrong. I'm sure there are plenty of unsung heroes from that time, as opposed to what the media did focus on.'

Miles, with the financial backing of Peter Asher, formerly of pop duo Peter and Gordon, began the Indica Gallery and Bookstore in January 1966 with John Dunbar. After a brief tenure at Southampton Row, Indica relocated to the staid surroundings of Mason's Yard in St James; an enclave of shops in the heart of Establishment stolidity. Dunbar's gallery was downstairs and Miles attended to the bookstore on the ground floor. Both gallery and bookstore were chock to the brim with fantastic accoutrements of hip. Paul McCartney donated wrapping paper and installed shelves for the shop. Kerouac, Corso, Pynchon and Trocchi vied for space with esoteric literature on a great number of topics, ranging from the most outlandish spiritualism to the subversive (and until recently illegal) Burroughs novels. Posters, Underground newspapers from America, like San Francisco's *Oracle* and New York's *East Village Other*, a select few records by the Fugs and Frank Zappa, were all available. Soon, the shop was an essential nerve centre for the growing hip constituency as yet unnamed. The Scotch of St James, a nightclub for the new aristocracy, namely the pop bands, was close by.

Duggie Fields says, 'There was a particular period that, culturally, has never been pinpointed, because it wasn't that documented by the media at that time. There were a lot of people of the same age, it was the boom from the post-War. A lot of very good-looking young people were around. There was this huge cultural difference between those who had started using drugs and the mass who hadn't. You could walk down the King's Road and you saw people who stood out. Groups of people who would stand out, and you had an empathy with them, and you would smile across the road. A year later, you might be best friends with them. But it wouldn't be important to say hello when you first saw them. You would recognise them and vice versa. There was that difference, and to find that difference is so hard. It wasn't so much the clothes, it was an attitude of a perception to life.

'There was definitely a group identity that was different. It wasn't that we were going to change the world, but it was that the world would change. And this was the start of it, of people relating in this way. I'm trying to find a word other than "vibe" for the communication between people, because there was definitely a way of relating that had very little to do with social structures. It was an empathy that you felt for people straight off or not. I'm always reluctant to say it, but it does have to do with drugs. Or it did during that period.

'The idea of an alternative culture was definitely viable then, which it hasn't been since, and wasn't before. There was a big difference between the "us" and the "them". It was drugs-based for a period, the social divide. It took a while for it to sink in that some of the people I knew that didn't smoke dope were fabulous while some of the people who did smoke dope were idiots. There were various late-night cinemas that you would walk into and everyone in there was stoned, everyone. There would be giggles going round the cinema for no reason at all, other than everyone was high. There was a visual difference, where you would recognise others on the streets as fellow heads. There was a musical difference as well. Now the divisions are much less marked.'

Peter Wynne-Wilson says, 'Today is analogous to the fifties, when the Beat movement started as a reaction away from the Establishment. That grew into the sixties where there was a feeling of cohesion. Music was a convenient vehicle for that, clothes and drugs also; it had a unifying factor. As winter turned slowly to spring, the urge was to capture the immediacy of the moment, and clubs were filled with the millions of under-thirties who suddenly seemed to be on every street corner, or filling the drab tube trains with the laughter, ebullience and colourful clothes.'

Barrett, meanwhile, had moved from Highgate to Earlham Street, near Covent Garden, following David Gale. With him, he brought his girlfriend Lindsay Korner, whom he'd known from Cambridge. She would remain his central love interest for the next two years. Syd's other girlfriend was Jenny Spires, also from Cambridge. Gale explains, 'At Earlham Street, I lived with Susie Gawler-Wright, Peter Wynne-Wilson, John Whitely, his then-girlfriend Anna and Jean-Michelle Kaminsky, a pornographer and jack-of-all-trades. When Jean-Michelle's equipment burned down, the fire brigade came and found his charred pornography in the flat. He had to leave and I took over his refurbished room. And Earlham Street became another nexus for people to come and stroll about town and meet each other.' (Kaminsky's 'pornography' consisted of reprints of the Parisian Olympus Press risque books, which at the time were contraband in the UK.)

Peter Wynne-Wilson says, 'I'd met Susie Gawler-Wright and we were living in Earlham Street. The first time I met Syd was when he came to live in Earlham in early 1966. He was with Lindsay [Korner, but Jenny Spires was around. Syd had this particular musical gift, and a poetic gift, but he didn't stand out from the group of people that were around. There were a lot of very interesting people. Kaminsky had been living with a semi-titled girl who was quite an accomplished artist, an illustrator. They were living in the room which Syd and Lindsay ultimately had. Also living there was Ponji, Susie and myself. There were a lot of people passing through, though. It was a focal point, like Cromwell Road or Egerton Court. My first acid trip was in Earlham Street in 1966 with John Whitely and Anna Murray, his girlfriend at the time, as well as Imo from Cambridge. After acid experiences, the idea of getting seriously consumed by politics seemed completely ludicrous to me.'

Miles sought to articulate the momentous feeling of occasion he'd felt at the Albert Hall in a piece he wrote for a magazine he and Hoppy published at the very end of 1965, called *Long Hair*. The magazine was given the quaint sub-title suggested by Ginsberg: 'NATO: North Atlantic Turn-On'. Miles said, 'In my editorial I was suggesting that it was time that there was some kind of cross-pollination of ideas, between all the people then involved in the scene in London. There was a lot going on: in fashion, rock'n'roll, theatre, movies, poetry, literature. What we wanted to do was to put these people in touch with each other; there was actually a need, quite a strong need for some sort of vehicle for their ideas.'[1]

Between the first and second issues, the content, typography and graphic design became slightly looser, more playful and less serious. Hoppy and Miles printed up a batch and took them down to the Aldermaston March in March 1966. They sold hundreds of copies of this second edition, entitled 'The Long Hair Moon Edition of the International Times', and it struck an immediate chord.

Miles says, 'Hoppy and I published something called *Arazt.* I had co-edited *Tzara* magazine with Lee Hardwood, so then I did *Arazt.* It had a text by Burroughs, some photos by Hoppy. We had problems getting it printed because Hoppy's photos were of his girlfriend naked, and in those days you couldn't get stuff printed by offset litho because they were new machines, a new technology. So we had to have the whole thing done on letterpress, with all the illustrations done on copper plates. Hoppy then bought a used offset litho machine for 100 quid. The first thing we printed was *Long Hair Times*, to see if it worked. We had to do it offset litho, because that was how the American Underground papers were done, and you could do just so many more things. It was much easier, and if you needed to touch something up, you could just literally type it up and it would print. You could do black and white photographs, illustrations.

'The first eight issues of *IT* [*International Times*] we did by letterpress until Hoppy found that machine. The next thing we did was a conventional magazine called *Long Hair* with mostly Ginsberg's piece on Angkor Wat. But Hoppy and I wrote a long editorial that was a precursor of *IT,* it stated what we believed in and I'm sure would be very embarrassing to read today. We were on the cusp there between literary magazines and what was to become the Underground press.'

The Goings-On, which opened in January of 1966, was a club in Archer Street organised by Liverpool Beats Pete Brown, Johnny Byrne and Spike Hawkins for poetry readings with musical accompaniment. Poets Pete Brown and Mike Horovitz had been persistent in their efforts at striking a balance between poetry and jazz, with over 300 performances, since their fateful meeting at the Beaulieu Jazz Festival in 1961. The Pink Floyd played at the Goings-On in January 1966, according to Miles. His wife Sue Miles recalled, 'The very first thing was the Goings-On, which was Sunday afternoons. The first time I ever heard the Pink Floyd. "Squeak, squeak," I told Miles, "They'll never catch on. . ." Anybody could get up and do anything they wanted. It was actually very good in a funny sort of way.'[2] One of the highlights was a poet doing a reading accompanied by a stripper. The poet was a bit flummoxed when the stripper began to attract more attention than his poem from the thirty odd people in attendance. Miles says, 'The Goings-On didn't last long, but it was the forerunner of the Spontaneous Underground.'

This was now the era of 'happenings', art events that were innovative for their sometimes anarchic, sometimes awkward structures. Hoppy says, 'The idea of an open-ended event where you didn't quite know what was going to happen, but the elements were in place, was very fetching. And obviously a lot of other people saw that as well. You'd have a bit of this and some of that, you'd have smoke going of, coloured lights, some poetry. "Happening" was a good label, because anything could happen.'

A precedent for the London-based happenings was Fluxus, the New York- and Cologne-based arts group which included Nam June Paik, Yoko Ono and George Maciunas. Taking their cues from composer John Cage's chance operations, Fluxus boldly struck out on a programme of conceptual and performance art, mixing humour with a Zen-like emphasis on spontaneity.

In San Francisco, meanwhile, a loose collective of anarcho-pranksters called the Family Dog had been organising dances and concerts at Longshoremen's Hall since October 1965. The shows, featuring the Jefferson Airplane and Lovin' Spoonful, led to the three-day-long Trips Festival, which began on 21 January. The event attracted hundreds of young 'hippies'(as the mainstream newspapers had derisively labelled them) to hear the Grateful Dead, Big Brother and the Holding Company and witness the Chinese New Year Lion Dancers and Drum and Bugle Corps, to jump on the Stroboscopic Trampoline, and be dosed with legal LSD by Ken Kesey and his Merry Pranksters. 'Can you pass the acid test?' was their motto. News of events like these would spread across the Atlantic and inspire people like Hoppy, whose 'fancy dress and flowers' ethos was more in line with Ken Kesey than George Maciunas. The arrival of Suzy Creamcheese (neé Zieger) from the scene surrounding Frank Zappa and the Mothers Of Invention from Los Angeles into Hoppy's life was another catalyst.

A more immediate forerunner for English Underground happenings was Mark Boyle's (formerly of the Hornsey Light and Sound Workshop) happening at the ICA on Dover Street. 'Oh, What a Lovely Whore', as it was piquantly titled, in Boyle's words, was 'outrageously successful. I don't think anyone who was there has ever forgotten it. I was amazed. They did smash the place to pieces, but they did it in a kind of ritual way that was astonishing. I think everybody regressed to about the age of five, it was an extraordinary experience for everybody. I still meet people who were there.'[3]

Hoppy certainly came away impressed; a few weeks later he caught up with Boyle and introduced himself. He breathlessly explained that he was working a series of happenings at the Marquee with a fellow called Stollman. He asked them to get involved, saying, 'Everyone's going to be in fancy dress, and it's going to be a jazz!'

Hoppy's partner in crime for these events was Steve Stollman, a New Yorker, and brother of Bernard Stollman, owner of the *avant-garde* jazz record label ESP, who had migrated to London with an eye to putting on events where ESP's marginal, brilliant players could perform. Hoppy says, 'Steve Stollman was an interesting guy, young, active, and moved about in all different circles. He'd say, "What about this, what about that?" and he put on the first event where the Floyd first played to the general public, at the Marquee.'

Stollman approached the owner of the Marquee Club, the famed mod and

R&B club at 90 Wardour Street in Soho, with the idea of putting on an invite-only event on Sunday afternoons. Dubbed the Spontaneous Underground, the Sunday sessions were to prove highly influential, injecting a dose of the arty 'happenings' into the club circuit, and injecting the spirit of pop frivolity into the happenings.

Nigel Gordon says, 'I met Stollman at John Esam's flat. I went round one day and there he was. They were talking about these Sunday afternoon sessions. Stollman wanted to bring over some of the *avant* jazz bands on his brother's ESP label.' Stollman mentioned that he was looking for good bands to book. Gordon immediately suggested the Pink Floyd Sound. Stollman said, 'Sure, give them a ring and ask if they'll come.' Nigel Gordon laughs as he recalls, 'We got the Pink Floyd to come and play these strange Sunday afternoon happenings at the Marquee. The Pink Floyd's first London gigs, so they have me to thank.'

The *Melody Maker* carried an ad for the first Spontaneous Underground on Sunday 30 January. It ran from 7.30 to 11 p.m.: 'A giant mystery happening! By invitation only, limited number available from Marquee. Music, dancing, painting, sculpture, etc., etc.' The missing link between the Albert Hall poetry reading and the flamboyant clothes, loud rock music and loon dancing that took place later in the ballroom at UFO, Steve Stollman's Spontaneous Underground sessions were the precursors for many of the things that followed. Along with the subsequent All Saint's Hall gigs, the Spontaneous Underground sowed the seeds for what came to be known as the psychedelic Underground.

Barrett, Waters, Mason and Wright arrived at the Marquee in their beat-up old van with their rudimentary equipment. Roger Waters said, 'The whole mixed media thing started happening in 1966. We had a Sunday afternoon at the Marquee with film going and us banging and crashing away. John Hopkins and his merry men were there.'[4] Miles says, 'I first saw them at the Spontaneous Underground in January 1966. I actually wrote the first review of the Pink Floyd for the *East Village Other*, the New York Underground newspaper.'

Miles adds, 'A good address list was important in those days, because not everyone had a telephone. You'd mail fliers out and they would tell people, which was how Stollman promoted the Spontaneous Underground. He used Hoppy's address list and sent out these funny envelopes filled with slices of text from Alex Trocchi's *Sigma* portfolio and pages from *Long Hair* magazine and Marvel comics, along with one mimeographed advertisement.' The invites that had circulated around London read:

'TRIP, bring furniture toy prop paper rug paint balloon jumble costume mask robot candle incense ladder wheel light self all others. March 13th 5 PM, marquee club 90 Wardour street W1 5/-'

Small things like this invite for the Spontaneous Underground best capture the spirit of the emerging Underground. The light-hearted and festive air of the sessions took the best from Fluxus and created a sense of occasion where otherwise there wouldn't have been anything but a silent club. And one has to admire the ingenuity of the Underground, doing a lot with very little. Miles smiles, 'We had to.'

He remembers Syd coming into the Indica Bookstore to purchase a Fugs album, which was issued by ESP Records in New York, run by Steve Stollman's brother Bernard. The anarchic wit and Lower East Side sophomoric satire of Sanders and Kupferberg appealed immensely to Barrett. Influenced heavily by Frank Zappa and the Mothers Of Invention's *Freak Out!* album, the Byrds and the Fugs, Syd started to jettison R&B. The band began a profound shift in focus, with Barrett's songwriting and guitar coming decidedly to the fore. He later told *Melody Maker's* Chris Welch, 'I really dig the Byrds, Mothers Of Invention and Fugs. We have drawn quite a bit from those groups'.

It was at the Marquee that Barrett and the Floyd began to draw out their instrumentals, doing covers of Bo Diddley songs like 'Roadrunner' with 'freak-out' explorations in the middle. At the Spontaneous Underground, they were expanding the parameter of what was considered acceptable in pop. The Kinks released their single 'Dedicated Follower of Fashion' in March, and it established a precedent for Barrett's subsequent use of musical hall styles in his own songs. Ray Davies, the Kink's principal songwriter, also paved the way for Barrett in his use of English eccentricities as subject matter. Concurrent with the rise of peculiar, topical pop songs was a new era of hard rock, engendered by such singles as the Troggs' 'Wild Thing' and the Spencer Davis Group's 'Keep On Running'. This tremendous season in British pop music was bracketed by the Beatles' hard driving, rhythm oriented singles 'Day Tripper', released in December 1965, and 'Paperback Writer'(with its astonishing B-Side 'Rain') released in June 1966.

The Yardbirds, with their triumvirate of guitarists Eric Clapton, Jeff Beck and Jimmy Page, also pushed the envelope. Jeff Beck was held in awe as he unfolded solos of complexity, rhythmic fervour and unparalleled atmospherics. The solo on 'Shape Of Things To Come', which was broadcast by the pirate stations relentlessly in March 1966, was a milestone, signalling the way to the psychedelic era ahead. In a film of the Yardbirds performing this track at the annual Wembley *NME* pollwinners show, singer Keith Relf sings an apocalyptic lyric laced with a strong environmental message. This in itself was advanced, but when Beck hits his solo, he stomps on a distortion pedal and kicks the figurative door wide open. Indian modal scales collide head-on with Elmore James, flamenco and Stockhausen. Relf, upon hearing the riff, starts bopping like a frenzied elf while the girls begin to scream. British guitarists were able to inject hard rock with surprising doses of melodicism, due in part to the influence of native folk songs of the British Isles as well as solid grounding in the blues and a wide ranging ear for new, exotic sounds. It was the new era of guitar effects, 'deep' lyrics and a strong push against the more mundane pop songs of the era.

Despite his initial debt to Bo Diddley (himself an innovator in his milieu) and

R&B, Barrett would depart radically from the formulaic scales and structures which would continue to inform his peers such as Clapton and Townshend. Of all the musicians of his generation, perhaps Syd Barrett owes the least to black American music. The familiar blues scales that a guitarist's hands so comfortably gravitate to are conspicuous by their absence in Barrett's oeuvre.

In his superb analysis in *Trouser Press*, writer Kris DiLorenzo states: 'Syd borrowed no familiar blue licks as the young Eric Clapton, Jeff Beck and Jimmy Page were wont to do. Barrett used to cite Bo Diddley as his major influence, yet these inputs are no more than alluded to in his music . . . funky rhythm churn up speeding riffs that distort into jazzy improvisation. At times an Eastern influence surfaces, blending vocal chants, jangling guitar.' Barrett began to use contrasting dualities in his music, using lyrics to counterpoint melody, innocuous lyrics coupled with forceful, distorted guitar. Barrett was a master at such contrasts. DiLorenzo adds, 'His trademark (and Achilles heel) was sudden surprise: trance-like riffs would slide abruptly into intense, slightly offbeat strumming . . . harmless lyrics skitter over a fierce undertow of evil-sounding feedback and menacing wah-wah . . . Stylised extremes made Barrett's guitar the focus of Floyd's early music; his instrumental mannerisms dominated each song even when Syd merely played chords.'[5]

At the Marquee they began to play new Barrett compositions such as 'Astronomy Domine', which began with a conventional intro, verse and chorus before it slipped into an improvisation which had no conventional structure to speak of, standing out sharply from the work of his contemporaries. The effect was stunning and the response must have been good, because Stollman asked them to return on the 27th. Stollman and Hoppy dropped more envelopes in the post, which were opened by the amused and bemused, the hipsters and the soon-to-be hipsters. The flier for the 'Mad Hatter's Tea Party' that tumbled out trumpeted:

'Who will be there? Poets, Pop singers, hoods, Americans, homosexuals (because they make up 10 percent of the population), 20 clowns, jazz musicians, one murderer, sculptors, politicians, and some girls who defy description. (For 3/-) costume, mask, ethnic, space, Edwardian, Victorian, and hipness generally, face and body makeup certainly.'

The reference to Lewis Carroll's Mad Hatter from *Alice's Adventures In Wonderland* was apt, for according to Miles, a typical performance would involve a cellist playing Bach whilst having her hair cut, a troupe of Ginger Johnson's African drummers, sitar players from the Indian Institute, various poets, and Donovan. Nick Mason said, 'And I think we were caught up in the time with Syd's writing and the whole interest in the London Underground. We were in the right place at the right time. I don't think there is a simple reason why it all happened, there is always an element of luck and just fate.[6] There were elements of the Underground that we did tune into. The main one was mixed media. We may not have been into acid but we certainly understood the idea of a Happening. We supplied the music while people did creative dance, painted their faces, or bathed in the giant jelly. If it had been thirty years earlier Rick would have come out of the floor in front of the cinema screen playing the organ.'[7]

The Pink Floyd Sound returned throughout April and May. Hoppy recalled, 'That was where I first heard the Pink Floyd, May 1966. They were playing stuff that nobody had ever heard. I thought they were wonderful.'[8]

At one of these Spontaneous Underground gigs, an avant-garde jazz group named AMM played. For Barrett, it was most fortuitous. AMM, and particularly their highly experimental guitarist Keith Rowe, proved to be perhaps his greatest influence, enabling his improvisations to take a quantum leap forward. 'Keith Rowe was doing very abstract improvisations with feedback and the guitar,' notes Joe Boyd. Although Miles liked the Pink Floyd, he says, 'I was more impressed at the time by AMM, because I was very keen on John Cage [American avant-garde composer].'

The roots of AMM date to 1965, when Lou Gare (tenor saxophone) played in the Mike Westbrook Band, with Eddie Prevost (percussion), Keith Rowe (guitar, radio) and John Tilbury (piano). Theorist/composer Cornelius Cardew joined later. Christopher Hobbs, Lawrence Sheaff, and many others would be part of AMM briefly, but the core was Prevost, Rowe and Tilbury. Keith Rowe says, 'AMM was always a radical, marginal, improvising group, which was owned by no one, completely free and responsible only to themselves.' They continue playing to this day. 'Our heroes were David Tudor, Merce Cunningham, John Cage and Rauschenberg, plus some of the American jazz performers, like Cecil Taylor.'

AMM would often play with the similarly inclined Spontaneous Music Ensemble at the Little Theatre Club, Monmouth Street, in London's West End. In 1966, AMM was approached by composer and theorist Cornelius Cardew, who was looking for additional musicians for a performance of his piece *Treatise*.

'AMM had an intellectual structure to support their improvisations,' says Hoppy. 'I knew Cornelius Cardew at Oxford; his starting point was classical music, as opposed to jazz. I'm sure he was a devotee of Cage. He leaned towards Cage and had nothing to do with jazz as far as I understood, from the beginning to the end of his career. Just a different way of hearing things.' Pete Brown says, 'We used to do gigs with Cornelius Cardew, who was a very good friend of Michael Horovitz and Michael Westbroook. Cardew started off as a John Cage disciple, then got into the more political areas, then joined up with AMM.'

'I remember going to listen to AMM when they played,' says Hoppy. 'They were doing something which I'd never heard before, which was to take music and turn it into sound and take sound and turn it into music. So Keith Rowe could drop a book on the piano or the floor and it would make a certain sound, or if someone came in and slammed the door, that was part of it, or coughed or farted or turned the radio on. It was rather like a drug trip, though you didn't need to be on drugs.

'Their performances would last forty-five to sixty minutes and in that time the musicians would go through a whole lot of self-expression, relating to each other musically, socially, and then it would just reach a point where it stopped. I was very excited by this, it was a new experience with music and sound. The nearest I could relate it to was John Cassavetes, whose film *Shadows* [one of the first 'lifestyle' movies] I saw on Oxford Street in the very early sixties, and I remember coming out of the movie house with the feeling that I was still in the film.'

Indeed, one measure of a successful artistic performance, whether it be film, music or theatre, is if the spectator forgets they are watching a performance, are transported from their seat into the scenario, losing consciousness of their surroundings. Thirty years later AMM still matches this criteria. Aptly enough, AMM's début album *AMM Music*, was subtitled *Extracts From A Continuous Performance.*

AMM, outside of sympathetic venues like the Spontaneous Underground, faced an incredible amount of confusion and even hostility from audiences. The Pink Floyd themselves would soon run into the same problem. 'Promoters would tell us to push off in no uncertain terms,' says Keith Rowe, 'on the basis that we hadn't played. Very aggressive, very abrasive. We'd say, "No, we've played, that is our music," and we'd have to take them to court to get our money.'

AMM took many of their cues from the visual arts. Keith Rowe explains, 'It was for us the equivalent of synthetic cubism, where Picasso or Braque would glue pieces of cigarette packets or newspaper on to a canvas. The radio in our performances, for me in particular, in the very early days, was based on synthetic cubism, the ideas of analytical cubism . . . see, we always had this problem, we didn't want a jazz group with a soloist. The philosophical model in my head, the way to get around this problem of background/foreground, was in cubism, they would take the pot, the flowers, the apples, the cloth in the back, and they would say, there was a democracy in that where everything could be the same; the cloth was just as important as the flower. In jazz, the soloist was the flower, and the piece of cloth the drummer, piano and bass, the back line. How do you integrate all these things together? My model for doing that was analytical cubism; you break all the parts of the landscape or still life and reconstruct it on a completely democratic even base where there is no centre point of view or perspective, but held together by use of tone. And that was quite a powerful thing.'

Waters pointed to this as the time when the Pink Floyd, inspired by their contemporaries and Barrett's own experimentalism, began to strike out on their own path. 'In June or July of 1966 . . . we'd already started to do the things that we continued to do. Even though we were still amateur, we stopped playing blues and started thrashing about making stranger noises and doing different things.'[9] Miles said, 'The Floyd were using some very unconventional techniques: playing the guitar with a metal cigarette lighter, rolling ball-bearings down the guitar neck to give an amazing Bo Diddley feedback sound and feedback in continuous controlled waves which added up to complex repeating patterns that took ages before coming round again.'[10]

The source of Barrett's experimental inspiration was guitarist Keith Rowe of AMM. Techniques such as the rolling of steel ball bearings down the neck of the guitar developed straight out of Rowe's head. The 'seagull' noises that Barrett and the post-Syd Floyd both utilised were also the creation of Rowe, who used metal objects and distortion to make an astonishing variety of sounds.

'Those techniques came from being a painter, a visual artist,' Rowe explains, 'because the idea of laying the guitar flat came from Jackson Pollock. You had the abandonment of the easel technique, with the small brush and lots of detail. When you give that up what you're given in its place is the horizontal canvas, which you can work on top of and use gravity. So that was one idea, to stop using the normal guitar technique, that linear technique, and work more with an idea of a more gestural, developmental idea of working, combined with an interest in Marcel Deauchamp. If I take a utilitarian object and I put it in an exhibition and call it art, it becomes art. Just by changing its context. I change its culture. I change the way you look at it. I liked the idea that when you look at it, this thing you had taken and called art had an ambiguous feeling about it. If you took the same object, I couldn't tell the difference between your object and mine, because both would look the same. I liked the idea of taking a knife or metal object, an everyday object I knew very well and putting it in the guitar strings and hitting it. I was fascinated by the idea of 'what do you hear?' Do you hear Keith Rowe playing guitar? Do you hear a guitar, or a knife? What do you hear? It has an ambiguity which I like. At the time I was trying to get away from an ego-driven music. I was interested in developing an ambiguous kind of music, and an anti-technique driven music. So ball bearings . . . after a while you develop an eye and I would know what to pick up for the guitar.'

Meanwhile, summer bloomed in unexpectedly bright hues. Miles claims, 'The Summer of Love in Britain was really in 1966, not in 1967, and Syd was very much a part of that.' Various factors served to make that summer memorable, from the healthy state of the economy to the World Cup victory of the English football team over the Germans on 30 July. In addition there was the plenitude of acid and marijuana circulating through London. Fittingly, the two singles that eptiomised the topsy-turvy atmosphere of that summer were the Kinks' 'Sunny Afternoon' and the Rolling Stones' menacing 'Paint It, Black'.

In June 1966, legislation was introduced in Parliament to shut down the pirate radio stations which had sprung up outside coastal waters, relaying a constant stream of pop music, inane chatter and advertisements to the new youth.

By 1966 more young people listened to Radio Caroline than to the BBC. In a sense, the introduction of legislation to put down the pirates was a tacit recognition of the emerging power of the youth that pirate radio was reaching.

Meanwhile, Peter Jenner, Hoppy, Ron Atkins and Alan Beckett set up DNA, what Miles terms an independent record production company. Their first record was *AMM Music for a Continuous Performance* by AMM, released by Elektra in January 1967. Peter Jenner said, 'It was a very, very good far out record,' remarking that AMM came from 'the avant-garde/classical/weirdo scene.[11] The sessions took place at Sound Techniques Studio in Chelsea produced by Joe Boyd and engineer John Wood on 8 and 27 June 1966. With Cornelius Cardew variously playing piano, cello and manipulating a transistor radio, Eddie Prevost on percussion, Keith Rowe on electric guitar and transistor radio, Lawrence Sheaff on cello, accordion, clarinet and transistor radio and Lou Gare playing endless scales on his sax or violin, AMM managed to get an incredible amount of gear into a very tiny studio. AMM did a twenty-one-minute 'Later during a flaming Riviera sunset', followed by a twenty-minute 'After rapidly circling the plaza'.

Boyd says, 'I produced AMM with Hoppy for Elektra at the same period. Peter Jenner and Hoppy were all involved with AMM as well, so there was an awareness of those avant garde things. 'It was something that was in the air,' Peter Jenner said, 'The idea of the label was that it should be avant-garde music, break down the barriers between classical music, folk music in its widest definition, and pop music. Modern, progressive, avant-garde music.' DNA's next production, an album's worth of sessions for Steve Lacey, the soprano saxophone player, was ultimately never released. Finances were the problem of course; avant-garde music just didn't generate the sums needed to bankroll studio time, record pressing and distribution. 'We needed huge volume and it was only going to be through a group that was in some way pop that we'd do this. So what we wanted was an avant garde pop group.'

In one of those serendipitous twists of fate typical of the sixties, Jenner found just that. 'While I was marking some exam papers at the LSE I needed a break and I walked over to the Marquee and went to this gig, a private gig on a Sunday, at which there was the Pink Floyd Sound. It was May 1966.'[12]

Jenner says, 'I wandered round the stage, trying to work out where the noise was coming from, just what was playing it. Normally you could hear something: that's the bass, that's the drums, that's the sax, that's the trumpet, you know where everything was. But the Floyd, when they were doing their solo bits, I couldn't work out whether it was coming from the keyboards or from the guitar and that was what interested me.'[13]

Andrew King, who was to become Jenner's partner, was working at for British Airways, but like Jenner was looking for a band to manage. 'I heard about the Pink Floyd, and I thought, that's the one to manage. You had a tough cookie in Roger, a man who if he hadn't been in rock'n'roll I'm sure would have been an enormously successful architect. You had Nick, with a wonderful show-biz instinct, and Rick, giving it the basis of the musical skills. And you had a genius in Syd. . . So it was a lucky combination.'[14]

Jenner and King couldn't have chosen a better time to 'discover' the band, and approached them after the show, greeting them with, 'You lads could be bigger than the Beatles.' Roger Waters recalled that the band dubiously replied, 'Yes, well we'll see you when we get back from our holidays.'[15] The band, ironically, had been talking of whether they would even bother getting back together after the summer holidays. They had been together for a more than a year and were *still* not pop stars, so the effort of lugging their broken-down equipment from gig to gig hardly seemed justified. Jenner blurted out, 'You should stay together and sign to my label.'

Waters responded if they were so keen on signing them, they should come and see them after their holidays. Jenner and King agreed, and true to his word, a month later Jenner wandered down the maze-like streets leading to Leonard's Highgate house. The band were surprised to see him. Waters immediately started in with, 'What we really need is a manager because otherwise we're going to break up . . . We don't have enough equipment, we need someone to help. . .' Jenner, guided by gut feeling, went home to Edbrooke Road and rang Andrew King, somehow talking him into using his severance pay from BEA to buy the Pink Floyd Sound new WEM speakers, guitar leads, cymbals and other equipment. Within weeks, of course, the entire lot was stolen from their truck.[16]

'Who are my idols?' said Syd Barrett. 'Well, Steve Cropper is an obvious choice, and so is Bo Diddley. In the old days, he was a great influence on both me and the group. I don't think they influence me now. At least, I'm not conscious of it.'[17] Steve Cropper, of Memphis-based Stax soul instrumentalists Booker T. and the M.G.'s is an interesting and telling choice. His favoured guitar was the Fender Telecaster, with its distinctly trebly tone. Barrett would achieve renown using Telecasters as well, and his tone betrays a debt to Cropper. On their soul instrumentals such as 'Green Onions', Cropper would use single-note, repetitive riffs to carry along the rhythm, using his guitar almost as a percussive tool. Barrett was to employ these percussive phrases in his own right, particularly on the Pink Floyd's first album repeating one short phrase for what seemed an eternity, slightly ahead of the beat, creating an atmosphere of tension.

Eventually, one of Barrett's trademarks and indeed breakthroughs would be to utilise the guitar as neither a rhythmic or melodic instrument, using short repetitive phrases laden with echo and slide to create atmosphere, using his guitar as what critic Simon Reynolds called 'a texture and timbre generator'. Barrett transformed the clichéd solos of R&B into textural washes, as if he had taken his painting technique and transferred it to music *a la* Keith Rowe. On 'Late Night' from his solo album 'The Madcap Laughs' or on Rick Wright's 'Remember A Day' one can hear how Syd would use these atmospheric washes of sound, sliding up and down the fretboard, from octave to octave, creating backgrounds on which to layer more conventional rhythm or lead guitar. Very subtle but very effective. What AMM did in the world of avant-garde jazz, Barrett took upon himself to do in the pop/rock medium.

Kris DiLorenzo notes, 'Barrett's music was as experimental as you could get without crossing over entirely into free-form jazz; there simply were no other bands extending the boundaries of rock beyond the basic 4/4 sex-and-love themes.'[18] Restlessly improvising with rhythm, building cross rhythms, dancing around the beat, sneaking in mechanical repetitions that would disorient the listener, then morph into an almost oceanic, lulling riff. What Syd's solos lacked in technical skill would be more than compensated for in the intensely atmospheric sounds he would coax out of his Telecaster.

'In 1966, it had been ten years since "Rock Around The Clock",' says Keith Rowe, 'but it took ten years, especially in London, for something to happen where you felt you could cast off the luggage. It was the epoch of having an open mind towards things, as if you were shedding the skin of pre-rock players. Humorous pop songs had no relevance for us at all. There were definitely people who were in the fast lane, trying things out. At that point, there was alternative or "new wave" music, which covered an enormous amount of categories, from the avant-garde right through to the experimental rock groups. The categorisation hadn't begun to form, so a group like AMM could easily be confused with a group like Pink Floyd, though not for long. But there was this period where there apparently was the same kind of thing. It wasn't yet clear how it would turn out, therefore one had concerts in London which had the AMM and you had rock groups which were trying to make career moves and becoming famous, like Geno Washington and the Ram-Jam Band, Cream, Pink Floyd, the Bluesbreakers and AMM would all be playing the same gigs. By 1969-70 this wasn't possible any more. AMM would be invited to play parties in London where members of the Beatles would be there, relaxing on the sofa and AMM would be playing, which is quite an odd juxtaposition. Later on, Lennon took part in performances which would involve people like Trevor Watts and John Stevens. The free jazz edge would overlap with people like Lennon because of the influence of Yoko Ono, who was more avant-garde.'

'No one was doing work quite in the same vein as AMM in 1966,' adds Keith Rowe, 'but there were associated groups like Sonic Art Union of New York, which we would have some correlation with, or the electronic music of Musica Electronica Viva in Italy, the Taj Mahal Travellers of Japan, which would have a very similar outlook. But we were the only ones doing pure, absolute improvisation. We realised, and very consciously knew, that we were not black or American. For us the task was to develop a unique music which was European. We had enormous respect for what black jazz musicians had done. They developed their music, and the great jazz musicians who weren't appreciated never just slavishly copied the generation before them. They always developed their own languages, ideas and forms. And that for us was a very powerful inspiration for us to do the same thing.'

One of the notable characteristics of the era was the strong symbiotic link between the Underground scenes in America and the UK. Hoppy says, 'We listened to a lot of American avant-garde music. In the early sixties it was Coltrane and Rollins, then Ornette Coleman. I went to the Newport Jazz Festival in 1963-64 because Joe Boyd was working as assistant to George Wheelan, who ran it. Boyd has been staying in Westbourne Terrace with me and invited me to come to the Festival, and I got a job from *Melody Maker* taking photos. I saw Cecil Taylor, Archie Shepp, Carla Bley and Mike Mantler. When I was in NY, I went to see Archie Shepp and he gave me a poem for $5. When Ornette Coleman came to London he stayed with me in my flat in Queensway; they were sort of nice. The avant-garde NY jazz musicians, most of them, appeared on the ESP label run by Bernard Stollman. Stollman gave me a dozen LPs when I went to visit him in New York, and which I then brought back to London and we all sat around listening to and trying to understand what was going on. At the same time there was the Velvet Underground which I'd come across because of the New York avant-garde film cultural scene. Kate Heleczer brought a tape and we'd often go to bed and listen to this tape.

'The part of English culture that I was from, and there were many different parts, we allowed ourselves to be very influenced by American culture. American beat poetry and writing, Ferlinghetti, Kerouac, Ginsberg, Burroughs, were formative influences whether you liked them or not. We felt very receptive to things American. Nowadays what America puts into the global culture is a bit different, but they were definitely leading edge at the time. Miles married Sue and although she was English, she had been brought up in the States and she had a bit of an American accent, and a bit of American behaviour. It seemed to be exactly the right thing that Miles would marry Sue. Later on I married Suzy Creamcheese, from California, and that seemed to be the right thing to do at the time. The pollination went both ways. The avant-garde cinema had a lot of interesting people in it. Paolo Leonni, an Italian film maker. Warhol, Pierre Heleczer. They had an impact on people who were doing similar work and led to the formation of the Filmmakers Co-op.

'It wasn't as if English culture was only in England or American was only over there, there were people going back and forth and an interchange of ideas. Chet Helms and the Family Dog at the Avalon Ballroom, and Bill Graham at the Fillmore. We heard about what those people were doing and thought, "That's interesting", and that what we were doing was in some way similar. UFO was the first all-night dance club. The way UFO came about wasn't people sitting down and planning a cultural event. Drugs were very important as a cultural subset. Personally, I think, looking back, a lot of what happened in the sixties is really down to acid. Albert Hoffman was one of the most important people of the twentieth century.'

Peter Wynne-Wilson says, 'The consciousness-expanding experimental movement was a conviction for me and for many others, but not for all. It was certainly drug related, to what extent it was drug *clouded* I couldn't tell. Certainly it would be ludicrous to say we didn't take LSD and cannabis for recreation, but it was always really with the feeling in the back of your mind that they would ultimately lead to something which might or might not require more drugs. There was definitely a transcendental goal. In a way it sounds crass, but it was a very serious thing at the time. A lot of established mysticism was drawn upon, and a lot of quack mysticism too. There is no doubt that in some cases it did bring people to some kind of spiritual life, though post-drugs I would think. It was totally wonderful to encounter strangers in your own country or in others who were operating on extremely similar lines to yourself, which was quite different from the society created by our parents.'

Peter Jenner said, 'Syd was the most creative person I've ever known. It was extraordinary, in those few months at Earlham Street he wrote nearly all his songs for the Floyd and the solo albums. It was all very casual, done off the top of the head. No tortured genius sweating through his pain, as far as I could see. When people just write without any inhibitions, they write so much better than when they start getting concerned that they're great writers.[19] The strongest image I always have of Syd is of him sitting in his flat in Earlham Street with his guitar and his book of songs, which he represented by paintings with different coloured circles. . . . Syd did this wild, impossible drawing, and they turned it into the Pink Floyd.[20]

'[Syd's] influences were very much the Stones, the Beatles, Byrds and Love. The Stones were the prominent ones; he wore out his copy of *Between The Buttons* very quickly. Love's album too. In fact, I was once trying to tell him about this Arthur Lee song I couldn't remember the title of, so I just hummed the main riff. Syd picked up his guitar and followed what I was humming chord-wise. The chord pattern he worked out he went on to use as the main riff for Interstellar Overdrive".'[21]

Barrett's love of the massed spiky guitars on the coda of the Byrd's 1965 "Eight Miles High" and "Have You Seen Her Face", from the 1965 album *5th Dimension* is evident in his latter playing. *5th Dimension* in particular was a favourite, its jangle guitar and tight choral work ringing out in Barrett's room in Earlham Street. The Rolling Stones' *Between The Buttons* established a precedent for the Pink Floyd's music with the faux-Elizabethan and mysterious air of 'Lady Jane' contrasted with the eleven-minute electric blues jam of 'Going Home' on the flipside. Barrett seized on this duality at once. Nick Mason remarked, 'We were listening to Cream and the Who, Hendrix, that sort of stuff. That was what turned me on to being in a band again.'[22]

Wynne-Wilson says, 'There were periods of an incredible amount of lyrics and songs flowing out of Syd in space of a few months. I can remember him writing "Astronomy Domine", which wasn't a one-evening scene, it was concentrated but not an outpouring. He worked on it quite hard; there was a lot of *I-Ching* going on at the time, Syd threw it quite a bit. There would be periods when he would focus on songwriting to the exclusion of other things, but sometimes with the inclusion of other things, like the *I-Ching*. "Astronomy Domine" was a case in point.'

Peter Jenner said, 'The Pink Floyd were the *only* psychedelic band. Various bands came along later to copy, but at that time it was the Pink Floyd. They had this improvisation, this spirit of psychedelia which I don't think any other band did. Even the Grateful Dead, they had improvisations but they seemed a perfectly ordinary group, playing with chords. The Floyd didn't play with chords.'[23]

Regarding the Pink Floyd's headlong plunge into improvisation, Peter Jenner joked at the time, 'My guess is that this wasn't even intentional, they are a lazy bunch and could not be bothered to practice, so they probably had to improvise to get away with it.'[24] Roger Waters said at the time, 'With us, it depends on the club's atmosphere to start with as to how we go down. Our music is light and sound. We don't want any particular image. Our managers said we should find one, "It's important" they said, but we're not prepared to be pigeonholed like other groups. We were a blues group, but then we suddenly stopped playing ordinary music and started improvising around single chords. This gave us a lot more musical freedom.'[25]

Syd's look was developing at the same time as the music. 'He came out in this outrageous gear,' said Peter Jenner. 'He had this permanent, which cost £20 at the time, and he looked like a beautiful woman.'[26] Joe Boyd says, 'My impressions were of his clothes; tight velvet trousers, military jackets, curly hair, very handsome and attractive. He had a bandanna around his neck, knotted like a cravat. You got the feeling that girls would adore him, which they did.'

Peter Wynne-Wilson, Susie, Syd, Lindsay and Alan Beam attended the annual performance of Handel's *Messiah* at the Albert Hall. That night, the full impact of the times they were living in struck them. Before they went they each took a drop of acid; Wynne-Wilson said, 'I can't speak for anyone else's mental experience, but the *Messiah* on acid was quite the most extraordinary thing I'd encountered.'[27]

On 29 September 1966, a strangely dressed black man arrived at Heathrow Airport from New York. Carrying one bag of clothes and with his manager, Chas Chandler of the Animals carrying his guitar in order to avoid work permit questioning by Customs, Jimi Hendrix had come to England. In English music his arrival was nothing short of a revolution. Every guitarist in England would feel his influence within weeks. It was probably the most notable landing since Rudolf Hess parachuted in during 1941. And just as unexpected. When Hendrix showed up at a Cream gig a few days later, having already jammed with Zoot

Money and his band, the shock was acute. Hendrix jammed with Cream and within a few bars, a shaken Eric Clapton, up until then referred to as 'God' by his acolytes for his guitar skill, retreated to the wings. 'He's that good?' said a stunned Clapton to Chandler.

Hendrix's influence was massive. Within weeks Townshend, Page, Beck and Clapton were always at Hendrix performances, soaking in Hendrix's electric gypsy blues. Hendrix's flamboyant clothes and Afro were emulated by Clapton, and later, Barrett. Barrett simply said, 'Hendrix was a perfect guitarist.'[28]

Hendrix played a new, unique variant of the blues, having taken the best of his thousand odd gigs as a member of the touring band for nearly every soul or R&B act in US, including Little Richard, the Isley Brothers. Hendrix brought over the dazzling pyrotechnics of blues guitarist Buddy Guy. Joe Boyd remembers seeing Buddy Guy in Chicago in 1964, and hearing him use heavy distortion. But Hendrix differed from most every other American black guitarist; he was equally influenced by Dylan, the Stones and the Beatles. And soon he would be not only influencing the new breed of British guitarists, but would also be influenced by them. For Barrett, seeing and hearing Hendrix in late 1966 helped map out his new direction. Barrett was unveiling a new electric blues of his own, the blues of a Cambridge art student steeped in children's literature, nature, Joyce and his own odd percolating mind that saw things a bit differently than others. And it's safe to say Barrett influenced Hendrix; Barrett was already pushing the envelope before Hendrix arrived.*

On 30 September, the Pink Floyd, now informally managed by Jenner and King, played at the London Free School. The organisers of the Free School, including Jenner, King and Joe Boyd had realised that they needed money to pay for the newspaper they had set up, the *International Times*, and to pay off the debts they had accumulated. The answer was a fund-raising concert. In the basement of the All Saints' church hall, Powis Gardens, Notting Hill Gate, Barrett and the Floyd refined their growing experimentalism.

On 14 October Nick Jones from *Melody Maker* attended the Pink Floyd's second All Saints' show, and wrote their first review in the music weeklies: 'Last Friday the Pink Floyd, a new London group, embarked upon their first "happening", a pop dance incorporating psychedelic effects and mixed media ... The slides were excellent, colourful, frightening, grotesque, beautiful, and the group's trip into outer space sounds promised very interesting things to come. Unfortunately it all fell a bit flat in the cold reality of All Saints' Hall. The Floyd need to write more of their own material. "Psychedelic" versions of "Louie, Louie" won't come off, but if they can incorporate their electronic prowess with some melodic and lyrical songs, getting away from dated R&B things, they

*Hendrix witnessed the Pink Floyd's performance at UFO on 30 December 1966. He had come to see the Soft Machine play, joining them onstage for a jam session. A close examination of tracks like Hendrix's 1967 'Third Stone from the Sun', with its frenetic noise-drenched coda, suggest a Barrett influence.

could well score in the near future.'

The set list from that night's performance survives. The band played all Syd Barrett originals bar two. During the first set, they opened with 'Pink', of which no known recording exists, followed by 'Let's Roll Another', which would soon resurface as the B-Side of their first single under the new title of 'Candy And A Currant Bun'. The band followed with their old mainstay from Bob Close's days in the band, Bo Diddley's 'Gimme A Break'. 'Stoned Alone' is known only to have featured the line, 'Sitting here all alone I get stoned', showing Syd Barrett in a candid, autobiographical mode. Bo Diddley's 'I Can Tell' was followed by 'The Gnome', one of Barrett's most playful songs, drawn from his childhood favourite *The Hobbit* by J.R.R. Tolkien. The band ended the first set with 'Interstellar Overdrive', the group instrumental effort that Waters characterised as 'an abstract piece' and which would be the centrepiece of their live shows for the next eighteen months. The second set began with the Floyd's first recorded song, Syd's slightly paranoid ode to love gone wrong, 'Lucy Leave'. Roger Water had tried his hand at writing and had come up with 'Stethoscope', a lengthy instrumental which would surface on their first album. The unknown 'Flapdoodle Dealing', was followed by the equally mysterious 'Snowing'. 'Matilda Mother', Barrett's haunted ode to childhood bedtime stories, was followed by 'Pow R. Toc H.', another group effort and instrumental freak-out. The closer was the powerfully atmospheric 'Astronomy Domine'.

Joe Boyd saw the Pink Floyd perform that night and was given a tape of the band by Jenner and King. Impressed with what he heard, Boyd petitioned his boss, Jac Holzman, chief of Elektra, to sign the band. Holzman refused. Boyd saw parallels between the Floyd and the band whose début he had just produced, the Incredible String Band. Released in June 1966, *The Incredible String Band* was a remarkable album, melding traditional folk with proto-psychedelic lyrics and bizarre instrumentation layered atop the acoustic guitars of Robin Williamson, Clive Palmer and Mike Heron. Barrett, like many songwriters of the era, was deeply influenced by this album and the subsequent and brilliantly titled *5,000 Spirits Or The Layers Of An Onion*, released in 1967. They are both fascinating albums, and their pastoral folk-psychedelic vision influenced songs like Barrett's 'The Gnome'.*

The Pink Floyd took two large steps forward at All Saints' Hall. They began to discard the bulk of their R&B covers in favour of Syd's increasingly brilliant originals, and they also incorporated a light show as an integral part of their live performance. Tracing the origins of the light shows that became such a key part of both Pink Floyd's stage show and the Underground scene is akin to

*The liner notes for the Incredible String Band's debut are a classic of the genre and reveal a sensibility that Barrett was very much in tune with: 'Ever since their meeting with a magic blackbird one day, the Incredible String Band have led lives of a rather strange nature. From dawn's first pale whisper till the sun's wick burns low, the logs on which they spend every waking hour splash whitely down the river. Everywhere they go, they leave bits of themselves lying about all over the place, and if you didn't look at them very closely, you might quite easily think they were songs.'

deciphering Mayan hieroglyphics by candlelight, but it appears that under the influence of psychedelics, they began showing up everywhere, as if by spontaneous generation. It's impossible to trace the originator of the light shows, if there ever was one person. Light shows were the result of the efforts of dozens of people working far afield with lights since the fifties. What is true, with this most perishable of all sixties artforms, is how easy it is to forget how stunning, colourful and artistic the work of Mark Boyle, Peter Wynne-Wilson, John Marsh, Mike Leonard and Joe Gannon was.

Peter Jenner said, 'Two guys turned up from America and did the blippy lights, the oil slide show. They just turned up and said they were from San Francisco and they did lights, so we said, "Great, come and do lights."'[29] According to Miles they were Joel and Toni Brown, associates of Dr Timothy Leary at his experimental acid retreat, Millbrook, in upstate New York, who came to London, bringing water slides. When they showed up at the London Free School, their effects were swiftly incorporated into the general mayhem taking place. The band mentioned Leonard and the Hornsey Sound and Light Workshops to Jenner and King, who put two and two together and realised it was a great idea to have the band play with a full lighting accompaniment.

Nick Mason remarked, 'The light show was due to various influences, like someone coming over from the States, heard the band and liked it, and had got a projector and knew how to make a water slide and did so. At the begining there was the music with a few people flashing lights over it, but the lights were insignificant because no one had got into powerful bulbs and so on.'[30]

Peter Jenner, his wife Sumi, and Andrew King built the first light show for the Pink Floyd. They bought closed-beam spotlights which they mounted on wooden boards, wired together, and had a domestic light switch. Jenner said, 'If you put them a long way away they had no impact, so we put them right in front of them. The result was these hugely dramatic shadows behind, which I'm sure everyone thought was brilliant. Of course, it was a complete fuck-up and mistake as all the best things are.'[31]

The band's first lighting engineer, was Joe Gannon, then only sixteen years old. Jenner recalls him as 'a young bullshitting fresh-faced kid with an incredible amount of energy and loads of verbal who just whizzed in and whizzed out again.'[32] Hoppy says, 'Certainly the first person who did light shows was Joe Gannon, who was a bright teenager, and who had already made a film about Notting Hill. People were travelling and they brought their artefacts with them. There was also Jack Braceland, from the nudist colony in Watford, and Mark Boyle, who was at the time a lecturer at Reading University.' Hoppy adds that acid was important in the development of the light shows; the expanded panorama of LSD demanded visual accompaniment to music.

Joe Gannon said at the time, 'I design the slides, basing them on my idea of the music. The lights work rhythmically, I just wave my hand over the microswitches and the different colours flash.'[33] Gannon left soon after for California and was succeeded by Russell Page, Syd's old Cambridge mate. Pip Carter, another friend of Barrett's from Cambridge, was taken on as roadie, lugging the band's new equipment from Jenner's Edbrooke Road flat to the band's old black van and to their gigs. Peter Wynne-Wilson, Syd's friend and flatmate at Earlham, was mechanically inclined, so Syd also volunteered him to help out. John Marsh was a young mod who hung around the All Saints' Hall and asked to help out and was taken on as well.

John Marsh said, 'Light shows in those days were desperately unsophisticated. Pre-laser, even pre-video era. Everything very crudely mechanical, very crudely assembled, but for the time, pretty effective. All kinds of strange stories got around: there were electronic links between the lights and the band, absolute nonsense: the whole thing was very primitive and in the case of the Floyd, as in most bands, relied 90 per cent on liquid slide projection, a certain amount of use of things like Kodak carousels with pre-programmed cassette changes. Also two effects, both built by Peter Wynne-Wilson: one called the Daleks, the other the Flashes and these were the two things that the Floyd had which no other band had and which put them in light show terms streets ahead of everybody else. But this was still manually operated, switch-oriented kind of stuff. '[34]

The light show became an integral part of Pink Floyd's live act. 'Ours is a sort of light-sound show,' explained Roger Waters in an interview in 1967. 'As for our music, it's pop but very free and full of improvisation. Some of our numbers have been known to run at least half an hour. We started on this lighting idea a couple of years ago. It seemed that visual images are just as good a thing to give an audience as sounds. Visual images can be really stimulating to you when you're up on stage playing.[35] There is no preconceived arrangement. Perhaps there was an idea dreamed up in using images as well as sounds, but otherwise it's all improvisation.'[36] Nick Mason remarked, 'We were very disorganised until our managers materialised and we started looking for a guy to do the lights full-time. The lighting man literally has to be one of the group. When we were in our early stages we didn't play a lot of our electronic "interstellar" music and the slides were still rather amateurish. However, this has developed now and our "take off" into the mainly improvised electronic scenes are much longer, the slides have developed out of all proportion.'[37]

Duggie Fields says, 'Musically what the Pink Floyd was doing was very interesting, but they had no rhythm. Great sense of theatrical showmanship, and obviously inventive and experimental. But they couldn't dance. And to look at the Pink Floyd, they weren't much to look at except for Syd. Syd was the only one worth looking at. I saw the Pink Floyd at All Saints' Hall, a very memorable performance for me, the most potent. People used to do light shows in Cromwell Road and also at Earlham Street, and so I was used to the light shows being done in a home and hanging around watching them. I liked watching the Pink Floyd with no audience, because I could hear them clearly. There couldn't have been more than fifty people. I remember one guy dancing, and no one ever danced to the Pink Floyd. He was dancing on his own, and he was amazing. I'd never seen anyone dance like that, very stylishly dressed. It was very potent music, what they were doing, definitely. The Pink Floyd were doing something which extended away from the basic R&B.

'The Pink Floyd you didn't look at, you looked at effects around them, whereas everyone else you looked at the band, and the band wanted you to look at them. The Pink Floyd didn't want you to, they wanted you to be distracted from looking at them. The light shows were entertaining, but there was a big difference between people who have charisma on-stage and use it and those who deny any charisma. Pop performers usually play with it, but the Pink Floyd wouldn't. If they had it they didn't let it develop.

'Of the group, Syd was the only one who became a friend as such. Syd was much more charming and entertaining. Syd was a great wit at that time. On a personal level I got on with Syd in a way that I never got on with Roger. Roger I always found difficult. Rick was a nice guy, but I don't remember him being anything more than that. And Nick didn't register, we never formed a relationship particularly.'

Pete Brown remembers the All Saints' Hall gigs as haphazard affairs, 'There was a gig at Powis Square where we all ended up jamming. Mick Farren, Alexis Korner, Nick Mason, Arthur Brown and me all singing "Lucille". It wasn't music. It was nonsense, really, but it was funny.' Yet they quickly created a buzz around the band. Each concert in the tiny church hall was sold out.

'We none of us knew what had hit us.' Peter Jenner recalls. 'It was probably seven shillings and sixpence at the door. It was a tiny church hall, it couldn't have held more than 300. It was heaving. You couldn't move. Originally it was all word of mouth, all our mates, the community. Suddenly it hit a responsive chord.'[38]

Jenner and King took a small ad in the back pages of *Melody Maker* and *IT* to announce upcoming Pink Floyd gigs at the London Free School. They used Timothy Leary's catchphrase, 'Turn On, Tune In, Drop Out' as their slogan in the ads, which acted as a draw to those in the Underground who had actually read Leary and Alpert's *The Psychedelic Experience*. Nick Mason said, 'The London Free School was important because it was the first time we were booked in under our own name, and actually drew a crowd on that name.'[39] Roger Waters said, 'There were about twenty people there when we first played, the second week one hundred and then three or four hundred and after that you couldn't get in.'[40] Rick Wright said of the All Saints' Hall gigs, 'That was a very special time. Those early days were purely experimental for us and a time of learning and finding out exactly what we were trying to do. Each night was a complete buzz because we did totally new things and none of us knew how the others would react to it. It was the formation of the Pink Floyd.'[41]

Of the Free School, Peter Wynne-Wilson says, 'There were a lot of, in retrospect, grandiose ideas around at the time. It never seemed to me to be a practical project.' Hoppy concurs, 'The Free School never really got off the ground and it's an idea that really shouldn't be inflated with too much content, 'cos there really wasn't too much content.'[42]

Meanwhile, Miles' and Hoppy's *Long Hair Times* had evolved into something a bit different. Inspired by the example of the *Village Voice* in New York's Greenwich Village, Hoppy and Miles, in association with Jim Haynes and Jack Henry Moore of Edinburgh's Traverse Theatre and Paperback Bookstore, began a layout for what Miles termed 'a mass communication paper'. Trying to capture the zeitgeist of the times, and also providing a crucial listing of what was going on, this new newspaper would feature articles, artwork and editorials emanating from a decidedly Underground perspective.

On 15 October the new Underground newspaper the *International Times* or simply *IT*, as it came to be known, was launched on a cold night with a huge event at the Roundhouse in Chalk Farm, London.

Hoppy explains how he first discovered the Roundhouse as a possible venue. 'The Roundhouse was very cold. Arnold Wesker was a playwright who came to prominence in the late fifties and early sixties. And he considered himself a socialist. He made a successful interaction with the trade union movement, providing "art for the masses". And he set up Centre 42, which was based on the Trade Union manifesto, section 42. His main interest was theatre and theatre is a very difficult art form to propagate to the masses at anytime, even then. He was on a roll and he managed to persuade the Gilbey's Gin company to let him take over the Roundhouse. He wasn't able to materialise his vision of the Roundhouse as a trade union people's cultural theatre. I worked for Wesker as a photographer, taking pictures of the Roundhouse, when it was still a gin vat warehouse. Although Centre 42 had acquired the Roundhouse, he didn't do anything with it. I said, "Arnold, look, here's £50, let us use the Roundhouse." He didn't participate, he was in a different space altogether. He was serious, probably still is!'

Recalling the event, Miles says. 'The Roundhouse was a complete fire trap. It hadn't been used since before the War . . . It was grimy and very, very cold, because it was October.[43] We did fliers for the *IT* launch to publicise it, printed on letterpress, with the actual IT girl on it, Clara Bow. We printed thousands and gave them away or mailed them to people.' Using Hoppy's address book, Miles and Hoppy sent out invitations that circulated among the hip coteries of the emerging Underground. It promised:

'*Pop/Op/Costume/Masque/Fantasy-Loon/Blowout/Drag Ball. All night rave to launch* International Times, *with the Soft Machine, Pink Floyd, steel bands, strips, trips, happenings, movies. Bring your own poison and flowers & gas filled balloons & submarines & rocket ships & candy & striped boxes & ladders & paint & flutes & feet & ladders & locomotives & madness & autumn & blow lamps.*'

Perhaps ninety-nine per cent of today's estimated million a week club-goers in the UK don't know about this milestone event, the very first rave, paving the way for all that came later. Miles stood at the top of the staircase which curved around the brick façade of the Roundhouse, greeting each guest with a sugar cube, which was assumed to contain LSD. They didn't, but there was plenty on offer inside, dispensed by the new street pharmacists who congregated by the thin, fluted steel pillars inside the Roundhouse and sold them or gave them away. Joe Boyd notes, 'The Underground spirit was made manifest at the London Free School concerts, and the *IT* launch.'

The giant six foot jelly at the *IT* launch was a classic English thing,' says Miles. 'We're having a party, let's make a great big jelly!" The one at the launch was made out of a bath. The Pink Floyd backed their van into it and knocked it over. But Steve Abrams said it never set, it was still sloshy, and it was gelling on a big plastic sheet so when it was done one could pull it out. But Steve said that the bath was being held up by wooden supports and Syd and Pip Carter pulled away some of the wood to use for their light show, and the whole thing collapsed, splashing jelly everywhere. There was body painting, Mike Westbrook did an imitation of Yves Klein. He got naked and covered himself in paint and crawled along a sheet of wall paper. I paid the Soft Machine £12 10 shillings, and £15 to the Pink Floyd, because they had a light show. The Soft Machine, however, did have a motorcycle on which they had contact mikes, and which they gave people rides on.'

The *New Society* noted that Marianne Faithful was 'wearing what appeared to be a fair imitation of a nun's habit, which didn't quite make it to the ground: in fact it didn't even cover her bottom; this must have been the shortest of the evening, if not the barest.'

Poet Kenneth Rexroth, one of the American forefathers of the Beats, filed the following report for the 4 December 1966 *San Francisco Examiner* under the headline 'Making the Rounds of Way-Out London'. 'The bands didn't show, so there was a large pick-up band of assorted instruments on a small central platform. Sometimes they were making rhythmic sounds, sometimes not . . . . I felt exactly like I was on the *Titanic*. Far be it for me to holler copper, but I was dumbfounded that the London police and fire authorities permitted even a dozen people to congregate in such a trap.'

Peter Jenner said, 'Paul McCartney was dressed as an arab in a hood. It was very dark. The total power supply in the Roundhouse at that time was about as much as there was in the average kitchen, probably much less. So the Floyd frequently put all the lights out; we frequently blew the power. If you saw the place in daylight you would have been horrified. It was dank, really cold and wet and filthy and horrible, but the excitement at that gig was enormous. It was like "Wow! This is our place." There was this great feeling; it was a classic gig, a terrific gig.'[44]

The *International Times* reported '2500 Ball at IT-Launch': 'Two and a half thousand people dancing about in that strange, giant round barn. Darkness, only flashing lights. People in masks, girls half-naked. Other people standing about wondering what the hell was going on. Pot smoke. Now and then the sound of a bottle breaking. Somebody looks as if he might get violent. There was a lot of tension about. The Pink Floyd, psychedelic pop group, did weird things to the feel of the evening with their scary feedback sounds, slide projections playing on their skin (drops of paint run riot on the slides to produce outer space/prehistoric textures on the skin), spotlights flashing on them in time with a drum beat. The Soft Machine, another group with new ideas, drove a motor bike into the place, in and around the pillars that held up that gallery we had been warned wasn't all that safe. A large car (some said it was Oldsmobile, others a Cadillac) in the middle of it all, painted bright pop art striped and explosions by Binder, Edwards and Vaughan, New York interior decorators, who someone said, put stripes over everything. The car was previously seen parked inside the Robert Fraser Gallery. Simon Postuma and Marijke Koger, the Amsterdam couple who are opening Karma, designed an interesting cubicle with coloured screens and nets, and within the box one of them, in suitable dress, read palms and told fortunes.'*

IT continued, 'In another part of the Roundhouse, Bob Cobbing and the London Film Coop gave an all-night film show featuring films like *Scorpio Rising, Towers Open Fire,* under the most difficult of conditions. The audience stood in front of the projectors, on top of the cables, on top of Bob Cobbing. Yet the films went on. It may, though, have been just the right setting for those particular films. Burroughs' inner-space disappearance in *Towers Open Fire* somehow had more impact because of the vibrations from the "party". "Famous" people turned up: Antonioni and Monica Vitti, Paul McCartney disguised as an arab, Kenneth Rexroth. Of course several things went wrong. There was that narrow entrance for an unpleasant start. That communal toilet that ended up in flood. A giant jelly made in a bath for the party was run over by a bicycle . . . After the party, the crowds caused a traffic jam in the streets outside. It should be said here that throughout the event the police were cooperative . . . Perhaps it was just relief that something has at last happened in the Roundhouse. It was a good party, and just to prove something really IS going on in London, another, bigger, better one is currently being planned.'

Daevid Allen of the Soft Machine called the launch 'one of the two most revolutionary events in the history of English alternative music and thinking. The *IT* event was important because it marked the first recognition of a rapidly spreading socio-cultural revolution that had its parallel in the States. It was its London newspaper. The new year came . . . bringing an inexpressible feeling of

*Simon Postuma and Marijke Koger, a.k.a. "The Fool", used to come around to 101 Cromwell Road,' says Duggie Fields. 'They were friends of mine, and when I later went to New York I visited them in Washington Square Mews and we would go around New York with their multicoloured painted Rolls. They painted the big mural at the Apple Shop in 1968.

change in the air.'[45] Allen noted that two separate stages had been set up, and facing them was the first light show gantry seen in London. All around milled the crowd in their 'fancy dress'.

The Soft Machine played their first gig as a quartet, going on at 9 p.m. They had borrowed a motorcycle, parked it on-stage and fitted it with contact mikes on the cylinder head, and its short bursts of noises as it was revved echoed throughout the Roundhouse at intervals through their performance of their psychedelic-laced jazz improvisations. Halfway through their set, all the lights were shut off, and in the darkness came the amplified voice of a Japanese woman. It was Yoko Ono, staging a Fluxus-style happening.

'Touch the person next to you . . .' she said, and the startled audience responded, reaching in the dark for the person next to them. A flurry of embarrassed giggles and then the lights came back on and the Soft Machine continued their set. Ono, who had been active in the German/American experimental arts movement Fluxus in the early sixties, was a familiar figure in the nascent Underground. On 9 November, just a few weeks away, she would meet John Lennon at Miles' and John Dunbar's Indica Art Gallery. Lennon had come down to see her 'Unfinished Objects And Paintings' show.*

As the Soft Machine finished, the Pink Floyd began their set on the stage set up on the opposite side of the Roundhouse. With the house lights off and their light show on, Barrett and co. began with the low, ominous rumble of 'Astronomy Domine'. Their light show, though primitive, made quite an impression on the assembled crowd, not least of all Paul McCartney, who made his approval plain.

On 30 October the *Sunday Times* wrote, 'At the launching of the new magazine *IT* the other night a pop group called the Pink Floyd played throbbing music while a series of bizarre coloured shapes flashed on a huge screen behind them. Someone had made a mountain of jelly which people ate at midnight and another person had parked his motorbike in the middle of the room. All apparently very psychedelic.'

Andrew King told *The Times*, 'We don't call ourselves psychedelic. But we don't deny it. We don't confirm it either. People who want to make up slogans can do it.'[46] Of their act, Roger Waters gushed, 'It is totally anarchistic. But it's cooperative anarchy if you see what I mean. It's definitely a complete realisation of the aims of psychedelia. But if you take LSD what you experience depends entirely on who you are. Our music may give you the screaming horrors or throw you into screaming ecstasy. Mostly it's the latter. We find our audiences

*'Yoko One came around to Cromwell Road,' says Duggie Fields, 'she wanted me be in her *Bottoms* movie which I found uninteresting. Now I wish I'd gone and talked to Yoko when she came to Cromwell, even had my bottom filmed, because she was a very interesting woman.' Keith Rowe of AMM says, 'We had a very good relationship with Yoko. She used to stay at Cornelius Cardew's flat, and the AMM played at the opening of her exhibition. We knew her quite well.' Not everyone felt the same enthusiasm; Hoppy remarks, 'Yoko Ono's happenings were boring, she was the most boring artist I'd ever met.'

stop dancing now. We tend to get them standing there totally grooved with their mouths open.'[47]

On 31 October Blackhill Enterprises, the Pink Floyd's management, was founded. Peter Jenner said, 'The company name came from a little farmhouse called Blackhill Farm in the Brecon Beacons which Andrew [King] and I had bought for £1,000. So we called the partnership after that. It wasn't a company, it was a partnership between ourselves and the Floyd, very cosmic. Which made it very tricky when we broke up. We did buy the hippie thing. We were going to be alternative, all working together and everything was going to be democratic and groovy. We didn't know any better about resolving the problems that arose. We were incredibly inexperienced in things like cash flow and business management.'[48] Nick Mason remarked, 'We don't get all that much money now because our earnings are split six ways, us four and our two managers. We buy all our own equipment, not to mention hire purchase payments, so our present wage is quite small.'[49] Robert Wyatt of the Soft Machine said, 'The Pink Floyd were with a lovely bunch of people, Blackhill and they were very nice and I think they were an honourable exception to the shady rule about managers. I think they were nice people and really cared about the people they worked for. I think that most of us were less lucky than that.'[50]

June Childs, later the wife of glam-rocker Marc Bolan, began working for the Floyd in 1966. 'Peter Jenner and Andrew King were trying to get work for the Floyd. They had a telephone and the phone kept ringing all day, and because I was on the dole I answered the telephone. This went on for two or three months and I'd write down all the messages. One day I said, "Look, this is a joke. You need a secretary. Pay me fifteen quid a week." So I became the secretary.'[51]

Straight after signing with Blackhill, the Pink Floyd cut their first studio demo at the rather grandly titled Thompson Private Recording Company, at Hemel Hempstead. They also recorded 'Interstellar Overdrive' and Barrett's 'Stoned Alone', 'Silas Lane' (perhaps an early working title for 'Arnold Layne') and 'Let's Roll Another One'. The first being a group effort, and the latter three all Barrett compositions.

Jazz saxophonist John Coltrane was a marked influence on Barrett, especially as his instrumental explorations became more daring. Coltrane was a Barrett favourite during his tenure at Earlham Street; his mythic scales and stacked chords were inspirational for players as diverse as Paul Butterfield, Keith Rowe and Roger McGuinn, all inspired by Coltrane and applying this inspiration to their music. One precedent for the feedback and echo-laden improvisation both AAMM and the Pink Floyd pursued, was, according to Keith Rowe, John Coltrane's 'sheets of sound'. 'The notion of a block of sound. It was the antithesis of punctuated hi-hat sound, and there is a natural response to clear some space for yourself, you have to have a new area. The new area would be a very long continuous drone [like La Monte Young], and there are still people interested in that. Music that saxophonist Evan Parker would describe as "laminal"; layers of material, stacked like laminated wood. This comes from a number of sources, such as Coltrane, but also a notion of Eastern time signatures, not Afro-American.'

In 'Interstellar Overdrive', the Pink Floyd's live centerpiece throughout the rest of Syd's tenure in the band, the influence of jazz players like Coltrane comes through strongest. Barrett's brutal barre chord riff, itself a precursor for the sludge riffs of heavy metal, echoes the thunder of rocket engines roaring to life. In the wide open improvisation that is bracketed by the opening riff and restatement at the end, the listener could conjure up a plenitude of images. Here, Barrett achieved a quantum leap in pop music – how far pop had travelled from the innocuous chorus of 'yeah yeah yeahs' just three short years before.

Barrett was a primitive, a wonderfully uninhibited one, compared to technically correct guitarists like Clapton or John Mayall. A parallel would be Gauguin travelling thousands of miles from his homeland to the South Sea Islands and 'going primitive', expanding his palette of colours to dazzling reds, yellows and blues, eliminating the baroque trappings of European painting and returning to a basic spectrum of simple yet intense colours. Where others were trapped by form, Barrett dispensed with it. To paraphrase Peter Jenner, when no one tells you what you are doing is wrong, your creativity, technically flawed though it may be, flourishes. A clever songwriter turns to music of greater complexity for succour. The musician's ear is inexorably drawn to arrangements that revel in detail and difficulty.

'Interstellar Overdrive', suggests, if nothing else, the vast loneliness of space, both inner and outer. It evokes images in sound, of a rocket being launched; the central riff, whatever its origin, suggests nothing so much as a countdown. With each successive note, we are readied for takeoff into realms of abstraction and improvisation. After the thunder and flash, *sturm und drang* of takeoff, we the listeners are propelled by Syd into a strange world of mathematics, sound, silence, suggestions, indeed intimations of space. The song is arranged like a jazz song, it goes from head-solo-head; statement of theme, exploration, restatement of theme. There were definite parallels between free jazz and Barrett's Floyd. AMM's Keith Rowe was beginning to move even past the standard format of jazz improvisation in favour of completely open improvisation, without the constraint of winding everything down into a coherent restatement of the central theme.

'Interstellar Overdrive' is perhaps Barrett's most important work, and the most difficult. It's no accident that he linked the title with the piece, for from the scalar riff to the vast complexity of sounds he generates in the improvisation, to the thunderous restatement of the theme, the song mirrors the turbulence of take-off, as well as the infinitely vast reaches of space, both inner and outer. John Coltrane was at the same time making a connection between improvisation and outer space. He was approaching the end of his life, and his steady methodical quest for perfection had led him to a remarkable, and difficult at times, musical expression. On 15 February 1967, he recorded several songs which would later surface on the album *Stellar Regions*; the titles of the pieces parallel the content of his playing: 'Seraphic Light', 'Sun Star', the title track and 'Tranesonic'. On his penultimate session on 22 February, a beatific Coltrane laid down a stunning set of tracks, 'Mars', 'Venus', 'Jupiter' and 'Saturn', which together would comprise the album *Interstellar Space.* Listening to Coltrane, his wife Alice on piano, Jimmy Garrison on bass, and Rashied Ali on drums, one easily pictures the sound of massive Apollo rockets rocketing into the stratosphere then breaking apart in the absolute silence of space, falling away in graceful motion.

Roger Waters refuted the notion that Syd Barrett invented the genre known as 'space-rock', as epitomised by later bands ranging from Hawkwind to Flying Saucer Attack, saying, 'All that stuff about Syd starting the space-rock thing is just so much fucking nonsense. He was completely into Hilaire Belloc, and all his stuff was kind of whimsical, all fairly heavily rooted in English literature. I think Syd had one song that had anything to do with space, 'Astronomy Domine', that's all. That's the sum total of all Syd's writing about space and yet there's this whole fucking mystique about how he was the father of it all. It's just a load of old bollocks, it all happened afterwards. There's an instrumental track which we came up with together on the first album, 'Interstellar Overdrive', that's just the title, you see, it's actually an abstract piece with an interstellar attachment in terms of its name.'[52]

There is some validity to what Waters says, for in an interview from the time Waters and Barrett stated that they favoured reading science fiction and fairy tales respectively. Waters' statement however addresses only Syd's lyrics and concise, more structured songs, and not the instrumental improvisations that are also very much part of the Barrett legacy and the legacy of later Pink Floyd as well. Barrett said that the outer-space angle to the Pink Floyd's music was derived from listening to radio shows like *Journey Into Space* and *Quartermass*; 'Which was when I was about fifteen, so that could be where it came from.' Barrett's 'Astronomy Domine' mentions Dan Dare, the hero of science fiction comic books Barrett read as a child.

Another strong influence for the Pink Floyd's increasingly lengthy improvisations was the Butterfield Blues Band, an American blues-based band led by stellar guitarist Mike Bloomfield, which had just released their epochal album *East-West.* The album's eponymous title track, a thirteen-minute improvisation based on equal parts blues, Indian raga and Coltrane, was a product of an acid trip Bloomfield had had in Boston in 1965. During November they swept through England, promoting the album, which was released on Elektra. Joe Boyd, still heading the English branch of Elektra, took them around the various clubs to hear new bands. They saw the Move with Boyd and were stunned by the new directions being taken in British music. Boyd says, 'I remember taking

Paul Butterfield and Mike Bloomfield down to the Marquee to see the Move and they were completely astonished by what was going on. It was a different aesthetic than the American blues based rock and roll. They were promoting the release of *East-West.*' The Butterfield Blues Band played the trendy Blaises nightclub on 8 November, followed by a gig at the hallowed Marquee on the 10th. Whether Syd Barrett saw them perform live or not is unknown, but their song 'East-West' was a tremendous influence, certainly one of the most important for him. Syd absorbed the Butterfield Blues Band's 'East-West' in its thirteen-minute entirety; his understanding of that epic song's textures and subtleties is absolute. Barrett's interweaving of that song's broad improvisational sweep into his own playing put him miles ahead of his peers. He coloured his compositions with as equal dexterity and attention to dynamics as did Michael Bloomfield, freely transcending the perceived limits of the genres.

On 18 November the Pink Floyd played one last event at Hornsey, a gig called 'Philadelic Music for Simian Hominids'. Wright noted, 'At Hornsey College of Art . . . they were into a much more serious mixed media thing of light and sound workshop with special projectors and special equipment. We never really got into that in the same way that they did. They were taking it seriously [laughs] and we were far too busy being a rock'n'roll band who were getting some success.' But Wright acknowledged that the light show 'became a very essential part of us – it represented Pink Floyd and an attitude to life'.[53]

Roger Waters said, 'We take all the lighting equipment and get it set up before the show starts. Then our lighting manager takes over while we're playing and it's up to him to choose light sequences which strike him as being harmonious with the sounds being produced by us. Before we start, the whole room is blacked out and then the lights go into operation. We link sounds together which aren't usually linked and link lights which aren't usually linked.'[54]

On 19 November, the Pink Floyd played their first major out-of-town gig, at Canterbury Technical College in Kent. The college newspaper reported, 'Flashing lights, slide projection, thunderous atmospheric sounds and incense were the essence of the psychedelic Pink Floyd concert held on Saturday. The opening curtains revealed the group on-stage wearing neutral shirts to reflect the coloured lights and standing in semi-darkness. Behind them was a fifteen-foot-high tinfoil Buddha. On either side, sets of filtered spots sprayed various colours over the stage whilst modern art slides were projected behind. This weird conglomeration of sight and sound added up to a strange result. Those watching were a little mystified but after the first rather frightening discordant notes began dancing and gradually relaxed. It was an enjoyable if somewhat odd evening.'

Rick Wright told the newspaper's reporter, 'It was completely spontaneous. We just turned up the amplifiers and tried it, thought about it, and it developed from there. But we still have a long way to go before we get exactly what we want. It must still develop further. There is probably more coordination between the members of our group than in any pop group. We play far more like a jazz group than anything else because we have to be together to produce the right sound, we have come to think musically together. Most of our act is spontaneous and unrehearsed. It just comes when we are on-stage. It does sometimes get to a point where it's a wow. That is when it works, which isn't always. Then we really feel the music is coming from us, not the instruments, or rather the instruments become part of us. We look at the lights and the slides behind us and hope that it all has the same effect on the audience as it does on us. As we are a comparatively new group and are projecting a really new sound, most people just stand and listen at first. What we really want is that they should dance to the music and with the music and so become a part of us. When some people do experience what we want them to, it gets a bit of a jungle, but it's harmless enough because they are wrapped up in the music and themselves. It's a release of emotion but an inward, not an outward, one and no one goes into trance or anything.'

In the *International Times* a 'What's Happening' section was begun, relegated to the back page and printed in letters so small that a magnifying glass was needed to discern what was hip and trendy in the Underground. None the less, the section was a first, and each issue served to connect various groups: painting, music, dance, photography, politics and lectures. The editors of *IT* made a conscious effort to try and link up emerging Underground scenes in cities like Amsterdam, Prague and New York. Hoppy comments on *IT*'s success at connecting various different scenes together, 'About thirty two per cent. [laughs] But clearly it was an expression of the cultural interchange, and put it down on paper, so it then became a thing it itself. I suppose it was partly successful. You have to put it in its context; the *East Village Other*, the *Village Voice*, then *Oz*, which was very interesting. There were various other papers in non-English speaking countries. In a way English was the lingua franca of that particular movement.'

The Pink Floyd were listed as follows:

> *psychedelia: the pink Floyd –*
> *mixed media show. London*
> *Free School at All Saints'*
> *Hall, Powis Gardens, W11, 8 PM.*

But their tenure at the Church hall was at an end, on 29 November, the Pink Floyd played their last All Saints' Hall gig. Miles was there that night and wrote in the *International Times,* 'Since I last saw the Pink Floyd they've got hold of bigger amplifiers, new light gear and a rave from Paul McCartney. This time I saw them at Powis Gardens, W11, on Tuesday 29th, the last of their regular shows here. Their work is largely improvisation and lead guitarist Syd Barrett shoulders most of the burden of providing continuity and attack in the improvised parts. He was providing a huge range of sounds with the new equipment, from throttles shrieks to mellow feedback roars. Visually the show was less adventurous. Three projectors bathed the group, the walls and sometimes the audience in vivid colour. But the colour was fairly static and there was no searching for the brain alpha rhythms by chopping the focus of the images.' Nick Mason recalled that review thirty years later, with a deadpan, 'I remember that night and I never could quite put my finger on where we went wrong. Looking back, I blame the lighting man.'[55]

Joe Boyd by this time had parted from Elektra and had set up his own independent Witchseason Productions. In collusion with Jenner and King, he began to scout around for a record contract for the band. Boyd was to produce their début. He says, 'I brought Alan Bates, who was working for Polydor at the time, down to see the Pink Floyd at Powis Gardens. He then brought other Polydor executives down to another gig, and then we started drawing up a contract. During that time, there were sessions in the Polydor Studios in Stratford Place, which were rehearsals and not recorded. Polydor basically had a studio which wasn't being used, and the group was using it as a rehearsal room.'

In December 1966, Cream released their single 'I Feel Free', perhaps the song that truly lies right on the boundary between the R&B/blues mod era and the psychedelic era. Its strength lies in the duality between the lyrics and the arrangement. The song established a precedent for many of Barrett's own songs. The lyricist was none other than poet Pete Brown, who recalls, 'It's a weird song, I didn't really know what I was doing yet. It was psychedelic, I suppose. Most of my lyrics were, to start with, very much inspired by film imagery. My head was absolutely filled with film imagery, I used to spend all my time at the movies. My post-drugs lyrics were actually more drug orientated than my drug-time lyrics, when I think about it. I had taken quite a lot of drugs up until 1967 when I quit them all.' Barrett also had a flair for cinematic imagery, with the absolutely precise description of 'Arnold Layne' or 'Scarecrow', as if describing a scenario in a screenplay. 'I Feel Free' was a whole piece, and solid arrangement. Musically, that made it successful. It defies the production, or attempts to do anything with it. When Jack Bruce wrote it he had a vision of how that should be; a melody and an arrangement in his head. He put it down in such a way that, although they had the worst producer in the world, Bruce could get around it by creating something that couldn't be destroyed by shitty production. Bruce set out to make a very hard rhythm track and on top of it, put a very soft melody. That's the contrast that really makes things work. That's the astounding thing about it, it's got a real design,' says Brown.

Cream was a great influence on the Pink Floyd's rhythm section, Mason and Waters. Mason was particularly enamoured of Ginger Baker's jazz-influenced drumming. Waters also recalls Cream as a powerful influence, 'Cream had been such a turn-on when I saw them . . . the curtains parted and there was a big bank of Marshall gear and it was an all-enveloping, loud, powerful bluesy experience.'[56]

On 3 December, the Pink Floyd played at the 'Psychodelphia vs. Ian Smith' 10 p.m. to dawn rave at the Roundhouse. The adverts announced, with due solemnity, *'Screaming THOUSANDS, Underground films, poets, HAPPENINGS, with the Pink Floyd and the Ram Holder Messengers. Bring your own happenings and ecstatogenic substances. Drag optional.'* December 12 marked the band's first appearance at the Royal Albert Hall for an Oxfam charity benefit called 'You're Joking'.

The success of the *IT* launch and the vibe that had emerged from the All Saints' Hall prompted Joe Boyd to suggest to Hoppy that they move their operation to the West End. Hoppy says, 'I was working with Joe Boyd, and he said, "This is going well, if I find a place in the West End, why don't we do it there?" We said we'd try it for two occasions to see if it worked, and we were amazed that it did. The ostensible reason for doing it in the first place was to pay some debts from a scam that didn't work out. It wasn't because we had our heads full of, "I want to be like Bill Graham or Chet Helms", it was more like a simultaneous synchronicity, a global culture. If it wasn't us it would have been someone else, looking back there was no grand plan.'

None the less, Hoppy was enthusiastic, and Boyd found an Irish pub on Tottenham Court Road, off Oxford Street, whose owner was willing to rent out the ballroom downstairs. Initially, Hoppy and Boyd couldn't decide whether to call the new club 'Night Tripper' (Boyd's play on both the Beatles' 1966 hit 'Day Tripper' and a reference to New Orleans R&B pianist Dr. John, known as the 'Night Tripper') or UFO (Hoppy's choice), so in a move typical of their collaboration, they combined the two. Hoppy, Boyd, Kate Heleczer and Nigel Waymouth took a stack of handbills and handed them out in the Portobello Road.

On 23 December 'UFO Presents Night Tripper' opened its doors, and the heat from the several hundred punters that gathered there was intense. That night it ran from 10:30 p.m. to 4:30 a.m., and the Pink Floyd played. It would become the focus for their activities during the next months.

Their set that night, amidst a backdrop of light shows, was followed by a screening of an Akira Kurosawa film. The response was immediate; 400 people showed up. Joe Boyd said, 'It was great. It was packed from the first night. It was a lot of people who didn't know that there were that many of them recognising each other. I wasn't surprised, but I was pleased. I thought there was an audience there. You could tell, you didn't have to be a genius to look around the streets and see there were a lot of people dressing in funny ways, the success of Granny Takes A Trip. There was a tremendous amount of energy. I was very excited by the whole scene . . . very stimulating, very interesting, very fertile.'[57]

The club was known ever thereafter as UFO, pronounced 'u-fo' by those in the know, and 'u-f-o' by those that weren't.

Artists Michael English and Nigel Waymouth, known under the psychedelic nom de plume 'Haphash and the Coloured Coat', were commissioned to design a poster, featuring Peter Townshend's girlfriend Karen. Their subsequent posters for UFO attempted to capture the ephemeral lysergic mood engendered at the All Saints' Hall. Haphash and the Coloured Coat were responsible for some incredible posters in the next year or so. Showing the typically stunning British flair for design, Waymouth and English conjured up mystical connections to nineteenth-century illustrators William Morris and Aubrey Beardsley, whose opium-laced visions of flora and leaves were drawn in interlaced patterns, hypnotic motifs and arabesques. It was small wonder the nascent hippie illustrators, fuelled by LSD and cannabis, made designs that resonated with those of their forebears. Indian influences, including paisleys and the vivid colours of non-synthetic dyes, and the complex geometric patterns of Islamic art were taken in and regurgitated in a psychedelic wash of colours unseen before or since. There was a revival of the exotic Orientalism of the nineteenth century, much as the San Francisco hippie graphic designers conjured up the dormant ghosts of both Art Nouveau and the Wild West.

English's and Waymouth's posters, when they first appeared, heralding the arrival of UFO, simply reflected their community's interest in style, exuberant colours, quasi-mystical books and arcane philosophies, tinged with the strong wind blowing from the East. These posters truly captured the feeling of the time, precisely because they had been made with no intention of doing so, just as it was doubtful that Bob Dylan ever envisaged himself as 'the voice of a generation' his admirers cited him as, these psychedelic artefacts simply mirror the ethos of the era. Like all movements, this one was characterised by an exceptional feeling of camaraderie and a sense that others not only shared your views but shared them passionately. Their ravishing motifs, fluorescent colours, spidery lettering so oblique only the 'turned on' could read it, and rich English illustration all conveyed that mood of the emerging effervescent Underground. A new constituency of hipness, the Underground, at least in the theory then being defined, was far more egalitarian than the rigid mod hierarchy of clothes, collectors' R&B and purple-heart amphetamines.

Artist Martin Sharp, fresh from satirical magazine *Oz* in Australia, had travelled with the editor, Richard Neville, through Asia en route to London. Their trip, through Angkor Wat and the tea houses of Katmandu, rife with dope smoke, had proved eye opening, and they arrived in London in September 1966 with vivid ideas and schemes. Neville launched *Oz* in England soon after, with Sharp's richly decorated works adorning the inserts. *Oz* was *IT*'s satirical counterpart, and each issue was a stunner, always courting controversy with its writing and art. Several Australians made their mark on those pages, not least of which was Germaine Greer. They were young, vibrant and brought tremendous energy and vitality with them. The Australians joined the bubbling Americans, liberal Swedes, artistic Germans, radical French, aesthetic Japanese and other recent arrivals to give London a dazzling cosmopolitan dash. There was the sense in the air that something, as yet undefined, was happening, of which UFO was the focus.

Because of the stringent nature of licensing laws more than any desire to foster an élite clientele, UFO instituted membership charges of 15 shillings, or simple admission for a reasonable 10 shillings. On opening night, in keeping with the emerging spirit of the times, free memberships were given out. The club opened its doors at 10:30 p.m. and often ran till dawn, long after the English capital's underground trains had stopped running at midnight. There was no alcohol, though there would eventually be plenty of intoxicants of varying potency, including a plentiful supply of high quality acid. Soft drinks, coffee, bananas and candy floss were dispensed from one corner. The ads placed in the back pages of the *Melody Maker* promised 'films, slides, heat and food'.

Hoppy says, 'We found a film distributor called Connoisseur Films, and they had a very interesting catalogue. When we played those films, we didn't play the soundtrack. They were all 16 mm films, which now you never see anywhere. Whereas nowadays you have computerised and automated light shows, with video and projectors, before you needed an army of people with light shows, projectors and slides. Nowadays one person can do a whole club. It was always a bit hair-raising, wondering if you'd get enough people there to pay the expenses at the door. If you are a promoter, that's always your secret concern, that you won't make enough money at the door to pay for everything and make a profit. If the events couldn't pay for themselves you'd have to stop them because you couldn't keep on losing money. It's all very simple; when the buck stops at you then you have to be careful. Mind you, we weren't very careful in those days. Sometimes money was short.'

On Saturday 23 December, the Who, the Move, and the Pink Floyd all played another 10 p.m. till dawn rave at the Roundhouse. Joe Boyd told the *Melody Maker's* Chris Welch, 'The object of the club is to provide a place for experimental pop music and also for the mixing of media, light shows and theatrical happenings. The club has grown spectacularly and we've already had to close membership so now we've got to find larger premises. The kids who go are the London psychedelic crowd who come from Notting Hill and Bayswater. There is a very *laissez-faire* attitude at the club. There is no attempt made to make people fit into a format. If they want to lie on the floor they can, or if they want to jump on the stage they can, as long as they don't interfere with the group of course.'[58]

Miles wrote in the *International Times*, 'December 23rd saw "Night Tripper" at Tottenham Court Road, advertised by a poster and a display as in *IT*. There was no indication as to who would be there performing; the audience attended because they "knew" who would be there and "knew" what was happening. The name change to UFO occurred the next week and the first UFO advertised the Pink Floyd, Fanta and Ood, the Giant Sun Trolley and Dave

Tomlin improvising to government propaganda. UFO was created by and for the original "Underground", posters from Messrs. English & Waymouth, and an *IT* stall by the cloakrooms. The first UFO also had a Marilyn Monroe movie, karate and light shows. UFO was a club in the sense that most people knew each other, met there to do their business, arrange their week's appointments, dinners and lunches, and hatch out issues of *IT,* plans for Arts Lab, SOMA, and various schemes for turning the Thames flow and removing the fences in Notting Hill. The activity and energy was thicker than the incense.'[59]

Chris Welch of the *Melody Maker* was the first in the mainstream press to cover the scene, and he reported, 'Today in London the Bell People already have their own headquarters, and UFO (it stands for Unidentified Flying Object or Underground Freak Out) is believed to be Britain's first psychedelic club. Happy young people waving sticks of incense danced Greek-like dances, waving frond-like hands with bells jingling, neck scarves fluttering and strange hats abounding. There were pretty slides casting beams of light over the oily throng who stood or squatted in communion, digging the light show or listening to Love being relayed at sensible non-discotheque volume. There were frequent announcements warning patrons to be cool and that the fuzz might pay a call. In fact two young constables did pop in and seemed wholly satisfied that all was well, and in fact all was well.'[60]

Nick Mason remarked, 'It's got rosier with age, but there is a germ in truth in it, because for a brief moment there looked as if there might actually be some combining of activities. People would go down to this place, and a number of things, rather than simply one band performing. There would be some mad actors, a couple of light shows, perhaps the recitation of some poetry or verse, and a lot of wandering about and a lot of cheerful chatter going on. It seems really strange looking back on it, really hard to describe. Endless rock groups, that's what "Underground" meant to the people, but that wasn't what it really was. It was a mixture of bands, poets, jugglers and all sorts of acts. It was the beginning of talk about mixed-media events, music and light shows and we happened to have a light show. It just happened, in the same way that everything happened. I mean, there was no direction, policy or planning or anything. Things just happened.' Roger Waters interjected with, 'There was so much dope and acid around in those days that I don't think anyone can remember anything about anything.'[61]

On 29 December the Pink Floyd played at the Marquee. The band that opened for them was Syn, whose Peter Banks would later play with Yes. Banks recalls the events as being rather less than successful, with few punters who did come looking bemused by the Pink Floyd's strange lighting and thirty minutes songs.

Banks himself was taken aback by the band. 'The thing I remember most about Syd Barrett was that he always wore mascara. He had a lot of eye shadow and mascara and I wasn't into all that because Syn was still playing Motown stuff . . . Later I saw them at the Roundhouse and they suddenly got very professional. I remember they were all very middle-class and aloof, even at the Marquee they had this art student vibe about them . . . They'd show up, play and then leave. They always had good-looking women with them, and that impressed us. We thought they were very upper-crust and they didn't mix like pally musicians. But then, we didn't regard them as proper musicians. We thought they were a bunch of guys just making a lot of noise . . . and wearing make-up.'[62] David Bowie, in an interview with *Penthouse*, recalled seeing Syd at the Marquee Club, 'There was Syd Barrett with his white face and his black eyeliner all around his eyes – this strange presence singing in front of a band that was using light shows. I thought, "Wow! He's a bohemian, a poet, and he's in a rock band!"'

Nick Mason said, 'My memory of the Marquee is that we weren't really Marquee material. I remember us being sort of demolished by people like Marmalade and proper bands with nice suits. We would have been doing what can only be described as early "Pink Floyd", which is rather abstract rhythm and blues, performing rather nasty operations on Chuck Berry material.'[63]

On 30 December the Pink Floyd played again at UFO. Hoppy had contracted Mark Boyle to provide lights for the club, and that night he began with a light show that was based on the four elements. The Soft Machine opened and halfway through their set, Jimi Hendrix jumped on-stage to jam with them. Hendrix stayed for the Pink Floyd's set as well, soaking up elements of Syd's style just as he was doing with all the bands he was dashing from place to place to watch and jam with.

The next night the Pink Floyd were once again at the Roundhouse, for 'Psychedelicamania: New Year's Eve All Night Rave' with the Who and the Move. In their usual understated style, the advertisements read, '*WHAT IS A FREAK OUT? When a large number of individuals gather and express themselves creatively through music, dance, light patterns and electronic sound. The participants, already emancipated from our national social slavery, dressed in their most inspired apparel, realise as a group whatever potential they possess for free expression. IT'S HAPPENING MAN! Suzy Creamcheese presents a DOUBLE GIANT FREAK-OUT BALL*'.

Nick Jones of the *Melody Maker* reported, 'Despite the freezing cold, large numbers of revellers turned up to watch the Move destroy two televisions and a car, the Who blow out the Roundhouse's pitiful electrical system twice and Pete Townshend destroy his guitar and amps.' Two hippie girls tripping on acid, moved by the anarchic performances, took off their shirts and danced topless, oblivious to the cold. The Pink Floyd's performance was a bit anticlimactic perhaps, but Jones none the less noted, 'The Pink Floyd have a promising sound, and some very groovy picture slides which attracted far more attention than the group, as they merge, blossom, burst, glow, divide and die'.

1 Unedited transcripts of interviews with Miles by Jonathan Greene. *Days In The Life: Voices From The English Underground, 1961-1971*. Minerva, 1988
2 Jonathan Greene. *Days In The Life: Voices From The English Underground, 1961-1971*. Minerva, 1988
3 Ibid.
4 *ZigZag*, July 1973
5 'Syd Barrett Careening Through Life'. Kris DiLorenzo, Trouser Press, February 1978
6 Danish television interviews with Pink Floyd, 1992
7 *Mojo*, July 1995
8 Unedited transcripts of interviews with Hoppy by Jonathan Greene. *Days In The Life: Voices From The English Underground, 1961-1971*. Minerva, 1988
9 *Georgia Straight*, October 14-21, 1970
10 Miles & Mabbett, Andy. *Pink Floyd: The Visual Documentary. Omnibus* Press, London 1994
11 *ZigZag*, July 1973
12 Unedited transcripts of interviews with Peter Jenner by Jonathan Greene. *Days In The Life: Voices From The English Underground, 1961-1971*. Minerva, 1988
13 Ibid.
14 *Omnibus* special on Pink Floyd, 1994
15 *ZigZag*, July 1973
16 Jonathan Greene. *Days In The Life: Voices From The English Underground, 1961-1971*. Minerva, 1988
17 *Beat Instrumental*, October 1967
18 'Syd Barrett Careening Through Life'. Kris DiLorenzo, Trouser Press, February 1978
19 Schaffner, Nicholas. *Saucerful Of Secrets*. Delta, 1991
20 *Mojo*, May 1994
21 *NME*, 13 April 1974
22 *ZigZag*, July 1973
23 Unedited transcripts of interviews with Peter Jenner by Jonathan Greene. *Days In The Life: Voices From The English Underground, 1961-1971*. Minerva, 1988
24 *Disc & Music Echo*, July 22, 1967
25 Miles & Mabbett, Andy. *Pink Floyd: The Visual Documentary. Omnibus* Press, London 1994
26 Jonathan Greene. *Days In The Life: Voices From The English Underground, 1961-1971*. Minerva, 1988
27 Schaffner, Nicholas. *Saucerful Of Secrets*. Delta, 1991
28 *Rolling Stone*, December 1971
29 Unedited transcripts of interviews with Peter Jenner by Jonathan Greene. *Days In The Life: Voices From the English Underground, 1961-1971*. Minerva, 1988
30 Miles and Mabbett, Andy. *Pink Floyd: The Visual Documentary*. Omnibus Press. London 1994
31 *Dancing in the Streets*, BBC series, 1996
32 Jonathan Greene. *Days In The Life: Voices From the English Underground, 1961-1971*. Minerva, 1988
33 Miles & Mabbett, Andy. *Pink Floyd: The Visual Documentary. Omnibus* Press, London 1994
34 Jonathan Greene. *Days In The Life: Voices From the English Underground, 1961-1971*. Minerva, 1988
35 *Disc & Music Echo*, 25 March 1967
36 *Disc & Music Echo*, 8 April 1967
37 *Melody Maker*, 14 January 1967
38 Unedited transcripts of interviews with Peter Jenner by Jonathan Greene. *Days In The Life: Voices From the English Underground, 1961-1971*. Minerva, 1988
39 *Omnibus* special on Pink Floyd, 1994
40 Miles & Mabbett, Andy. *Pink Floyd: The Visual Documentary. Omnibus* Press, London 1994
41 Schaffner, Nicholas. *The British Invasion*. McGraw-Hill, 1982, p.142
42 Unedited transcripts of interviews with Peter Jenner by Jonathan Greene. *Days In The Life: Voices From the English Underground, 1961-1971*. Minerva, 1988
43 Ibid.
44 Ibid.
45 Allen, Daevid. *Gong Dreaming*. GAS,1994
46 *Sunday Times*, 30 October 1966
47 Ibid.
48 Unedited transcripts of interviews with Peter Jenner by Jonathan Greene. *Days In The Life: Voices From the English Underground, 1961-1971*. Minerva, 1988

49 Miles & Mabbett, Andy. *Pink Floyd: The Visual Documentary. Omnibus* Press, London 1994
50 Jonathan Greene. *Days In The Life: Voices From the English Underground, 1961-1971.* Minerva, 1988
51 Unedited transcripts of interviews with June Bolan by Jonathan Greene. *Days In The Life: Voices From the English Underground, 1961-1971.* Minerva, 1988
52 *The Pink Floyd Story*. Six-part documentary broadcast on Capital Radio, London, Dec 1996 – Jan 1997
53 Ibid.
54 Miles & Mabbett, Andy. *Pink Floyd: The Visual Documentary.* Omnibus Press, London 1994
55 *Mojo*, July 1995
56 'Treading Waters' by Scott Cohen, *Spin*, September 1987
57 Unedited transcripts of interviews with Joe Boyd by Jonathan Greene. *Days In The Life: Voices From the English Underground, 1961-1971.* Minerva, 1988
58 Taylor, Derek, *It Was Twenty Years Ago Today,* Fireside, 1987
59 *International Times 9*
60 Taylor, Derek, *It Was Twenty Years Ago Today,* Fireside, 1987
61 *ZigZag,* July 1973
62 Welch, Chris. *Pink Floyd: Learning to Fly*. Castle Communications, London 1994
63 Macdonald, Bruno, editor. *Pink Floyd: Through the Eyes of. . .* Sidgwick & Jackson, London, 1996

Stage Three: The Piper at the Gates of Dawn (January-July 1967)

'In winter the life energy, symbolised by thunder, the Arousing, is still underground. Movement is just at its beginning.'

'All movements are accomplished in six stages, and the seventh brings return. Thus the winter solstice, with which the decline of the year begins, comes in the seventh month after the summer solstice; so too sunrise comes in the seventh double hour after sunset. Therefore seven is the number of the young light, and it arises when six, the number of the great darkness, is increased by one. In this way, the state of rest gives place to movement.'

Chapter 24: Fu/Return – The Turning Point
The I-Ching or Book Of Changes

At the very beginning of 1967, the Canadian Broadcasting Company sent an interviewer to profile the Pink Floyd. Her piece offers an interesting view of the band just as they were about to ascend to fame. 'Some call it free sound,' she said, 'others prefer to include it in the psychedelic wave of "isms" already circulating around the Western Hemisphere. But this music, here and now, is of the Pink Floyd, a group of four young musicians, a light man, and an array of equipment sadistically designed to shatter the strongest nerves. The Pink Floyd are new on the London scene, they've stupefied audiences at all-night raves, in church halls, at the Albert Hall, and at various tours around Britain. They've yet to make their début on records, but perhaps the Pink Floyd themselves are best qualified to tell you what it is all about. . .'

'We didn't start out trying to get anything new,' said Roger Waters, 'it entirely happened. We originally started as an R&B group.' 'Sometimes we just let loose a bit and decided to hit the guitar a bit harder,' said Syd Barrett, 'not worrying so much about the chords.' 'It stopped being third-rate academic rock,' said Waters, '[and] started becoming an intuitive groove, really.' 'It's free form,' said Barrett, 'in terms of construction it's almost like jazz, where you start off with a riff and then you improvise.' 'The difference from jazz is in jazz if you improvise on a sixteen-bar number,' said Waters, 'you stick to sixteen-bar choruses, and take sixteen-bar solos, whereas with us it starts and we may play three choruses of something that lasts for seventeen and a half bars each chorus, and then it will stop happening and it will stop happening when it stops happening. That may be 423 bars later . . . or four.'

'It's not like jazz because we all want to be pop stars, we don't want to be jazz musicians. We play for people to dance to,' said Barrett, adding with a smile, ' [though] they don't seem to dance much now. That was the initial idea. We play loudly, with electric guitars, so we're utilising all the volume and effects you can get.' 'But now we're trying to develop this by using the light [show],' said Waters. 'But the thing about this jazz thing is we don't have this great musician thing. We don't really look upon ourselves as musicians, as such. Period. Reading the dots, all that stuff.'

'How important is the visual aspect of the musical production?' asked the interviewer. 'Very important,' said Barrett and Waters in unison. 'It's quite a revelation to have people operating something like lights while you're playing,' said Barrett, 'and as a direct stimulus to what you're playing. It's audience reaction, except on a higher level. You can respond to the lights, and the lights will respond back. There are various sorts of lights, there are simple flashing spotlights that are worked off a control board sort of like a piano, so they can be used very rhythmically. And there are effect lights, usually coloured or wet slides which have some sort of liquids on them, so you get some movement.' Waters added, 'Or they may be actual movies as such, which have their own set speed and sequence that can't be altered by the operators. This changes the formation to some extent, because we tend to play to that.' This response highlights a major difference between Barrett's and Waters' approach to the Pink Floyd; Barrett emphasising spontaneity in response to their effects, while Waters seems to favour a pre-programmed approach.

The interviewer asked, 'What happens at a performance, what happens with your audience, what's the feel you get?' 'Well,' said Waters, 'if we get very excited when we're playing very well, then the audience get very excited as well.' 'Do they dance?' she asked. 'They may dance,' said Waters, 'it depends on the sort of number and what's happening.' 'Anyway,' said Barrett, 'you hardly ever get dancing right from the beginning. That you usually get as a response to the rhythm. Usually people just stand there, and if they work themselves into some sort of hysteria while they are there. . .' 'Yes, the dancing takes the form of a frenzy,' added Nick Mason, 'which is very good.' 'They don't stand in a line and do the Madison,' said Waters. 'The audience tend to be standing there,' said Mason, 'and maybe one or two people might suddenly flip out and rush forward and start leaping up and down.' ' "Freak-out" is what they call it,' said Waters.

Rick Wright said, 'It's an exciting thing, because this is what dancing is.' Nick Mason laughed, 'This is *really* what dancing is.'

To sum up, the interviewer posited, 'Is this then the music destined to replace the Beatles? Are the melodic harmonies, poetic lyrics and soulful rhythms of today to be swept into the archives? Totally undermined by a psychotic sweep of sound and vision such as this displayed by the Pink Floyd. Large pockets of enthusiasts from all over the country are determined that it shall, despite the powerful opposition of the majority of disc jockeys. But the most enthusiastic fans of all, quite fittingly, are the Pink Floyd's managers.' Peter Jenner stated, 'I think the records will be very different from the stage shows. With records there is a three-minute limitation, and you can't walk around the kitchen humming to the Pink Floyd. If you had the sort of sound they are making in the clubs come over the radio while you're doing the washing up, you'd probably scream! I suspect that the records will have to be much more audio, written for a different situation, of listening to a gramophone in your home or on the radio is very different from going into a club or watching a stage show. They are two different things, and require a different approach. And we think we can do both.'

And so Syd Barrett's songs struck a deep, resonant chord in his audience, much as Tolkien's *The Hobbit*, rehabilitated from its status as a children's book, had. It was a music with overtones of mysticism, as if Kenneth Grahame's vision of vibrant Nature had chosen to channel itself through Syd's songs and Syd himself. Andrew King recalled that Syd told him he'd had a sort of mystical experience whereby Pan, the mischievous sylvan deity of nature, 'had given Syd insight and understanding into the way nature works. It formed itself into his own holistic view of the world'.[1] Syd assumed the persona of the Piper at the Gate of Dawn, his presence illuminating the psychedelic dawn. Eventually, only the echoes of his presence would be left to linger in the minds of those privileged few who witnessed his live performances. There were moments of ineffable beauty amidst the cranked up distorted roar, which the audiences at UFO would have seared into their collective mind.

Syd put immense amounts of energy into illuminating his performances with the vibrant and immutable magic that was his trademark. Blinding lights, visions of space, AMM's spontaneous jazz, Cantabrigian folk, mutated Bo Diddley's riffs, the jangle of the Byrds, Bloomfield's blues-raga epics, all rechannelled through the ears of one with a hand on the very pulse of Nature. Experiment, whimsy and spontaneity were his great contribution to the new music. And the buzz at UFO extended from person to person, as the punters took back breathless accounts to their more staid flatmates in Fulham, Notting Hill, Chelsea and Muswell Hill. Dave Gale notes, '1967 was the year of Syd's strongest compositions. Syd's music was very different from what became the later Floyd's music. It's not anthemic, dirge-like or protracted. His most emotional compositions were bouncy, jolly, quirky melodies with absurdist, amusing lyrics.'

Joe Boyd noted, 'Syd Barrett set the tone for what people think of as psychedelic guitar playing. His sound and feeling had all those qualities of spaciness and abstraction.'[2] Boyd adds, 'The Pink Floyd didn't have a thorough knowledge of Karlheinz Stockhausen or John Cage [avant-garde composers]. Barrett, at the time, didn't strike me as someone who studied things very much. Though astute, he was a very spontaneous character, not a scholastic kind of guy. He had a real glint in his eye, a sparkle, and a real joyous energy about him.' Peter Wynne-Wilson says that at that time, 'I wouldn't have said there was a wide gulf between Syd and the others. They were all nice middle-class boys; well, middle-class boys at any rate. Syd seemed younger than the others, though it was a difference of attitude more than of age, particularly.'

On 5 January, the Pink Floyd played at the Marquee Club, where a reporter from *Record Mirror* opined, 'Excellent and extremely exciting. But I couldn't help thinking how dangerous this sort of free-form thing could be in the hands of not such good musicians'. Nick Mason reflected, 'I'm fascinated by how often people thought we were accomplished musicians. We must have been quite convincing.' Mason adds that part of their success was based on the premise that 'if you find an interesting idea then the technique is not that important'.[3]

In an interview with *Record Mirror*, Roger Waters stated the band's ethos, 'What we really want is for complete audience participation. You don't just get it at the Marquee. What we want isn't just lights flashing on us but on the audience as well, and they should react spontaneously and not simply dance around as they would to normal music. Another good thing would be if we could get a theatre and all the proper equipment. We could go two ways as we are at the moment. The one is to pure abstraction with the sound and light, but the other is to complete illustration, pure evocation: like playing to a vase of flowers.' Nick Mason said at the time, 'It's only lately that the Pink Floyd have been doing much work. In the past we played about one date a fortnight and spent the rest of the time sitting in pubs and saying how nice it would be to be famous.'[4]

The Pink Floyd played at the UFO at least nine times between December 1966 and April 1967. They became synonymous with the venue; the house band. On 6 January the band played a gig elsewhere in London and hurriedly packed their gear back in the van and drove back across town, cramped and cold. Parking on a side street off Tottenham Court Road, on one of those small Fitzrovia roads, they unloaded the drum kit and speakers. The band and their managers hurried across the road and down the steps of the Blarney Pub, light emanating in tiny slivers from the rotating iron drum punctured with holes, which hung over the narrow staircase. The heat percolating out of the basement was accompanied with a blast of Monteverdi on the turntable while the last band packed up. Smiling girls in gauzy dresses, many carrying flowers, drifted by. Manfred, a heavy German with a beard and dressed in a kaftan, had concocted a batch of LSD he dubbed 'White Lightning' and had given away hundreds of doses by midnight. Artist Mark Boyle and Jack Braceland from the nudist colony in Watford had separate light shows rigged up in each corner. Boyle, in plastic gloves and goggles, mixed mad chemicals in a glass petri dish over a blazing projector, sweat dripping off his brow.

The long room had a low ceiling, and that bland white acoustic tiling on the walls typical of the sixties. It was absolutely packed with people wearing the most outrageous dress. One hippie walked by holding a smouldering bunch of joss sticks, giving them out. A small concessionary corner in the back dispensed tomato rolls, tended by a girl with long straight black hair parted in the middle, a bland expression, and wearing a Pucci mini skirt. Everywhere small groups stood talking, and some of them were very young indeed. The more courageous stood near the edge of the stage and danced, eyes closed, bobbing in place, blissfully oblivious. There was constantly traffic in and out, with people edging past each other slowly on the stairs. Some would go out to smoke a joint or catch a breather while others would go down to Braceland's Happening 44 and return later on. Chris Rowley tended a small stand that sold issues of *IT* and silk-screened psychedelic posters by the likes of Haphash and the Coloured Coat. Notable by their absence were the hard core yobbos who hung around at the end of the bar at pubs, menacing and drunk.

Colin Turner was a young mod on the loose in London. He and his mates somehow or another caught wind of the strange goings-on at Tottenham Court Road. Deciding to chance it and venture on down to UFO one Friday, Turner recalls, 'As we approached the club we saw a long-haired guy dressed in only his underpants, and strings of tiny bells; as if this wasn't strange by itself, he was spinning around and around in the middle of the road. We were later to discover that he (and many others) had taken a cocktail of LSD and speed. I remember thinking at the time, should we go in? The people milling around were totally different to the people I usually associated with, but certainly they were very friendly. Nothing ventured, nothing gained. So down a steep flight of steps we went and paid our £1 admittance fee. Into the double doors on the left and into a new world! The noise from the crowd was deafening, the smell of incense overpowering, and the heat . . . It was a cold night but the heat being generated by sweaty bodies was awesome. Just about everyone was wearing tiny bells and either sitting staring into space (stoned) or prancing around (also stoned) or just plain stoned.'

Wynne-Wilson and Russell Page would set up a little platform, where they would unload and set up their lighting gear, mixing inks, oils, water and chemicals and project them through the darkness on to the bare, small stage. Pip Carter and June Bolan would set the Floyd's AC-30 speakers up and wire them to the rat's nest of wiring behind the stage, looking like it was going to explode if one more extension was plugged into the outlet.

Colin Turner recalls, 'It was the early hours, and in walked another group of long-haired musicians, basically all carrying their own equipment. Across the floor they walked, stepping up on to the stage.' (No curtains or wings, just a plain old stage about three feet high.) The band stepped on-stage as the light show began to swirl over them, the house lights beaming down on them, refracting through the haze of smoke and heat. *Twang!* Turner says, 'They started to tune up, playing some very weird chords. "This could be good," someone said. "Hello, we're The Pink Floyd," one of them said. And away they went.' Mason counted off with a hushed, 'And a one, and a two. . .' and they were off. Syd dropping into 'Astronomy Domine's riff with tremolo picking and waves of echo. Turner wasn't immediately impressed, 'Although they were different, the music had a very "jazzy" feel to it and I have never been a great lover of jazz. I remember thinking that it was a strange combination of rock and jazz they were attempting. However as they went along I realised that this band had something . . . They launched into a piece that must have lasted at least forty minutes, an early version of "Interstellar Overdrive". I think everyone around had the same thought: brilliant in parts, but mainly boring. They were using a very rudimentary light show which consisted of a slide projector, with printer's ink placed between two slides. As the ink heated up it "popped" between the slides, projecting bubbles of colour on the band and the back of the stage.

'The Floyd's session that night lasted for about two hours, which was very long by other bands' standards. One hour in those days was considered good, two hours was unheard of! They left the stage with little fuss, once again carrying their own gear, I think they may have had just one roadie, but I do remember them packing up their own stuff. So that was it, I had seen my first Pink Floyd gig, what did I think of it overall? Unique, jazzy, boring and brilliant. I had to see them again. I saw them many times after this night, it wasn't love at first sight but they had certainly teased me into coming back for more.'

The light show was developing quickly, with Peter Wynne-Wilson and Russell Page bringing technical expertise to the proceedings. Barrett stated unequivocally that the lights were a conduit for the music, 'We use lights to get the audiences used to the type of music we play. It's hard to get used to it, actually, because it's a new type of music. But because it *is* a new type of music, we realise that it takes a lot more time to get used to it. The crazy lights help, I think. Anyway, I like looking at them.'[5] Nick Mason stated, 'The trouble with the projected slides is that everybody tends to ignore the music . . . To us the sound is at least as important as the visual aspect.'[6] However, the band also grew to relish the anonymity that the lights afforded. Rick Wright later noted, 'From the earliest days, when we used oil slides projected on to the band, which hid us, we were always faceless musicians, and that idea developed and developed. Even in UFO days [audiences] came for the experience, the lights plus the music. We were happy not to be in the limelight.'[7]

'After a while I knew the music very well,' says Peter Wynne-Wilson. 'I knew the band musically very well, not that I'm any musician. When it was good, it was a terrific experience to be doing the lighting with such interesting music, and developing along with the music. Because it was unusual for any light show to be touring with a specific band, as opposed to it being at a particular venue. That was one aspect of it. The technical aspects, apart from the controls that I'd made for some of the lights, were extremely sensitive. The light bulbs and lanterns reaction time was very rapid. The thicker the wire in a filament, the slower it is to come up to temperature. If it's low voltage, it's relatively big and if it's high wattage, it's relatively thin. This was relatively low wattage and, in terms of those days, absurdly low wattage. So it did react very fast, and the control was extremely sensitive and fast. It was a real rush to do that. They were very efficient lanterns, set very close to the band, but it wasn't like having a lighting rig.

'The base of the slides we made were with using water-based inks. We would use a whole slew of different chemicals and powders. There were various actions taking place in a given slide. There would be the action of bubbles occluded in the liquid, which would tend to rise, falling on the screen. There would be chemical reaction between different liquids in the slide, there would the heat of the projector itself; different colours as well as chemicals would react at different speeds due to the heat of the projector. We would speed things up or slow them down using a hair dryer on Hot or Cold. We used a gas torch. The projectors were main voltage projectors, 1000 w, which were quite an item then. Those lamps were very fragile. It was before the days of heat-reflective coatings, so the heat was absorbed. They were hot, and since we'd be leaning over them to mess with the slides, it was a hot business, particularly in somewhere like UFO with a low ceiling and relatively packed out, but that came with the territory.'

The Pink Floyd's residency at UFO quickly earned them the sobriquet of 'the Underground's band'. Roger Waters said, 'You could describe us as the movement's house orchestra because we were one of the first people to play what they wanted to hear . . . It's not difficult to convert the audience to this presentation. It's very beautiful to watch. It takes them right away.'[8]

Mike Leonard says, 'When the Pink Floyd began playing at UFO, that was where their reputation was built. They became the icons of the alternative society.' 'UFO was a very blank room,' says Peter Wynne-Wilson, 'partly because the stage was on a side wall rather than on an end wall. And that had a good effect because it was a much softer set-up. The stage was slightly raised and in the middle of the room. The stage was fairly small, even though it was primarily a show-band stage, though I can't imagine how they could get a show-band on to that tiny stage. When the focus was on the stage, without the house lights up, it was a very cosy environment. But you wouldn't think so if you went into the Blarney Pub in daylight. It was quite long, not very wide. It would have been a squash with a few hundred people. There was a bar arrangement at the Tottenham Court Road end of it. It fell into different areas. There was a little dressing-room beyond the stage and then a slightly L-shaped bit where Mark Boyle would often do his lights. It was a completely unremarkable room. A terrific atmosphere was created there.'

Syd Barrett recognised UFO as his musical base, saying, 'Everything was so rosy at UFO. It was really nice to go there after slogging around the pubs and so. Everyone had their own thing. It's been interesting to see things turning out the way they have.[9]

Jenny Fabian, wrote in *Groupie*, 'The [Floyd's] shows were always packed. Underground groups were suddenly commercial, and straight industry people were moving into our scene and exploiting it. Imitators changed their equipment, got light shows, and followed where the [Floyd] led.'[10]

One such band was the Move. 'The Move played at UFO,' says Miles, 'and the crowd didn't like them at all. There was booing, and it was the first time I'd ever heard booing there. The Move were much too aggressive, they smashed up television sets. It was a fickle audience, and they saw the Move as terribly commercial. Tomorrow were just as commercial though, really. They began as the In-Crowd, just a typical Denmark Street pop band. Only the addition of Twink [live-wire drummer] made them a psychedelic band.' Steve Howe, then with Tomorrow, later of Yes, remarked, 'The 1967 period of psychedelic music brought it all in. All the young guitarists and other musicians felt they could play on these planes . . . long improvised solos. Improvisation was really expanding the whole idea of what a song had been up to then . . . [With] the change from the single to the album, there were more people trying to get out of the rut of playing a song that repeated its first strain and then its middle eight and then the first eight again . . . It was becoming a much warmer thing where people could improvise much more freely.'[11] The improvisational ethic was deeply ingrained in Barrett, an extension of his belief in unfettered freedom. He was a restless improviser, and like Charlie Parker, who never played a solo the same way twice, Barrett was too creative to be tied to any pattern. Barrett loathed rehearsing and adhering to formats of any sort; his restless native intelligence compelled him to seek out new and often exquisite variations of a theme.

The psychedelic era dawned very quickly, and many were caught unaware, on- and off-stage. There were those who exchanged their mod suits or PVC raincoats for a bell and a caftan; changing from one fashion to the other. Jenny Fabian remembers the sudden influx of people on the scene, 'The new punters were OK, there was no problem, the more the merrier really. They weren't tourists as such on the scene, though there were those we called "plastic hippies" and "weekend hippies", but looking back, poor things, they probably were the people who had the nine to five jobs who just enjoyed the environment. There must have been ordinary people who just liked the music, it couldn't have been just the people who took acid.'

Nick Mason stated that the Underground 'didn't influence much of our recorded stuff, but it gave us a launching pad, a record deal, which we wouldn't have got if everyone hadn't been so fascinated by the new changing culture in London. The Underground scene gave us a home base to work from, but as a way of developing ourselves around the country it was pretty useless.[12] We weren't loyal supporters of the Underground. Even then, we were occupied with being a band, going the route. The Underground was a launch pad. Yes, there was UFO, but for every UFO there were twenty gigs up the motorways at the Top Rank Ballroom, Dunstable, or whatever. Essentially, the Underground was a London event. By the time it moved out to the provinces it was much more a commercial enterprise, much more to do with the music than, perhaps, the intellectual aspirations. But for us, the buzz of being involved was enormously helpful. Timing is very important to any band.'[13]

'I expected the band to be much more into the Underground scene and they weren't remotely interested in it,' says Wynne-Wilson. 'Roger and Nick were certainly not into any hip ideal of any kind; that's my observation, though I don't know what they were thinking themselves. Syd, yes. But for a relatively short time, because as soon as there was any money around it became quite a different attitude. Syd didn't really make time for it. So although they were adopted by the Underground, I don't think they were of it, at all. Maybe Andrew and Peter were more.' Nick Mason said, 'I don't think even Syd was a man of the times. He didn't slot in with the intellectual likes of John Hopkins and Joe Boyd, Miles, Peter Jenner; the London Free School people. Probably being middle-class we could talk our way through, make ourselves sound as though we were part of it . . . But Syd was a great figurehead. He was part of acid culture.[14] I didn't know what was going on. Peter and Andrew and the kind of Joe Boyd figures that were around then were probably part of it in a way that I certainly wasn't. All four of us . . . we were the band, that's all. There was no community spirit whatsoever, all we were interested in was our EMI recording contract, making a record, having a hit. At UFO we felt like the house band, and it was by far the nicest gig and what everyone asked about in the interviews, but I certainly wasn't into the lifestyle of the whole thing, because I was too busy being part of the new rock'n'roll movement which was a different thing.'[15]

'The Arts Lab was right at the end of Earlham Street on Drury Lane,' says Wynne-Wilson, 'a seriously alternative establishment, with artistic rather than political aspirations, run by Jim Haynes and Jack Henry Moore, which opened in very early 1967. And I don't remember Syd being there very much. Rick might have ventured down there but I don't think Roger or Nick did.' Syd later remarked, 'I haven't been to the Arts Lab or anything, so I don't really know what's happening. There are just so many people running around doing different things and no kind of unity. It doesn't really bother me.'[16]

On 8 January, the Floyd played at the Upper Cut, Forest Gate. The next day they squeezed in an intensive rehearsal for their first major studio session scheduled for the 11th. Peter Whitehead, director of *Wholly Communion*, the film of the 1965 Albert Hall poetry reading, was at work on a new film called, *Tonite Let's Make Love In London,* which took its title from a line in Allen Ginsberg's poem

'Who Be Kind' that he'd read at Wholly Communion. The inspiration for *Tonite Let's Make Love In London* was simple: 'Protest movements, life and everything!' Whitehead had begun making pop promos for *Top Of The Pops* and fell in with the Rolling Stones, who commissioned him to film their 1965 Irish tour. The resulting film, *Charlie Is My Darling*, has been rarely seen but is well worth seeking out. *Tonite Let's Make Love In London* began as an effort to capture the spirit of Swinging London, but ended instead documenting the rise of the nascent psychedelic Underground. 'That was probably because for me the Underground was closer to my whole life,' Whitehead explained. 'The wider scene [which included interviews with Julie Christie and Michael Caine] I filmed with tongue in cheek. It was hard to make two films at once but that is probably what I tried to do.'

Something exciting and original was taking place Underground. 'Everything was exciting, and expanding and imploding in all directions.' The light shows, with their multi-coloured bubbles expanding and imploding amoeba-like, in constant flux, was an apt metaphor for much of the goings-on at UFO and in the Underground. Whitehead and Stern captured stunning footage of the Pink Floyd on-stage, of Mark Boyle's light shows and the young Underground groovers, which is included in their Pink Floyd '66'-77 video.

Peter and Anthony Stern, whom Syd had had a painting exhibition with in Cambridge Town Hall in 1962,[17] shared a flat, and they had kept links with their old Cambridge friends. Among them was a girlfriend of Syd's, Jenny Spires (Syd was still seeing Lindsay Korner though; Jenny and Lindsay were friends). 'I had an affair with Jenny,' says Whitehead, 'who was still with Syd at the time, though he was already out of touch most of the time.' The idea to feature the Pink Floyd in Peter's film came about 'in bed with Jenny Spires. She suggested it, being sexually unfaithful to him made her try to be extra faithful in marketing and promoting him.' Whitehead told *Record Collector*, 'I first saw the Pink Floyd at the Royal College of Art, and then caught them several times at UFO, because of Jenny Spires. I was fascinated with the music, but I didn't think they'd last! Nor did she, alas!'

On 11 January, the Pink Floyd packed their gear into the van which Syd had written 'Pink Floyd' in spidery pink ink over the front wheel, and drove down to Old Church Street in Chelsea. At Sound Techniques Studio, Peter Whitehead set up his camera and the Floyd began playing. 'I agreed to pay for the session so that I could have music for my film. I just decided to run off a roll of film and ended up only using five seconds in the film! They did "Interstellar Overdrive" in one take and didn't want to do it a second time. As I had booked and paid for two hours they agreed to do an improvisation just for fun and out came the song they agreed to call "Nick's Boogie", as it had been Mason that had led the music from the start, its mood especially. It was a pure improvisation on the spur of the moment, for me, to fill up the time. I said I liked it and might use it so it was included in my contract. Of course, it wasn't used until I released the

London 66-67 Pink Floyd video.*

The film and soundtrack of the session, released on video, is fascinating. Syd sits in the centre of the drab little studio on a stool, with his Telecaster and Binson echo unit, flanked to his left by Rick Wright at his Farfisa organ and his own Binson, and Roger Waters and Nick Mason on the right. The only known footage of the original Floyd in the studio, it shows the delicate interplay between four individuals. Syd seems the focal point, yet conversely, the odd man out. He sits on the stool hunched over his guitar, his head bobbing to its own rhythm, looking a bit like a spastic child, quite stoned. Nick Mason, looking uncomfortable in purple turtleneck and bowl cut, drums out his accompaniment, largely riding the cymbals, with Wright duly filling in with freaky glissandos, showing elements of the prowess he was soon to develop on-stage at UFO and in the sessions for the first album. Roger Waters stands solemn and impassive, playing with marked intensity. His composure slips towards the end of the nearly seventeen-minute 'Interstellar Overdrive', gritting his teeth and strangling his bass. One Floyd associate says, 'I remember that film session and I thought it was appalling, because Roger was getting stars in his eyes. So it fell apart. Roger strangling his bass would have been performance rather than music making. Syd could be relaxed and uninhibited in a way that none of the others could be. To that extent he was completely different from the other three. I don't remember seeing any of them moving in any situation, apart from Roger doing his funny thing which was studied and not spirited.' As the band reach the end of 'Interstellar Overdrive', an exhausted Syd's head drops and he raises a weary hand to his face, rubbing his eyes.

Whitehead seized upon this image, using it as the cover for the video and CD released thirty years later. It's a chilling frozen image, seeming to encapsulate all the woes ahead for Barrett. He literally seems to be pushing himself relentlessly to a musical apogee that is forever tantalisingly out of his grasp.

It should be noted here that Barrett was still fully in possession of his faculties, increasing LSD and cannabis use notwithstanding, and his best work was still ahead of him. Many of the ideas contained on this version of 'Interstellar Overdrive' were to be refined in the following weeks and months, emerging as a finished cut on their first album in radically different form. In the short film Barrett is shown to have clearly absorbed a large portion of Keith Rowe's technique. Rowe sat and watched the video with the author in 1996 and pointed out four or five techniques he'd developed. He detunes and retunes one of the tuning pegs, channelling the sound through the Binson in dramatic ascensions and descensions. The Binson echo unit became an instrument in its own right, as Andrew King stated, with Barrett the skilful manipulator. In two years he had

*Twenty four years later, in 1991, Colin Miles of See for Miles Records recalls unearthing 24 minutes of unreleased Pink Floyd music 'the most incredible find'. 'Peter Whitehead brought in this 7 inch tape with green mould growing all over it and I thought, "Oh dear, what can we do with that?". But it was so tightly wound the sound quality was absolutely superb.' (*Radio One, 12 Dec 91*)

mastered the stodgy little machine. Altering the tuning of his strings as he played was a creative act that belies the criticism Barrett later received for detuning his guitar on stage, too often cited as a sign of his growing madness. It may have been madness, but a madness that sounds suspiciously like inspiration. And during this session Barrett is clearly inspired. His playing clearly outpaces the others' contributions, save for Mason's surprisingly delicate soft mallet fills on 'Nick's Boogie'.

The artistry of Syd's work is still not fully understood, and it takes many, many listens before the approach Syd was using becomes apparent. Barrett loses himself in abstraction with his guitar and effects, creating never before heard soundscapes and textures. In 'Interstellar Overdrive' and 'Nick's Boogie' from these Whitehead-funded Chelsea sessions, Barrett is simultaneously everywhere and nowhere, as elusive as the Cheshire cat. Examination of those pieces leaves the casual listener wondering if they are hearing Barrett or just an echo sample, its frequencies pitching wildly across the octaves.

'Interstellar Overdrive' is Pink Floyd's most difficult song and one of their most rewarding listens once the ear has grown accustomed to its illusory harshness. The several extant versions of 'Interstellar Overdrive' are a veritable loadstone of information, and perhaps the key to understanding the arcane processes of Barrett's thought before its irremediable fracture. Deceptively chaotic Telecaster flights, sketch filigrees of distortion, with Rick Wright's organ crafting instant counterpoint. As Wright's organ style gradually became less stiff and more fluid, it would prove to be an ideal counterpoint to Barrett's Telecaster flights. Wright has never received enough credit for his work with Barrett, sometimes matching him note for sustained note. With Barrett, Wright achieved his most relaxed and least constrained playing. When he forgets himself, he manages to echo Bill Evans, pianist in Miles Davis's classic quintet who recorded the 1959 *Kind Of Blue*. Like Jimi Hendrix's drummer Mitch Mitchell, Wright alone could accompany the rapidly alternating melodicism and cacophony of Barrett's guitar.

The 'rhythms in flux', orderly in their chaos, constant and yet unsettled, predominate. Barrett traces ever changing progressions through tempo and time signature with all the deftness of an alchemist approaching the formula for the transmutation of matter. He takes the leaden central riff and elaborates on it in myriad ways, tracing trails of gold through the ether. Pete Townshend said, 'I once got Eric Clapton to come down to UFO because I thought what Syd was doing was very interesting. We both enjoyed him.'[18] Barrett's extensive use of minor-second and flatted fifth-chord changes, and proclivity for ominous tritones is perhaps his single most pervasive influence in modern rock. Tritones, once banned by the Roman Catholic Church for being 'of the devil', swept through Barrett's work like dread currents. Barrett's descending minor chords reverberate through the work of guitarists such as Tony Iommi of Black Sabbath, Graham Coxon of Blur, Nick McCabe of the Verve, Robyn Hitchcock,

Kevin Shields of My Bloody Valentine, Bernard Albrecht of Joy Division, and on and on.

On 13 January, 'The Return Of The Dreaded UFO' welcomed back 'the monstrous Pink Floyd' to the psychedelic ballroom. *'Gape at the film "Marilyn Monroe", thrill to the Giant Sun Trolley, gasp at the horrible crawling slides!'* ran the breathless *Melody Maker* ad. Here was their constituency, a club that has become mythic for its relaxed and enthusiastic air, charged with the positive energy of its members. Colin Turner, the mod punter who had come to UFO out of curiosity and found himself irresistibly drawn to its air of freedom, recalls, 'Syd would often go off in his own direction leaving the rest of the guys wondering when he would come back and play something they could identify, so they could join back in! They often lounged around at the back of the stage (which was very small with nowhere to hide) waiting for Syd. It was pretty obvious even then that they were Syd's band. They were also not consistent in that in most songs on most nights they played like nothing you had ever heard and yet other times they would produce crap.'

Chris Welch of *Melody Maker* went to UFO to investigate, and spoke to Joe Boyd, who said, 'We started the club in December, and it's basically a home for groups that are doing experimental things in pop. The object of the club is to provide a place for experimental pop music, and also for the mixing of medias, lights shows and theatrical happenings. We also show New York avant-garde films.' Boyd noted the original constituency, the psychedelic cadre, came from Bayswater and Notting Hill rather than Chelsea, but that now new people were starting to arrive en masse. 'We are getting a lot more observers rather than people who participate.' Welch walked around noting, 'A boy danced about playing maracas, a fat girl wandered about spreading love and happiness by smiling cheerfully. Nobody swore, nobody sneered, adopted threatening poses to bolster sagging egos . . .'

Joe Boyd says, 'Hoppy and I ran UFO together, we were partners from the beginning. My attitude was the same as it had always been. I was sympathetic to the socio-political mood but my real interest was in the music. One of the reasons that it also began was that I was fired by Elektra, and I had to choose if I was going to stay in London or not. Managing the Incredible String Band wasn't bringing in enough money for me to live on. And Hoppy was always broke. Both of us were looking for cash flow. I don't know if there was any difference in our respective needs for cash. Not that we made a lot of money, but after paying the expenses, rent and the groups, we'd take whatever was left and put half of it in his pocket and half of it in mine, every Sunday morning at 7 a.m., and that's how we lived. There wasn't a big philosophical divide, but Hoppy's interest in the club was in its atmosphere, the spirit, the political connection of it, the centre of the Underground.

'One symbol of this difference was in one of the few arguments we ever had, which was over the Deviants. Hoppy had gone to Middle Earth and seen this anarchic Underground group and thought they were great. We drove down in a blizzard to the East End to hear them rehearse and I thought they were terrible. I said, "They're going into the club over my dead body," and Hoppy felt they represented something we should encourage! An anarchic spirit, working-class kids from across the tracks. After so much pressure from Hoppy, we booked them at 5 a.m. We always had a band on at 5 a.m. and paid them £5. In February I was standing at the door and this little mod kid in a three-piece suit with flares and big eyes ran down the stairs and introduced himself, saying he was the DJ at [R&B bastion] Tiles, Jeff Dexter. He was like a delegate, come over to see what was happening. He thought the place was great and demanded that I come back and visit his club. We went and he showed me around and offered me a black bomber.'

Syd Barrett and the Pink Floyd didn't occur in a vacuum, there was plenty around to feed the madness of their brilliant improvisation. Another band that often shared the stage at UFO with the Pink Floyd was the Soft Machine, whose blend of jazz and psychedelic rock was innovative and musically solid. The Soft Machine and the Floyd, though professionally amiable rivals, were mutual admirers. The Soft Machine declared to the *Melody Maker*, 'We dig the Pink Floyd very much because they have got their own scene.'* The Soft Machine also stated, 'They haven't copied anybody else; they've gone out and they've found themselves and taken a big chance.'[19]

Arthur Brown was another experimental performer who played at UFO. 'Our first UFO gig was a memorable one,' Daevid Allen recalls, 'I was standing in the doorway of the dressing room, as a band called the Crazy World of Arthur Brown launched into a jazzy keyboard-dominated intro. Suddenly a wild figure appeared in the corridor with the entire top of his head on fire: Arthur Brown. He plunged on to the stage and began declaiming in an operatically bottomless voice, I am the god of hellfire!"

Syd Barrett simply said, 'Freedom is what I'm after. That's why I like working in this group. There is such freedom artistically.'[20] He had largely given up painting, because it could not 'transcend the feeling of playing at UFO and those sort of places with the lights and that, [and] the fact that the group was getting bigger and bigger.'[21] Roger Waters said, 'We're playing something completely different from what has gone before. Like jazz musicians, we improvise all the time, both vocally and instrumentally.'[22]

Pete Brown says, 'The musical content of psychedelia comes from trying to do a simpler form of jazz. It was quite a jumping scene in 1967, where you had the psychedelic scene happening at places like UFO, Middle Earth and Happenings 44. And then you had the Little Theatre Club and the old Ronnie

*Interpretation of the precise meaning of the word 'scene' as used in this context, will be left to future historians, but it seems to indicate a certain camaraderie.

Scott's, where younger musicians would play the more experimental jazz. It was quite interesting going from one to the other. I've come to the conclusion that rock people like Syd Barrett, and people who have been inspired by Syd, were really trying to do a form of jazz, maybe without so many chords and with different structures. Syd, apart from writing songs, as a player, probably had more knowledge than the others in the band. And within his limitations, he could improvise and be inspired in the same way that a jazz musician could be inspired. That's what he was trying to do. Whether it was drug-driven or not, whenever I saw Syd playing, he always seemed on a high level of inspiration, which was beyond what the rhythm section could do, to be brutally honest. His stage act at UFO was pretty wild.'

'Syd actually had a job playing in a dance band in Cambridge [Geoff Mott And The Mottoes],' says Pete Brown, 'which suggests that he had a larger knowledge of music, even in a limited way, than the others did. He wasn't coming from that British amateur point of view, as the others were. That fits very well with my image of what he could do. Even with that small degree of competence, he had more knowledge of chords and chord changes. It suggests that he had some old-fashioned musical ability, and could probably even read music up to a point. Which makes it all the more remarkable what he did.

'I've never rated the rest of the Pink Floyd as musicians, very much. I never thought they had that much to say musically. The rhythm section couldn't compare to those of competitors like the Soft Machine and Dantalion's Chariot, who had it and were great. The Soft Machine also came from a very artistic and experimental place, Canterbury, deliberately questioning everything and changing things. And compared to them, the Floyd didn't play very well, except for Syd. Syd was the only one who was holding it down. His timing was very good. I'm not sure how much support he had within the band.' None the less, the others in the band established a leaden base which Syd transformed into gold. The architecture students built a solid framework for Barrett's most baroque flourishes.

Duggie Fields says, 'I never thought they had any rhythm, and that was the least appealing part of them.' Brown says, 'British rock rhythm sections always had funny timing. They don't any more, because it gets sorted out in the studio, but live they still can't do it. Right from the start of the Liverpool scene, those who had no musical training and jumped right into it, all had funny timing. Even on their records. Even on Pink Floyd records. In rock, with the exception of people coming into it from jazz, it's mostly about people working within their limitations. I don't know how many chords Syd could play. I don't know whether Syd was listening to Indian stuff, which has a lot of improvising on one chord and drones. People were listening to a lot of Indian music, for a lot of people of that generation Indian music and jazz and blues were what they listened to. There was the trance element as well. Trance today has its roots not only in psychedelia but also in dub reggae. That improvising on one chord, if you are out of your mind, it's easier not to think about chord changes. It's like Jamaican musicians getting into a heavy ganja groove and staying in one or two chords for a hell of a long time. It's comfortable, you can get off on it, the longer you stay inside it, the better you feel. Syd was probably creating grooves in his own mind rather than working off anything the others were creating. The others could play simple things.'

World music, as it later came to be known, played a part in Barrett's sound, albeit often second-hand, filtered through the ears of Mike Bloomfield, John Coltrane and Yusef Lateef. 'The Master Musicians of Jajouka, Morocco, have a lot in common with the live music of the sixties,' says bassist Jack Monck, who later played in a band with Barrett. 'A lot of improvisation, but unlike jazz, not based around a theme. Repetitive improvisation where things gradually evolve, where you have layers and textures, modulating in a rhythmic rather than harmonic way.'

'Jethro Tull played support to the Floyd,' said Ian Anderson, the band's singer and flautist, 'when Syd Barrett was in the band. They were genuinely amazing. It wasn't their songs as much as the way they broke down all musical and presentational barriers. I never did any drugs, so I wasn't particularly interested in the psychedelic aspect of what they were doing. But the way they seemed to mix rock and folk and Eastern influences was fascinating. Very eclectic. It prompted me to pick up an instrument again.'[23]

Barrett's particular genius was one of unschooled technique, his restless improvising unhampered by any formal technique. Barrett eschewed the obvious clichés of R&B for a naive, intricate web of echo-laden glissando, spitfire arpeggios and short, punchy phrasing. At his peak, Barrett was experimenting constantly with tonality, exploring micro-tones right down to their essence. His intake of acid augmented his dissection of the notes, as if he was trying to find the very source of music. Ultimately, the process would subsume his native gifts not only for rhythm but also for lyrical description, melodic inventiveness and instrumental prowess.

Syd's stage presence and playing indicated an musician courting his muse with imaginative quicksteps. Anything seemed possible, no boundaries had been set yet. Like in any dynamic generation or movement, the few, the luminous, were compelled by inner agitation to push the envelope, to look beyond. To open Pandora's Box, to open the Doors of Perception. And make no mistake, the sheer volume used filled the ballroom at UFO with an other-worldly miasma of evolving textures. Sound and light, in perfect contention or in harmony, the runs emanating from Syd's Telecaster seemingly acting as a catalyst for the chemicals used in the light show. Small wonder the music evoked visions of astral travel, it mirrored the stellar nebulae's airless shift with its flashes of turbulent liquid. Action and reaction, in equal measure. Andrew King said, 'It was the most intensely creative time of Syd's life. He was not like a dominant band leader so much as he was Hale-Bopp and they were dragged along in the tail. I remember watching him mixing on the 4-track desk. He played it like it was an instrument.'[24]

Syd, the strange attractor, was the piper who had exchanged his pan flute for a silver-mirrored Telecaster. And his influence was acutely felt by aspirant young musicians who crowded the Pink Floyd's shows at UFO as Barrett succeeded in breaking the rigid formats laid down before. Barrett's luminescent pop seemed to trace the very fallout of the cosmos; little did he imagine he would be drawn into its relentless tide.

Peter Whitehead and Anthony Stern came down to the Institute of Contemporary Arts on 16 January to film the Pink Floyd's gig there.* The performance was followed by a discussion between the band and the audience, many of them earnest arts students who presumably could appreciate the intermedia spectacle of the Floyd in full flight.

Of their music that night, Whitehead says there was 'no future in it, but it was an interesting passing phase, and very appropriate for the UFO scene. One wanted long jazz-like music rather than aggressive pop. I personally liked the jazz feel because I never really liked pop music as such.'

This was to be a key in winning the early Floyd many unlikely converts. The jazz and classical snobs were handed an aural spectacle utterly unlike anything in pop music. Echoes of Schoenberg or Coltrane's 'sheets of sound' caught the ear of people like classical concert promoter Christopher Hunt. Hunt was intrigued by the Floyd, after having heard of them through Sumi Jenner, Peter Jenner's wife, who worked as his secretary. Hunt extended the Pink Floyd an offer to play at the Commonwealth Institute on the High Street in Kensington. This prestigious location, usually reserved for high profile and serious conferences on socialism in Sikkim and the like, was taken over on 17 January for a multimedia event dubbed 'Music In Colour: Pink Floyd'. At 8 p.m. on a cold Tuesday, the serious and the hip filed in for the aural assault of the Floyd. 'I like what they do,' said Christopher Hunt in the press release issued for the event. 'I usually just deal with classical chamber music but I believe that the Pink Floyd are something quite different from normal pop music. In fact I have no interest at all in any other pop groups.'

On 1 February, the Pink Floyd officially went professional, abandoning their schooling for music, and two days later they played the Queen's Hall in Leeds. Peter Wynne-Wilson was slowly assuming the reins of the light show overseer from Russell Page, Syd's old Cambridge friend. Wynne says, 'Russell did lighting for a comparatively short time and I was always rather impatient, not necessarily directly with him, but I knew I wanted control of it rather than him. Russell was much more laid-back than me. He did the light shows a few times

*His black and white film of the gig was subsequently lost or stolen. 'Someone will have it somewhere,' deadpans Whitehead.

at UFO. I can remember Russell doing the light show in Leeds in a tram shelter. Already at that time he was finding it a bit distasteful. It was quite a drunken scene there, and dirty. That Leeds gig wasn't bad at all, but it was an extremely highly charged atmosphere. I don't know that the Floyd were the lead band, but they went down very well. The reaction to the Pink Floyd in the provinces was not invariably hostile. There was, however, nothing like UFO in the provinces, apart from some of the college gigs. They certainly weren't hostile at those, they were appreciative. There would generally be quite a small proportion of hip audience members, but perhaps they weren't accepted on the level that the band themselves thought they should have been accepted. But it wasn't like UFO or the Roundhouse at all.'

On 12 February, Rolling Stones Keith Richard and Mick Jagger were arrested by the police drugs squad at Richard's cottage, Redferns. George Harrison of the Beatles narrowly avoided being arrested himself, having left shortly before the arrival of the police. The police were increasingly interested in rock bands' use of drugs, and a systematic witchhunt began.

The Pink Floyd returned to Cambridge on 17 February to play at 'the Dot', the Dorothy Ballroom, where Dave Gilmour's Joker's Wild had often played. Many of Waters' and Barrett's friends were in attendance and witnessed the Pink Floyd in a spectacular homecoming gig. Gilmour and Joker's Wild meanwhile, bending to the changing sound of the times, had begun playing covers of 'Hey Joe'. Soon they would tour France under the unfortunate moniter the Little Flowers.

The next day the Pink Floyd played a memorable, if for all the wrong reasons, out-of-town gig at the California Ballroom, in Dunstable. Waters remembers, 'They were pouring pints of beer on to us from the balcony. Most unpleasant and very fucking dangerous too.'[25] He added at the time, 'I think the reason that we've been employed by so many of these freak-out merchants is only because we have lots of equipment and lighting and it saves the promoters from having to hire lighting for the group. Anyway, a freak-out should be relaxed, informal and spontaneous. The best freak-out you'll ever get is a party with about a hundred people. A freak-out shouldn't be a savage mob of geezers throwing bottles.'[26]

Nick Mason stated, 'You must never underestimate how unpopular we were around the rest of England. They hated it. They would throw things, pour beer over us. And we were terrible, though we didn't quite know it. Promoters were always coming up to us and saying, "I don't know why you boys won't do proper songs". Looking back on it, I can't think why we persevered.'[27] 'We got jolly annoyed but we weren't really scared. We just went on and on. We never said, "Fuck this, let's pack it in." We just trudged around for a daily dose of broken bottle.'[28]

Roger Waters told the *Melody Maker* at the time, 'We're being frustrated at the moment by the fact that to stay alive we have to play lots and lots of places and venues that aren't really suitable. This can't last obviously and we're hoping to create our own venues. We all like our music. That's the only driving force behind us. All the trappings of becoming vaguely successful, like being able to buy bigger amplifiers, none of that stuff is really important.'

Probably the band member who was least aligned with Barrett in either temperament or outlook, Nick Mason was driven by a strong work ethic and, in his own words, 'lust to succeed'. 'We were rejuvenated every time we came back to London and got that fix of finding that there was an audience for us.'[29] In a candid interview with *Disc & Music Echo*, Mason stated, 'I take life easy because I'm a bit of a paranoiac, I feel everyone has a down on me. I want to be successful and loved in everything I turn my hands to.'[30]

Syd's time at Earlham thus far had been largely idyllic, save for his growing intake of LSD. It was progressing from recreational use to a frequent escape and diversion from the growing trials and tribulations of touring. Joe Boyd says, 'I ran into Syd outside the flat at Earlham Street, where he was living with Lindsay. It was a warm day, and I saw him sitting on the kerb with a bunch of people, looking very stoned. And Lindsay, whom I always liked and was always very keen on, said to me, "Wow, Syd's just taking acid every day, it's just incredible how much he's taking." Syd took a great deal of drugs.' Boyd adds, 'People were aware of the strength of the acid experience. Taking it once, I couldn't imagine taking it every day. It was beyond my comprehension how people could want to do that. It was obvious to me that if you did it every day, you were jeopardising the wires that held everything together in your mind.'

On 17 February, the Beatles released their epochal single 'Strawberry Fields Forever' b/w 'Penny Lane'. 'Strawberry Fields Forever' was such an incredible melange of sounds, tempos and instruments, and coupled to such an unusual, abstract lyric that it constituted nothing less than a revolution in pop music. So far removed from anything on the pop charts, it failed to reach the number one spot, but none the less its impact was immediate. 'Strawberry Fields Forever' stylistic antecedent was Lennon's own 'Tomorrow Never Knows', the final track off 1966's *Revolver*. 'Strawberry Fields Forever' influence on Barrett's writing was immediate, and most timely as well. Its distinctive stamp is evident in the version of 'Arnold Layne' that the Pink Floyd would shortly record.

Joe Boyd said, 'Jenner and King retained the Bryan Morrison Agency to be their agents. Morrison, Steve O'Rourke and Tony Howard all came down one night to see a rehearsal and we all met for the first time. The next day, Jenner rang me to say that Morrison felt he could get the group a better deal with EMI than the one that was on the table with Polydor. Within a short space of time, it was clear that we were losing the Polydor deal. I was going to be included as the producer with the Polydor deal. Bryan Morrison then said that the best way to get the best deal was for the group to make their own master of a single. Take a finished record to EMI. Then the group asked me if I would produce the single for them. At this point, as far as we knew, there was still no direct contact with

EMI. So I arranged for a session at Sound Techniques Studio in Old Church Street, Chelsea. I had to get Bryan Morrison to write a letter to Sound Technique guaranteeing the bill. Then an agreement was drawn up which stipulated I got a percentage of whatever the group got for the single. And then we did the session.'

The band went to Sound Techniques Studios on 27 February to record a set of six songs in order to send a demo around to various record labels. Joe Boyd was the producer, along with superb engineer John Wood. Another version of 'Interstellar Overdrive' was also recorded, which would form part of the finished album version.

Joe Boyd said, 'We went into the studio to do "Arnold Layne" and we did it pretty much in one day for recording, it was four-track, so we had to put the rhythm section on one track and overdub a few other things.[31] I remember having fun with "Arnold Layne", bringing up the organ for one thing, and then pulling something down. Making the production fit into the group personality was [important], and that was successfully done on the records that came afterwards. It's hard to put your finger on what the quality of the sound was, but there was a clarity and a richness that wasn't quite the same as other groups at the time.'[32] Boyd adds, 'After the Pink Floyd session I even discussed with Peter Jenner doing a solo record with Syd, though nothing came of it. When I talked or dealt with the band, I dealt with Roger rather than Syd.'

The reaction from EMI was positive and the band decided to sign with them. 'Basically, I think we felt, "Let's be on the same label as the Beatles", so we signed to EMI.'[33] The Pink Floyd's deal with EMI had set a new precedent – in a time when singles still dominated the market, the deal allowed for the band to record an entire album at an unhurried pace. The Pink Floyd's deal followed suit. 'We were signed up with a £5,000 advance over five years,' said Waters. 'It was a bloody stupid deal. Ken East was managing director at the time at EMI and we all went in there and signed the contract and then they wheeled in Norman "Hurricane" Smith and said he was going to be our producer. It was all jolly nice and polite.'[34] Jenner said, 'If we had started out with just any old banger group, we'd have been finished within a year, because we had so little idea of what we were doing, but fortunately the Floyd had all this talent. Andrew and I just played everything by ear; goodness only knows what the established record-biz poseurs must've thought about us . . . I suppose that when we left their offices they just looked at each other and collapsed in disbelief at our naiveté.'[35]

Norman Smith, the A&R man who would be responsible for the Pink Floyd at EMI, recalled his first exposure to the Pink Floyd, 'I went [to UFO] and what I saw absolutely amazed me. I was into creating and developing new electronic sounds in the control-room, and Pink Floyd, I could see, were into exactly the same thing. It was a perfect marriage.'[36] Rick Wright noted, 'I was just very very excited; doing your first album, putting down your music on to tape. And knowing that the Beatles are next door, doing *Sergeant Pepper*. I was a bit of a snob before that, a "jazz-o". And I didn't really believe that pop music meant any-

Syd Barrett and Lyndsay Korner at 101 Cromwell Road, South Kensington, spring 1967

The EMI signing photo session, 1 April 1967. From left: Roger Waters (bass), Nick Mason (drums), Syd Barrett (guitar and vocals), Rick Wright (keyboards)

Waving or signalling for help? A previously unseen shot of Barrett and the Pink Floyd, taken in a scrap yard, August 1967

Spiralling, spiralling ... Rick Wright takes note of Syd Barrett's proto-punk hairdo as the band begins to enter rough waters, October 1967

A weary Pink Floyd face the camera in November 1967.
The distance between Barrett and his bandmates is already apparent

A rare shot of the five-man Pink Floyd, featuring Syd Barrett and his old Cambridge friend, David Gilmour, January 1968

The Lost Weekend that stretched to a year ... August 1968

Barrett during the recording of *The Madcap Laughs*, 1969

An outtake from the legendary *The Madcap Laughs* photo session by Mick Rock, Earl's Court, London, 1969. One of Barrett's paintings hangs on the rear wall

Syd Barrett on holiday in Formentera, Spain, with Imo Moore and a friend, 1969

The exile begins: Syd Barrett on his ill-advised press junket, 1971

Barrett holds the object which had become increasingly foreign, and a burden, to him: his Fender Telecaster. His return to Cambridge is imminent, 1971

thing at all. When I heard *Sergeant Pepper,* it changed my attitude as to what people like us could do.'[37] Joe Boyd's role as producer was taken over by EMI's Norman Smith, a common occurrence at the time. EMI executive Beecher Stevens had gone down to UFO with Norman Smith to see the band and noticed with some apprehension that, 'One of the boys in the group, and some of the people around them, seemed a bit strange, which is one reason I wanted Norman Smith as their producer. I thought he was close enough to their music to keep a firm hand on the sessions.'[38]

Stevens must have been at a loss as to what to do with the Floyd. He was an old-school record company executive, most of who saw pop music as a lucrative but ultimately disposable commodity.

Nick Mason stated, 'Sounds a little bit naive, but I was probably unaware of the politics of Joe Boyd going on over that period, because what happened was that Joe Boyd was the initial producer and then was really rode out when we signed to EMI.'[39] Joe Boyd said, 'EMI in those days had a policy of using their own studios, own producers. Once you signed to EMI, you were "in-house", and so I was very much shut out.'[40] King said, 'It's interesting that it didn't occur to us to make a fuss about who was going to produce us. We didn't say, "No, that's our decision, it's nothing to do with you." We said, "Yes, OK,"'[41]

Peter Jenner, however, believes that the change of producer was the right decision. 'I suspect that Norman was rather better for them. He had been the Beatles' engineer up to that time and had graduated to become a producer and he tapped them into that Beatles tradition. He helped them make good records. It's quite likely that Joe might have let them become more indulgent, because he didn't have the age and the experience at that time. There was enough madness flying around and the sanity and the boringness of Norman helped ensure that the Floyd made hits.'[42] Joe Boyd's percentage on 'Arnold Layne' went unpaid for decades. He dryly notes, 'It took a long while before I got the percentage, but I'm now on the EMI computer.'

'We were given Norman Smith by EMI, no arguments,' Mason told *Mojo*. 'So Joe Boyd, our original producer, got written out of the thing. Norman was more interested in making us sound like a classical rock band. It was a bit like the George Martin thing, a useful influence to have. But I think Joe would have given Syd his head, let him run in a freer way. We spent three months recording it, which was quite a long time in those days. Bands used to have to finish albums in a week, with session players brought in to play the difficult bits. But because the Beatles were taking their time recording *Sergeant Pepper* in the studio next door, EMI thought this was the way people now made records.'

On 3 March, the Pink Floyd, AMM and the Soft Machine all played at UFO. Surprisingly Keith Rowe said, 'AMM never felt much kinship with Barrett or the Pink Floyd. I'm not sure why. It was probably more of "us and them", all the pop/rock musicians. What they wanted and we wanted were ultimately very different things. We set out with the agenda of developing a form of music which hadn't existed before, a set of techniques to go with that. From the very early days, that was the agenda, and not to become rich and famous. In fact, the art school that I went to, the ultimate success was to become middle-aged and obscure, and hanging out wasn't part of AMM's scene. Getting gigs at any price, being popular or understood, wasn't part of our agenda, [even] to this day. Being marginal and unappreciated, at that point it was seen as a positive thing. When you're so close to it, and up to your eyes in it, you don't know. Those obvious things are too close for you to see them.'

On Saturday 4 March, the Pink Floyd played the Poly Rag Ball, a benefit for War on Want and Cancer Research at the Regent Street Polytechnic, London. Jenner and King were highly reluctant to book the Pink Floyd for benefit gigs, but the occasional one did crop up. The next day the Pink Floyd played the stately Saville Theatre on Shaftesbury Avenue. Photographer Tony Gale of the Pictorial Press said, 'Pink Floyd were on the bill supporting Lee Dorsey alongside the Ryan Brothers and Jeff Beck. This was probably the first time the gelatin 'psychedelic' light effects were used in a major theatre. Photographers, used to bright spot-lights, were caught off guard by the low-key lighting and had relatively slow films in their cameras, hence the somewhat blurred static images which, in retrospect, actually added to the intended effect.'

On March 7, the Pink Floyd appeared on Granada's *Scene Special* – 'It's So Far Out, It's Straight Down!' – performing on 20 January versions of 'Interstellar Overdrive' and 'Percy The Ratcatcher' filmed at UFO. The special was an off-shoot of the early-evening *Scene At 6.30* news-magazine programme. Among its other highlights was Paul McCartney stating, 'The straights should welcome the Underground because it stands for freedom . . . it's not strange, it's just new, it's not weird, it's just what's going around.' The programme, which highlighted the burgeoning Underground, was only broadcast in the north of England, which must have been the first exposure to the strange goings-on in London for many people in the provinces. Indeed one could liken it to culture shock. The influence of programmes like *Scene At 6.30* was immense, and the clip of Syd and the Floyd on-stage at UFO, was beamed into thousands of homes, bringing their name to a much wider audience than their tours had done.

The supplements in the Sunday newspapers were also a vanguard for the media's reportage on all they perceived, sometimes mistakenly, to be fashionable and hip. The *Observer* published a memorable insert on the Underground, replete with photos and quotes from prime movers like Hoppy, Miles, Joe Boyd, Pete Brown, Caroline Coon, Mike Horovitz and others. The supplements arrived on suburban doorsteps with a merciful dose of colour.

Reporters for the *NME* and *Melody Maker*, though initially viewing the Underground from a comfortable piss-taking distance, slowly came around. As Chris Welch and Nick Jones of the *Melody Maker* reported on the Pink Floyd and UFO, the Moody Blues and the Move, Donovan and Hendrix, their own views broadened. The writers at *IT* and *Oz* meanwhile pushed boundaries with their riotous exhortations and reportage, with the redoubtable Germaine Greer, the playful Richard Neville, the catalytic Miles and the provocative Mick Farren all chronicling the tenor of the times.

Rock records also spread the word of the Underground around the world. Musicians in the other epicentre of psychedelia, San Francisco, had a strong feeling of musical unity with England. The Grateful Dead heard 'Tomorrow Never Knows' in early 1967 with amazement, its revolutionary sounds and textures altering their own music instantly. The impact of British imports the Stones, Beatles and ironically, Jimi Hendrix was immense and immediate in the USA. In LPs, newspapers and television, the interchange of ideas was becoming close to instantaneous for the first time in history. The DJs, musicians and Underground newspaper writers all had a pulse of the new youth movement. Pirate radio, and particularly shows like John Peel's *Perfumed Garden* on Radio Caroline, with his hip jargon and propensity to play side-long album tracks, was key in promulgating the fruits of this intense musical symbiosis between the USA and the UK. 'Somebody To Love' by Jefferson Airplane, or Country Joe And The Fish, resounded out of the windows of Earlham, Egerton and Cromwell, every radio in the house tuned to Peel's show. Duggie Fields says, 'At the same time we were just hearing Janis Joplin for the first time, and the Doors, the Velvet Underground.'

The vanguard formed at Wholly Communion, by *Revolver*, All Saints', *IT* and UFO needed clothes shops. Several young designers, branching out from the mod boutiques such as Mary Quant and the more esoteric Carnaby Street designs, began to purvey 'threads' to the 'hippies'. Frock shops gave way to boutiques with names such as Granny Takes A Trip. Nigel Waymouth, expanding from his involvement in graphic design, opened Granny Takes A Trip, buying up military waistcoats, lace dresses and hats from the antiques markets, and combining them with its own satin, silk and velvet creations.

The impetus for the revolution in fashion had begun with shops like Michael Rainey's Hung On You in Chelsea, which had outlined a new standard in flamboyance and extravagance, as if casting off once and for all the drabness of the post-War period. Author Nik Cohn in his superb 1971 analysis of post-War English fashion, *Today There Are No Gentlemen*, also points to the stall run by Vernon Lambert and Adrian Emmerton in the Chelsea Antique Market. They practically began the vogue for antique clothing. Boutiques such as I Was Lord Kitchener's Valet and Dandy, and designers such as Mr Freedom, Mr Fish, Thea Porter, and Zandra Rhodes began to service the Underground's wild revellers, who were as clothes conscious as their mod predecessors, but infinitely less constrained and rigid in their choice of wardrobe.

The extremes of mod and hippie dress reflects a duality in English society. The rigid hierarchy of immaculately tailored three-button suits, Chelsea boots, strict colour schemes, and short haircuts of mod were in stark contrast to the ebullient excesses of early hippie clothes, with their generous cuts, bizarre prints, satin, silk and velvet materials and radical colours. It was no coincidence that as time went on some mods would either become die-hard hippies or, ultimately, skinheads. Skinheads could be seen as the logical conclusion of the less salient, and essentially fascist, aspects of the mod ethic; the uniformity, the xenophobia, the rigidly defined code of music and dress. The mods, though, who 'saw the light' and grew their hair out, turned on and truly grasped the spirit of the Underground were the diametric opposites of more rigid peers, and shed their mod accoutrements rapidly in favour of the lotus-eating pleasure ethic of UFO, marijuana, meditation and psychedelic music.

On 9 March, the Pink Floyd played the Marquee, doing the tiring 7.30 to 11 p.m. slot; as opening band the Thoughts worked their way through the first set, the Pink Floyd heard about the day's Underground news. Earlier that day a sinister portent of things to come occurred when the offices of *IT* were raided by the police. Copies of the subversive paper had found their way to the police, and the nudity, cartoons, frank discussions of drugs, racism and police harassment running side by side with satiric pieces besieging the columns of the Establishment proved a bit much. Every single piece of paper, plus the typewriters, contents of the ashtrays and accounting ledgers were taken.

Miles says the *IT* staffers were stunned, 'We weren't waiting for it to happen. We were very naive. An interview we did with Dick Gregory in issue four, where he said "kill the whites" or something triggered it. They waited three months before reading it, so it took a while after it had come out for someone to be outraged enough for the police to come down looking for their payoff or whatever it was they were looking for. The intention was to close us down, they took everything away, even the phone books, the editor's address book. They stripped the office, there wasn't anything left, just an empty room with a few chairs. They took away the contents of the ashtrays, and searched the book shop upstairs. They kept everything for three months and then brought it all back with no charges. That's police tactics you would expect in South Africa or Indonesia, a police state activity. Closing down a newspaper. Imagine them going into the *Guardian* and taking away all their lists of advertisers, you'd never hear the end of it. But the English press did fuck-all about *International Times* getting raided. But that was to be expected, we were an alternative Underground press; so we didn't expect it and we didn't get it.'

Meanwhile, for the Floyd, the gig schedule was unrelenting, with performances on 10 March at UFO and the next evening at Canterbury. At long last though, on the 11th, their first single was released, the seminal 'Arnold Layne'. At UFO, the loyal psychedelic ravers got an advance screening of the Pink Floyd's film clip for 'Arnold Layne'; *'See the Pink Floyd go pop!'* trumpeted the UFO advert. The assembled ravers were treated to the sight of the Pink Floyd carrying a shop window mannequin on a windy beach.

'Arnold Layne' was reviewed by Nick Jones in *Melody Maker,* who described it as 'an amusing and colourful story about a guy who got himself put inside while teaming of the birds and the bees . . . without a doubt, a very good disc. It was interesting to see how the Floyd were going to fare with the problem of having to make a commercial single, but with their electronic sound, which takes an unexpected twist, they have made a good single. Pink Floyd represent a new form of music on the English pop scene. So let's hope the English are broad minded enough to accept it with open arms.'

'"Arnold Layne" is nothing but a pop record, it wasn't intended to represent anything in particular.[43] I just wrote it,' Barrett told Jones. 'I thought Arnold Layne was a nice name and fitted well into the music I had already composed. I was at Cambridge at the time I started to write the song. I pinched the line about "moonshine washing line" from Roger, our bass guitarist, because he has an enormous washing line in the back garden of his house. Then I thought "Arnold must have a hobby" and it went on from there. Arnold Layne just happens to dig dressing up in women's clothing. A lot of people do, so let's face up to reality. About the only lyric anybody could object to is the bit about "It takes two to know" and there's nothing smutty about that! But then if more people like them dislike us, more people like the Underground lot are going to dig us, so we hope they'll cancel each other out.'

'"Arnold Layne" was a song about a clothes fetishist, which was pretty go ahead for the time, come to think about it,' said Roger Waters. 'Both my mother and Syd's mother had students as lodgers because there was a girls' college up the road. So there was constantly great lines of bras and kickers on our washing lines, and "Arnold" or whoever he was, had bits and pieces off our washing lines. They never caught him. He stopped doing it after a bit, when things got too hot for him.'[44]

The band had been given no choice in choosing their initial single, as Nick Mason relates: 'In fact, we really didn't want "Arnold Layne" to be our first single. We were asked to record six numbers and pick the best two, then find a recording company that would accept them. We recorded the first two and they were snatched away and we were told, "That's it." By the time "Arnold Layne" was released, we had already progressed and changed our ideas about what a good hit record should be. We tried to stop it being released but we couldn't.'[45]

Roger Waters said, 'It's a song about a clothes fetishist who's obviously a bit kinked. A very simple, straight forward song about one sort of human predicament.[46] I'm upset when people say it is a smutty song. The attitude is the type of thing which leads us to the kind of situation which the song is about. It is a real song about a real subject. It isn't just a collection of words like "love", "baby" and "dig" put to music like the average pop song. If all the members of the group hadn't liked it we wouldn't have done it. That's obvious. The song was written in good faith. I think it's good. If we can't write and sing songs about various forms of human predicament then we might as well not be in the business.'[47]

Tetchy Waters was already beginning to get upset about the various stupidities that were part and parcel of pop stardom, giving him plenty of grist for future works such as 1975's bitter 'Welcome To The Machine'. The band was under the standard intense pressure from EMI to produce saleable products. The British pop music scene was still singles-driven, and a band was only as good as its last single. Bookings, TV appearances and press coverage depended on how well a single fared in the charts. The Pink Floyd, like all other bands, acquiesced to the pressure imposed by its label. They participated in the most inane photo shoots, being told to jump in the air or do leg-kicks in unison outside EMI's Manchester House. Welcome to the Machine, indeed. In these early promotional shots, the band would be photographed 'playing' their instruments on a small stage; of course, none of their instruments would be plugged in. Barrett, incidentally, was featured in one session wearing what is perhaps the ugliest shirt ever known to mankind.

Strangely, pirate Radio London banned 'Arnold Layne', purportedly because of its subject matter. The staid BBC however played it often. Radio Caroline, having not received enough payola money from the record pluggers, deigned to give it only the occasional airing. Regardless, it went to number twenty in the charts on 22 April. The Pink Floyd had a little help. Andrew King said, 'It was banned by Radio London because it had references to transvestism and also to nicking underwear. But we hyped it a bit, with the help of a gentleman whose name I wouldn't dream of revealing, who in those days could help you improve your chart positions for a comparatively small expenditure. We managed to hype it to number twenty.'[48] In an 11 February article in *Melody Maker*, Radio Caroline admitted that it accepted payment for playing pop singles on its programmes. Caroline charged a minimum of £100 a week for sixty plays of a single. In their defence, Caroline argued that EMI, Philips, Decca and Pye 'spent hundreds of thousands of pounds every year on Radio Luxembourg . . . to present shows built round their own records'. Money, rather than merit, ruled the waves. Rick Wright took it more personally, complaining bitterly to *Melody Maker*, 'The record was banned, not because of the lyrics, because there's nothing there you can really object to, but because they're against us as a group and against what we stand for'.

'It's only a business-like commercial insult anyway,' said Syd Barrett, trying to mask his growing disenchantment with the commerce inextricably linked to the art of making music. 'It doesn't affect us personally. The music is all coming straight out of our heads and it's not too far-out to understand. If we play well on-stage I think most people understand that what we play isn't just a noise.'[49]

Inevitably, some of the more militant factions in the close-bound clique in the Underground derided 'Arnold Layne' as something of a 'sell-out'. 'At UFO,' said Waters, 'people there are bored to death with "Arnold Layne" because it's become a pop song. Yet in other clubs this song is the only song of ours they know and enjoy.'[50]

'What bothered me was the complete shift in the phase of the music made at UFO versus the music made at Abbey Road Studios,' says Peter Wynne-Wilson. 'I would have said Syd was under pressure from Roger, though I don't know to what extent EMI applied pressure directly to him. I was quite aghast at "Arnold Layne", it really took me by surprise . . . Anybody that hung around their gigs at UFO, which was their primary place of making music, would have chosen "Interstellar Overdrive" as a first record if one was to be made. I'm sure that must have given Syd a hard time. Certainly he was very fed up with having to play "Arnold Layne" and "See Emily Play" at gigs because they were little pop ditties.'

Waters said, 'No one interferes with us when we're in the studio. They just leave us, more or less, alone to get on with what we want.'[51] Which would suggest either the band or their managers were pressuring Syd to write commercial songs.

Yet there can be no doubt that 'Arnold Layne' was a breakthrough in British pop music. Along with the Kinks' 'Waterloo Sunset' and 'Dedicated Follower of Fashion' and the Beatles' 'Strawberry Fields Forever'/'Penny Lane' single, 'Arnold Layne' was the first thoroughly English pop song. 'The early Pink Floyd,' said David Gilmour, 'under Syd's tutelage, was quintessentially English, in the same way that Ray Davies is. It wasn't your usual rock'n'roll, R&B stuff, which is very American-oriented.'[52]

Pete Brown was particularly inspired by the song, and directly as a result of hearing 'Arnold Layne' began work on 'White Room' for Cream, a lyric with a distinctly English slant. 'Along with John Lennon and Ray Davies, Syd Barrett was one of the first English songwriters. They looked at English subjects and phenomena, and didn't use overtly American styles, but at the same time they were influenced by American blues and R&B, and its lyrical content, which was inspiring. Because the blues is a very personal form, people have always made their own version of it, from Robert Johnson to Peter Green. Once you heard that, and understood that you too could something with that, there was the liberation. You could actually do your own thing and stretch it to include things about your own environment. Nobody had looked at that way of doing things before Lennon and Barrett in particular, because everyone else was working in a completely American idiom, albeit it with flashes of Britishness. "Arnold Layne" had nothing to do with the blues on one hand, but somewhere distantly behind it is a lyrical liberation that comes from knowing about the blues. When the Kinks started they were your basic R&B band until they started doing English subjects. I started liking the Kinks when they did "Waterloo Sunset". Certainly, Barrett was closer to me because of the people we had in common. His music made more of an impression on me. Obviously "Strawberry Fields/Penny Lane" was an important record as well.'

The bands in the tightly insular British music scene of the mid sixties were constantly influencing each other. It's easy to forget just how small London and England were in proportion to the musical, fashion, social and cultural influence it had. The English music weeklies reported minute trends in exhaustive detail every week, informing both the public and musicians. Bands influenced each other to a degree uncommon elsewhere. It was as if Britain was a laboratory where innovations occurred daily. There was a closed feedback loop between the Floyd and their contemporaries.

The B-side of the single was 'Candy And A Currant Bun'. The song had begun as 'Let's Roll Another One', an unsubtle ode to the joys of smoking dope, but EMI balked. Once again, the Floyd were forced to acquiesce. 'We had to change all the lyrics,' said Waters, 'because it was about rolling joints. It was called "Let's Roll Another One" and we had to change the title to "Candy And A Currant Bun" and it had lines in it like, "Tastes good if you eat it right . . ." No, they did not like that at all.'[53] When told to change the words to 'Let's Roll Another One', a mischievous (and rather annoyed) Syd snuck in the word 'fuck' into the rewritten version. 'Candy And A Currant Bun', none the less, was still a drug song, and everyone on the scene knew what Syd meant. Like Toad in *The Wind In The Willows*, Syd was being a playful rascal, but it seems now that he was beginning to chafe at the bit. At this point, however, he was playing along with the pop star routine, keeping one eye on the charts. It wasn't until the steamroller of fame picked up momentum though, that *Top Of The Pops* and endless out of London gigs began to seem an extremely onerous chore.

On 'Candy And A Currant Bun', Syd already was in full possession of the technical skill that would fire their début album, *The Piper At The Gates Of Dawn*. His masterful guitar and Binson manipulation techniques were firmly in place. Indeed, 'Candy And A Currant Bun' is often overlooked, especially in light of the fact that very few people have heard it due to its limited availability, but the composition contains some of Barrett's most fully realised guitar effects. It's said to be derived from the Yardbird's version of 'Smokestack Lightning', but a more direct precursor would be the Byrd's 'Eight Miles High', from which Barrett borrowed the final ascending riff in that song's coda. The song is quite advanced, with sinister minor chords in the choruses that predate Gothic rock by twenty years. Waters augments the menacing feel of the song with a droning one-chord bass line below the choruses, giving the song a menacing feel.

Sessions for the untitled début album began at EMI on 15 March, with versions of 'Chapter 24' and a short version of 'Interstellar Overdrive'. These were two-track demos. The following day, work began on 'Flame' (which would metamorphose into 'Flaming').

On 'Interstellar Overdrive' Norman Smith used the recording levels on his console with deft skill, carefully drawing out the subtleties of one layer while obscuring the more dissonant textures from the other. The mix is a successful combination of potentially jarring individual tracks, something his mentor George Martin was particularly adept at. Barrett would expertly counterpoint Waters' massed chords with sharp, echo-repeated single-note stabs. The stage was set for Pink Floyd's future explorations; the central jam in 'Interstellar Overdrive' could almost segue into 'Let There Be More Light' on Pink Floyd's second album, 1968's *A Saucerful Of Secrets.*

We are fortunate to have several different versions of 'Interstellar Overdrive', including the early 1967 Whitehead version, an acetate of the short version recorded on 16 March, at least one UFO version, a snippet from Canadian radio in late 1966 and two live versions. The rendering on *The Piper At The Gates Of Dawn* was a combination of the first version, recorded on the 16th, and a second overdub on the 22nd; an acetate survives of Pink Floyd's *The Piper At The Gates Of Dawn* version of 'Interstellar Overdrive' without the overdubbed second layer. It's haunting for the pregnant shades of silence and space when the band drops into their improvisation. Syd's guitar slows down in increments, like Apollo rockets separating in a silent burst. It highlights his genius at atmospherics and ambient tonalities. Wright, thinking in tandem, drops the volume, slipping into the lower registers on his organ, complementing Barrett's guitar excursion. It's a musical exploration of the first order. At seven minutes into 'Interstellar Overdrive', the composition ranks with Stravinsky's *Rites Of Spring* in its mapping out of a new parameter in music. Barrett rides a crescendo of glissando guitar, giving way to an exploratory improvisation of the first order, one single note repeated to hypnotic effect with organ, and Binson echo layered in the background. It's remarkable the wonder Smith and Bown were able to produce, considering the technical limitations of their four-track equipment. The choice of Smith would be a mixed blessing. The downside was his stolid and defined ideas of production, the plus was his underrated ear for ambience. Peter Bown, the engineer, also brought great skill in mixing to the production of the first album. Engineer Peter Bown recalled his arrival at the studio that night, his first night's work with the Pink Floyd: 'I had certainly never heard anything quite like it, and I don't think I ever did again. It was very exciting.'[54]

The finished album rides a see-saw of moods, with tightly compressed guitar parts such as the opening riff to 'Lucifer Sam' contrasting sharply with the free-form 'space' sections of 'Interstellar Overdrive'.

One of the things that makes *The Piper At The Gates Of Dawn* an enduring work is its evocation of a very specific and thoroughly imaginary world, that inside Syd Barrett's mind, a strange light refracted through the prism of his eyes. The album evokes a slightly claustrophobic Victorian house of strange deserted rooms filled chock a block with mysterious ephemera. On 'Matilda Mother' Barrett's image of 'the doll's house darkness, old perfume' captures this slightly sinister evocation of childhood. Even on the oceanic middle passages of 'Interstellar Overdrive', where the mood evokes the infinite reaches of space, the feeling is one of being on-board the spaceship in Kubrick's *2001: A Space Odyssey* or in Tarkovsky's *Solaris,* claustrophobic in the midst of vast, empty space.

Smith and Barrett would have a contentious relationship in the studio, especially towards the latter half of 1967, with Smith questioning Barrett's more *outré* ideas. But there was method to Barrett's madness, even as he strummed endless solos, sitting barefoot in EMI's Studio Two. Although the sessions were the source of apparent indifference to him, and his Zen-like insistence on 'first take, best take' spontaneity irritated Smith, the songs themselves were tightly structured, well thought out and had been prepared in Earlham Street after days or weeks of continual playing. The ideas came quickly to Barrett, but the refining process took ages. Like Hendrix, Barrett later became excessively orientated towards jamming as a method of accessing the creative muse. But in Earlham Street, Barrett was judiciously editing and reworking his compositions before he tried them out on-stage or in the studio.

Despite the personality differences between Smith and Barrett, there was common ground as well. Smith had engineered all the Beatles albums through 1965's *Rubber Soul* and was adept at the arduous cut-and-paste editing required for their four-track masterpieces. Having learned his craft under the tutelage of Beatles' producer George Martin, he was singularly qualified to handle the Pink Floyd epic soundscapes. This was to be his first album as producer and he would take pains to ensure a high-quality recording.

As an added surprise to their first EMI sessions, Roger Waters said, 'I remember the first sessions we did at Abbey Road on four-track. The Beatles were making *Sergeant Pepper* in the other studio. At about five-thirty in the afternoon Ringo, Paul and George came into our studios and we all stood rooted to the spot, excited by it all.'[55] Rick Wright told German newspaper *Hannoversche Allgemeine Zeitung*. 'I remember John Lennon was extremely unfriendly, Paul McCartney on the other hand showed interest.' 'We were taken in to meet them once,' says Mason, 'while they were recording Lovely Rita". It was a bit like meeting the Royal Family.'[56]

Miles was also on hand. 'It was really extraordinary because the Floyd were so naive, they were saying "Can you hear me?" because of the soundproof glass, not realising that the mikes were on. It was complete innocence, very touching really. And Paul was patting them on the back, saying they were great and were going to do fine. He wasn't being patronising; it was almost like the Beatles passing on the mantle, at least some of it, and acknowledging the existence of a new generation of music. In my discussions with him, McCartney had always been convinced that there would be a new synthesis of electronic music and studio techniques and rock'n'roll. He didn't see the Beatles as being quite the vehicle for that. But the Pink Floyd, he thought, were the very stuff that we'd been talking about.'[57]

Paul McCartney said, 'You'd go down UFO and see the early incarnation of the Floyd. They'd be down there, a lot of projections, lots of people sort of wandering about, that was nice; it was all like a trippy adventure playground really. Chaplin films going here, Marx Brothers here, Floyd up there, conjurer over here or something, just a nice circus-cum-adventure playground.'[58]

On 20 March, the Pink Floyd started work on Roger Waters' 'Take Up Thy Stethoscope and Walk', Barrett's playful 'The Gnome' and evocative 'The Scarecrow'. Work also began on 'Pow R. Toc H.'. The following day work continued on 'Pow R. Toc H.', and on the 22nd, they once again tackled 'Interstellar Overdrive'.

'Pow R. Toc H.' draws its title in part from the 'Toc H' huts where soldiers in the First World War used to gather between breaks in the fighting. The song, a live showcase throughout 1967, along with 'Interstellar Overdrive', is the closest approximation we have on their début album to the live Floyd sound during 1967. Crude versions of the song exist on the two known recorded 1967 concerts. The album's 'Pow R. Toc H.' features Roger Waters and Syd doing vocal effects which mimic the sound of a train's steam whistle. Steam whistles of trains turn into a salvo of strange Fenland animal noises and croaking frogs, illustrating how deeply rooted Syd and Roger's sense of nature was. The sonic mayhem, drawn from the sounds of their youth, calling up images of walks in the Fen Causeway during the idle torpor of summer. Waters was instrumental in helping develop these sound effects. Nick Mason said, 'How "Pow R. Toc H." started was just one geezer would go up to the microphone and go, "Ba boom chi chi, Ba boom chi chi" and everyone picked up on it, and then the drums picked up and that was more or less that.'[59] Even at this early stage, Andrew King noted: 'Roger and Syd were already working at a tangent to each other. I remember watching Roger do his strange vocal parts on "Pow R. Toc H." and being slightly worried because it was so far removed from Syd's more lyrical stuff.'[60]

The Piper At The Gates Of Dawn is rife with sound effects facilatated by Norman Smith and Peter Bown, drawing from a long tradition of technical experts fascinated by the vagaries of sound. The sound effects emerge like radio emissions from the ether, like an errant reception of Radio Caroline.

'The "Scarecrow"'s clip-clop effects are Roger's and Syd's evocation of horses' hooves cantering down the deserted back roads of Cambridge's Fen Causeway. Echoes of ancient folk tunes with its plaintive flutes. 'The Scarecrow' was a prophetic song in a sense. A scarecrow, a lifeless and inert approximation of a man, is a superb metaphor for the catatonia that would strike Barrett during his breakdown. In the song, the very birds the scarecrow is supposed to scare away stand on his head, picking out the straw that holds him together, the very stuff of which this shadow of Syd is made. The scarecrow stands in a field with his straw scattered around him, but he doesn't care. The wind and mice, both negative archetypes, are the only signs of life. Barrett seems to have presaged his own literal and mental exile using clever poetic metaphor.

Syd's deep immersion in his work was a gift and a curse. His creations were such an inimitable extension of his self that his very fate might have been bound up in their success or failure. His songs began to determine his persona as much as his persona determined his songs. This lack of division would ultimately erode his own perhaps already fragile sense of self. In a sense, his fate was tied to the quality and clarity of his output. As he himself became disorganised, afflicted by the chaos of excessive LSD use, so would his songs reflect this turbulence.

Like Jeff Beck or Pete Townshend, Barrett was carrying rhythm and lead guitar roles simultaneously, and while this better allows the guitar player to bend and experiment with rhythms, it can become an onerous chore, making it difficult to maintain steady tempo. The rhythm guitarist in a standard four-piece rock band give the lead player a sounding board on which to test ideas, to keep steady time, and to alleviate the task of reproducing all the guitar parts live. The Pink Floyd endlessly experimented on-stage with riffs and phrases developed during their lengthy improvisations. Pieces were freely taken from their longer pieces for insertion into what would become the songs on their first album.

Roger Waters's bass picks up the rhythm, often helping to carry the melody, something that provides 'Set The Controls For The Heart Of The Sun' with its strong rhythmic pulse. Waters may not have had the best ear, or the best timing, but he's an effective bassist, drawing from feel rather than expertise. At his best, he provides a solid counterpoint to Barrett's guitar. It's noteworthy that on the *Piper* version of 'Interstellar Overdrive', the rhythm section, Mason and Waters, are mixed to the right, while the melodic team of Wright and Barrett are mixed to the left. The split in the stereo spectrum mirrors the split in the Pink Floyd's music; part of the edginess that seeps into their tracks comes from the contention, both musical and personal, between the two sides of the group.

An April Fool's Day press reception was held at Manchester Square's EMI House. Hoary old executives, Beecher Stevens, Ron White and Roy Featherstone, presided and presented their latest pop sensations to the overground media. In their press release, EMI announced the Pink Floyd as 'musical spokesmen for a new movement which involves experimentation in all the arts, including music'. The record company's old guard were the day's April Fools, however, as they concluded, 'The Pink Floyd does not know what people mean by psychedelic pop and are not trying to create hallucinatory effects on their audiences'. Even in the early spring of 1967, the term 'psychedelic' alarmed EMI; they were anxious to avoid having any drug connotations associated with the band.

Mason was dubious of the psychedelic tag, 'You have to be careful when you start on this psychedelic thing. We don't call ourselves a psychedelic group or say that we play psychedelic pop music. It's just that people associate us with this, and we get employed all the time at the various freak-outs and happenings in London. Let's face it, there isn't really a definition for the word "psychedelic". It's something that has taken around us, not within us.'[61] Later, 'psychedelic' would have cheap trendy connotations. It was a term designed to describe an experience but became a new way to package a product, for the same reasons records have bar codes. Artists especially resent labelling; there has always been a tug of war between art and commerce regarding labels – labels make it easier for the businessmen to sell their product, and artists instinctively distrust this. In the up-and-down pop music market of 1967 musicians were especially wary of having their music labelled, knowing that labels carry expiration dates. Barrett said, 'People can call it anything they like, we don't like labels to be stuck on things, but as long as they listen, I don't object.'[62]

That evening the Pink Floyd rushed off to play a gig at the aptly-named Birdcage in Portsmouth. 'The others were happy to make the money and happy to take the money,' says Peter Wynne-Wilson. 'And I don't know if that was their goal from the start, but it certainly very rapidly became the focus. That's not to say that Syd didn't enjoy spending money; he did. Probably spent it more recklessly than the others did. And not that there were great amounts of it around really, very small quantities really. But with the record contract there was a decided shift in atmosphere. I probably would have said they began to take themselves too seriously, but I don't know that that's necessarily fair because they had very serious success, so it would be silly to say that they took themselves too seriously. It most certainly wasn't an Underground scene then.'

The money from their EMI advance went quickly. They purchased a Rolls Royce. 'I was the only person who drove it because nobody else was insured. It cost about a grand,' said secretary June Bolan, 'not very much. It was the band car, very smart, very grand. A proper old Rolls Royce. Automatic drive, power steering.'[63] 'I splashed out a couple of hundred on a new guitar,' said Syd Barrett.[64] Shown holding this new guitar in the signing photo sessions, Syd rarely played the Danelectro.

On 3 April, the Pink Floyd appeared on radio's *Monday, Monday* for a live session broadcast from the BBC Playhouse Theatre, and played both sides of their single. Their film clip for 'Arnold Layne' was screened on *Top Of The Pops* as well.

Meanwhile, Syd and Lindsay Korner had taken up residence at 101 Cromwell Road. The pair had been an on-again off-again couple since Cambridge days, but had been living together since Earlham Street, and had settled into a steady relationship. Jenny Gordon says, 'Syd and Lindsay were in Cambridge when they first started going out.' Maldwyn Thomas, a former mod who was drawn into the Underground, recalled the residents of the fabled flat, 'They were a Cambridge lot, Cambridge freaks. Duggie Fields painted abstracts in tiny little dots, rather like Seurat. But it was very much Syd's place. He was the central figure there. "Going down to 101, man?" "Think I will." It was very handy for the Cromwellian club, which was nearby.'[65] The Cromwell flat, since 1965, had been a critical nexus for Underground (and illicit) activities of every shade and stripe. Painters, musicians, eccentrics, mystics and freaks mixed with film stars, pop icons and slumming hip young aristocrats. Duggie Fields remembers when Syd moved in, '[The Pink Floyd] used to rehearse in the flat, and I used to go downstairs and put on Smokey Robinson as loud as possible. I just remember suddenly being surrounded by the Pink Floyd and hundreds of groupies instantly.'[66]

Nigel Gordon says, 'We didn't really care about LSD being made illegal. I wasn't on any particular quest to have drugs legalised. We lived outside the law anyway, it was just another thing that the authorities were doing.' Jenny Gordon agrees, 'Because *we* were illegal, the police were always coming round. People wanted to put acid in the water supply. One of the Ormsby-Gore's had put LSD in the tea of the woman next to her at the hairdressers!' Nigel Gordon says, 'There were great trips I took there. Trips were very personal anyway. As long as you are in the right set and setting, without hostile people.' Dr Timothy Leary's advice to users of psychedelics was to observe the basic guidelines of 'set and setting'; basically that one's mental state ('set') and actual physical surroundings and company ('setting') were a key in having a positive acid trip. 'I used to sit and stare into honey pots and watch the light bend and refract, watching the universe being reborn, stirring it slightly. I used to discuss alchemy with Stash de Rola. We got off on the quest for the Holy Grail, Arthurian legend, alchemy, the elixir of life,' explains Nigel.*

Jenny Gordon says, 'Bill Barlow was the master renter. Nigel and I, John Tate (who built a tiny room in the attic, earning him the name 'The Spider'), Chris Case, who was also at Cambridge but didn't finish his degree; all on our floor. Briony Pane lived there as well, she lived with Bill Barlow. There would be other people who would come in all the time.' Nigel Gordon says, 'People were in and out all the time because of the LSD. In between our rooms, there was peculiar man called Alberto Poliblanc, who was a lecturer, a total mystery and a hermit. There was a flat on the top where Duggie Fields lived, and Dick Bett. Upstairs, where Syd lived they were all students.'

Nigel Gordon says, 'I remember one occasion when Vince Taylor, the rock star, came back from being in France and came over to Cromwell. It turned out that he had been taking a lot of LSD and had figured out this grand cosmology where all the different rock stars represented Greek mythological deities. A pantheon of gods which he'd figured out, and were interchangeable. He figured he'd take over P.J. Proby's place in this pantheon! His explanation went on for hours,

*'I wrote a script for Mick Jagger, about this quest for the Holy Grail, something Marianne Faithful could star in. I was trying to make films all the time. Mick Jagger gave me some money for it, I wrote it, and finished it in India, and when I got back I read it to him and he liked it. I don't know why the film on the Holy Grail never got made, but there was another attempt to do it, with Donovan. Marianne Faithful was going to play the Lady of Shallot. Donovan wrote the music and we filmed him on his boat all around the Greek Islands.'

and was very entertaining.'

'There were always people at Cromwell,' says Jenny Gordon, 'there was one gorgeous girl who was sixteen, if that, who spent one whole summer rolling opium, smoking it, and not going out. We didn't see her as dysfunctional. Her mother had a bit of a problem with it, and called the police. We had a girl who turned up who was definitely mentally subnormal, about eleven, and we don't know where she came from. Hester Page and Sue Kingsford found her on the street and brought her in, we kept her for the weekend, and then she went home but kept running away to Cromwell and the police were always after her. She was in care somewhere and she had never had such a good time as when she was with us. She was allowed to be part of things.'

On 7 April the Pink Floyd played the Floral Hall in Belfast, where the Irish lost their collective head over the band. In light of the mainstream success of 'Arnold Layne', for the first time they had a brigade of screamers, swooning and calling out 'Syd!' or 'Rick!' The next day they played at the Rhodes Centre, Bishops Stortford, before driving back to play at the 'All Night Light Show Continuum' at the Roundhouse, another 10 pm to dawn rave with the Flies, Earl Fuggle and the Electric Poets, the Block and Sandy and Narda dancers, Sam Gopal tabla, films and lights by Patrik Trevor. The Flies, whom Miles has cited as the world's first punk band and who performed their ragtag songs wearing palm-leaf skirts and warpaint, stood by the side of the stage screaming 'Sell Out!' at the Pink Floyd for the duration of their performance; it seems the Pink Floyd had committed the heinous crime of releasing a pop single. Syd was particularly taken aback by these freaks, and the image of flies would crop up later in his songs as symbols of death and decay.

On 11 April, the Pink Floyd were back at EMI to work on 'Astronomy Domine' and 'Percy The Ratcatcher' (alias 'Lucifer Sam'). 'Astronomy Domine', destined to be the opener for the album, was a staple of their live set since the Spontaneous Underground. The introduction featured manager Peter Jenner reading off the names of horoscopes and planets through a megaphone, double-tracked and mixed to the right of the stereo spectrum, in a presumably accidental approximation of the never fully-audible chattering voices of schizophrenia. Barrett's staccato Telecaster riff thunders to life with an ominous staccato rhythm, while Wright leans in with Morse-code blips played on his organ and fed through his Binson unit. Mason enters with a drum roll which sets the stage for Barrett's opening lead, bleeding to the right in the stereo spectrum. The organ, bass and guitar are pushed to fore in the sheer intensity of the statement of the central riff, with its thunderous and compressed Rickenbacker bass. Wright and Barrett, carrying the melody on the left, while Barrett's frenetic choppy rhythm guitar skates uneasily over Mason and Waters' rhythm section, Waters playing swooping bass lines evocative of the Who's John Entwistle. The verse opens with Syd and Rick intoning 'Lime and limpid green...' set to a droning E that drops to Eb, leaving us hanging in expectation. Like a roller-coaster rising to its apex with slowly grinding gears, Syd lands with a thud on G. He backtracks to A before landing back on the opening E, but only for a moment, because then he's back on G, which gives the false impression of resolution, sweetening slightly to G#, and then – he's off! Awash in echo delay, Syd descends into the bridge, free-falling through the octaves with barre chords until he lands with a full stop on E. The band falls away, all except for Wright's swelling organ chord. Syd's Binson rings out with a sampled note, and with great instinctive musicianship Barrett plays counterpoint to himself, each secondary note ringing out from his Telecaster a millisecond faster than the 'sample' emanating from the Binson. The echo swells to a thunderous crescendo, arriving at the very cusp of distortion before Syd tears away, off on another tangent altogether. A stark solo with those trebly notes and glissandi which approximate a bow being drawn across a violin ensues. A chant emerges in the song's coda based on a two-note metronomic phrase, both monotonous and trance-like, as Barrett and Wright intone in relay chorus: 'Lime *and* lim*pid* green the *sound* sur*rounds* the icy wa*ters* under*ground*'. Barrett's genius is laid out here for all to hear, startling with the brilliance of his Binson echo-unit experiments. Barrett here sounds unlike any of his peers; the closest parallel would be producer King Tubby's or Lee Perry's dub reggae work. Critic Simon Reynolds noted in *Wire* magazine, 'This is a genuine post-rock, because the guitar is no longer kinetic (a riff machine) but atmospheric (a texture and timbre generator). Fed through effects pedals and signal-processing devices, the guitar effectively becomes a kind of analog synthesiser. Syd Barrett with his use of slide to create a fractal chaos . . . got to this re- or un-invention of the guitar first.'

The discordant squalls, composed of echo-drenched notes churning out of space for a second, rising to the brink of distortion, only to be reabsorbed an instant later; with the imprimatur of genius, Barrett makes it all sound so simple. The complex is rendered simple by a few deft strokes of a master's brush. The complexities of the logic behind the inner machinations are hidden by the cloak of simplicity. The solid rhythmic grounding provides the basis from which Barrett's glissando guitar can trace filigree patterns through the air like the mathematician bordering his page of equations with a pattern of ornamental leaves . . . The listener, from the very first bars of *The Piper At The Gates Of Dawn*, is utterly compelled to follow Barrett's tangents, as if being led by a ten-year-old Roger Barrett into the wild woods at the edge of town that your mother told you to never play in.

There was a marked dichotomy between the short cannabis-inspired songs of Syd Barrett, such as 'The Scarecrow', and the Pink Floyd's extended freak-out jams, like 'Interstellar Overdrive'. The short songs dated largely from Cambridge and early London days in Highgate and Earlham Street; these were Barrett's songs of innocence and largely bewildered experience, as he explored dualities between lyrics and melody. The improvisations on themes like

'Interstellar Overdrive' were born out of his increasing usage of acid.

Gale says, 'The kind of meandering style that they pioneered presumably grew out of LSD because it was music to be contemplated at that great length, while See Emily Play", for example, was a more jolly cannabis song. It's worth looking into whether Syd's early compositions were inspired by cannabis, and the longer pieces, where he and Waters and Wright started hacking out vast oceanic washes of sound, were LSD-inspired.

But there was a growing schism also reflected in this duality. The short songs, perhaps, had been the product of Roger Barrett, Cambridge youth and aspirant London musician. The long jams were the product of this half-invented apparition Syd Barrett, a creature who danced under the psychedelic lights at UFO, the veritable Piper at the Gates of Dawn, exchanging his pan pipes for a guitar.

There was a conflict between the two sides. Syd was under pressure to make saleable material; as Peter Jenner noted, in the short-term this was probably beneficial, in that it forced him to condense his voyages of the imagination into concise descriptions. These short songs were melodic and lyrical. His UFO freak-outs were primarily instrumental, alternately harsh and ethereal. They gave Barrett a chance to explore a potent form of non-verbal communication with his audience, a chance to discover subtle nuances between tones and feedback. The struggle between Barrett's lyrics-driven songs and his electric glissando guitar distortion epics reflected the conflict within Barrett himself. The freak-out jams were largely intuitive and spontaneous, aiming to break the barriers of consciousness expansion. The short, playful, mystic songs were logical, precise in their evocation of images through lyrics. Syd's solo songs have a curious habit of being incredibly specific in their detail, yet completely vague. His concentration on minutiae rather than conventional narrative reflects the destabilising effect of acid.

'Barrett's rhythms were usually unpredictable; one never knew what process in Syd's brain dictated when to speed up or slow down the pace, when to sweeten or sour the sound, and when to wrench the tempo totally out of joint, shifting gears to turn rhythms inside-out,'[67] wrote Kris DiLorenzo.

One of acid's features is its ability to induce oscillations in time/space relationships. Time alternately slows or speeds, and for a musician, this affects tempo and time signature as well. For the next year, Barrett was able to use this to his advantage. Eventually though, LSD's time and space distorting effects would cripple his ability to manipulate tempo.

On *The Piper At The Gates Of Dawn*, this duality is pointed up by the juxtaposition of 'Interstellar Overdrive' segueing directly into 'The Gnome', its metronomic bass intro and tight structure a stabilising and startling change after 'Interstellar Overdrive's free-form looseness. 'The Gnome' was a playful ode to the sort of creatures found in Tolkien's *The Hobbit*; 'a no-name grimble gromble', a grimble being a gnome in Old English. 'The Gnome', of all Barrett's songs, most closely echoes the Cantabrigian folk songs or nursery rhymes of his childhood.* 'The Gnome' draws inspiration from the faux-Elizabethan air of the Rolling Stones's 'Lady Jane', as well as the pastoral stylings of the Incredible String Band.

These short cannabis-inspired songs dated back to lazy summer days by the River Cam or in the unpressured surrounding of 2 Earlham Street. In contrast to his solo outings, they are playful and happy songs. The UFO live material was free-form, experimental to the point of anarchy, chaotic. This was in sharp contrast to the concise musical and narrative structures of Syd's short songs. The sound effects in these songs are drawn largely from, and heavily grounded in, the parallel worlds of nature, childhood and dreams. The long improvisations were largely abstract, mechanical, electronic and evocative of the other worldly, of the interstellar.

'The Floyd were playing the perfect music for what was happening at that moment, it was getting looser and looser,' Peter Whitehead told *Record Collector*. 'People were going to UFO, stoned out of their minds on acid, and that just changes your perception of time. You're not interested in songs that last for two minutes thirty-seven seconds. There is no point. They were taking a number of basic elements from pop music, but Syd was pushing it into as many directions as he could away from all that. Roger was trying to hold that back.'

Syd's increasing drug use was beginning to alarm his bandmates. The others hardly touched drugs. Nick Mason stated, 'Well, possibly a tiny bit of dope smoking but certainly not tripping on the same scale the management certainly were![68] Some of us never really did it. Syd was the big acid freak. It was never a big thing, and it stopped very early.'[69] 'Roger wasn't into LSD, nor was he enthusiastic about it,' says David Gale. 'He had a much stronger, inflexible ego structure. Syd by temperament was highly experimental and hedonistic. He was very fit and healthy, he always seemed to bounce back.' Rick Wright had taken acid once, before joining the Pink Floyd. Waters didn't trip until 1969, when he, Wright and Nigel Gordon all tripped while travelling around the Greek islands. Wright never took acid again, and Waters was to have only one other trip, in the early seventies, before forswearing it all together. Mason said, 'Syd was a walking example of why not to.'[70] Peter Wynne-Wilson says, 'I didn't ever take a trip with Rick, but I'm sure he would have taken acid at that time, though not on a regular basis. Not that I knew what "regular" means in that context. Rick definitely smoked, quite a lot, but he was quite introverted. Roger smoked a bit, but only as an adjunct to alcohol.' Peter Jenner said, 'None of them did drugs when I met them, except Syd, and he would only smoke dope. Then with the Summer Of Love and all that bollocks, Syd got very enthusiastic about acid, and got into the religious aspect of it, which I never did. The others were very straight. They were much more into half a pint of bitter than they were into drugs.'[71]

*Fittingly, Neil the Hippie lampooned 'The Gnome' on television's 'The Young Ones'.

On 17 and 18 April, the Pink Floyd laboured once more on overdubs for 'Astronomy Domine'. On the 18th, the Pink Floyd tried out a song that has never seen the light of day, 'She Was A Millionaire', and work on 'Percy The Ratcatcher', now renamed 'Lucifer Sam', was completed. Cliff Jones noted the influence of Bo Diddley's 'I Ain't Got You' on this track. Barrett, alluding to the undertow of paranoia in the song, cryptically said, '"Lucifer Sam" didn't mean much to me at the time, but then three or four months later it came to mean a lot.'[72] An ode to a cat named Lucifer Sam, who stirs Syd's paranoia as he pads around, always underfoot and watching with fixed staring eyes, the song bears a resemblance to the Byrd's 'Eight Miles High', opening with a chord suspended for an instant, before Syd's enters with a descending scale, Mason riding the cymbals and Water playing thunderous bass. 'Lucifer Sam' also betrays a debt to surf rock, particularly the Ventures 1960 'Walk, Don't Run', a popular tune for Cambridge amateur bands. Syd rises and falls through scales, perpetually ascending and descending – a Barrett trademark – similar to Coltrane's 'sheets of sound'. 'Lucifer Sam' pre-dates the urgency of punk, as Barrett plays frenetic rhythm guitar with lightning-fast fingering, approximating a cello being rapidly bowed. Its intense rhythm sounds like a cross between a Bo Diddley rave-up and the Beatles' 1966 'Tomorrow Never Knows', the very song that helped psychedelia reach critical mass. Of all Syd's Pink Floyd era songs, it sounds the most contemporary. 'Lucifer Sam' is still given an occasional airing in London clubs like 'Blow Up', where it fits in seamlessly with other exotica on offer, and people dance to it on crowded dancefloors.

The *Melody Maker* ran an announcement of *The Life Story Of Percy The Ratcatcher*, a half-hour film which the Pink Floyd were going to start shooting sequences for on 24 April, revolving around the cat who would later be featured in 'Lucifer Sam'. Unfortunately, nothing came of it, but it illustrates the Pink Floyd's growing interest in multi-media. Waters in particular was to retain an interest in film and larger theatrical events.

On 22 April, 'Arnold Layne' peaked at number twenty on the pop charts. But at a gig at the Feathers Club, Ealing Broadway, on 24 April an unfortunate incident occurred. 'The worst thing that ever happened to me was at the Feathers Club,' said Roger Waters. Some yobbo from the audience, perhaps indignant at having to pay seven shillings and sixpence to hear thirty minutes of 'Interstellar Overdrive', reached into his pocket and threw a heavy penny coin directly at Roger Waters' forehead. 'It made a bloody great cut in the middle of my forehead. I bled quite a lot. And I stood right at the front of the stage to see if I could see him throw one. I was glowering in a real rage, and I was going to leap out into the audience and get him. Happily, there was one freak who turned up who liked us, so the audience spent the whole evening beating the shit out of him and left us alone.'[73] The Pink Floyd's twenty-plus-minutes freak-out jams were bound to cause confusion and hostility in their unsuspecting audiences. The

Floyd were simply light-years apart from the hard driving, amphetamine-fuelled mod R&B of such contemporaries as Geno Washington and the Ram Jam band.

Early in the morning of 29 April, an exhausted Pink Floyd departed for the Netherlands, where they were filmed for an appearance on a Dutch TV show called *Fan Club*. That very same night they were scheduled to close the multi-band extravaganza known in hippie lore as the 14 Hour Technicolor Dream. They drove back from Holland that night, doing the tedious ferry crossing over the English Channel, stopping in briefly at Edbrooke Road, where an exhausted Jenner and Syd each dropped a tab of acid before driving to north London's Muswell Hill in their cramped car.

Like the 1965 Albert Hall poetry reading, the event marked a turning point in the London Underground, and was indeed a highlight event of the sixties. An estimated 7,000 punters crowded into the massive Alexandra Palace, which was hired out for the night by Hoppy and Dave Hewson. The idea of renting out this vast place had been germinating in Hoppy's mind since he had first been there when the Stones and John Lee Hooker played in 1964. The Technicolor Dream had been envisioned by Hoppy as a 'giant benefit against fuzz action', as the ads carried in the *Melody Maker* attested. 'Fuzz action' was the sort that had attempted to shut down *IT*, and the ostensible purpose of the Technicolor Dream was to raise funds for *IT's* legal defence fund. It began at 8 p.m. and went through until 10 a.m. the next morning. Hoppy and Suzy Creamcheese stood at the door, collecting tickets and, in their inimitable style, greeting everyone.

The armies of nascent hippiedom duly congregated at the gates and filed in. Much of the audience came in ties and blazers, with a generous assortment of kaftan and bell-wearing ravers among them. For many it proved to be an epochal experience, as they saw for the first time that they weren't the only freaks in London. Two film crews were on hand to film the proceedings. Peter Whitehead, director of *Tonite Let's Make Love In London*, fought for vantage points with a film crew from the BBC, who presented a live airing of the event on BBC2.

Indica gallery owner John Dunbar was at John Lennon's home that evening, 'We were all down in Weybridge, and we were watching TV and suddenly saw that this thing was going on. So we thought, fuck it, let's go! We ended up at this place where everybody I'd ever known in my life swam before my eyes at one time or another. All eyes were vaguely on us because we were with John, and I literally saw people I'd last seen at kindergarten and hadn't seen since.'[74]

This was perhaps the high-water mark for the Underground; a party the Underground threw to celebrate itself. The Underground and the vibe cultivated at UFO certainly went overground on this night, gathering momentum, but, some would argue, losing its integrity. The small London coterie would send out ripples that would affect many of the world's young people one way or another in the coming years; but this was to be the grand night of all nights for the

Underground. It was certainly a show of force, as Wholly Communion had been, simply by virtue of having so many young people under one roof. This wasn't a gig or mundane pop show, rather this was an event like the poetry reading that galvanised the Underground and brought diverse pockets of 'freaks' and 'hippies' out of the woodwork.

Word of the event had spread throughout London, and expectations were high. Two stages had been erected inside the cavernous hall: a smaller central stage designed for poets, performance artists and dancers, jugglers, the Tribe Of The Sacred Mushroom, Philippine dancer David Medalla and the Exploding Galaxy dance troupe, and the larger stage for the main events was built along the back wall, flanked by the large glass windows of the Palace. Jack Henry Moore and a small army of technicians were constantly dashing from one spot to another, fixing lights and wiring speakers. The fluted columns that rose to the high ceiling resembled, if one was stoned enough, Aubrey Beardsley's lilies, rising forty feet above the concrete floors. Light shows galore lit up every inch of available wall space from a massive gantry in the centre of the hall. Underground films, notably the horrid *Flaming Creatures*, were screened on billowing white sheets taped with electrician's tape to the scaffolding housing the Alexandra Palace organ. The centrepiece was a helter skelter, rented for the night, which people clambered to the top of and spiralled down.

The first of the forty-odd bands, poets, artists and dancers who played that night, was the brilliantly abysmal agit-rockers the Social Deviants , who took the stage at 8 p.m. For the better of the night and morning, two bands played simultaneously on the two stages, often causing an unexpected merger of styles but mostly causing a headache as the sound reverberated off the walls. Some bright spark of a chemist had chosen the event as the world première of STP, an insane drug which makes you feel like one of the bulls at Pamplona, charging around with a head full of steam. None the less, the mood was very positive, as smiling, colourfully dressed people endlessly milled with chemical quicksteps from corner to corner of the vast edifice. A plastic igloo had been set up in one corner, where a laughing Suzy Creamcheese dispensed banana-skin joints, touted for their hallucinogenic effects. A bitter aftertaste really was all it left one with, but one simply had to laugh at the incongruity of standing in the midst of this mad, milling throng smoking a banana!

The acts on hand included American black comedian/activist Dick Gregory, Yoko Ono, artists Binder Edwards and Vaughn (famous for painting pop stripes on a Cadillac and displaying it in a gallery), Ron Geesin (who later did the orchestrations for Pink Floyd's 1970 *Atom Heart Mother*), Barry Fantoni, Scottish author Alexander Trocchi of *Cain's Book* fame, Christopher Logue, poet Michael Horovitz and his New Departures team, the 26 Kingly Street group, (the brilliantly titled) the Utterly Incredible Too Long Ago To Remember Sometimes Shouting At People, Alexis Korner, Champion Jack Dupree, Graham Bond, Ginger Johnson and his African conga drummers, Savoy Brown, 117, the

Pretty Things, the proto-punk band the Flies, the Purple Gang, the Crazy World Of Arthur Brown, the Soft Machine and, top billed, the Pink Floyd.

Mick Farren of the Deviants, said, 'It was damned good, the Alexandra Palace was such a beautiful place anyway. And there were mounds of speakers and light. And everybody who had been fucking around in a small environment got to go completely nuts . . . There were about 10,000 in the audience and a certain kind of exponential curve seemed to be setting in, which led some people to believe that we would now conquer the planet.'[75]

Peter Jenner remembers the 14 Hour Technicolor Dream: 'That *really* was a psychedelic experience. That really was the most psychedelic experience that I've ever been to. At least half the audience were doing acid. I was doing acid. We'd had to take a long drive to get there from a gig in Holland, and I did the last bit of the drive in the van. We dropped in at home and I did some acid before we went, and by the time I got to Alexandra Palace the old acid was beginning to go and trying to drive the van was getting quite exciting.[76] It started coming on as we were being directed in. I had to steer the van in through something very tiny with lots of people wandering around absolutely out of their crust.'[77] Nick Mason stated, 'We'd played a gig in Holland that same night and we didn't get to Alexandra Palace till three in the morning . . . More like, "Someone take me home now, please."'[78]

Syd wandered through the crowd, tripping on LSD, the endlessly milling crowd sweeping slowly and curiously up and down the vast, airy expanses of the Alexandra Palace. They would pause to see the light shows flickering on the dancers, the helter skelter ride in the centre of the hall or the punters climbing the scaffolding to peer into the massive pipe organ that was being repaired. Hoppy had to stop the bands and make an impassioned announcement, asking them to kindly *get off*. The light-bulb installation, a billboard arranged on a stage, displayed handy sound-bites in lights, like 'Vietnam is a sad trip'.

Nick Jones of the *Melody Maker* noted, 'There was [a lot of] noise, and the Alexandra Palace wasn't the best place for acoustics, most of the sound echoing up into the high dome and away.' Some people spent the whole night in one corner, watching the light shows, or climbing on the scaffolding. Others decamped to one corner, where they laid their coats on the hard floor and lay down, staring at the ceiling and its acid-induced arabesques, chatting, sleeping or snogging. There were a lot of people milling about who were very straight, wearing suits and ties, looking slightly at a loss. One Underground luminary recalls, 'One of the organisers, who was gay, spent the whole time under one of the stages having sex with his motorbike boys, for hours and hours.'

Joe Boyd said, 'The 14 Hour Technicolor Dream was great, though I don't remember it too clearly. The Alexandra Palace was a big open hall. I was a bit stoned and had been up all night because we had had UFO the night before.' DJ John Peel said, 'It was like paradise, it was wonderful. You spent a lot of time rushing around saying, "Brian Jones is here, Hendrix is here, where, where?"

Rushing around to see famous people; you were still that much of a dickhead. But it was just a great event. All these bands came on, a lot of them were awful. There were a few that were really good, but it was the sense of community, of occasion, the sense that anything was possible.'[79]

Yoko Ono staged a happening in the style of the Fluxus events she'd been involved with in New York in the early sixties. A model, quite stoned, was seated on a stepladder with a blazing spotlight shining on her. Audience members were handed a pair of scissors, outfitted with a microphone plugged into the sound system, and instructed to snip off her clothes. Bit by bit her clothes fell away, with a crowd of bemused (largely male) punters swarming around her. Some looked on lecherously, but most just seemed confused. The sound of the amplified scissors echoed across the hall until the model sat, in all her glory, completely *dishabille*. Keith Rowe, who performed with AMM that night, says, 'I remember the 14 Hour Technicolor Dream as very violent. There was violence towards Yoko quite often when she performed those pieces with the men ripping away her pants, I found it unpleasant. A quite powerful emotion. The violence shown to her was quite out of order. She had racism and sexism against her. Even today it would probably be illegal to go on-stage and take someone's clothes off, but with a pair of amplified scissors, it's possible.'

'I don't have particularly good memories of the 14 Hour Technicolor Dream,' says Peter Wynne-Wilson. 'I can't quite picture the scene, I can remember being up scaffolding there and I can remember someone doing watch-glass overhead projections. Roger Waters was in a bit of a state about something. I can remember taking equipment up, but I don't remember doing any lights there. There was fairground stuff, a lot of drugs, a *lot* of drugs. I can remember thinking that the drug situation had got extremely messy and perverted because there were people completely in a state because of drink and drugs. And it seemed to me to be a real falling apart, I didn't like it at all.'

Miles says, 'The 14 Hour Technicolor Dream was quite boring by virtue of the fact that it went on for fourteen hours. There is a limit to how many dodgy bands you can listen to, and it was also cold. There weren't many things to do, and there was nowhere to sit except on the floor. Not very nice, but it was a heavy socialising scene. Obviously the more people you know the better time you had. I knew a tremendous number of the people there, so I had a tremendous time. It's improved with age, at the time I never saw it as anything fantastic. Only later on did it start to take on a life of its own, whereas with the Albert Hall poetry reading, that was a significant event. The 14 Hour Technicolor Dream was no different than a UFO, only a big one; and I would have preferred UFO anytime.'

The Soft Machine took the stage. Daevid Allen said, 'I had found a miner's helmet with a lamp set above the brow. Robert Wyatt had set his drums sideways and Kevin Ayers was wearing make-up. The stages were set at opposite end of the cavernous venue facing each other, and more often than not two bands were playing at once. We only heard the band opposite us when we stopped, so it was supportable . . . just. After we had finished I wandered about amongst the huge crowd. All my life I had felt myself to be an outside, a freak, totally at odds with my time. Now, suddenly, I realised for the first time that I wasn't alone. I was surrounded by thousands of other versions of myself. I was part of a tribe, a movement, a gigantic soul. We looked around and saw ourselves reflected in multiples and we felt our power to change the world. This was the beginning of a peaceful revolution! As this realisation took hold of my entire being I became aware of a celestial orchestra playing over a slow beat. I was drawn to the far stage where, unopposed by a simultaneous band, a group of slightly embarrassed musicians played symphonic slide guitar under the camouflage of vividly hypnotic light projections. From the edge of the stage I watched, fascinated, as a young guy with mad staring eyes stroked his guitar with metal objects. The music thus created was almost Wagnerian in its emotional power. It welled up, expanding through the swirl of liquid light . . . '[80]*

Colin Turner, the one-time mod who had found a portal into a new world at UFO, was on hand, 'Then the dawn arrived in a triumphant pink hue, the light came cascading in from the huge windows and amidst this awesome display of nature Pink Floyd took the stage. They were wearing outfits with flared trousers and satin shirts that I hadn't seen them wear before. People began to awake and hold hands as the first notes of "Astronomy Domine" reverberated through the massive hall. The atmosphere was electric. There was an extraordinary connection between the band and the audience. Then the magic happened. Syd's mirror-disc Telecaster caught the dawn's pink light. Syd noticed this and with drug-filled eyes blazing, he made his guitar talk louder and louder, higher and higher as he reflected the light into the eyes of his audience and christened those of us lucky enough to be there, followers of Pink Floyd for life.'

Peter Jenner said, 'The band played at dawn with all the light coming through the glass at the Palace, the high point of the psychedelic era for me.[81] It was a perfect setting, everyone had been waiting for them and everybody was on acid; that event was the peak of acid use in England . . . Everybody was on it: the bands, the organisers, the audience, and I certainly was.'[82]

Miles memorably wrote, 'Their music was eerie, solemn, and calming. After a whole night of frolicking and festivities and acid came the celebration of the dawn. A lot of people held hands with their neighbours. The Floyd were probably not that good but in the moment they were superb. They gave voice to the feelings of the crowd. Syd's eyes blazed as his notes soared up into the strengthening light. As the dawn was reflected in his famous mirror-disc Telecaster. Then came the rebirth of energy, another day, and with the sun a burst of danc-

*This was a life-changing moment for Daevid Allen, who henceforth adapted Barrett's glissando technique, and refined it over a thirty-year stretch with various incarnations of Gong. In many ways Gong, which still exists today, is the most direct remaining link to Syd Barrett and his music, and Barrett's humour, guitar style and approach all live on in the band.

ing and enthusiasm. It was quite an event.'[83]

However, Syd was tired, very tired, and tripping too.' It was at moments like this when one's grip on reality begins to loosen. Daevid Allen spoke of the uncomfortably eerie vibe as the Pink Floyd played, 'The glissando guitar stroker looked as though he wasn't there. It wouldn't be long before he wasn't.'[84]

'Shadowy and ghostly' is how Peter Whitehead remembers Syd at this time. 'Syd was already starting to cultivate this as a deliberate image. It was partially the way he functioned with people and also as a means of self-protection. He never found it easy to communicate with people.' Syd's mystical vibe was partially the result of the glassy-eyed distance of the cannabis and LSD head, but also a strategy to beguile, while simultaneously creating distance. Miles says, 'Syd wasn't that different than quite a few other people around at the time until he started to burn himself up with acid. There were a lot of people around like that by that time. Acid was Syd's drug of choice. He had a real twinkle of the eye which later came to be a bit mystical. Again that became quite a common thing.'

Daevid Allen said, 'Mostly Syd Barrett sat around looking completely manic with staring eyes. In fact, it was very fashionable for everyone to sit around with staring eyes, like everyone was demented and totally out of their minds.'[85] Mark Boyle noted, 'People really did believe that people who took drugs were pioneers of inner space.'[86] The idea was popularised by Timothy Leary, as well as Alex Trocchi who wrote in the early sixties about drug users being 'cosmonauts of inner space'. It was an unfortunate mythologisation of drug use, giving a romantic veneer to burning your brain out.

Whitehead told *Record Collector* that signs of Syd's impending breakdown 'had been evident for a while, especially as I got the whole inside story from Jenny Spires, who was a bit cagey but it was clear to us all that he might not hold it together. He was just out of it, around the clock, every day. When it reached his stage efforts, it was clearly the beginning of the end.' The 14 Hour Technicolor Dream was the last time Whitehead ever saw Syd.

On 10 May, Keith Richard and Mick Jagger of the Rolling Stones entered court to stand trial on trumped up drug charges. It was a brilliant media circus of a trial. In the early days of the trial, the pair arrived in sober suits, but soon each successive hearing would see Richard and Jagger arriving at the Old Bailey in their Bentleys, wearing the most incredible apparel. The media loved it, printing day-by-day reports of their clothes. Marianne Faithful, in her autobiography, said that the media coverage of these flamboyantly attired dandies swayed public opinion in their favour, making the Establishment look as if it were crushing a pair of butterflies. Perhaps it was Underground fashion's finest moment. Richards in a three-button pinstripe suit with flared bell-bottoms and a white fake fur coat, a wide-brimmed fedora on his head, and sunglasses. Jagger resplendent in satin shirt, Savile Row suit specially modified for a looser fit, and definitely shaggy hair.

On 12 May the Pink Floyd performed their first major concert, called 'Games For May', at the Queen Elizabeth Hall, on the South Bank in London. Organised by Jenner and King in collusion with Christopher Hunt, the classical concert promoter who staged the Pink Floyd's 'Music In Colour' concert at the Commonwealth Institute, 'Games For May' was a landmark for the Pink Floyd. The concert was carefully planned, and advertisements in the music press announced, *'Games For May: Space-age relaxation for the climax of spring, electronic compositions, colour and image projections, girls, and THE PINK FLOYD.'*

The press release outlined the band's idea, 'The Floyd intend this concert to be a musical and visual exploration, not only for themselves but for the audience too. New material has been written and will be given for the first time, including some specially prepared four-way stereo tapes. Visually, the lightsmen of the group have prepared an entirely new, bigger-than-ever-before show. Sadly we are not allowed to throw lighting effects as planned on to the external surfaces of the hall, nor even in the foyer. But inside should be enough!'

Certainly, during this intensely experimental time, Roger Waters was finding his raison d'être. His interest in the more theatrical aspects of a rock'n'roll concert was beginning to take shape, and over the next thirty years he would develop further the ideas from this time.

In a 1967 interview Nick Mason recalled, 'We went on to the stage in the morning to try and work out our act; up until then we hadn't thought about what we were going to do. Even then we only got as far as rehearsing the individual numbers, and working out the lighting. So when it came to the time of the performance in the evening, we had no idea what we were going to do. We just took a lot of props on stage with us and improvised. Quite a bit of what we did went down quite well, but a lot of it got completely lost. We worked out a fantastic stereophonic system whereby the sounds travelled around the hall in a sort of circle, giving the audience an eerie effect of being absolutely surrounded by this music. And of course we tried to help the effect by the use of our lighting.

'Unfortunately it only worked for people sitting in the front of the hall, still this was the first time we'd tried it, and like a lot of other ideas we used for the first time at this concert, they should be improved by the time we do our next one. Also, we thought we'd be able to use the props and work our act out as we went along, but we found this to be extremely difficult . . . Another thing we found out from giving the concert was that our ideas were far more advanced than our musical capabilities.'

Andrew King said, 'The Games For May concert was in two parts: there was a Floyd set and a number of individual efforts. The individual efforts came in the first half. They were basically pre-recorded tapes; Roger and Rick got some together, but no one else did really because Syd was in the middle of writing "See

Emily Play" which was like a theme song for that show; "games for May" comes in the lyric. The released version was lyrically altered a bit, but it was basically the same song.'[87]

Roger Waters recalled the preparations for Games For May, 'I was working in this dank, dingy basement off the Harrow Road, with an old Ferrograph. I remember sitting there recording edge tones off cymbals for the performance, later that became the beginning of "Saucerful Of Secrets". In those days you could get away with stuff like chasing clockwork toy cars around the stage with a microphone. For Games For May I also made "bird" noises recorded on the old Ferrograph at half-speed, to be played in the theatre's foyer as the audience was coming in. I was always interested in the possibilities of rock'n'roll, how to fill the space between the audience and the idea with more than just guitars and vocals.'[88]

He said, 'We did a lot of strange things, although it was much less controlled than it is now. But we even used a form of quadraphonic sound then. I think everyone in the group was into doing something different, and at that time we did some really lunatic things. I can remember spending quite a lot of time moving a bunch of flowers from vase to vase because I couldn't think of anything else to do at the time; I'd run out of potatoes to throw at the gong, and I thought that if I kept moving then nobody would take any notice of what I was playing.'[89]

Peter Wynne-Wilson says, 'Games For May was a theatrical setting, a concert hall setting as opposed to a club setting. There was definitely a feeling that we were putting on a show, but I felt it was legitimate within the scene, as it were, because it was "art" as opposed to . . . well, it could have been "art". It was quite stressful, because they were recording it at the time, I do remember someone in the sound booth, the BBC, I think. So it was quite a new thing having to operate within a framework. There was a sense of occasion, but it was one of those strange gigs. There was this *frisson* that we were playing for the "legitimate" market and imagining that we were respected in some way.'

Says Joe Boyd, 'I remember walking outside on the South Bank before the concert, outside the Queen Elizabeth Hall, running into people, and looking at the poster. It was the first time I saw Roger with the really big gong.' Mike Leonard was in the audience as well, 'I went to Games For May, it was slightly stilted. They started by sawing a big log of wood, with the sound amplified. And everyone looked slightly uncomfortable. It didn't flow.'

Games For May marked the inauguration of a box called the Azimuth coordinator, which was designed to send quadraphonic sounds effects around the hall. Mason said, 'Games For May was a very important show. It was the beginning of the concept that we ended up spending the next twenty-odd years doing.'[90] The Azimuth coordinator, which has remained an integral part of Pink Floyd's shows to this day, was a 360-degree sound system where a series of speakers situated around the hall, controlled by the sound engineer's joystick, allowed the band's sounds to be swept in a circle around the hall, creating a three-dimensional effect. Sound effects assembled by Waters were played on the coordinator, sending bird sounds culled from Abbey Road's formidable sound effects library circling the hall, and stunning the audience. The idea had begun when Waters and Barrett had gone to one of the maintenance engineers at Abbey Road and explained their idea. The boffins at EMI were intrigued and designed the quadraphonic apparatus. It has remained a staple in their live show ever since.

Duggie Fields says, 'The Pink Floyd started playing games with technology, bouncing the sound all around the hall.' Peter Jenner, 'We got this guy from EMI to erect speakers at the back of the hall, too, which was like the predecessor of the Azimuth coordinator. We had an incredible light show by then as well, and the concert, which was the first pop show ever held in the hall, was just unbelievable. At one stage, one of the roadies came on dressed in admiral's gear and tossed armfuls of daffodils up in the air . . . it was just amazing, and everybody went berserk.'[91] Sadly, this action got the Pink Floyd banned from ever using the Queen Elizabeth Hall again. Roger Waters said, 'It seems we contravened a regulation. We were told that people might have slipped on the flowers we threw into the audience. Someone I know was sitting next to two old ladies who sat there still and silent until the interval. Then one turned to her friend and said, "They're very good, aren't they?"'[92]

International Times also reviewed Games For May under the headline 'Floyd Play Games', 'The choice of the Queen Elizabeth Hall for the Games For May event was really good thinking, for it was a genuine twentieth-century chamber music concert. Acoustically, the hall is probably better for amplified sound than natural sound and the cleanness of presentation of the hall itself was perfect for the very loose mixed media. The performance consisted basically of the Pink Floyd, a tape machine, projections, flowers and the Queen Elizabeth Hall, all combined rather leisurely. The first half was a fairly straight presentation of their sound and light show, but the second half moved right into the hall and into the realm of involvement. Musically, the second half was really bordering on pure electronic music and very good at that. On the whole it was good to see the strength of a hip show holding its own in such a museum like and square environment. More of this.'

Games For May set the groundwork for their incorporation of musique concrete and sound effects, which would be woven into their 'heavy concept' albums later on. The band considered Games For May a success, even if they had been intimidated by the sheer solemnity of putting on a concert at the Queen Elizabeth Hall. Jenner and King issued a statement to the music weeklies saying that plans were afoot for a follow-up at Chiswick House in June. In a radical departure, it was to be called Games For June. It never happened, but the seeds were sown for larger concerts, and the post-Syd Floyd would go on to build arguably the most stunning concert set-up.

Roger Waters said, 'With us, lights were not, and are not a gimmick. We believe that a good light show enhances the music. Groups who adopted lights as a gimmick are now being forced to drop them, but there's no reason why we should. In this country, groups were forced to provide their own light shows, whereas in the States, it was the clubs who provided the lights.'[93] Syd Barrett said, 'Really, we have only just started to scrape the surface of effects and ideas of lights and music combined; we think that the music and the lights are part of the same scene, one enhances and adds to the other. In the future, groups are going to have to offer much more than just a pop show. They'll have to offer a well-presented theatre show.'[94] Prescient, isn't it? Barrett was no fool.

On 14 May the Pink Floyd appeared on *Look Of The Week*, a late-night arts programme on BBC2. They opened with 'Pow R. Toc H.', followed by a spectacular 'Astronomy Domine' with a smiling Syd waving his arms in the air, shadows from Peter Wynne-Wilson's lights casting spectral shadows on the walls in time with the thunderous music. They also played an incredibly loud version of 'Interstellar Overdrive'. On hand that night was eminent musicologist Dr Hans Keller, a rather taciturn German who followed his disdainful introduction of the band with an absurd question and answer segment.

The good doctor began with, 'Well, if I may first turn to Roger, I want to ask one fundamental question, of which our viewers may not be fully aware of because they didn't see all of it: why has it all got to be so terribly loud? For me I just can't bear it, I happened to have grown up in the string quartet, which is a bit softer. Why has it got to be so loud, so amplified?' Roger Waters, eyes rolling sykward, answered, 'Well, I guess it doesn't have to be. That's just they way *we* like it, we didn't grow up in the string quartet. I guess that could be one of the reasons why it's loud. It doesn't sound terribly loud to us.' Keller haughtily said, 'Not everyone who hasn't grown up in the string quartet turns into a loud cock . . . er, pop group, so your reason isn't altogether convincing, except that you like it. What I'm saying is that if one gets immune to this kind of sound, one may finder it difficult to appreciate softer types of sound. Syd, yes, no?'

Syd Barrett, suppressing a smirk, said, 'I don't think that's so. I mean, everybody listens. We don't need it very loud in order to be able to hear it, and some of it is very quiet in fact. I personally like quiet music just as much as loud music. We play in large halls and things where obviously volume is necessary, and when people dance volume comes in on its own.' Keller asked, 'Well, that's interesting, "when people dance. . ." You did start, if I'm not mistaken, as a group that accompanied dancing?' Barrett replied, smiling, 'Yes, you could say that.' Keller continued, 'How have you turned into a concertising [sic] group, if I may use that term?'

Roger Waters said, 'Well, we've only done two concerts, because I guess pop music is the scene we're in at the moment. You play gigs around ballrooms and dance halls, and that sort of scene. Because that's how it works at the moment. But we felt that there was no real reason why we shouldn't play an organised concert in a large hall where people can actually listen to what we do. Because dance halls aren't, generally speaking, very good places to listen to the music. Most people come along and the music, for most of them over the past few years, has just been a background noise that they can shake about to.'

Keller asked, 'Were those two concerts successful, Syd?' Barrett answered, 'Yes, I think so. The way the act has developed over the last six months has been influenced rather a lot by the fact that we played in ballrooms, which was obviously the first market. But concerts give us a chance to see that maybe the music we play isn't directed at dancing like normal pop groups in the past.' Keller: 'Have you encountered any hostility towards your creation?' Waters replied, 'Well, yes we have, but I guess there has been quite a lot of hostility going on in odd places in the country. The only hostility we've actually seen has been from the professional knockers in the press like . . .' and here Waters fixes the camera with a fearsome expression, before hissing the name of the dreaded *NME* writer, '*Robert Pittman*!'

Keller asked, 'Do you, in turn, feel aggressive towards the audience?' Barrett and Waters answered in unison, 'No, not at all!' Keller asked, 'In spite of all the loudness?' 'There's not many young people who dislike it,' said Barrett, curtly. Keller: 'There's no shock treatment intended?' 'No, certainly not,' said Barrett, aghast, 'some people think we deliberately try to shock the audience, or use the volume to keep them quiet. This is not so.' Dr. Hans Keller concluded lamely, 'Well, there it is. I think you can pass your verdict as well as you can. My verdict is that it is a little bit of a regression to childhood, but after all . . . *why not?*'

The Pink Floyd returned to their old haunts at Sound Techniques Studios on 21 May to record 'See Emily Play'. They had failed to maintain the spirit which had fuelled Joe Boyd's production of 'Arnold Layne' and trouped down to the Chelsea studio to try and recapture it. Barrett's wayward muse was beginning to become elusive, and later it would take more than a change of locale to inject the sessions with the necessary illumination. On the horizon ominous clouds were beginning to form, reflected in the lyrics of song, which contained subtle foreshadowings of madness; 'You'll lose your mind and play free games for May,' sang Barrett.

'I remember I really started to get worried when I went along to the session for "See Emily Play",' recalled David Gilmour.[95] 'I don't know at quite what point Syd started to go very strange, but I know I came back from France and I called Syd up while I was there and he said why didn't I come down [because] they were doing a recording session. And I went down to the studio and he didn't even recognise me.[96] He gave me a complete blank.[97] Syd was still functioning OK, but he definitely wasn't the person I knew. He looked through you. He wasn't quite there.[98] Syd just looked straight through me, barely acknowledged that I was there. Very weird.[99] The change was sort of devastating. Syd was a different person to the one I'd known very well. It was tragic.'[100]

Syd's semi-mystical glazed look had progressed to a piercing and rather disconcerting stare. His immense eyes stared blankly at whoever he was facing, unnerving all in his immediate circle. Most worrying was that he seemed to be staring but not seeing, his mind elsewhere, wrapped in its own private enigmas.

He returned for a brief visit home; his sister Rosemary said, 'The next time I saw him he'd changed so much that I couldn't reach him. The brother I knew had disappeared. After that meeting I just couldn't enjoy the music any more.'[101]

On the 21st the band completed 'The Bike Song' (aka 'Bike'), intended to be the forthcoming album's closer. Cliff Jones wrote, 'The tempo changes at the end of every verse. The rising glissando note that finishes each chorus was achieved using a crude oscillator and varispeeding the tape down while the track was running.'[102] The lead vocal on 'Bike' is set far enough apart from the lead to disorient the listener. One fears the vocal tracks will become unglued and drift farther out of phase than they already are. Artificial double tracking was developed at EMI to save the trouble of recording a separate back-up vocal. The song started out as a playful Barrett ditty in the style of 'The Gnome', but the haunting coda imbues it with a prophetic, sinister overtone. The finale of the song proper is a parody of the sort of fanfares to be found at the end of an operetta by Gilbert and Sullivan or in English vaudeville. Waters, Wright and Barrett join in on a campy chorus, inviting the girl 'who fits in with my world' into Syd's 'room of musical tunes'. At the beginning of the coda, footsteps echo down a long hallway, a door opens with a heaving creak and a most extraordinary sound collage free of melody or harmony erupts; as if Barrett was trying to let everyone else hear the sounds in his head: a wash of cymbals, discordant string instruments, clockwork echoing the bell towers of Cambridge.

The final ingredient in this sonic bouillabaisse is a repeated loop of shrill and horrific laughing voices, rising discordantly as the 'room of musical tunes' fades back into the recesses of Syd's mind. Slowed down by half, the loop reveals itself to be a roughly edited loop of bellowing laughter. It resounds from the speakers like the riotous drunken laughter of pub regulars ringing in the ear of one fleeing a pub into a cold, raining night. The twisted laughter is both funny and frightening, disarming you as it hits home. And it's eerily reminiscent of the runout groove on *Sergeant Pepper's Lonely Hearts Club Band*, which Syd and the Floyd were directly inspired by when they heard a special advance copy. Indeed, the day *Sergeant Pepper* was released, the Floyd were at Abbey Road working on a version of 'Bike'.

Norman Smith was alternately impressed and dismayed with Barrett's *modus operandi* in the studio. He commented on 'Bike', 'It's the most fantastical muddle of sounds, time signatures and yet somehow Syd makes it all make perfect sense. "Bike" was one of the last tracks where Syd was truly in control.'[103]

On 24 May Syd was interviewed by *Melody Maker's* Chris Welch for the paper's 'Blind Date' column, in which pop stars reviewed new releases by trying to guess who the artist was. Welch, in his book *Learning to Fly*, recalled, 'I found Syd perfectly chatty and amiable, although a little worried and frightened. Syd crouched in a small darkened room as I arrived with my crude portable record player and inky notebook, to play a suitably daft selection of records.' As King and Jenner watched uncertainly from the next room, Barrett ran through the singles, dropping a few interesting asides: 'The new wave of music is all-embracing. It gets across and makes everybody feel good', 'If you want your own hit it's best to make your own sounds', and 'It doesn't matter if an artist is dead or alive about records being released'. One also gets a feel for Barrett's bossy and somewhat imperious airs, as he orders Welch to remove a particularly offensive pop platter. 'Fade it out!' he demands of a Vince Hill single. As for Barry Fantoni, 'I don't want to hear it again!' Convinced that he was in the right, Syd could be inflexible in his views, and petulant and demanding when he wanted to be, often to the annoyance of the others in the band. But his irritability masked a palpable unhappiness. Welch said, 'When Syd finally smiled, I thought of him as a prisoner in a cell, someone I should have gone back to visit and try to help, if only by making him laugh again.'[104]

Peter Wynne-Wilson said, 'Syd had a quality, sometimes, a slightly ethereal quality. He had a really devastating smile which wasn't used a lot, but it was a really a lighting-up smile. Later on, when he was getting into a state, he would sometimes use the smile, or almost that smile, to pretend that he was okay; but it was different.'

Syd derided Jim Reeves' 'Trying To Forget' as, 'A very way-out record. I think I tapped my foot to this one. I don't know who it was. Well, let me think, who's dead? It must be Jim Reeves! It's another that would sound better at 33⅓' Barrett must have crushed his acolyte, David Bowie, when he commented on the latter's 'Love You 'Til Tuesday' single, 'Yeah, it's a joke number. Jokes are good. Everybody likes jokes. The Pink Floyd likes jokes. It's very casual. If you play it a second time it might be even more of a joke. Jokes are good. The Pink Floyd like jokes. I think that was a very funny joke. I think people will like the fact about it being Monday, when in fact it was Tuesday. Very chirpy, but I don't think my toes were tapping at all.'[105] This short review is psychologically noteworthy for the fact that Barrett is using what psychologists refer to as clang association, a pattern of words or a single word repeated like a bell being clanged incessantly. Barrett repeats the word 'joke' eight times in nine short sentences, a pattern reminiscent of clinically defined schizophrenic speech patterns.

On 25 May, the Pink Floyd played a gig at Abergavenny, Wales, where they were rapturously received. Ethnologists perhaps will one day determine why the Welsh felt such a warm affinity for increasingly ragged thirty-minute sonic assaults of 'Interstellar Overdrive'.

The Floyd joined the Jimi Hendrix Experience, the Move and Cream for a gig at 'Barbecue 67', at Tulip Bulb Auction Hall, Spalding, on 29 May. Admission was £1; whoever was in the audience certainly got their money's worth.

*

The Beatles' *Sergeant Pepper's Lonely Hearts Club Band* was released on 1 June. The Pink Floyd had been creating their début while the Beatles spent nearly 700 studio hours forming and refining their masterpiece in the adjacent Studio Two. In the UK and in America, the release of *Sergeant Pepper* signalled the beginning of the Summer Of Love and within days the refrains of 'Lucy In The Sky With Diamonds' and 'With A Little Help From My Friends' could be heard resounding out of hippie 'crash pads' from Notting Hill to Haight-Ashbury.

There was excitement in the air, and the Pink Floyd had a big party at the Jenners' house to listen to their advance copy of the album and celebrate, fuelling them to even greater heights on their own forthcoming album. June Bolan recalled that night fondly, 'The day *Sergeant Pepper* came out we got a pre-release copy, because the Floyd were signed to EMI [the Beatles' label], it was unbelievable.'[106]

In a sadly ironic twist, Hoppy, the bird-like impresario of the Underground and the spark behind so many ventures, was gaoled on the very day *Sergeant Pepper* was released. Hoppy embodied the freewheeling sprit of the Underground, and was its primary catalyst. He would walk into a room and sparkle with ideas and energy. With Suzy Creamcheese at his side, they set London alight. The London Free School, the All Saint's Hall, UFO, the 14 Hour Technicolor Dream, *IT* . . . without Hoppy most of these ventures would have joined the countless number of great ideas that never developed further than a stoned conversation or two. While dope generated many ideas, it often robbed one of the capacity for realising them. Hoppy was an exception.

Hoppy once memorably said, 'There's something about England that I've never fathomed, but I'm sure it's true, which is: if you've got the bottle to go out and do something, anything, it's like a magnet.'[107] A magnet in every sense, as Hoppy's successes caught the attention of both the Underground and the Establishment. 'One of the slogans we had, which of course isn't true, was "There are no leaders". Of course there are!' Hoppy certainly was one, and it didn't take terribly long before the powers that be realised it. Hoppy's imprisonment didn't bode well for the Underground either.

Things were changing, and quickly. This strange psychedelic movement, blossoming quickly in an explosive flash of colour, already seemed to be withering slightly. Its momentum was to be felt everywhere in the world, but the original Big Bang, so to speak, was nearing an end. Like an extinguished star, its light would continue to illuminate for a long time. And indeed it still does today.

Steve Abrams, of SOMA, the lobby for the decriminalisation of marijuana, says, 'When Hoppy's trial came up, he insisted on pleading not guilty, though he had no defence. He had a previous conviction for possession of cannabis but insisted on a jury trial, which meant going before a judge of the Crown Court and risking a longer sentence than one year.' Hoppy completed a classical recipe for self-imprisonment by lecturing the court on the need to legalise cannabis.

Sentencing him to nine months imprisonment, the Deputy Chairman of Inner London Sessions, A. Gordon Friend, said, 'I have just heard what your views are on the possession of cannabis and the smoking of it. This is not a matter I can overlook. You are a pest to society.'[108]

'I found going to gaol was very traumatic,' says Hoppy. 'I wasn't ready for it. I had some acid in my body actually when I went into gaol, enough acid for several days. It was stashed in a convenient orifice. I was completely freaked, I started feeling the horrors. I would cry, I was very upset. They put me in hospital pretty soon after I arrived in gaol. When I was in gaol, they gave me a lot of Largactyl, which just wipes you out.* It neutralises you. But in a way, looking back on it, I landed in gaol really because of my own actions. I didn't really look ahead and see that's what would happen to me. John Esam really took hold of his situation, he was caught, but he made a successful outcome. I was the opposite. I didn't see it coming, and when it did it hit me right smack in the face. And I think it had a very deep effect on my life afterwards. And some of that effect was negative. I suppose it must have come out in my attitudes. When I was in gaol, Suzy Creamcheese was in a nuthouse. She was in a private insane asylum, put there by her parents, and they wanted to give her shock treatment and she managed to talk herself out. A very strong person; weaker people wouldn't have been able to.'

On 2 June, the Pink Floyd returned to UFO for what was in essence a homecoming party thrown by the Underground for their house band. The posters that night announced, *'My watch stops, my radio is silent . . . but what do I care . . . at UFO?'* Also promised was 'all-nite intermedia', one of those funny sixties buzzwords. Joe Boyd said, 'The news that the Floyd were going playing meant that it was absolutely jammed, there were queues around the block.'[109]

'They arrived and because of the crowd . . . there was only one way in and you had to go through the crowd to the dressing-room and they came past, sort of just inside the door and it was very crushed, so it was like faces two inches from your nose. They all came by. "Hi, Joe! How are you?" "Great!" I greeted them all as they came through, and the last one was Syd. And the great thing with Syd, when I had known Syd and worked [with him] on "Arnold Layne" and in the early days of UFO, was that if there is anything about him that you really remembered it was that he had a twinkle in his eye; he was a real eye-twinkler. He had this impish look about him, this mischievous glint. And he came by, and I said, "Hi, Syd", and he just kind of looked at me. I looked right in his eye and there was no twinkle, no glint. And it was like somebody had pulled the blinds, you know, nobody home. And it was a real shock. Very, very sad.'[110]

Between uncomfortable drives up and down the motorway to endless small gigs

*Largactyl, a phenothiazine, can reduce one to a catatonic stupor. It is still used indiscriminately in mental hospitals to reduce 'troublesome cases' to utter, vacant docility.

where the audience reaction was often indifferent or hostile, the Pink Floyd still toiled away on their début album. Sessions continued with work on a new song, 'Chapter 24', distinguished for its celestial coda, spiralling heavenward in multi-layered vocals, saturated with melody, echoing through an evocation of clouded skies. Barrett's vocal arrangement on the song is immaculate, not technically, but stylistically; where usually the listener would expect the massed voices to trail off in the fade-out, instead they rise in a celestial crescendo, a truly transcendent sound. It's reminiscent of Brian Wilson's pioneering work on his unfinished symphony *Smile* the year before, where chord progressions would ascend right into the fade-out, never peaking. Lyrically the song was lifted nearly verbatim from Richard Wilhelm's 1924 translation of the Chinese oracle *The I-Ching – The Book Of Changes*. Barrett had been given a copy by Seamus O'Connell's mother when he was living in the flat on Tottenham Street and his interest in Eastern mysticism had only grown in Earlham Street's sanctuary of creativity.

Nicholas Schaffner notes that Syd and Lindsay used to play long running games of the Chinese board game 'Go' in their flat at Earlham Street. '"Chapter 24",' recalled Barrett, noting the prophetic tone of the lyrics, 'was from the *I-Ching*, there was someone around who was very into that, most of the words came straight off that . . . it didn't mean much to me at the time, but then three or four months later it came to mean a lot.'[111] Rick Wright and Syd harmonised on the chorus, their voices ascending skyward. One often overlooked aspect of Barrett's songwriting skill is his gift for vocal arrangements, augmented by substantial input from Wright and Waters. Their voices strike resonant notes, wavering in pitch slightly, evoking the timbre and tone of Indian swordmandels and sitars.

Along with 'The Gnome' and 'The Scarecrow', 'Chapter 24' draws forth potent images of the Cambridgeshire countryside. Wind wafting through the woods, the scent of snapdragon. The scent of freshly mown summer grass rising through the air, the ephemeral shift of the seasons, capturing the sensation of summer coursing through the air, threading promise and wonderment.

The band also completed a four-track master for one of the earliest Barrett originals performed by the Pink Floyd. 'Matilda Mother' had progressed from performances of it at All Saints' Hall to a full-blown freak-out on-stage at UFO. On the 23rd, Norman Smith and Peter Bown made a mono-mixdown of the song, earmarking it for inclusion on the album. 'Matilda Mother' is one of Syd's masterpieces; the descending chromatic jangle guitar in the intro, the background vocals echoing the drawn out word *'waiting'* in shrill falsetto. Wright's fairground organ undergirds the song's harmonic structure, and he does a solo vocal on the verses.

The song is filled with tiny audible edits, and mistakes, such as laughter between verses. Smith and Bown were kept busy trying to edit the various tempi together. Barrett, in collusion with Smith, devised a call response break, whispering *'shhh'* in the left channel and responding with a muted *'pow!'* in the right. It's a tiny segment, of the sort that often goes unnoticed, but epitomises Barrett's subtle artistry. 'Matilda Mother' touched directly on Barrett's childhood, using a first-person narrative to recall childhood stories being read to him by his mother. The undercurrent of fear that pervades the song is no accident. Later on, it wasn't a coincidence that the more autobiographical the song, the more tortured Barrett's delivery or lyrics would be.

The song is superb in its evocation of what author Ian McDonald, writing about the Beatles' 'Cry Baby Cry' in *Revolution In The Head*, called 'its deceptive sunshine and mysterious laughter behind half-open doors'. 'Cry Baby Cry' itself was probably inspired by 'Matilda Mother', with its lyric allusions to childhood stories, its chorus derived from 'Sing A Song Of Sixpence' and its use of eerie chords played waltz-time in the verses, echoing with a ringing finality.

The Pink Floyd played a double-header on 10 June, performing at Lowestoft before driving back to play at UFO. Barrett was beginning to feel reservations even about playing there. He said, 'I remember at UFO, one week one group, then another week another group, going in and out, making that set-up, and I didn't think it was as active as it could've been. What we were doing was a microcosm of the whole sort of philosophy and it tended to be a little bit cheap.'[112] I only know the thing of playing, of being a musician, was very exciting. Obviously, one was better off with a silver guitar with mirrors and things all over it than people who ended up on the floor or anywhere else in London. The "general concept" I didn't feel so conscious of as perhaps I should. I mean, one's position as a member of London's young people's Underground wasn't necessarily realised and felt . . . from the point of view of groups.'[113]

On 16 June, a crew from Rediffusion TV filmed the Pink Floyd performing 'Astronomy Domine' for inclusion in a thirty-minute documentary called *Come Here Often?* about DJ Mike Quinnin of the Tiles nightclub on Oxford Street, London. It was a joyous day, perhaps the last fully joyous day that Syd Barrett was to know with the Pink Floyd. That same day their second single, 'See Emily Play', backed with 'Scarecrow', was released. 'Arnold Layne' had reached number twenty in the pop but their second single 'See Emily Play' was a top-ten smash that summer. The cold days of October 1966, when the Pink Floyd had taken the freezing stage at the Roundhouse, were gone; they were soon to be fully fledged pop stars. 'See Emily Play' would stay on the national charts for seven weeks, reaching number six on 29 July.*

Barrett told the *Melody Maker*, 'Singles are always simple . . . It was probably me alone [who wanted singles], I think. Obviously, being a pop group one wanted to have singles. I think "See Emily Play" was fourth in the hits.'

'I was sleeping in a wood after a gig up north,' he joked, when asked about

*This would be the highest placing for any Pink Floyd single for thirteen years, until 'Another Brick In The Wall (Part II)' hit number one in 1979.

the song's origins by the press, 'when I saw a girl coming through the trees, shouting and dancing. That's Emily!' In truth, Emily Kennett was one of the so-called 'psychedelic debutantes', neophyte ravers 'on the scene' at UFO. Without being condescending, Barrett subtly reproaches her with one of his more astute lines; 'Emily tries, but misunderstands. She's often inclined to borrow somebody's dreams till tomorrow.'

Pete Brown says, 'See Emily Play" was based on this schoolgirl. This English thing, the cult of the schoolgirl in the fetish uniform, has always been around. It's part of the more dubious side of English culture, allied with British repression and fetishes. Emily was actually someone I went out with a couple of times. I was friends with her because originally I had gone out with one of her friends. They all went to the same school. [Actress] Anjelica Huston was at the same school, and used to hang out with Emily as well. I used to meet them walking down the Portobello Road. I was doing poetry gigs in schools at that time. I was quite young, in my twenties, and some of these girls were seventeen or eighteen. Of course, I used to go out with them, and English schoolgirls in the sixties were very forward looking. They were in the process of discovering their own sexuality. I guess it was a good time, which might sound sexist. As the sixties progressed, I think women got pushed into too much. The burden on them was quite a lot, they didn't have as much freedom as people think they did.'

'Although it sounds a bit gimmicky, hardly any special effects were used,' said Rick Wright in 1967 of 'See Emily Play'. 'That "Hawaiian" bit at the end of each verse was just Syd using a bottleneck through echo. The part that sounds speeded-up, though, was speeded-up. John Woods, the engineer, just upped the whole thing about an octave. On stage, we . . . cut that particular bit out, but then I don't think the audience minds if our reproduction isn't 100 per cent accurate . . . I don't think the success of "See Emily Play" has affected us personally. Sure we get more money for bookings, but the next one could easily be a flop. When I first heard the playback in the studio, I had a feeling it would go higher than it did, but I'm not complaining.'[114]

'See Emily Play' was Syd's commercial high point, but perhaps that wasn't enough any more. 'Pink Floyd got a hit with "See Emily Play", and for a few months they were moderately overground,' said David Bowie, who was himself undergoing a transformation from mod David Jones under the inspiration of people like Syd and choreographer Lindsay Kemp. 'Syd just didn't want any part of that, so he opted out. And I understood why. I thought, "They're being accepted, nobody wants that."'[115]

'The Pink Floyd may have been the darlings of London,' said Peter Jenner, 'but out in the suburbs it was fairly terrible. Before "See Emily Play" the Pink Floyd would have things thrown at them on-stage. After "See Emily Play" it was screaming girls wanting to hear the hit song.'[116] Roger Waters said, '"Arnold Layne" and "See Emily Play" were both minor hits, and we wouldn't perform them live because we considered the three-minute form irrelevant to the idea of live performance. So we did a lot of gigs where people would stand on the balcony and pour beer on us because we wouldn't play [our singles].'[117]

Nick Mason stated, 'There would be this revolving stage, and the audience out front all hoping to hear "Arnold Layne" and "See Emily Play", and a host of other hits which we couldn't, of course, play. We had a repertoire of strange things like "Interstellar Overdrive" which carried us through about half the set. I just remember the stages going round and the whole audience just appalled by what they saw in front of them. The whole thing was fantastic anyway, because what was then considered to be our audience could never get into these places because you had to have a tie. And there was this whole business of not letting us drink at the bar because we hadn't got collars and ties, and various outrages which used to drive us all mad.'[118]

Studio sessions continued with 'Flaming', stylistically derived from 'I Come And Stand At Every Door' which was written by Gene Clark on the Byrd's 1966 *5th Dimension* album. The alternating pastoral, acoustic moods and hard electric rhythm were also highly inspirational for Barrett, setting a clear precedent for the Floyd's new album.

The intro on 'Flaming' echoes those seemingly eternally long moments of hypnagogic sleep suspended between dream and reality. Syd's artificially double-tracked voice again, as in 'Bike', shadows his original vocal far enough out of phase to produce a dream-like disorienting effect. The effect on the listener is to feel as if they've just woken in a sylvan dale at dawn to hear the mystic refrain of the Piper's flute echo across the mist of morning grass. 'Alone, in the clouds, all blue . . .' sings Syd, here assuming an earthly incarnation of Pan, the true Piper at the Gates of Dawn. The song delves into the mystical angle of sunrise, as night turns to day. Astronomers speak of a phenomena known as the dawn chorus, where the electrical static of the cosmos rises in crescendo with the first rays of the new rising sun, creating a celestial 'music'.

In *The Wind In The Willows*, Mole and Rat are greeted by the Piper with his mystic pipes. The ephemeral satyr of Nature draws up the dawn in spidery tendrils, the plaintive melody heralding the day. The flaming lysergic dawn casts the night away in rays of preternatural luminescence. 'Lying on an eiderdown,' sings Syd, the song's lush harmonics calling forth visions of droplets of waters condensing on blades of grass, dissolving skyward. 'Yippee! You can't see me, but I can you,' sings the Piper, leaving Mole and Rat with no memory of ever seeing them, but leaving them with the powerful feeling of a dream that lingers half remembered long after they wake, colouring their day in unexpected hues. 'Flaming' is an elegy to Nature.

Jenny Fabian, meanwhile, had managed to penetrate the Floyd's inner circle, catching Syd's attention. But she notes, 'Syd had just about gone by the time I got anywhere near him. Or was going.' It is to Fabian and her autobiographical novel *Groupie*, that we owe a vivid description of the Pink Floyd's 25 April gig at the Oxford Summer Ball. 'There were all these students and deb chicks in long dresses looning about with guys in DJs, all getting stoned on strawberries and cream and champers . . . [The band] said it was all too much for them, and as they had plenty of time before they were due to play, we decided to split down to the river and turn on. I managed to sit with [Syd] on a punt somewhere apart from the others and rolled some spliffs for him. There was this warm mist creeping along the river, and the sounds of the water lapping against the sides of the boat made us both feel relaxed and peaceful. I told [Syd] how groovy it was to be here with him, and quite suddenly he put his arm around me and started talking about Japanese temples . . . I was afraid to speak, and I didn't want to interrupt his voice or spoil the almost transcendental mood I was in . . . I didn't really understand what [Syd] was talking about, but it didn't matter. We stayed there until it was time for them to go back and play.'[119]

After weeks of hearings, on 29 June Keith Richard and Mick Jagger were convicted on drugs charges. There was an uproar in the courtroom, as the hipsters in the galleys shook their fists in anger at the severity of the sentences; these were later overturned after William Rees-Mogg wrote an infamous editorial in *The Times* 'Who breaks a butterfly on a wheel?', a tacit acknowledgement of their innocence by the Establishment.

Steve Abrams wrote at the time of the convictions, 'There was a spontaneous demonstration outside the *News Of The World* building in Fleet street. No one had cared enough to demonstrate in Fleet Street since the First World War, and no one would ever care enough to do so again. The police turned dogs on the demonstrators and six people were arrested. The demonstrations continued into the early hours of the morning. The next day, Richard and Jagger were released on bail. It being Friday, the members of the Underground club, UFO, over a thousand persons in extravagant dress, marched at midnight from Tottenham Court Road to the statue of Eros at Piccadilly Circus, where they were joined by several hundred members of other West End clubs. We then formed up and marched to Fleet Street. Again the police turned dogs against us, and one demonstrator was bitten.

'On Saturday the *News Of The World* demonstrations continued for the third night running. A picture of part of the crowd, myself among them, appeared on the front page of the *News Of The World*. Mick Farren, a future editor of *IT* and lead singer of the Social Deviants, was beaten by the police and a number of others were arrested, including Suzy Creamcheese.'[120]

That night at UFO, Tomorrow played for a highly charged audience. All the talk centred on the convictions, and the sense of anger was palpable. Twink jumped from behind his drums and grabbed the microphone, shouting 'Revolution! Revolution!', the chorus of their new single; he kept shouting 'Revolution!' until the entire club was chanting along with him, shaking their fists.[121] Joe Boyd, speaking to Nick Jones, remembered that night. 'From 12 to 3 a.m. the club just emptied and went down to Piccadilly Circus to demonstrate about the Stones' convictions.' The crowd mobbed the *News Of The World* building, writing inflammatory slogans on car windows with black tar soap. Ending up at Piccadilly Circus, the crowd protested loudly, to the bemusement of the night-time trade of prostitutes, bobbies, junkies, cruising gays and tourists at Piccadilly. Caroline Coon and Rufus Harris, among those in the throng, resolved to set up an organisation to defend the growing number of young people on drugs charges. Release was the organisation and it continues to this day.

The entire crowd returned to UFO at 5 a.m. 'It was absolutely jam-packed to the ceiling,' Boyd told the *Melody Maker*. It's worth noting that the UFO pro-Stones demo was probably one of the handful of times club culture has acted on a principle other than hedonism.

Peter Wynne-Wilson says, 'There were demonstrations from time to time, but the heavy hard-nosed political thing was later, which was potentially violent. Our scene was non-violent. I could remember tension when the Stones were arrested. Everyone felt that as an attack. You could put up with the regular prosecution of drug offences, but that seemed to be a deliberate attack. I don't know why we took it so personally. It was over within a couple of days, and it wasn't a particularly big thing but it was very emotional at the time. The hip attitude was that the revolution was an internal thing anyway, a personal rather than political thing. Because as far as I was, and am concerned, politicians are completely discredited anyway, so I wouldn't take an alternative politician any more seriously than an established politician.' What the Underground shared was a view that conventional politics were corrupt. In the immortal phrase of Jack Henry Moore of the Arts Lab, which even today Hoppy still loves to quote with relish, 'Politics is pigshit'.

Barrett was finding that pop stardom wasn't all he'd imagined it to be. Touring was very demanding, and the excessive touring of the sort Pink Floyd did in 1967 didn't help Syd's fraying nerves at all. With so many gigs they must have all blurred together, the audiences' faces blending into identical masks. Night after night of playing to sometimes indifferent and sometimes hostile provincial audiences began to take a toll on Syd. The others made it through a bit better, with Nick Mason describing his driving force as 'fear and rum'.

Peter Wynne-Wilson says, 'The gigs weren't remotely well scheduled, particularly given the fees paid then. There was only one motorway and we seemed to be pounding it every night, so there wouldn't be a linear run of gigs; it was right upcountry and then down. Syd would get frustrated that the gigs were often so completely unsuited to the band's music. And I don't know if he saw himself as a frontman. Although Syd would be singing, Roger would always try to be a pop star. So I don't know that fronting the band was a particular pressure on Syd, but certainly the travelling was very, very arduous. And Syd would tend to smoke his way out of that. Certainly not the only one.'

David Gilmour later remarked on Nick Mason's list of Pink Floyd gigs, 'It's ten yards long and it's quite extraordinary when you look at the gigs got through, four or five a week . . . On-stage monitors were unheard of, and musicians could barely hear what they were playing, leading to tremendous frustration. In 1967 no one realised that sound could get better. There was just noise and that's how rock'n'roll was. As soon as you educate people to something better, then they want it better, permanently. PAs were terrible in those days.'[122]

Roger Waters told the *Melody Maker* in 1967, 'We've had problems with our equipment and we can't get the PA to work because we play extremely loudly. It's a pity because Syd writes great lyrics and nobody ever hears them. Maybe it's our fault because we are trying too hard. After all the human voice can't compete with Fender Telecasters and double drumkits. We're a very young group, not in age, but in experience. We're trying to solve problems that haven't existed before. Perhaps we should stop trying to do our singles on-stage. Even the Beatles, when they worked live, sounded like their records. But the sort of records we make today are impossible to reproduce on-stage so there is no point in trying.'[123]

Like the Beatles, who quit touring in the year before, the Pink Floyd had found the strain of reproducing their intricately crafted pop hits arduous. In this era of growing reliance on the studio, there were sounds that were simply impossible to reproduce with the limited technology at their disposal. Roger Waters said, 'We still do "Arnold Layne" and struggle through "See Emily Play" occasionally. We don't think it's dishonest because we can't play live what we play on records . . . We've got the recording side together and not the playing side. What we've got to do now is get together a stage act that has nothing to do with our records, things like "Interstellar Overdrive" and instrumentals that are much easier to play. It's sometimes depressing [when we fail to communicate with an audience] and becomes a drag.'

Nick Mason remembered trying to play both 'See Emily Play' and 'Interstellar Overdrive' in their live shows. 'We thought they fitted, but audiences quite often turned hostile, about twenty to thirty minutes into the set. Sometimes it was expressed by the throwing of objects, sometimes by their leaving the facility. Therefore, the conclusion must be that either they didn't fit or the audience didn't understand. But we weren't demoralised. It was very curious. If the public treated us like that now we'd retire hurt immediately.'[124]

The growing rift between the demands of the pop market and the band's growing desire for experimentalism would be unsatisfactorily resolved until the Pink Floyd decided to stop making singles altogether several years later.

On 6 July, they appeared on *Top Of The Pops*, their first of three appearances. 'See Emily Play' had crashed into the charts, bolstered by heavy air-play from the pirate radio stations as well as the BBC. It became one of the theme songs of that magical, long-gone summer. Yet Barrett was growing increasingly dissatisfied with the demands of being in a commercial pop band. Peter Wynne-

Wilson says, 'Syd was already very dissatisfied with the way the whole band scene was going by the time of the first *Top Of The Pops* show. *Top Of The Pops* seemed like a very pedestrian and commercial thing to be doing. He need a lot of "smoothing" to go to that. That would have been before he'd had any really substantial amounts of acid. I think that although a common belief is that it was an acid-induced problem, that wasn't necessarily so, unless he reacted particularly badly to it.' Did Syd have a great conflict about commercialism? Wynne-Wilson says, 'Yes, I would think so. More than the others.'

Susie and Peter began to realise that something was wrong with Syd, beyond the freewheeling madness of the time. 'The first time I registered that was at *Top Of The Pops*, that day. There had often been times when you would get a strange look in Syd's eyes, just fleeting, but he was definitely disturbed [about *Top Of The Pops*]. It might've been an element of panic. What little he articulated about it was that he didn't feel *Top Of The Pops* was the sort of thing they should be doing.'

The band appeared on the show with Barrett and Waters sitting cross-legged on burnished steel pillars, like a space-age parody of the Lewis Carroll's caterpillar reclining on his toadstool. Mason and his drumkit were placed in front. Wright, to Syd's left, sat imperturbable at his organ. Syd was clad in full pop star clothes, looking a bit uncomfortable. Waters was wearing a red suit with what looks like curtain fringe sewn on to the cuffs. Behind them are silver plastic sheeting stretched on frames. A decidedly odd session.

On 8 July, Pathe Newsreels aired a promotional film for 'Scarecrow', an interesting little glimpse of the Pink Floyd parading a scarecrow around the countryside of Suffolk in summer. The three-minute colour film features the group clowning around, striking horror film poses. Barrett lopes along gamely, his gait a bit heavy, as if a certain stiffness had taken hold of his limbs.

The following day, the Pink Floyd performed at the Roundhouse, Chalk Farm, and a live performance of 'Astronomy Domine' was filmed by BBC2, according to the 29 July *NME,* for inclusion on *Man Alive.* So it was an exhausted Pink Floyd which embarked on a gruelling drive to Scotland to begin a mini-tour. On 20 July, they played the Red Shoes in Elgin, and were billed on posters for the gig as *'The group that brings its own lighting to set the scene oscillating and vibrating with* WAY OUT SETS'. The Scottish tour was a fiasco of sorts. Roger Waters wasn't pleased, 'Terrible stage. We're going to give up ballroom gigs. Conditions are so bad. We'd really like to set up in a big tent, circus style, and take our show around the country.' It was a case of the music not fitting the environment. Even in 1967, Waters was envisioning something much more grandiose. The feeling of playing in small clubs for witless punters must have irked Waters to no end.

He told the *Melody Maker*, 'We're trying to play music of which it can be said that it has freedom of feeling. That sounds very corny, but it is very free. We can't go on doing clubs and ballrooms. We want a brand new environment, and we've hit on the idea of using a big top. We'll have a huge tent and go around like a travelling circus. We'll have a huge screen 120 feet wide and forty feet high inside, and project films and slides. We'll play the big cities, or anywhere, and become an occasion, just like a circus. It'll be a beautiful scene. It could even be the salvation of the circus! The thing is, I don't think we can go on doing what we are doing now. If we do, we'll all be on the dole.' Here were the origins of later concepts such as the Wall. He said, 'We've got a name of sorts now among the public so everybody comes to have a look at us, and we get full houses. But the atmosphere in these places is very stale. There is no feeling of occasion. The sort of thing we are trying to do doesn't fit into the sort of environment we are playing in. The supporting bands play "Midnight Hour" and the records are all soul, then we come on. On the club scene we rate about two out of ten and "Must try harder".'[125]

The *Disc & Music Echo* followed the band up to Scotland. Syd told their reporter that he loved fairy tales and outrageous clothes, and believed in total freedom. He said he hated to impede or criticise others and hated others to impede or criticise him. He also stated he didn't care about money, and wasn't worried about the future.[126] On the surface seemingly a throwaway set of answers to a reporter's probing, Barrett unintentionally infers that he was being 'criticised and impeded by others'. Not being worried about the future implies he was thinking of a coming change, and the reference to 'total freedom' suggests he wasn't feeling very free at the time.

Disc & Music Echo, 29 July, reported that the Pink Floyd 'are four unpretentious, easygoing, and unaffected boys. Roger Waters, quiet and seemingly cultured, Syd Barrett, quiet and seemingly shy, Rick Wright, and Nick Mason, pile into a car at Great Yarmouth at darkest night on Wednesday and drive through the night to arrive near Elgin at a seaside hotel in Lossiemouth at 4 p.m. on Thursday.'

Roger Waters said, 'I suppose it's odd, us being up here when we've got a big hit going. Still we're staying up here a couple of nights. Be a break really. No, the hotel people don't mind our clothes and hair. Think they'd be a bit disappointed if we didn't turn up in fancy dress.'[127]

On 20 July, the Pink Floyd's pre-recorded second *Top Of The Pops* appearance was screened. Syd appeared in a plain red shirt and black trousers, dispensing with the pop star clothes of the previous show.

The next day they played at Nairn and on 22 July at Aberdeen. On 23 July, the Pink Floyd played the Cosmopolitan Ballroom, Carlisle, where their performance was recorded for a broadcast on pirate Radio Carlisle. Fragments of the recording have survived, and the Floyd played versions of 'Reaction In G', an unmemorable improvisational snippet with Barrett doing Bo Diddley-esque runs on his Telecaster, and a new Waters' composition, 'Set The Controls For The Heart Of The Sun'. 'Reaction In G' would metamorphose into a proto-metal live powerhouse, as a live recording from the era illustrates.

In response to Hoppy's gaoling, Steve Abrams, whose Society for Mental Awareness had once held meetings at 101 Cromwell Road, organised an interesting project. On 24 July, against all odds, a full-page advertisement appeared in the conservative *Sunday Times* with the headline 'The law against marijuana is immoral in principle and unworkable in practice'. Calling for the decriminalisation of marijuana, the signatories came from all walks of life, including all four Beatles, psychologist R.D. Laing, photographer David Bailey, activist Tariq Ali, painter David Hockney, eleven medical doctors, a reverend, two MPs and author Graham Greene. It was a remarkable document, immediately prompting debate in Parliament, and ultimately leading to the Wooton Report and rescindment of the harsh penalties for marijuana users.

Blackhill Enterprises announced on 25 July the Pink Floyd's third single, 'Old Woman In A Casket' backed with 'Millionaire'. The proposed single was later scrapped, and both songs would remain unreleased.

Roger Waters said, 'We are simply a pop group. But because we use light and colour in our act, a lot of people seem to imagine that we are trying to put across some message with nasty, evil undertones. It sometimes makes it very difficult for us to establish any association with the audience. Apart from the few at the front, no one can really identify us.'[128]

On 27 July, the Pink Floyd performed their third and final *Top Of The Pops* appearance promoting 'See Emily Play'. 'The first time Syd dressed up like a pop star,' said Peter Jenner. 'The second time he came on in his straightforward, fairly scruffy clothes, looking rather unshaven. The third time he came to the studio in his pop star clothes and then changed into complete rags for the actual TV spot.'[129] 'When "Emily" was a hit and we were in the top-ten for three weeks,' said Roger Waters, 'we did *Top Of The Pops*, and the third week we did it Syd didn't want to know. He got down there in an incredible state and said he was not going to do it. We finally discovered the reason was that John Lennon didn't have to do *Top Of The Pops* so he didn't.'[130] It was a bit more than that, in reality. The television and radio appearances had become a major bone of contention between Syd and the rest of the band and his managers.

Jenny Gordon says, 'When he had all the make-up, long hair and green velvet trousers, that really wasn't him. I don't think he was a "dresser". He was a nature boy. It didn't seem to be him at all, all dressed up.'

Top Of The Pops was, as it remains now, a frenetic, plastic, highly commercialised joke, albeit with a huge audience. Nick Mason stated, 'When we started out that's what we wanted to be [a three-minute pop band]. We wanted to be on *Top Of The Pops*, we back-combed our hair and all that.'[131] '*Top Of The Pops* was definitely one of the worst things I did,' said Rick Wright. 'It was horrible to be on it [and] a real drag.'[132]

The entire experience had left Syd sour, and he'd had enough. He sought to distance himself from the banal spectacle of such things as *Top Of The Pops* and found that he couldn't. He was obliged to be there, in body if not in mind. The gruelling Scottish tour, being forced to do *Top Of The Pops* against his will three times, the constant travelling, and a furious intake of drugs to cope with it all were all pushing Syd to the edge of a breakdown.

Genius is a word that has slipped into overuse, but it is all too simple to focus on Barrett's downfall while forgetting his extraordinary intelligence and unique talent. His sensibilities allowed him to view things from a different angle and express what he saw or heard through words and music. Arguably, genius veers across the fine line into madness when these ideas can no longer be expressed. Perhaps the difference between a genius and a madman is that one can express his visions and ideas and the other can't. And this flow of ideas has been bolstered by initial, mild use of drugs. At least some of the appeal of drugs lies in the contrast they offer from reality, and part of the downside of drugs is that they simply become another reality from which to escape.

Eventually after long abuse, the drugs bring forward ideas that are so specific and tangled up in a web of supposition and meandering thought that they become muddled and unclear. Immense time and energy are used up trying to explain what is inherently uncomplicated. Brian Wilson once said that ultimately the combination of hash and speed wouldn't let him get past one chord on the piano when composing. Like Syd he would focus on one note or chord for ages, eventually only succeeding in confusing himself and others. Waters and co. would get exasperated with Syd's variations on a chord. It points up the irony of Barrett playing on-stage on acid while his band mates were sober or slightly drunk. The gulf between their respective states of mind would begin to fray their collective spirit. In the end, even bonds formed in teenage years wouldn't be enough to maintain their *esprit de corps*. Syd's natural creativity had begun to flourish with the back-up of the relatively staid, dependable Waters, Wright and Mason. In the beginning, having three architectural students to underpin his flights of fancy must have served Barrett well. It was an accident that worked brilliantly.

The drugs that had opened doors for Syd were now beginning to close them, one by one. The blur of fame with its gruelling tours, endless photo sessions and interviews, newspaper spreads, groupies and unsteady rhythm was beginning to occlude Syd's vision. Syd was just twenty-one when he became famous, and at twenty-one a person normally has time to reflect on where they are going or whether they want to be going there. There was no time for Syd to do this; the others in the band were two years older at a time in life when two years seems a near eternity. Barrett scholar Scott Frank notes, 'Syd never had time to build a framework.'

There were, according June Bolan, periods when the clouds that seemed to hover over Syd would part, and the familiar radiant light would re-emerge, giving him that familiar impish smile. And make no mistake, Syd was still executing incredibly tricky sonic somersaults on-stage with tremendous flair and vibrancy. But the pressures were intense. He was beginning to have major problems with fame and its excessive demands. As the momentum of fame increased, Barrett must have often longed for the tranquillity of Cambridge, where a walk will take in open green spaces where one can muse on the finer points of things. There was less possibility of doing this in London, so far from the unhurried pace of life in Cambridge.

Duggie Fields says, 'Fame wasn't something that I thought was particularly interesting, and I can't have been the only one. Material success wasn't a goal; if it happened, it happened. Fame wasn't something unusual in the world we lived in at that time. Fame and fortune were there, but they weren't seen as the great goals of life. Living life was the goal. Fame was kind of irrelevant, the media was seen as irrelevant. The media didn't reflect our lives; the media didn't inform and wasn't particularly relevant. It wasn't the same goal as people see it as now. I remember going to fancy restaurants without money, and being confident that someone would pay the bill. It didn't seem particularly relevant who would pay. Those who did have money didn't mind paying and didn't seem to begrudge if you were part of the group. And you were part of the group because of the vibe that you gave out more than anything, rather than what you did, rather than what you said. It was the vibe, whether you had an empathy with the others. People made music, people created, but that was the reward that one actually did it for. For Syd during the Pink Floyd, the "doing" and the responsibilities became a chore. A problem. Syd wasn't doing it for the vibe any more, he was doing it because he *had* to do it. The vibe wasn't right for him any more. There was a subversion by success, which I think is what happened to Syd. And resisting that is difficult for any creative individual. Success destroys creativity as much as failure.'

---

1 Jones, Cliff. *Echoes: The Stories Behind Every Pink Floyd Song*. Omnibus Press, 1996
2 *Guitar Player*, February 1997
3 *Mojo*, July 1995
4 *Disc & Music Echo*, 8 April 1967
5 *Go*, 4 August 1967
6 Miles & Mabbett, Andy. *Pink Floyd: The Visual Documentary*. Omnibus Press, London 1994
7 *Mojo*, July 1995
8 Miles & Mabbett, Andy. *Pink Floyd: The Visual Documentary*. Omnibus Press, London 1994
9 *Terrapin*, 7, 1975
10 Fabian, Jenny & Byrne, Johnny. *Groupie*. 1970
11 Bailey, Derek. 'Improvisation: Its nature and practice in music'. National Sound Archives; British Library, 1992
12 *NME*, 9 July 1988
13 *Mojo*, July 1995
14 Ibid.
15 *Sounds*, 17 August 1974

16 Giovanni Dadomo interview with Syd Barrett, 1970
17 Watkinson, Mike & Anderson, Pete. *Crazy Diamond: Syd Barrett & T he Dawn Of Pink Floyd.* Omnibus Press, 1993
18 Ibid.
19 *Melody Maker*, 9 September 1967
20 *Disc & Music Echo*, 8 April 1967
21 Giovanni Dadomo interview with Syd Barrett, 1970
22 *Disc & Music Echo*, 8 April 1967
23 *The Amazing Pudding*, # 58
24 *Mojo*, August 1997
25 *ZigZag*, July 1973
26 *Melody Maker*, 14 January 1967
27 *Mojo*, May 1994
28 *ZigZag*, July 1973
29 *Mojo*, July 1995
30 *Disc & Music Echo*, 8 April 1967
31 *Omnibus* special on Pink Floyd, 1994
32 Dancing in the Streets, BBC series, 1996
33 *Omnibus* special on Pink Floyd, 1994
34 Miles & Mabbett, Andy. *Pink Floyd: The Visual Documentary*. Omnibus Press, London 1994
35 *ZigZag*, July 1973
36 Welch, Chris. *Pink Floyd: Learning To Fly*. Castle Communications, London 1994
37 *Omnibus* special on Pink Floyd, 1994
38 *Pink Floyd* by Rick Sanders Futura Books, 1975 p.25
39 *Omnibus* special on Pink Floyd, 1994
40 Ibid.
41 Ibid.
42 Unedited transcripts of interviews with Peter Jenner by Jonathan Greene. *Days In The Life: Voices From The English Underground, 1961-1971*. Minerva, 1988
43 Macdonald, Bruno, editor. *Pink Floyd: Through The Eyes Of. . .* Sidgwick & Jackson, London, 1996
44 *ZigZag*, July 1973
45 Macdonald, Bruno, editor. *Pink Floyd: Through The Eyes Of. . .* Sidgwick & Jackson, London, 1996
46 *Disc & Music Echo*, 25 March 1967
47 Miles & Mabbett, Andy. *Pink Floyd: The Visual Documentary*. Omnibus Press, London 1994
48 *Omnibus* special on Pink Floyd, 1994
49 Macdonald, Bruno, editor. *Pink Floyd: Through The Eyes Of. . .* Sidgwick & Jackson, London, 1996
50 Miles & Mabbett, Andy. *Pink Floyd: The Visual Documentary*. Omnibus Press, London 1994
51 *Record Mirror*, 8 July 1967
52 *Interview*, 1994
53 *ZigZag*, July 1973
54 Jones, Cliff. *Echoes: The Stories Behind Every Pink Floyd Song* Omnibus Press, 1996
55 Miles & Mabbett, Andy. *Pink Floyd: The Visual Documentary*. Omnibus Press, London 1994
56 *Mojo*, May 1994
57 Schaffner, Nicholas. *Saucerful Of Secrets*. Delta, 1991
58 Unedited transcripts of interviews with Paul McCartney by Jonathan Greene. *Days In The Life: Voices From The English Underground, 1961-1971*. Minerva, 1988
59 Macdonald, Bruno, editor. *Pink Floyd: Through The Eyes Of. . .* Sidgwick & Jackson, London, 1996
60 *Mojo*, August 1997
61 *Melody Maker*, 14 January 1967
62 *Go*, 4 August 1967
63 Unedited transcripts of interviews with June Bolan by Jonathan Greene. *Days In The Life: Voices From The English Underground, 1961-1971*. Minerva, 1988
64 *Beat Instrumental*, October 1967
65 Jonathan Greene. *Days In The Life: Voices From The English Underground, 1961-1971*. Minerva, 1988
66 'Syd Barrett Careening Through Life'. Kris DiLorenzo, *Trouser Press*, February 1978
67 'Syd Barrett Careening Through Life'. Kris DiLorenzo, *Trouser Press*, February 1978
68 *Mojo*, July 1995
69 *NME*, 9 July 1988
70 *NME*, 9 July 1988

71 *Mojo*, May 1994
72 Giovanni Dadomo interview with Syd Barrett, 1970
73 *ZigZag*, July 1973
74 Jonathan Greene. *Days In The Life: Voices From The English Underground, 1961-1971*. Minerva, 1988
75 Ibid.
76 Ibid.
77 *Dancing In The Streets*, BBC series, 1996
78 *Mojo*, July 1995
79 *Dancing In The Streets*, BBC series, 1996
80 Allen, Daevid. *Gong Dreaming*. GAS, 1994
81 *Mojo*, May 1994
82 *ZigZag*, July 1973
83 Miles & Mabbett, Andy. *Pink Floyd: The Visual Documentary*. Omnibus Press, London 1994
84 Allen, Daevid. *Gong Dreaming*. GAS, 1994
85 Macdonald, Bruno, editor. *Pink Floyd: Through The Eyes Of...* Sidgwick & Jackson, London, 1996 244
86 Jonathan Greene. *Days In The Life: Voices From The English Underground, 1961-1971*. Minerva, 1988
87 *The Amazing Pudding*, # 56
88 Roger Waters Interview with Chris Salewicz, June 1987
89 '*Dark Side Of The Moon*'. Japanese CD edition liner notes
90 *Mojo*, July 1995
91 *ZigZag*, July 1973
92 Miles & Mabbett, Andy. *Pink Floyd: The Visual Documentary*. Omnibus Press, London 1994
93 *Melody Maker*, 9 December 1967
94 Ibid.
95 *NME*, 13 April 1974
96 *Sounds*, May 1983
97 Welch, Chris. Pink Floyd: *Learning To Fly*. Castle Communications, London 1994
98 *Mojo*, May 1994
99 Schaffner, Nicholas. *Saucerful Of Secrets*. Delta, 1991
100 MTV interviews with Pink Floyd, 1992
101 Watkinson, Mike & Anderson, Pete. *Crazy Diamond: Syd Barrett And The Dawn Of Pink Floyd*. Omnibus Press, 1993
102 Jones, Cliff. *Echoes: The Stories Behind Every Pink Floyd Song*. Omnibus Press, 1996
103 Ibid.
104 Welch, Chris. Pink Floyd: *Learning To Fly*. Castle Communications, London 1994
105 *Melody Maker*, 22 July 1967
106 Unedited transcripts of interviews with June Bolan by Jonathan Greene. *Days In The Life: Voices From The English* Underground, *1961-1971*. Minerva, 1988
107 Unedited transcripts of interviews with Hoppy by Jonathan Greene. *Days In The Life: Voices From The English* Underground, *1961-1971*. Minerva, 1988
108 Abrams, Steve. *Hashish Fudge: Soma and the Wootton Report*
109 *Omnibus* special on Pink Floyd, 1994
110 Miles interview with Joe Boyd, 1976
111 Giovanni Dadomo interview with Syd Barrett, 1970
112 *Melody Maker*, 27 March 1971
113 Ibid.
114 *The Amazing Pudding*, # 56
115 *The Amazing Pudding*, # 56
116 *NME*, 13 April 1974
117 *Dancing In The Streets*, BBC series, 1996
118 *The Pink Floyd Story*: Six-part documentary broadcast on Capital radio, London. December 1976-January 1977
119 Fabian, Jenny & Byrne, Johnny. *Groupie*. 1970
120 Abrams, Steve. *Hashish Fudge: Soma and the Wootton Report*
121 Miles interview with Joe Boyd, 1976
122 Macdonald, Bruno, editor. *Pink Floyd: Through the Eyes of...* Sidgwick & Jackson, London, 1996.
123 *Melody Maker*, 5 August 1967

124 *Mojo*, July 1995
125 *Melody Maker*, 5 August 1967
126 *Disc & Music Echo*, 22 July 1967
127 Ibid.
128 *Record Mirror*, 8 July 1967
129 *NME*, 13 April 1974
130 *Melody Maker*, 27 March 1971
131 *NME* 8 July 1988
132 *ZigZag*, July 1973

Stage Four: 'Like Summer Tempests Came His Tears' (July 1967-January 1968)

'There are people of a certain instability who feel a constant urge to reverse themselves. There is danger in continually deserting the good because of uncontrolled desires . . .'

Chapter 24: Fu/Return – The Turning Point
The I-Ching or Book Of Changes

By late 1967, the King's Road was becoming an institution. Mary Quant, Biba, Quorum, the Picasso Café, the Chelsea antiques market, Granny Takes A Trip, and Mr Fish were all part of the landscape, and new arrivals on the scene took it for granted. The hip philosophy, some began to suspect, was being watered down for mass consumption. The clothes began to represent something far different than they had in 1966. The cliché kaftan and bell, along with crushed velvet trousers, silk kerchiefs and satin shirts, had in 1966 been daring clothes, the far edge of this new dandyism, indicating flamboyance and individuality. By the tail end of 1967, a kaftan could be ordered out of the back pages of the *Disc & Music Echo*. They had become a uniform. Peter Wynne-Wilson says, 'The Kings Road was a decadent aspect of the Underground. Decadent in the literal sense, because that was the decay of the hip philosophy, if you like. Because there it had moved completely into garments and fashion, which wasn't a perversion of it because a lot of that confluence of music and philosophy and clothes was certainly identifiable, but "genteel" would be a word that I would apply to the Kings Road.'

Tourists and suburbanites began to flood the streets of Chelsea, or the Portobello Road. The same happened at UFO. The original vanguard at the club, in a fit of élitist pique, decried the invasion of their scene. The vibe that had spontaneously swollen from the ICA in 1964, Better Books and Wholly

Communion in 1965, the All Saints' Hall in 1966, and the Spontaneous Underground and UFO in 1967, had developed organically, powered by few concerns for money or prestige. The symbols and signposts of this new constituency had been erected and created in an unselfconscious way. The Underground was slowly being co-opted; the media had got hold of it, the merchants moved in to make money, the punters were drawn not by egalitarian ideas of peace and love but by the promise of drugs and free love and a new sensation.

And it was also going wrong from within; dissension and drugs, linked more often than people would care to admit, begin to fray the fabric that held it all together. The theft of ticket money from the 14 Hour Technicolor Dream and also from the Albert Hall poetry readings had highlighted the fact that not everyone was to be trusted. The new and dodgy drugs like STP and LSD cut with strychnine, and the old dodgy ones like speed and heroin, were becoming ubiquitous. New social strata were being erected in this new society, regardless of the claims of its theorists. The status symbols were drugs, money, fame and hip clothes. People began to change in unexpected and sometimes unpleasant ways. And some of the brightest lights were being snuffed out. Sadly but tellingly, one of the very brightest, Syd Barrett, was also one of the first to go.

On 28 July, the Pink Floyd were scheduled to record a session for BBC radio's *Saturday Club* at the BBC Playhouse Theatre, in London. In the studio that day were several bands, including the Spectrum, Amen Corner and Scott Peters, all recording for a session scheduled for broadcast on 12 August. Waters, Wright and Mason all showed at the studio, but Syd wasn't there. Waters recalled, 'I remember we had to do a radio show, and we were waiting for him, and he didn't turn up.'[1] Rick Wright said, 'We were supposed to do a session for the BBC one Friday, and Syd didn't turn up. Nobody could find him. He went missing for the whole weekend and when he reappeared again on the Monday, he was a totally different person.'[2] Roger Waters said, 'I believe Syd was a casualty of the so-called "psychedelic period" that we were meant to represent. Because everybody believed that we were taking acid before we went on stage and all that stuff . . . unfortunately, one of us was, and that was Syd. It's a simple matter, really, Syd just had a big overdose of acid and that was it. It was very frightening, and I couldn't believe what had happened, because . . . he didn't turn up. And then he came [back] and he was a different person.'[3]

What Waters referred to as 'a big overdose of acid', psychologists would call a psychotic break. Did Syd take that epochal trip from which he never fully came back? It's very likely that LSD aggravated an existing underlying problem, but to blame Syd's breakdown solely on LSD is facile. The factors in Syd's breakdown are numerous, and not all of them clear. But what was certain was that, except for brief flashes, from now on Barrett's haunted eyes would never waver from the immensely demanding, and all consuming, inner dialogue. The experiment slipped out of his hands; the criteria for exploration flew out the window. The Binson echo unit bouncing an endless loop of guitar brilliance while Syd sat staring at the psychedelic wash of lights, looking for a shadow of his elusive muse, ever more distant. Syd's performance persona, charismatic bordering on worrying, was out of step with the others, and it wouldn't be long before he was out of tune with them as well, both metaphorically and literally.

Syd did come back that night, however, for a performance at UFO. *Melody Maker* filed the following review: 'In a cacophony of sound played to a background of multi-coloured projected lights, the Pink Floyd proved they are Britain's top psychedelic group before the hip audience at UFO, on Friday night. In two powerful sets they drew nearly every conceivable note from their instruments but ignored their two hit singles. They included "Pow R. Toc H." and a number which received its first hearing called "Reaction In G" which they say was their reaction against their Scottish tour when they had to do "See Emily Play". Bass player Roger Waters gave the group a powerful depth and the lights played on to them set an impressive scene. Many of the audience found the Floyd's music too much to sit down to and in more subdued parts of the act the sound of jingling bells from their dancing masters joined in. It is clear that the Floyd prefer playing to UFO-type audiences rather than provincial ones and are at their best in an atmosphere more acceptable to them.'[4]

Jenny Fabian was there that night, and remembers it a bit differently. In *Groupie*, Fabian wrote a vivid and disturbing picture of Syd that night: 'He turned up at my place without any warning to take me to a gig, and looked really ill. He wasn't speaking to anyone and his face was deathly white and beaded with sweat. He went on to play and I noticed halfway through the first set he wasn't singing and hardly playing a note. [Roger Waters] was covering up for him well, so not many people noticed. After the first set [Syd] said he wanted to get away from the club and sit somewhere quiet. So we took a taxi cab back to my flat, promising to return in time for the second set. He sat down and suddenly started talking about all the people who were now putting down the group because they had made it. I told him there would always be people like that. But he believed the group had sold out, and he couldn't reconcile what he wanted to do with what he was actually doing. Commercialism had nothing to do with being a religious artist, he said . . . He seemed to have lost touch with reality, and there's no convincing someone like that.'[5] Syd returned for the second set, but spent the entire set sitting on the stage.

Roger Waters said, 'We went to UFO [and] it was more or less that we did [the] gig without Syd. He may have been on the stage but we really did it without him, he just stood there with [his guitar] hanging round his neck, which was something he was prone to do.'

The following night, 29 July, was where the severity of Syd's breakdown became clear, and from here on he would never be the same. Ironically, it was the day that 'See Emily Play' reached its highest position, number six, in the weekly music charts. The night began badly and ended worse. The Pink Floyd played two gigs that night, first at a miserable, grotty pub called the Wellington Club in East Dereham, Norfolk. Waters recalled, 'We actually had broken beer mugs smashing into the drum kit. I'll never forget that night. We did a double-header that night. First of all we played to a roomful of about 500 gypsies, hurling abuse and fighting, and then we did the Ally Pally.'[6] The furious provincial punters had clearly had enough. After cranking out a ragged 'Interstellar Overdrive' to violent lager louts, the lads gathered their guitars, the roadies brushed the broken glass and beer off Mason's drumkit and then hurriedly loaded the gear into the van, under cover of a furious rainfall, rushing at breakneck speed back to London for a massive, multi-act event called the International Love-In at the cavernous Alexandra Palace.

For Syd, this was to be the breaking point. He simply couldn't cope with the pressures of touring and playing two venues in one night, not to mention UFO and *Top Of The Pops* in the previous two days. His excessive acid ingestion had helped to render him nearly catatonic, priming him for his breakdown. This event was to be a crucial turning point for the Pink Floyd, Syd Barrett particularly, but Roger Waters as well. The events of this evening would haunt Waters for years.

The feeling at the International Love-In was captured by one James Vincent, in the audience that night, who wrote the following letter to the *Melody Maker*: 'What a tragic experience the Alexandra Palace Love-In proved to be. The most horrible yobs I have seen in years massed for an orgy of sneering . . . jeering, beating and swearing, and as love, Flower Power and music were ground into the litter-laden floor of the Palace, I felt here was the death of an ideal.'[7] The event was plagued by violence and bad vibes, a mini-Altamont. Bouncers were overzealous in their duties, faces were punched and heads were butted. Covering the event for the *NME* was Keith Altham, who characterised the Love-in as 'punch-ins (bouncers versus "flowerpot men"), smash-ins (beautiful people in the car park), raid-ins (the police took away substances to be analysed) and one stab-in . . . The main attraction, was the audience itself, aged between seventeen and twenty-five . . . Some came with faces painted blue, yellow, or green streaked by the torrential rain outside. Some wore floral jackets, some robes and brightly coloured scarves. Some wore beads and threw carnations about. Some came out of curiosity, some came because they believe and some because they thought it was an all-night orgy (and some proved it was!) . . . There were too many selling love in brown paper packets. There were too many flower children with smiles on their faces and nothing in their hearts.'[8]

Just before the band were due on stage, June Bolan found Barrett in the dressing room, frozen in catatonia, 'absolutely gaga, just totally switched off, sitting rigid like a stone'.[9] Roger Waters came into the dressing-room to see what was wrong. Immediately assessing the severity of the situation, Waters joined Bolan in trying to coax Barrett to stand up. 'And we're trying to get Syd up, and get him together to go and play. He couldn't speak; he was absolutely catatonic.[10]

Roger Waters and I got him on his feet, we got him out to the stage, and he had a white Stratocaster and we put it round his neck and he walked on stage and of course the audience went spare because they loved them. The band started to play and Syd stood there. He had his guitar round his neck and his arms just hanging down and I was in the wings and Peter was one side and Andrew was the other side and we're looking at each other and wondering what to do. And suddenly he put his hands on the guitar and we thought "Great, he's actually going to do it" and he stood there, he just stood there, tripping out of his mind. And he looked around. Syd couldn't even stand up for a set, let alone do anything else.[11] That's when you have to give Roger credit for what he did, he actually got the other two together and made sort of a half-assed version of a set. Peter Jenner and Andrew King were frantic; they were pulling out their hair.[12] They did three, maybe four numbers and we got him off.'[13]

Syd Barrett had made the break, eyes fixed on a spot in the indeterminate distance. His eyes frozen into a blank, frightened, and frightening stare. Peter Jenner quickly came across behind the stage and told June, 'Go and sit in the car'. Bolan hurried out of the back, money in hand, and got into the car. The promoter realised that the Pink Floyd weren't going to finish their set, and started shouting at Jenner and King for 'the chick with the money'. Jenner said, 'I'm awfully sorry, she's gone, she had to leave early.' With the promoter glowering in a rage, Waters and Jenner half-dragged Syd to the car, while Mason, Wright and King got all the guitars and ran out to it. Bolan, sitting in the driver's seat, started up the engine, and with everyone safely inside, she drove the Rolls-Royce out of the Alexandra Palace parking lot.

Waters was shaken by the night's events. Combined with another incident when Waters himself was given a 'jump-start' injection and pressured into performing despite a virulent attack of hepatitis during the early seventies, this episode formed the basis of a particularly horrifying scene in 'The Wall' where a catatonic Pink is given an injection by a dubious doctor backstage and then dragged on-stage to perform, tearing at his own skin.

That other symbol of psychedelic London, UFO, was imperiled as well. The *News Of The World*, published an exposé on 30 July. Under the headline 'The Flower Children', the *News Of The World* journalists painted a vivid if misinformed portrait of the famed club. After paying their £1 admission to an 'outrageously dressed flower girl with a bulging money box' the pair ventured into the psychedelic dungeon. 'The heat, music, noise and smell hit us like a left hook . . . Nearly everyone had smouldering joss sticks, giving off a sickly fragrance. Thumping music was so loud that the whole floor vibrated and violent coloured lights flashed in odd sequences. There was a crude stage at one end of the hall and old, Charlie-Chaplin-style films were projected on to a curtain. Two different records were played at the same time, assaulting the ears with discord. A youth nearby sprang up and began dancing on his own, sweat pouring down his face, his eyes closed, mumbling, "Let it flow, man, just move with it."' The music stopped and a poetry reading began, which the reporters duly noted was 'obscene'. 'A young girl in a wheel-chair, clutching a flower and taking in the scene while her American girlfriend kept rolling back her head and opening and closing her eyes.' The reporters gaped in disbelief as a Dalmatian roamed through the crowd. The female reporter ducked into the loo only to find two young hippie girls huddled under the sink, asleep.

Mr Gannon, the kindly old Irish proprietor of the Blarney Pub, UFO's locale, read the report in horror. He knew full well what was going on, but the media exposé was too much. He promptly rang Joe Boyd and told him, 'I'm sorry, boys, but I can't let you open on Friday.' The police at the station up the road had been leaning on Gannon for a while to evict UFO, and the exposé sealed it. Boyd was suddenly faced with having to find a new venue within a week, which he duly did. Ringing up Arnold Wesker, he secured a temporary lease for the Roundhouse. But there had been no time to change their weekly adverts in the music weeklies or in *IT* and *Oz*, so come Friday, Boyd had several people stand in front of the Blarney and inform the clubgoers of the change in venue. It was a bad start for the new UFO, which would run into one problem after another.[14]

On 31 July, the Pink Floyd played yet another date at Torquay, Devon, but King and Jenner realised something was terribly wrong with Syd, and decided to call a temporary halt to what was becoming an increasingly bizarre, Fellinesque spectacle. They cancelled a performance booked months in advance for the *Beat Club* programme on German television, as well as a string of scheduled gigs.

The gig was up, the cash cow exhausted. Syd Barrett's creative peak had passed, most ironically, just as his greatest achievement was released. On 5 August, at long last, after months of arduous work and editing, the Pink Floyd's first album, suffused with Syd Barrett's brilliance, was released. *The Piper At The Gates Of Dawn* was a stellar achievement. As Paul McCartney unequivocally stated, 'The new Floyd album is a knock-out'.

The Piper At The Gates Of Dawn remained on the charts for seven weeks, and reached number six. Along with Procul Harum's *Whiter Shade Of Pale*, the Beatles' *Sergeant Pepper*, Traffic's eponymous album and the Jimi Hendrix Experience's *Are You Experienced?, The Piper At The Gates Of Dawn* indelibly marks that moment in time when all seemed possible in the world of the young; that lysergic summer whose days seemed timeless.

The Piper At The Gates Of Dawn is one of those all too rare albums that rewards its avid listeners with a new surprise, a new subtlety or nuance, on every listen. Barrett would recall the making of the album years later in an interview; '*Wind in the Willows*,' he mused, recalling the book that provided the album with its title. 'That was very difficult in some ways, getting used to the studios and everything. But it was fun, we freaked about a lot. I was working very hard then; there's still lots of stuff lying around from then, even some of the stuff on *The Madcap Laughs*.'[15] Rick Wright said, 'If you listen to *The Piper At The Gates Of Dawn* there are some extraordinary songs in there, and that's what Syd did. He was an amazing person, and they were the kind of songs that no one had ever written before, childlike, but wonderful stuff. I can understand why people still want to know about Syd and the music we did then.[16] I love listening to it, just to listen to Syd's songs. It's sad in a way as well, because it reminds me of what might have been. I think he could have easily been one of the finest songwriters today.'[17]

The album was released in two versions, one monophonic and one stereo. Both are worth seeking out, as they are substantially different, with the mono mix of *The Piper At The Gates Of Dawn* being the one that Barrett and the Floyd had the greatest hand in helping fashion, with Smith, Bown and the band all participating in the mixing. A remastered stereo version was issued in 1994 and a remastered mono mix in 1997. The stereo mix, as was customary at EMI in those days, was mixed by engineers. Stereo was just beginning to be exploited fully, and some of the psychedelic era's tremendous overproduction can be attributed to the delight of engineers experimenting with the new medium. Heavy echo is added not only to Nick Mason's drums in the stereo mix, but on every vocal, guitar or organ part available. The mono mix is more compressed, owing more to the mod and R&B music of the preceding years. However, it lacks that wide horizon coupled with echo that gives the stereo *The Piper At The Gates Of Dawn* such resonance.*

Some tracks are noticeably inferior in the mono mix, particularly Barrett's more intimate, short narrative songs like 'Scarecrow' and 'Bike'; 'Matilda Mother' suffers from the lack of stereo ambiance. The rhythm section mixed to the fore in the mono mix, sometimes burying Barrett's more intricate guitar runs and sonic textures. The songs on *The Piper At The Gates Of Dawn* which echoed their live improvisations, notably 'Power R. Toc H.' and 'Interstellar Overdrive' benefit from the compressed mono mix, evoking the intensity of their live performances. The stereo mix, particularly on the 1995 remaster, is a marvellous production, despite its occasional faults. The 'more is better' ethos of psychedelic record production in 1967-8 certainly could have benefited from some restraint, but the stereo mix none the less has a majestic Spectoresque sweep.

'*The Piper At The Gates Of Dawn* was Syd; Syd was a genius,' said Waters.[18] Waters also tacitly acknowledged Barrett's role in a 1970 interview: '"See Emily Play" and "Arnold Layne" were Syd Barrett's songs, right, and it wouldn't matter who it was who played bass or did this or that, it's irrelevant. They're very strong songs and you just did it. It had nothing to do with the music, playing

*In the US the band's début was crudely resequenced, with two tracks being dropped in favour of their singles. 'Flaming' was issued as a single there as their US label, Capitol's subsidiary Tower, judged it the only track with any commercial potential. The single contains a different mix, with keyboards mixed to the fore.

that stuff, it has to do with writing songs and that was Syd who wrote those songs. I don't think we were doing anything then, if you see what I mean.'[19]

DJ John Peel said, 'That first LP obviously came about as a revelation.'[20] Cambridge friend Mick Rock said, 'What else could he have done after that? He'd already defined it all. There's nothing ever been done on God's earth like that, that's Art.'[21] Andrew King said, 'Syd was 100 per cent creative, and very hard on himself. He wouldn't do anything unless he thought he was doing it in an artistic way. [Syd] would throw the levers on the boards up and down apparently at random, making pretty pictures with his hands.'[22]

Norman Smith said, 'It was a pretty difficult job actually with Syd, because I think Syd used music with lyrical phrasing or lyrics with musical phrasing. It was a statement being made at a given time. That meant that if you came back five minutes later to do another take, you probably wouldn't get the same performance. You probably wouldn't get the same tune or musical composition. It made editing virtually impossible. We went through quite a few of Syd's songs, and it was very difficult to figure out which I liked and which I didn't like, so we'd come back to them and maybe try those songs again. Which made it even more difficult. It was a very slow, unwinding process.'[23] Norman Smith was able to do extraordinary things with the Floyd, though he instinctively lacked something his mentor George Martin had in spades, the ability to channel the ideas of his musicians, however bizarre or tangential, into concrete form. Martin essentially had faith in the Beatles' ideas, while it seems Smith didn't trust Barrett's instincts. Smith's area of expertise was largely technical, which is why he engineered the early Beatles' albums so well, but Martin himself was a musician, albeit an oboist, but a musician none the less.

Brian Wilson of the Beach Boys and Barrett's Floyd were both exploring the 'everything including the kitchen sink' approach to record production during 1967. If you had echo effects, use them! Why not overdub three guitars parts instead of two? Harmonies were rehearsed until every subtlety shone, some of them wholly in the minds of their creators. *Smile,* Wilson's unreleased 1966-7 masterpiece, and *The Piper At The Gates Of Dawn* share much in approach and in harmonic ideas. Brian Wilson was exploring the same terrain as Barrett but following a different path, harmonies instead of feedback, tight orchestrations versus improvisations, yet there are similarities in approach. The use of humour in music, American folklore versus English fairy tale whimsy, both seeking a distillation of moods through music; short melodic pieces, arduously edited together into a cohesive collage. Segments of epic instrumentation would alternate quickly with hushed vocals, plaintive piano or a solitary cello. The dualistic dynamics, loud to soft, overblown to subtle, give the music a much greater range than the simpler pop offerings of the time. Thundering strings and percussion, dropping out to reveal organ weaving a playful counterpoint to the guitar's monster riff. The ability to map out these peaks and troughs reveals a composer of great sensitivity, not only when making music but in the broader scope of their personal lives as well. The drugs accentuated this sensitivity; in moderation, the effects were pleasant and revealing, spurring Syd's creativity, in excess, his sensibilities became jarring and overwhelming. The vulnerabilities and frailties inherent in many creative minds leave the performer vulnerable in almost every way. Drugs, instead of being a spur to creativity, become an escape from its demands.

Jenner and King decided to send the band off on holiday, hoping that Syd would be able to get himself together, but one commitment remained. On 7 and 8 August the Pink Floyd went back to Abbey Road to try and record a third single, already overdue. The suitably tortured 'Scream Thy Last Scream' and Waters' meditative 'Set The Controls For The Heart Of The Sun' were recorded hastily and mixed to four-track.

'Scream Thy Last Scream', with its barrage of bells, crowd noises, scary echo-effect shadow vocal, and drumming reminiscent of Jewish wedding music, is dramatically overproduced, like all the best psychedelic records of the time. It is also a horrifying vignette of the turbulence in Barrett's mind; a truly frightening song. Like 'Jugband Blues' and 'Vegetable Man', its companion pieces recorded shortly thereafter, the song is much too much to absorb in one hearing. It reflects the overload of sensory stimuli its composer was experiencing. 'Scream Thy Last Scream' rings out like the aural equivalent of neurofibrillary tangles, collages of vast quantities of information coming and going without pattern. The disorientation of acid, where nothing feels as it should, where to paraphrase poet Arthur Rimbaud, all senses are deranged but none of their quintessence preserved. This disorientation becomes the *modus operandi*, supplanting reason and logic but leaving nothing to replace it in its wake.

The song might strike the casual listener as a mess, but much work and fevered thought courtesy of Barrett went into making this compelling, mad classic. It was a suitable song for stressful times, Barrett's most menacing song, with his voice fed back through his Binson to speed up his voice and causing it to pitch back and forth wildly, sometimes synchronised and sometimes spiralling off into the void, creating a dizzying disorientation. 'Scream Thy Last Scream' is quite an extraordinary melange of sounds, crowd noises echoing across the stereo spectrum, as Rick Wright plays some of his very best psychedelic Farfisa organ. Mason picks up an experimental marching rhythm. Syd freaks out with the Binson, feeding his vocal through and manipulating the 'swell' knob, skewing the falsetto shadow vocal wildly. It captured the feeling of their ragged state of affairs, particularly Syd's, before their unexpected summer holiday. It is a tone poem of madness.

'Set The Controls For The Heart Of The Sun' is a plaintive, meditative composition, a tonal inverse and diametric opposite to 'Scream Thy Last Scream's mad fanfare. Roger Waters' masterful ambient work was first performed during the summer of 1967 at places like UFO and on their July Scottish tour. 'Set The

Controls For The Heart Of The Sun' is Barrett's love of atmospheric soundscapes, a deft wisp of a melody, underscored by a filigree of one-chord bass. 'Set The Controls For The Heart Of The Sun' laid much of the framework for Pink Floyd's post-Syd work on albums such as *Meddle*; it was Waters' first significant composition, ignoring the forgettable 'Take Thy Stethoscope And Walk'. Peter Jenner said, 'It was the first song that Roger wrote that stood up against Syd's songs, which was significant at the time.'[24]

Waters proved himself to be a songwriter of tremendous potential. The song's structure is so slight as to suggest a whisper across an infinite nebula. The lyrics, derived from an ancient Chinese poem, and with a title lifted from a page of author William S. Burrough's *The Nova Express*, could be interpreted as a meditative allegory on Barrett's internal implosion. The interstellar voyager who had become an astral kamikaze. Waters explained the song was 'about an unknown person who, while piloting a mighty flying saucer, is overcome with solar suicidal tendencies and sets the control for the heart of the sun'.[25] In a hushed invocation of hypnotic brilliance, the song's single bass chord emulates the doomed spacecraft with its controls set for the heart of the sun.

The Pink Floyd finally made the cover of the *Melody Maker* on 12 August, but for all the wrong reasons. An enormous headline trumpeted, *'Pink Floyd FLAKE OUT!'*: 'Pink Floyd lead vocalist and songwriter Syd Barrett is suffering from "nervous exhaustion" and the group have withdrawn from all engagements booked for the rest of August. As a result they have lost £4,000 worth of work, but a group spokesman said they will resume making appearances in September. After recording tracks for their next single early this week, the group were due to leave Thursday for holidays in Spain, for two weeks.'

Barrett, Lindsay and Rick Wright flew to Ibiza on the 9th, where a severely traumatised Barrett tried to puzzle out his dilemma under the summer sun. In their absence, the Pink Floyd were featured on 19 August in the *NME* 'Lifelines' column, detailing their various likes and dislikes. The band cited the Beatles, Bartok, Cream, Thelonious Monk, Hendrix and the Stones as their favourites. Waters turned in a few sarcastic asides, citing his musical education 'as twelve years tuition on the spoons'. Barrett refused to answer anything but the odd question or two. He couldn't be bothered, and all aspects of the commercial façade, including ridiculous questionnaires, were beginning to annoy him deeply.

On 11 to 13 August, the 7th National Jazz & Blues Festival took place at Windsor, Berkshire. The three-day festival, featuring Cream, the Small Faces, the Move, Arthur Brown, Donovan, Jeff Beck, John Mayall, and Peter Green's Fleetwood Mac was a landmark show during 1967. The Pink Floyd had been scheduled to play and when it was announced that they had cancelled, a chorus of resounding boos rose from the audience. Peter Perrett, later of seminal New Wave band the Only Ones, was one of many in the audience who had hoped to see Barrett and came away deeply disappointed.

The pirate radios played their last set and shut down on the 14 August, a sad result of the Maritime Offences Act, which had been brewing in Parliament since June 1966, when legislation was introduced to close them down. The many pirate stations, which had reached more than 13 million listeners, ended their broadcasts at midnight, and with them went some of the impetus behind the psychedelic era's music. Shows like John Peel's *Perfumed Garden* had afforded all manner of marginal and/or experimental bands a valuable showcase. That mordant empty silence resounded down Earl's Court, Notting Hill Gate, Chelsea and Kensington, sounding an early death knell for the era. Times were changing rapidly. Even today in the UK, there is a certain amount of denial as to the political motivation behind the closures. Though the pirates weren't political in the literal sense, they had the ear of the youth, and as such, had inevitably come to be viewed as a threat by Parliament.

At the start of September, the Pink Floyd were back in London to play at a special UFO at the Roundhouse, a benefit for the drug offenders' defense organisation Release. The Crazy World Of Arthur Brown, Tomorrow, the Move and the Soft Machine were also featured, making it a sort of Underground festival. 'There were some very good nights at the UFO Roundhouse,' says Joe Boyd. 'The Roundhouse had a good, though different atmosphere than at Tottenham Court Road. The only problems UFO ever had, aside from the police, was at the Roundhouse. Pubs let out at 11 p.m. and the Irish from the Camden Town pubs used to insult or beat up people wearing kaftans. That was the problem of the Roundhouse.' One solution was to hire the Hell's Angels to protect the hippies, according to Colin Turner. Surprisingly it worked. Another menace for the hippies were the skinheads, the latest variant in youth culture. Emerging from the more extreme wing of the mods, the skinheads actually bore stronger resemblance to the teds of the fifties. Violence, lager and territorialism increasingly became the resort of those who couldn't grasp what the Underground was about. Hippies emerging from the Roundhouse and making their way to Chalk Farm tube station would have an unpleasant surprise.

With Hoppy in prison, the focus of UFO begun to shift under Boyd's guidance. It became more focused around music presentation, by Boyd's own admission, rather than the larger aspects of the Underground. Ultimately Boyd decided to close it down. Barrett said, 'I was really surprised that UFO finished. Joe Boyd did all the work on it and I was really amazed when he left.'[26]

Another attempt to meet the scheduled single release date on 8 September failed, as EMI vetoed the proposed 'Scream Thy Last Scream'/'Set The Controls For The Heart Of The Sun'. The Floyd flew off to Denmark for a five-day tour, arriving in Copenhagen on September 9, where they were interviewed by the Danish music papers and radio. The next day they played at the Boom, Arhus, and on 11 to 13 September they played at the Star Club in Copenhagen. On their last show there, they were recorded in an amateur recording, one of only two known Syd-era Pink Floyd complete recorded gigs, and although the recording is truly abysmal, it allows the listener that rarest of glimpses into Syd's live Floyd. The band ran through an abrasive half-hour set, which comprised 'Reaction In G', 'Arnold Layne', 'She Was A Millionaire', 'Matilda Mother', 'Scream Thy Last Scream' and 'Astronomy Domine'.

Then they took the ferry over to Stockholm, Sweden, where they played at the Gyllene Cirklem (Golden Circle), and from Sweden they flew directly to Ireland for a three-day tour. Jenner and King were anxious that the band break through in the rest of Europe as well. The reception was good, as it was always was in Ireland, where they were adored.

On 22 September, the Pink Floyd did a double-header, playing UFO at the Roundhouse, then racing down to Tiles on Oxford Street.

Things had evened out a bit, though Syd was still prone to strange shifts in mood. What was almost as unnerving as his breakdown, were the spells when he seemed to be perfectly fine. But photos from this time reflect the depth of Syd's inner traumas. He glowers in the posed photo sessions, staring with glassy, angry eyes into the camera. He had stopped washing his hair and it began to grow out in ragged spiky tufts, augmented with dashes of Brylcreem.*

On 25 September, the band recorded a session for radio's *Top Gear* at the BBC Playhouse Theatre, Northumberland Avenue, London; the session was an intimate reading, and a quality performance. It has the air of a sitting-room gig by the Floyd. That special air of timeless magic that Barrett imbued all his best work with is clearly in evidence here. On 'The Gnome', Mason's wooden blocks, Wright's muted drawn-out chords, and Syd's whispered vocals, all serve to impart that captivating Tolkienesque air, albeit with more plaintive *gravitas* and little of the whimsical joy of the original version. The Floyd shout out 'hooray!' in the background, Syd whispers, 'Look at the sky, look at the river . . .' During 'The Scarecrow' the cantering Cantabrigian horses' hooves effect is improvised live, at a slower tempo. Syd takes care to enunciate carefully, almost in waltz time, discarding his acoustic guitar coda. On 'Matilda Mother', Barrett's trebly Telecaster predominates; the guitar style suggesting that Syd played on Pink Floyd's 1968 'Corporal Clegg', itself a derivative of 'Scream Thy Last Scream'. A slower reading of 'Flaming' ensues with organ pushed to the fore. 'Apples And Oranges' is more fully realised than the soon to be issued single, showing why Roger Waters rather demurely called it 'a fucking good song ruined by the production'. Syd sounds in good humour, relaxed and in control, belying the view that he was permanently out of his head.

Peter Jenner said, 'The acid brought out his latent madness. I'm quite sure it was his latent madness which gave him his creativity. The acid brought out the creativity, but more importantly, it brought out the madness. The creativity was there, dope was enough to get it going. He wrote all his songs in about eighteen

*Syd's distressed late-1967 look doubtless was part of the inspiration for the transformation of Simon Ritchie into Sid Vicious a decade later by punk svengali/situationist Malcolm McLaren, a keen Barrett enthusiast to this day.

months, two years, including the ones on his solo albums.'[27]

Peter Jenner told *Melody Maker*, 'The group has been through a very confusing stage over the past few months and I think this has been reflected in their work. You can't take four people of this mental level, they used to be architects and an artist . . . give them big success and not expect them to get confused. But they are coming through a sort of de-confusing period now. They aren't just a record group. They really pull people in to see them and their album has been terrifically received in this country and America. I think they've got tremendous things ahead of them. They are really only just starting.'[28]

Jenner's words were prophetic, but little did he realise that Pink Floyd's future success would hinge on Syd's absence from the band. That there was conflict between Waters and Barrett is no secret, and as the months progressed, their essentially opposite natures were bound to bring them into further wrangling. Control and lack thereof, always a factor in Waters' professional relationships, was becoming a bone of contention within the band. Barrett's alienation not only from his bandmates but from the intrigues of fame, the record business and constant touring, continued apace. Whereas previously his dominion in the studio had been largely unchallenged, as Barrett's control slipped, Waters stepped to the fore.

'When I was with the Floyd the form of the music played on-stage was mainly governed by the records,' said Syd Barrett. 'With the volume used, they inclined to push me a little. Yes, there were hang-ups when I was with them, although it wasn't due to the travelling or anything, which you just put in the category of being a regular activity in that kind of job.'[29] 'Syd didn't talk to anyone,' said Peter Jenner. 'By now he was going on-stage and playing one chord throughout the set. He was into this thing of total anarchistic experiment and never really considered the other members of the band.'[30]

Tempers began to flare. Barrett was instinctively experimental to the extreme, but with the others in the band wanting to be pop stars, it would either be Syd acceding to the wishes of the others or vice versa. No one was willing to give any ground, and the others were beginning to doubt Barrett's musical instincts. Waters later said, 'The defensive barriers that are apparent in a small group of people who work together are almost heavier than everyday contact with the general public . . . in a small group, you feel more susceptible.'[31] Co manager Andrew King explained, 'Things got to be very nasty in the studio, it would literally be Syd in one corner and the rest of the band in the other. There had always been conflict between Roger and Syd but it had made the group what it was. Waters was conventionally forceful, and Syd had the power because he was writing the songs, so it worked.'[32] Peter Jenner said, 'Roger was very good with words, and you had to be skilled in semantics to beat him in an argument. Poor Syd didn't have that skill, and neither did any of the others for that matter.'[33]

Drugs were now becoming a serious problem for Syd. The strong dosages of

LSD in the sixties would tear the fabric of day-to-day reality. June Bolan observed that for Syd, meeting obligations became an almost insurmountable task; Barrett often had to be collected and taken to his various commitments. It was as if he had become a slightly errant piece of merchandise. Mick Rock told Nicholas Schaeffner, 'Syd was a totally pure artist; he couldn't deal with the business at all. That kind of vision, when it's that out-of-stage left, that original, can only come out of a state that has a tenuous hold on boring day-to-day reality.'[34] Pete Brown memorably remarked, 'The people least able to cope with acid were those who had the strongest imaginations. For people who had no imaginations, acid provided them with the illusion that they had one. For people who were already out there, it pushed them too far out in many cases.'[35]

The relative strength of LSD doses in the late sixties was a factor in Barrett's fracturing sense of self. 'Although I would go out on acid,' says Jenny Fabian, 'once I almost freaked out in the cinema, I had taken so much of something or other. We went to see *Fantasia* and I almost passed out when I saw how the music combined with the cartoons! But when I took the big doses, I couldn't *move* for the first hour. You were pole-axed, it must have shattered the central nervous system. It would shatter your body, and you could feel your mind going. Going into this great electronic buzz. And I used to wonder if I followed the buzz where I would go. I never quite made it, I used to go so far and then pull myself back. Presumably Syd followed the buzz all the way. No one has ever managed to find out what he saw. One looks for great revelations when maybe there aren't any. I think he'd gone beyond the safety zone, if there is one. He had gotten to the ultimate, he'd followed the noise out of the room, basically. The one that we always pulled ourselves back from.'

The freewheeling excess of the time was beginning to lead some of the Underground into rather sticky situations. Peter Wynne-Wilson had an acid trip which ended with him in a sanatorium. 'It was an unfortunate chain of circumstances. It was at a time when Susie and Syd were quite involved, and there was a girl who did some modelling and was hanging around Earlham. Her boyfriend was working in a Chelsea restaurant, and she said, "Let's go down there." It had gotten a bit of a name, this place, so it was quite an interesting place to go. We went there and had a terrific meal, and then I was handed a bill which completely threw me because I wasn't expecting to pay for it at all. I just had enough money, and then they said, "Let's go back to our flat," which was in Hammersmith, west London. We went back and took acid and after an hour or so this girl said, "We're going to get into bed, so you'll have to leave," which was very difficult as far as I was concerned, because I had no money.

'I was in west London at I don't know what time of night, so I thought, "I'll just have to walk back," as there was nothing else I could do, and that became quite an interesting adventure. It wasn't tiring, because I was completely out of my head, and it was quite a substantial dose of acid. I was barefoot. I don't know if I was dancing around, but I was into something sort of mystic, some sort of celestial scene. Not surprisingly, I was stopped by policemen who came by in a car. I didn't see them as a threat, but as they came over I tried to be as normal as I could be and they started to ask me questions I couldn't actually answer because I was off in such a space.

'They searched my pockets which I didn't particularly mind. I happened to knock off one of their helmets, completely unaggressively. It was just some sort of spacy gesture. And that really upset them so they bundled me into a car and took me to the police station. They were extremely unpleasant but not particularly violent. I can remember them hauling me downstairs and bumping my feet and legs and treading on my feet accidentally on purpose, and snidely apologising. But nothing particularly gruesome. Then someone said, "Oh, we'll cool him down" and they took me outside into a really unpleasant concrete yard and got a fireman's hose and stood me up against the wall and hosed me with this high pressure hose which was the most extraordinary experience. I could see it coming from miles away, I was extremely cold. I had a cotton shirt with big sleeves, jeans and a jeans waistcoat, but it really froze me.

'Then they took me from there and laid me down on a bench. I was seriously cold then, stiff with cold. I was there for ages. After they had turned the water on me, I had kept my eyes closed for the whole time. I heard someone say, "Have you killed him?!" So I thought, "Oh, that's what it is, I'm dead!" Some while later I felt what felt like someone cutting my chest open, which in reality was a stethoscope of a police surgeon they'd gotten in. I thought they were doing my post-mortem; it didn't feel bad, because I didn't feel any pain. I was fairly sure I'd died. He must have told them to take me into hospital, and I can remember being thrown, physically, into the back of a police van by two policeman. Arms and legs, up in the air and then down. That kind of physical movement on acid is unbelievable; I was falling for unbelievable time! I was bundled off in a police van, which was most unpleasant indeed, and taken to hospital.

'A delightful nurse undressed me, cleaned up a bit, and then put me into a warm bed. It was unbelievably gorgeous. She asked me the odd question or two but didn't give me any sort of aggravation, because I couldn't reply. That really relaxed me, a lot, it was most welcome. Then, when I was down from the trip, I got up and found my clothes, which the nurse had put on a radiator in the washroom. Then I started looking for a phone and I can remember opening a door. It was so funny, the door opened on to a canteen, and as I opened the door everyone who was eating looked up. It was then that I realised it was a mental hospital.

'It was the classic mental hospital, coloured with the slight hallucinations. It was really bad! I did get a little worried then, because I thought I'd been committed. I found a phone and rang Susie and she said she would come down with Syd and collect me. That sounded all right, so I found a lawn outside and did some stretching and yoga exercises, trying to sort myself out from this horrendous scene that I'd been through.'

Susie Wynne-Wilson said, 'Syd was very frightened to come in, because he was under the impression that they wouldn't let him out. Everyone was very, very on the edge then.'[36]

Peter Wynne-Wilson continues, 'It seemed like forever before Susie arrived, and what had happened was they'd set off in Syd's Mini for the hospital, and Syd couldn't find his way around anyway and as soon as he realised what the hospital was, he wouldn't go near it because it was a mental hospital and he was paranoid about all of that. At any rate, they picked me up and took me back to Earlham, and Russell Page looked after me for the rest of the morning. It was just one of those things that happened. Psychologically, it wasn't the worst trip I had, I had one that I found very disturbing and unpleasant.'

'101 Cromwell Road was the catastrophic flat where Syd got acided out,' says Peter Jenner. 'Acid in the coffee every morning, that's what we were told. He had one of our cats and they gave the cat acid. We rescued him from Cromwell Road, which was run by heavy, loony messianic acid freaks. I think there was a feeling that Syd ought to be taking lots of acid and they should help him.'[37]

Rick Wright said, 'Everyone knows the story of Syd; it's a sad story. I think he was brilliant. Acid certainly had something to do with his mental breakdown.[38] The point is, you don't know whether the acid accelerated this process that was happening in his brain, or was the cause of it. No one knows. I'm sure the drugs had a lot to do with it. I think Syd just got involved with particular people who were trying to turn him on. The whole thing in the late sixties was, like, taking acid, and it was a whole new world. He got caught up in it.'[39]

John Marsh recalls one such acid freak at Cromwell Road regularly spiking people's drinks with acid. He believes that nobody tried to stop Syd taking acid, because they would be considered 'uncool'.[40]

Jenny Gordon recalls the increasing chaos at Cromwell, 'Nigel was on probation and his probation officer would come by and we'd all be completely out of our minds and someone would say, "There's a little man in a suit at the door," and it would be Nigel's probation officer. He was quite nice and charming, and didn't seem to know what was going on, but there was a sense of danger, that we were being irresponsible. Yet it was great fun. I felt that what we were doing was quite dangerous. I felt at the time that we were playing with fire. I felt a lot of fear as well as having a great time. I think we were all very confused. For me, I couldn't have gone on with that. A lot of people were losing it. Syd certainly wasn't the first to fall, a lot of people had difficulties. John Esam was full of fear, because he'd already been busted in Paris and had been in prison, and was very bitter about that. He was very paranoid.'

Mick Rock remembered Cromwell as 'a burnt-out place, the biggest hovel, the biggest shit-heap; a total acid-shell, the craziest flat in the world. There were so many people, it was like a railway station. Two cats Syd had, one called Pink and one called Floyd, were still living in the flat after he left. He just left them there. Those were the cats they used to give acid to.'[41]

Nigel Gordon remembered the sharp denouement at 101 Cromwell, 'Johnny Johnson from Cambridge had tried to kill himself by throwing himself out of a six-storey window, and he lived, but you can imagine what he did to himself. He spent a year in hospital. When he came out he used to come and visit, take off his clothes and run around the flat with this horribly misshapen body. He was missing on one occasion, and I went down to the bathroom window and there, clinging to the drainpipes was Johnny, stark naked. It was raining too. I managed to talk him back in, but he'd gone mad. Schizophrenic, I think, heard voices and was very paranoid.'

Duggie Fields says, 'The most dramatic disintegration at Cromwell Road was Christopher Case. Christopher was one of the first people I knew who really freaked out. He took a lot of acid, not necessarily more than anyone else, but I remember him getting to a stage where you couldn't have a conversation with him because he would just quote a book he had read. He wouldn't necessarily say he was quoting from a book, he would just be parroting whatever he'd read. Everything that came from his mind by that time was something he'd read in a book.'

In the summer of 1967, Syd spent a weekend in Wales with the Gordons, Stash de Rola, and Lindsay. Nigel Gordon says, 'Syd was quite strange there. Definitely very very strange there, but we didn't take too much notice or worry about it. He was standing balanced on a wine bottle, rocking back and forth, his hands on the low ceiling, for hours.'

That Syd had suffered a destablising blow from an external or internal source or both was becoming apparent. His behaviour became highly erratic, even his high-spirited pranks and jokes became ever more unusual. Jenny Gordon says, 'He wasn't communicating with us there at all. He tripped with us in Wales, and just urinated out the door and said, "Wae-hey!"' Nigel Gordon says, 'He shit right outside the door as well, which was a bit strange, looking back. He just seemed like a bit of a nuisance at that time. Syd was just out of it, but we were out of our heads as well. It's just lucky any of us survived that. Lindsay was having a hard time there. Syd was a strange man, but we just thought that he was on acid. He became more of a court jester figure when we went to Wales than he was before.' Jenny Gordon says, 'He was sort a nuisance then, I suppose. I remember him *really* looking at you in the eye, and that being a bit odd.'

The acid weekend alternated between comedy and potential tragedy. Jenny Gordon says, 'We sent Stash out to get some logs, but instead he came back with some cans and mud all over his shoes and said, 'Let all mud be velvet!' At one point Stash was convinced that he could sit himself in the hearth, full of burning logs, and escape unscathed. Jenny recalls, 'Stash said, "I could sit on this fire and if you have faith I won't die." I was the one who said, "No, don't sit on the fire, you'll burn yourself." The policemen had already been there the day before, and I said to Stash, "The policemen might come back and they'll wonder where you are." Stash would have burned himself, everyone was being very irresponsible.

I stopped that happening. We all felt that if we all really loved each other and had faith then we could do anything.'

June Bolan said, 'Syd Barrett had this quality like a candle that was about to be snuffed out at any minute. Really all illumination. An extraordinary, wonderful man. Lots of people can take some LSD and cope with it in their lives, but if you take three or four trips every day . . . and then, because it was the done drug, you'd go round somebody's house for a cup of tea and they'd spike it. People did this to Syd.'[42] Duggie Fields notes, 'People did get spiked with acid, I never did. I never knew of anyone getting spiked with regularity, but I did know people who did get spiked. Some of the acid around then was very strong.'

Rick Wright said, 'Syd was very influenced by a lot of people around him, who encouraged him to take trips. There are a load of acid casualties out there. He wasn't alone. Back then, we had people like Timothy Leary openly advocating it: trip out and take it every day. Wrong? Yes. Misguided? Yes. It was wrong for me. I took two trips in my life. The first was quite enjoyable and that was before I was in the band. Then I took one more and I didn't enjoy it at all, so I never took it again. It certainly destroyed Syd and I think it has destroyed a lot of other people.'[43]

At twenty-one years of age, Syd was living without any stable framework in his life. His home life was transitory, disorganised; he was spending every day travelling, performing or in the studio. Since he had moved to London at eighteen he had lived in six different flats in less than three years. There was little regular pattern in his life other than it was becoming exhausting.

Regarding his intake of acid, Syd Barrett himself perhaps said it best when he said, 'There's really nothing to say.'[44] By that time, 1971, he had sworn off LSD. He seemed to realise it hadn't helped his precarious state of mental affairs. In another interview he skirted the subject of whether he had taken too much. 'Well, I don't know, it doesn't seem to have much to do with the job.'[45] Later in the same interview, Barrett alluded to LSD, saying, 'It was all, I suppose, related to living in London. I was lucky enough . . . I've always thought of going back to a place where you can drink tea and sit on the carpet. I've been fortunate enough to do that. All that time . . . you've just reminded me of it. I thought it was good fun.'[46]

Barrett and Lindsay moved into the Egerton Court flat. Jenner said, 'Syd, he got taken up by Storm and Po from Hipgnosis who put him up in their flat on Brompton Road just by South Kensington tube station. They knew him very well and they suffered with him going down: they were very supportive and tried to keep him with us.'[47]

Unfortunately, Egerton Court was becoming more like Cromwell by the day. David Gale remembers, 'We all embarked on an extremely acid-crazed period. We had this long thin flat, a long corridor with rooms off to one side only, just outside South Kensington tube station. Nigel and Jenny lived in the flat, in the end room. I lived in the room next to it, Po lived in the room next to that, Matthew Scofield lived in the room next to that, and Storm lived in the room next to that.

'Syd moved into Nigel and Jenny's room, next to my room, and he was now a pop star. I remember rock chicks who were into tailoring coming round and taking order for exotic late sixties rock'n'roll shirts for Syd. These were made of bizarre upholstery fabrics and strange satin curtains, and they had gigantic collars, puffed sleeves, ruffled fronts. Syd ordered a number of these because now he was a famous rock star. Syd lived in this room with Lindsay and I often used to hear Syd tickling Lindsay because I had the next room. And I used to think it was harmless lovers' play. And then I'd notice that sometimes he used to tickle her mercilessly and she would scream for him to stop. And then on one occasion, I remember hearing sort of thumping sounds, as though he were banging her head on the floor, possibly. I don't really know what he was doing, but she was screaming. And I thought, "Ah, a lovers' tiff."

'You have to understand that in the sixties it was considered uncool to interfere. Despite the idea of peace, love and community, it was nevertheless, in the same breath, considered uncool to interfere, rather like the attitude the police take towards what they call a "domestic".'

Lindsay Korner recalled that after the success of the first two singles and album, Barrett's 'chronic schizophrenia had set in'. Lindsay today refuses to talk about her time with Barrett, preferring not to focus on the past. Duggie Fields says, 'Lindsay lives a very different life these days, and the rock star boyfriend and the mattress on the floor is a long way from the grand house in the country. I don't remember their relationship being especially violent. I didn't actually live with Lindsay and Syd, though Syd could have been going out with her while he was at Cromwell Road.' A friend of Syd's says, 'Lindsay was a slender pretty blonde, not particularly engaged in Underground culture. She was rather a more decorative figure who didn't have much to say. She was a pleasant young woman but not much going on [in her head].' Others, more charitably, remember Lindsay as a charming person with a lovely smile and a very kind nature.

Peter Wynne-Wilson said, 'Syd and Lindsay . . . well, I would say Lindsay was more in tune with him than he was with her. She was pretty finely tuned to Syd, and also had a completely dazzling smile. She wasn't pursuing any sort of spiritual scene. But she wasn't a pretty groupie, she was very seriously involved with him and quite clearly so. She was extremely kind and generous of sprit. And incredibly beautiful. His violence towards Lindsay didn't seem in character at all to me. In Earlham Street I have a recollection of going into the room once and there being an atmosphere which I didn't recognise at all, which might have been after a violent episode but I've no idea about that. When I heard reports of violence in Egerton I was amazed, completely amazed, because I'd never seen Syd demonstrate violence of any kind whatsoever.'

David Gale says, 'As the months passed, Syd's mood very slowly changed. It should be observed that he was taking acid very, very frequently. There was a small subgroup that thought it was interesting to take acid daily. Most of us took it far less frequently. I had virtually stopped by then because I found it far too horrific. I think I had stopped completely, but everyone else was still swirling around doing it. Syd was one of the diehards who took it every day. He slowly became less jolly, more withdrawn, pale, bags under his eyes, he had trouble getting to sleep. He talked less, his sunny disposition was completely eclipsed. He started to beat Lindsay up. He did strange things like push her into the toilet and squeeze the toilet door against her, trapping her between the door and the wall. Punch her. He was also becoming surly. Lindsay got locked in a classic battered-partner syndrome, where all her friends would say, "You're crazy, all he does is beat you up and give you a hard time, he's crazy! Why don't you leave him?" And she couldn't. This went on and on. She somehow lacked the capacity to leave what had become an appalling situation. It wouldn't surprise me in the least if she's disturbed by those days.'

Jenny Fabian says, 'You can't put a date on when Syd broke down, it was just gradually you noticed things. Time was pretty timeless then anyway, but when he started going on-stage and not playing . . . Sometimes he'd play a bit and then sit down, or sometimes just stand there. I never heard him say much, so I must have come in towards the end. Yet Syd still felt the same, I know that there are stories that he did go a bit funny and hit Lindsay and things. But I suppose everybody does something like that at some stage in his life, but I never saw anything other than a gentle person. Syd and Lindsay were a living relationship, so there would have been more problems and more personal sadness.'

Lindsay affirmed that by Christmas 'Syd had started to act a little bonkers'.[48] According to Nicholas Schaffner, Barrett allegedly locked Lindsay in their room for three days, after a fierce argument that had ended in a beating. Rick Wright's wife Juliet and June Bolan rescued her. When Peter Jenner heard Bolan's account he was astonished, 'I couldn't believe it at the time. I had this firm picture of Syd as this really gentle guy, which is what he was, basically.'[49]

In late 1967, Barrett's latent violent streak, accentuated by prodigious intake of drugs and worsening mental problems, came resoundingly to the fore. One aspect of psychedelics lies in amplifying both inner and outer reality. An element in Syd's sudden violence was probably the intense frustration and fear he was feeling. Like a caged animal, removed from its habitat, all people began to look like potential predators, especially those closest to him. And knowing that you are having a mental breakdown, as he did, must have been ineffably frustrating. The dread certainty of an irreversible change for the worse must have augmented his psychological breakdown. So far removed from the safety and security of home, constantly on the move and surrounded by parasites, Barrett was at a loss as the line separating madness and creativity was beginning to blur, as the madness of his chaotic live shows crept into his studio compositions, and into his home. The free association of ideas conducive to creativity was a stone's throw from the loosening of associations typical of clinically defined schizophrenia.

The illusory nature of repeated acid trips could do little to bolster a mind in the process of fragmentation. To be objective, given the right mindframe, company and surroundings (Timothy Leary's 'set and setting'), LSD trips could potentially be eye-opening or profound. LSD works to amplify whatever its user is feeling or thinking, sometimes illuminatingly, sometimes frighteningly. LSD's presumed chemical action lies in the disruption of the brain chemical serotonin, which is believed to regulate moods. The visual hallucinations are believed to be something akin to a short-circuit in the way the eye processes information; a rapid influx of information unchecked by the normal barriers that affects every one of the senses. Conceivably, the acid experience could be beneficial in the right circumstances, but its widespread street abuse precludes any serious investigation into its possible positive uses. LSD could be likened to the box that Pandora opened in the fairy tale *Pandora's Box*, itself a retelling of the archetypal Eve and the apple Biblical parable. LSD itself holds no answers, as was widely assumed in the sixties; the 'quality' of the LSD experience is entirely subjective, and some minds are better equipped to handle it than others. For a creative mind in its formative stages, and in the absence of a substantial framework or foundation, Barrett's use ultimately imperiled him rather than empowered him. Perhaps he realised too late; songs like 'Jugband Blues' and his later solo 'Late Night' would suggest that he knew acid had aggravated his underlying psychological problems.

Like a beautiful and prized rare orchid, which can only survive in the most protected of environments, Syd's creative period was perhaps destined to be short. The dividing line between creativity and madness is perhaps determined by a level of conscious awareness and separation of the creative process from the one who engenders that process. When the creator becomes the created work and can't separate fantasy from reality, cracks begin to form. In a sense, the persona of Syd Barrett, pop star and Underground icon, was threatening to subsume its creator, Roger Barrett.

Oddly enough, blurred lines between fantasy and reality often fire the creative process. Many artists have abused drugs in an effort to 'derange the senses' and preserve the quintessence of their fractured experiences/experiments. Ironically James Joyce used elements of what would be regarded as schizoform language to create masterpieces of modern literature, whereas his schizophrenic daughter was drowning in a sea of silence, unable to use that same language to express herself.

David Gale says, 'Syd's rock'n'roll colleagues at that time will tell you that his behaviour on tour was becoming deeply peculiar. It finally occurred to us that perhaps something was wrong. We thought we must do something for Syd. We used to say things like, "Syd, we don't you think you ought to beat Lindsay up," and he would take no notice at all. A parallel strand at that time was an interest in the so-called "anti-psychiatric" school of thought of R.D. Laing, and his book *The Divided Self* was a hot read in our group, as well as Timothy Leary. By that time I was deeply interested in psychoanalysis, and had gone to Laing to see if he could help me sort out my own head. I had seen him talking at the Anti-University, and so I rang him up and said, "Look, I live in the same house as Syd Barrett and we think that he's in need of help, would you speak to him?" And Laing said, "Well, only if he wants to be seen, because there's no point in taking anyone to see an analyst if they don't want to go." But he did say he would see Syd. I said, "OK, we'll persuade him to see you, we'd better make an appointment, how about half-past three next Tuesday or Wednesday? We'll put him in a taxi and send him over to you," and Laing said, "OK, I'll expect him." We said to Syd, "Why don't you go see R.D. Laing, Syd, he could really understand what you're into." Syd didn't want anything to do with it. We even booked a taxi, and the driver came to the door in time to take him up to Harley Street, and Syd refused to get in it. As was his right, you could say. But he absolutely refused, so we sent the taxi away. So Syd never met Laing, but continued to be increasingly crazy.'

'Syd was well into his "orbiting" phrase by then,' said Peter Jenner. 'He was travelling very fast in his own private sphere and I thought I could be a mediator of some sort. Syd's madness wasn't caused by any linear progression of events, but more a circular haze of situations which meshed together on top of themselves and Syd. Me, I couldn't handle those stares though!'[50]

David Gilmour said, 'Syd functioned on a totally different plain of logic, and some people claimed, "Well yeah, man, he's on a higher cosmic level", but basically there was something drastically wrong. It wasn't just the drugs, we'd both done acid before the whole Floyd thing; it was just a mental foible which grew out of all proportion. I remember all sorts of strange things happening; at one point he was wearing lipstick, dressing in high heels, and believing he had homosexual tendencies. We all felt he should have gone to see a psychiatrist, though someone in fact played an interview he did to R.D. Laing, and Laing claimed he was incurable. What can you do, you know?'[51]

Jonathan Meades, a RADA student at the time, recalls Syd being locked in a linen cupboard when he was having a bad trip, although this is refuted by Duggie Fields and Jenny Fabian.

June Bolan said, 'I went through all of Syd's acid breakdowns. He used to go to the Youth Hostel in Holland Park, climb up on the roof and get wrecked and get spaced and he'd walk all the way to Shepherd's Bush where I was living. He used to come round to my house at five in the morning covered in mud from Holland Park when he'd freaked out and the police chased him. I meant money, meant wages, meant security to him.'[52]

In the aftermath of the trip to Wales, Nigel and Jenny Gordon were re-examining the course of their lives. Jenny says, 'Paul Charrier had told us about Sant

Mat when we were back in Cambridge, and I wasn't very interested until William Pryor and Ponji came back from India and told us about it. Dave Gilmour, Nigel, Stash de Rola, and Imo were all in our room at Egerton Court. Ponji and William walked in the door, back from India, and told us all about it. I just knew then that that was what I wanted to do, that was it. And Stash also, at that time. The Dera Baba Jaima Singh, meaning "the man who built his hut by the river", was the name of the ashram we went to. We stayed in Dera for three or four months, being with the Master and learning about it. We were initiated there. There were four principles: diet (no meat, fish or eggs); no alcohol or drugs; to lead a moral life, whatever that is; and the Master said no to sex out of marriage. Later, if you initiated, two and a half hours of meditation a day. No parallels with the Maharishi's system of mediation. By the time of the Beatles getting into TM, Paul Charrier had already come back from India. The way things were going, people realised you couldn't go on with that way of life. Certainly not for me. Acid was an indulgence, it was like going through the back door. Taking something without having the background would make people very wobbly. Taking LSD we would see, perhaps, things that we weren't ready to see. Through meditation you see a lot of these things, and that's probably why a lot of people gave up LSD.'

Sant Mat's meditation was designed to allow one to access higher states of consciousness, and investigate what lay beyond reality. Jenny Gordon says, 'You have a guide who told you what to look out for. In a way, people thought they knew what they were about, only to find out they didn't. The Master said, "Go out and live a normal life, marry, have children and a household." He said that being a hermit was actually a mistake.'

Nigel Gordon adds, 'People gave up tripping for meditation, and decided to [seek enlightenment] the hard way. The draw of the meditation was to get to the higher states of consciousness without the drugs. The drugs had shown that there were altered states, seemingly higher states of awareness. The Master was saying that, "Indeed there are higher states, higher and higher, and they are inside you, and the mind is just one level, and LSD is all to do with the mind." What Jenny says is right, that some people had taken enough. They had gone as far as they could with it. I wasn't so very frivolous with LSD. We did do it seriously, and conduct experiments with consciousness expansion. Doing it at the right time, in the right place with the right people. A lot of people didn't approach it like that, and maybe Syd was one of them. He didn't use it as a tool in his spiritual quest, perhaps. That questing was very serious, Syd wasn't on the same quest as Stash and I. We read our alchemy looking for the answer, it wasn't casual. How do you get to higher consciousness? I had the feeling that LSD could only take you so far before you came up against another door, and that there was another level supporting that one. But certainly Stash, Jenny and John Tate and all that lot viewed acid as part of the quest for the Holy Grail of higher states. That was what it was all about.'

On 1 October, the Pink Floyd performed at the Sunday At The Saville series of concerts at the Saville Theatre, London. 'Hippies rave over Pink Floyd,' reported *NME,* in a perfunctory review. 'The beautiful people and hippies turned up in their shawls, embroidered jackets, Indian head-bands and beads, to see the Pink Floyd at the Saville on Sunday night. Even the compère, Joe Boyd, was from UFO. The Pink Floyd were one of the first groups to experiment with weird light effects and they now have it down to a fine art, or rather their lighting man has. The flashing patterns and weaving silhouettes are an integral part of their music, which was very loud and mainly instrumental.'[53]

Nick Jones, on the other hand, wrote a very telling review in *Melody Maker*, 'The Pink Floyd, lights flicking nervously around their feet, with an eerie, full of promise first number. Unfortunately the impact of their opening was never continued. The Floyd themselves were never revealed, their personalities cut dead in the dark, and we saw that too-familiar, too impersonal performance. Certainly the Floyd have much to say, and their music is shatteringly original, taking off into a totally unexplored musical dimension of spacious, free electronic ideas and movements. However, their running order lacked fire or direction, nothing really seemed to get or go anywhere, and the Floyd didn't round off what could have been such exciting musical corners. There's a wealth of promises in the Floyd and their music, but only time will tell if they will come back.'[54]

On 7 October, Blackhill announced in a press release that the band were planning a major tour for March 1968, 'The Pink Floyd are to star in four concert spectaculars to be staged in major halls. They are developing a completely new-style show, incorporating a small orchestra and a choir of 100 voices . . . Next week the Floyd record their new single, another Syd Barrett composition.'[55]

A reporter from *Go!* magazine had dropped into a recording session to interview Barrett, who was padding around the studio barefoot. Trying to explain his motivation yet again, Syd said, 'It's better not to have a set goal. You'd be very narrow minded if you did. All I know is that I'm beginning to think less now. It's getting better.' The perplexed reporter said, 'Well, if you stop thinking entirely, you might as well be a vegetable.' 'Yeah!' was Barrett's startling comeback.[56] He was tickled by this encounter, and soon after followed the creation of one of his songs most clearly chronicling his inner fragmentation, 'Vegetable Man'.

'It was really stressful waiting for Syd to come up with the songs for the second album,' said Peter Jenner. 'Everybody was looking at him and he could not do it. The last Floyd song Syd wrote, "Vegetable Man", was done for those sessions, though it never came out. Syd was around at my house just before he had to go to record and, because a song was needed, he just wrote a description of what he was wearing at the time and threw in a chorus that went "Vegetable man, where are you?" It's very disturbing. Roger took it off the album because it was too dark, and it is. It's like psychological flashing.'[57]

'After he left the band, they all thought those songs were too intense,' said Jenner. 'They couldn't handle them. They were like words from a psychiatrist's chair – an extraordinary document of a serious mental disturbance . . . But I thought they were good songs and great pieces of art. They're disturbing, and not a lot of fun, but they're some of Syd's finest work, though God knows, I wouldn't wish anyone to go through what he's gone through to get to those songs. They're like Van Gogh.'[58]

Between 9 to 11 October, 'Vegetable Man' was recorded at Abbey Road. It's a list of rhyming couplets written made to order and out of necessity, one feels, rather than from any creative spark. Yet Barrett none the less conveys the arcane and mysterious processes of his thought as he details what he is wearing. Lyrics such as 'So I walk the street with my plastic feet' suggest intense mental dislocation. Syd breaks off from the song's martial rhythm with a middle eighth that is perhaps among his finest melodic and lyrical moments, singing, 'I've been looking all over the place/for a place for me'. He subverts that immaculate five seconds of melody with a self-mocking, 'But it ain't anywhere/It just ain't anywhere'.

When one pauses to consider the meaning of these few lines, it's clear these are the truest words Barrett ever wrote. Its poignancy is touching, the sad lyric refrain juxtaposed with a happy, jangling Byrds-derived guitar phrase. Self-mocking and ironic, with a bitter twist, all the more cutting because it is set to sing-song music that intentionally sabotages the severity of his message. Barrett's casual fans may think of him as an amusing lunatic, but these words are the credo of an exceptional person who truly never found his place in this world, and are among his most telling and saddest lyrics. He seemed to realise his essential alienation from the world around him.

'Vegetable Man' pre-figures the spooky echo repeats of dub reggae producers King Tubby and Lee Parry, the only others to have fully explored the revolutionary uses of echo as thoroughly as Barrett did. Some of the Binson echo tricks Barrett came up with are uncannily close to some of King Tubby's production work on records such as 'Real Gone Crazy Dub'.

Jenner and King had planned an American tour for the Pink Floyd months before, and with the band's departure for the States looming, they were informed that 'Vegetable Man' had been rejected as well. So on 20 to 21 October, at De Lane Lea studios, the Pink Floyd had a hurried session to record Barrett's 'Jugband Blues' and added overdubs to an out-take from *The Piper At The Gates Of Dawn*, Rick Wright's 'Remember A Day'. 'Remember A Day' is a beautiful song, with Wright playing some of his most memorable piano lines, and despite his claims to the contrary, the lyrics are charming. Syd creates a tremendous backing track of purely atmospheric Telecaster glissandi, which shadow Wright's melody but pay no mind to its general harmonic construction.

Barrett simply embellishes on Wright's right-hand fills with admirable restraint and grace.

Syd Barrett's ship had been sailing fast on LSD's uncharted seas, pitching and yawing on unsteady tides, swirling eddies and dread undercurrents. In the sixties LSD was largely an unknown proposition with its alternately placid and raging waters. Like the maps of sixteenth-century cartographers, the unknown areas simply bore the inscription, 'Here there be monsters indeed'. Syd's music began to reflect this shift into the unknown, as he began to reach the crumbling apex of his Pink Floyd-era compositions.

His final major contribution to the Pink Floyd was 'Jugband Blues'. In typical psychedelic production style, there were an incredible amount of ideas compressed to it, a potent parting salvo, directed not only at the intransigence of his producer, or the growing discontent of his bandmates, but at himself. It's akin to the sound of the band playing 'Closer My God To Thee' on the deck of the *Titanic* as it sank; a last mad fanfare when all is lost. As Nicholas & Schaeffner noted, it's filled with all the humour that is found to be often lacking in Pink Floyd's later *oeuvre*. 'Jugband Blues', with its discordant lyrics matched by the eclectic music's broad sweep of tempo, acoustic and electric guitars, wandering flutes, Salvation Army band, delirious Binson unit effects, and ebullient chorus, chiming middle eight – all descend to a fragile acoustic solo coda with a very vulnerable Syd singing and playing unaccompanied.

Syd sings of his impending exile, both literal and metaphorical, with an ironic smile. With sarcasm towards his bandmates, Barrett sings, 'It's awfully considerate of you to think of me here/And I'm much obliged to you for making it clear/That I'm not here'. Shortly after he calmly intones, 'And I'm wondering who could be writing this song', either a reminder to the others who was the songsmith in the band, or a statement of psychic detachment from the creative process, or both.

'Even at that point,' said Peter Jenner, 'Syd actually knew what was happening to him. "Jugband Blues" is the ultimate self-diagnosis on a state of schizophrenia.'[59] A really sad song, the portrait of a nervous breakdown.'[60] Andrew King said, 'Syd knew exactly what was happening to him, but was powerless to stop it. He knew he was going wrong inside.'[61]

The *Melody Maker* opined, '"Jugband Blues" is almost a poetic recitation by Barrett, with avant-garde sound effects by the group. The centre passage is almost free-form pop, with six members of the Salvation Army on the recording session told to play what you like".'[62]

Musically, 'Jugband Blues' is remarkable. Barrett jettisoned every conventional pop songwriting structure, in a sense finally achieving his goal of unimpeded freedom. But the apparent chaos of 'Jugband Blues' is deceptive; it's remarkably cohesive despite its episodic construction. It mirrors the abrupt mood shifts and perilously short attention span of its composer, but still manages to reflect the brilliance of his underlying concept. There is nothing else in popular music like it. Instructing the Salvation Army band to 'play whatever they want' is often painted as a ludicrous whim on Barrett's part, particularly by Norman Smith. It's not. It's an original and experimental gesture, reflecting Barrett's strong desire to capture spontaneity on tape or on-stage. After the last mad fanfare, long echoing repeats, atonal guitar scratching, a brief flash of Mellotron, the song fades into the abyss. And then almost imperceptibly, a lone guitar cadenza arises from the wreckage, playing an almost rudimentary two-chord passage as a fragile sounding Syd pointedly asks, 'And what exactly is a dream?/And what exactly is a joke?' The last strum hangs suspended in the air for a second, and then silence.

As a third attempt to find a suitable A-Side for their third single, one can only wonder what EMI made of it. It was promptly rejected, with a stern warning to the band and producer to write something commercial. The record business was right then on the cusp of transition. The singles charts were about to be superseded by an album-oriented market. The Pink Floyd were the very first band signed to EMI with an album deal. This was a prime innovation of the psychedelic era, and also one of its major faults. The musicians, producers and engineers were allowed a much freer hand, and given much more time to perfect on their instincts. Unfortunately, the legacy of all this extra time and space would be the bloated excesses of seventies pomp rock bands such Emerson, Lake And Palmer and ELO. But at this stage, singles were still seen as the barometer of success and marketability.

Peter Jenner said, 'I think we tended to underrate the extent of his problem. I mean, I thought that I could act as a mediator, having been a sociology teacher at the LSE and all that guff. One thing I regret now was that I made demands on Syd. He'd written "See Emily Play" and suddenly everything had to be seen in commercial terms. I think we may have pressurised him into a state of paranoia about having to come up with another "hit single".'[63] Roger Waters said, 'When you record a single, you aren't interested in showing the public how far you've advanced since the last record. You've got to please the recording company, apart from any other consideration, otherwise they won't release it.'[64]

The solution was 'Apples And Oranges'. Roger Waters said, 'It was a group decision and we definitely set out "Apples And Oranges" as a single. We all thought it was a really good song but the recording didn't come up as well. We've never been a singles band, "Arnold Layne" which I thought was a great single and "See Emily Play" which wasn't a great single, did very well and those are the only two that we've ever had. "Apples And Oranges" was a very good song; in spite of mistakes and the production, I don't think it was bad. "Apples And Oranges" was destroyed by the production. It's a fucking good song.'[65] Nick Mason added drily, 'It could have done with more working out.'[66]

With 'Apples And Oranges', Norman Smith was out of his depth; what could have prepared him for the ever changing tempos and odd tunings? Barrett's guitar is played out of tune, whether from perversity or just laziness isn't known. Nick Mason said, 'At that period we had no direction. We were being hustled about to make hit singles. There's so many people saying it's important you start to think it is important. It's possible on an LP to do exactly what we want. The last single, "Apples And Oranges", we had to hustle a bit. It was commercial but we could only do it in two sessions.'[67]

'Paintbox', the B-Side, was penned by Rick Wright, and is truly slight save for the coda, with Syd turning out the bare minimum in guitar work. Rick Wright's lyrics are banal, but the harmonies pleasant. But it was a throwaway, and quality control was forsaken as EMI put steady pressure on the band to produce the next Pink Floyd single after the rejection of 'Jugband Blues'.

On the morning of 24 October, the Pink Floyd, along with co-manager Andrew King, departed for their first American tour. Jenner opted to remain in England to sort out the mess over the new single. The tour was to be Syd's Waterloo. 'It was all getting too much with Syd,' said Peter Jenner, 'just getting too spacey. The American trip, which Syd went on, was quite extraordinary.[68] Syd was beginning to get seriously eccentric. That was when it became inarguable that it was a real problem.'[69] 'At the end of 1967 we went to the States for eight days,' said Roger Waters. 'That was an amazing disaster. Syd by this time was completely off his head.'[70]*

The Pink Floyd played on 26 to 28 October at the Fillmore in San Francisco on a triple bill with Lee Michaels and Clearlight. The band appeared on the 30th at a Fillmore benefit gig for pioneering FM radio station KPFA, from which DJ Tom Donaghue had disseminated a remarkable mix of new San Franciscan music. They were photographed in nearby Sausalito by Baron Wollman, and Syd appears brooding and distant, miles away from the band members sitting next to him. On the 31st they played a gig at the Pacific West High School auditorium in San Jose, two hours south of San Francisco. The Pink Floyd played at the Fillmore on the 2nd, then on 3 and 4 November at the massive Winterland with Janis Joplin's Big Brother And The Holding Company and Richie Havens on another triple bill. It was a big show, with a high demand for tickets, largely because of Joplin, but there was a sizeable contingent who turned out to hear the Pink Floyd.

Unfortunately, the Pink Floyd's atmospheric wash of lights and sound were lost in the cavernous hall. They compensated by playing a set of the loudest distortion and feedback they could.

'The Winterland was awesome, as they say,' says Peter Wynne-Wilson. 'It was certainly the biggest place we played there. Both the band and the lighting were very small, whereas Big Brother And The Holding Company were very big; a very big noise. Headlights were very big with masses of equipment. We had a

*The departure date of the band for the USA is unclear. They may have departed from the UK on the 29th, meaning the first three Fillmore shows were cancelled.

voltage problem there, they supplied us with a pathetic transformer with an earthing problem. From the lighting point of view it wasn't anything to remember. It was a tremendously interesting situation, though, because of Janis Joplin and a whole slew of other stuff. Roger was drinking phenomenal quantities of Southern Comfort produced by Janis Joplin. Janis was doing all kinds of stuff, she had a whole mess of stuff around her.' Janis Joplin, it seems, had introduced the lads to Bourbon, though one wonders if it was laced with codeine as was Joplin's wont.

Mason reflected years later on Barrett's disintegration. 'Obviously there were some incredible moments of clarity, like the wonderful American tour, which will live forever. Syd detuning his guitar all the way through one number, striking the strings and detuning the guitar, which is very modern [laughs], but very difficult for a band to follow or play with. Other occasions he more or less just ceased playing, and would stand there, leaving us to muddle along as best we could. At times like that you think, "What we need is someone else, or at least some help!"'[71]

When Syd stood on-stage picking out a single note with his plectrum, echoing like sonar through the darkened halls, or stood with arms hanging by his sides staring in glassy-eyed catatonia, it was the tell-tale signs of severe mental trauma, a particularly disturbing piece of unintentional performance art. Like the cracked Marine in Kubrick's *Full Metal Jacket*, 'He had the thousand-yard stare, like he'd looked beyond'.

When a performer steps on-stage, they become the centre of the crowd's focus. Energy pulsates into the performer, as well as radiating out, as with a trick mirror. The performer becomes a conduit, channel, refractor. The performer is simultaneously at the mercy of and in control of the audience. Barrett's on-stage blanks called to mind Friedrich Nietzsche's well-worn maxim (itself borrowed from a nameless Sanskrit sage), 'As you stare into the Void, so does the Void stare into you'. For the creative performer, there is no greater exhilaration; or fear, for it can be overpowering. Russian ballet dancer Nijinsky, in his final public performance, carried a chair on-stage, sat down, and faced the audience with the steely eyes of schizophrenia. For thirty minutes he stared at them in silence, and they were transfixed, bound in an equally profound silence. Through sheer concentration, he had succeeded in turning the audience into the performer. This silent reversal echoes the riotous performances of the Living Theatre, a theatre troupe popular in the sixties. Their performances were anarchic spectacles whereby the performers baited the audience with verbal and even physical antagonism in order to alert the audience of their relation to the performers. Was it a symbiotic relationship, or did it err towards the parasitic? The lines tend to blur. For Syd, in his maddened final season with the Floyd, the balance had swung against him. The sheer creative force he had channelled into making each performance unique and transcendent had overwhelmed him. And the audience, in a sense, were feeding off of him.

'Syd hanging with his arms limp,' says Wynne-Wilson, 'or banging out one chord did happen quite a bit, and it happened very definitely later on the tour with Hendrix. In the States was probably the first time Syd literally didn't play anything. But the amounts of drugs we were doing was quite considerable, DMT, STP, *et al.* I don't know about acid. There was never a shortage of hash or marijuana at Earlham, Egerton or Cromwell that I was aware of, but we had not encountered the prodigious Californian drugs scene, and because there was a lot of interest in the band we came under a lot of pressure, drugs pressure, and not remotely unpleasant. The Californian scene was *so* different from the English scene that Syd found it disorienting. I did, too, but I found it quite wonderful really. It was so different, even the people taking drugs had cars. In England, there was only one person in Cromwell, Egerton or Earlham who had a car. The sun shone, the archetypal Californian girls would just scoop you up and take you somewhere. Quite remarkable scene. It was just before the California scene really started to fall apart and become gruesome. Haight-Ashbury was teetering on the brink of whatever it fell into.'

'I went to San Francisco and stayed right on Haight-Ashbury around that time,' says Duggie Fields, 'which by then was one of the freakiest places I'd ever been to. You had to watch your back as you walked along the street, with people hustling to sell each other drugs the minute you stepped out your front door. "Smack! Acid! Speed!" in the most aggressive manner, people actually stopping your way as you walked down the street. I was very shocked at that.'

Barrett had his hair done at a trendy hippie salon, but it didn't come off very well. Wynne-Wilson recalls Syd looking decidedly ill at ease and tense, his botched perm and unwashed clothes highlighting his problems rather than drawing attention away from them. Not that the groupies who frequented the Winterland minded, for Barrett was, as ever, the recipient of their attentions. Roaming the rising and falling streets of the Haight well into the morning, being taken to crashpads where that strange timeless air that psychedelic drugs engenders prevailed, Syd was exhausted. The utter lack of anything familiar, his inability to get his bearings or even find his way back to the others was too much. But if San Francisco, with its plenitude of diversions, wasn't enough, Los Angeles, the next stop on the itinerary, was to prove overwhelming.

Los Angeles is an oddity of a city, a veritable catalogue of contradictions, simultaneously the terminus and starting point of the American Dream, and quite unlike anywhere else in the world. An air of unreality cloaks the city as thickly as the smog that never truly lifts. The number of musicians who have cracked up here, either temporarily or permanently, is remarkable. Brian Wilson scanning the hills for fire with fearful eyes, Phil Spector sitting behind razor-wire-lined high walls, Arthur Lee of Love firing his gun into the sky, Jim Morrison teetering at the brink of death on the parapets of the notorious Castle, Iggy Pop face-down in a gutter, John Lennon in a drunken haze during his 'lost weekend'.

It was here that the concept of all-engulfing fame was created. The kind of fame that can drive an unsuspecting soul round the bend with fear and paranoia. Los Angeles can be exhilarating or deeply worrying; it depends how one adapts to it. If you can't adapt, the city can vanquish your soul like no other city. Los Angeles, and its endless outlying suburbs, has been home variously to Disneyland, the Manson murders, Hollywood, riots, Beverly Hills, fires and earthquakes. It's also where on quiet nights warm Santa Ana winds blow and one feels a langorous bliss not found elsewhere. But the flipside is the haunting howling of coyotes in the distant hills that with a twist of the imagination seem to augur the very end of the world. Small wonder that the Pink Floyd's ill-fated trek through America reached its nadir here.

'On their first American tour the Floyd were being taken by some A&R man around Hollywood,' said John Marsh. 'They were taken for the classic tour of the stars' homes and so on. And they ended up on the corner of Hollywood and Vine. The band are looking around: "Hey, made it, Hollywood," and the A&R man's saying, "Yes, here we are, the centre of it all, Hollywood and Vine," and Syd's wandering around the place, wide-eyed, reckless and legged. "Gee," he says, "it's great to be in . . . *Las Vegas!!*"'[72]

'Syd was a big rock star now,' says David Gale, 'and behaving extremely weirdly indeed on tour, standing on-stage with an untuned guitar.' 'Syd went mad on that first American tour in the autumn of 1967,' said Nick Mason. 'He didn't know where he was most of the time. I remember he detuned his guitar on-stage in Venice, Los Angeles, and he just stood there rattling the strings which was a bit weird, even for us.'[73]

During the band's stay in Los Angeles, a city that must have seemed even more bizarre to Syd in his fractured state than it already was, they were supported by seventies shock-rocker Alice Cooper and his band, who invited the Pink Floyd for dinner at their communal house in Venice Beach. Cooper's guitarist Glen Buxton was left with vivid memories of Barrett. Barrett was entirely silent, only smiling a slightly quizzical smile, as they sat for dinner. Buxton sat next to the reticent musician with staring eyes, wild hair and blank gaze. Midway through the meal, Buxton passed Barrett the bowl of sugar. What Buxton noted was unusual about that was that Barrett hadn't actually asked him for it. But as Buxton handed it to him, Barrett acknowledged it with a slight smile. It was as if Barrett had asked him to pass the sugar by telepathy. Buxton was struck by Barrett's strange presence, as if he were simultaneously detached and yet very much in tune with what was going on around him.[74]

Glen Buxton also commiserated with Wynne-Wilson and Marsh, who complained that Barrett was either completely absent minded or careless. 'They'd fly a thousand miles, get to the gig, he'd get up on-stage and wouldn't have a guitar. He would do things like leave all his money in his clothes in the hotel room, or on the plane. Sometimes, they'd have to fly back and pick up his guitar.'[75]

The morning of the 5th, the Pink Floyd appeared on CBS television's *The Pat*

Boone Show. Boone, best known as the fifties white singer who scored big hits with watered-down versions of Little Richard's more raucous [read black] rockers such as 'Tutti Frutti'. *The Pat Boone Show* was a very straight scene indeed, being broadcast to a largely white, middle-class audience. The sight of the Pink Floyd, with a severely disoriented Syd Barrett must have been surprising, to say the least. Roger Waters said, 'By the time we went to America, Syd had gone, by and large. We did *The Pat Boone Show* and we were taping the show and we would do the run-through and Syd would stand there with his Telecaster with the silver bits all over it and mime happily. And then they'd go, "OK guys, we're gonna do it now", roll the tape, playback, and go!' And he'd just stand there and not move a muscle. He knew perfectly well what was going on, he was just being . . . *crazy*. And they did four of five takes like that. Eventually I mimed it.'[76] Roger indeed mimed it, looking decidedly nonplused. He complained bitterly to Andrew King after the gig. The others in the band were at loss; they wondered if Syd was sabotaging the tour on purpose. They really had no way to realise Barrett was ill and needed help that he wasn't likely to receive. The acid culture was just beginning to reap its harvest of fractured minds.

Boone came on-stage to talk to the band, and Syd Barrett stared blankly at him, his eyes frozen. America, which for the British seems larger than life at the best of times, must have been entirely too much for him. To be confronted with Pat Boone, even when not having just spent sleepless nights on Haight-Ashbury tripping on STP and sleeping with California blondes at the height of psychedelia, must have been deeply worrying for him. In tapes of the performance, Syd is shell-shocked as they began to mime to 'Apples And Oranges', his arms motionless, mouth ajar, head bobbing slightly. Watching a fragment of the taped performance reveals Syd staring out not with blank eyes, but with a deep penetrating stare, as if intently sending out a silent plea for help. Whether intentional or not, this stare was a powerful silent statement on the shallow spectacle, and high cost, of pop stardom.

That very same night the band performed at the Cheetah Club, in Santa Monica. 'I can remember Syd being on-stage but not playing a note,' says Peter Wynne-Wilson. 'I'm not sure if they didn't get in someone to play guitar for some of the gigs. The Cheetah Club in LA was a terrible stainless-steel discotheque. We hadn't seen that kind of club before, and I don't know what kind of music they usually played there, but it would have suited disco music rather than the Floyd's music. And at the Cheetah, Syd was in a bit of a state.'

The next day, 6 November, the Pink Floyd managed to better the previous day's performance with their appearance on ABC's Dick Clark's *American Bandstand*. Dick Clark, the seemingly ageless mannequin-like host, stepped up to interview Barrett. Syd must have been thinking, 'Didn't I just do this?' Another débâcle followed, with Syd refusing or being unable to form the words.

A third TV appearance, on *Beach Party*, was promptly cancelled by King, who had been watching the spectacle in horror from the wings. Everything that conceivably could have gone wrong, had. The rest of the tour was cancelled.

'It's easy now to look back on the past and try and give it some shape and some form,' said Nick Mason. 'But at the time you're in a total state of confusion, muddling about because you're trying to be in this band and be successful and make it work, and things aren't working out. You don't really understand why, and you can't believe someone's deliberately trying to screw it up; and yet the other half of you is saying, "This man's crazy, he's trying to destroy me!" Destroy *me*, you know, it gets very personal. You all get very worked up into a state of extreme rage.'[77]

The Pink Floyd's remaining gigs should have been on 9 November at the Fillmore and 10 and 11 November at the Winterland on a triple bill with Procol Harum and H.P. Lovecraft. But Andrew King, in despair, had decided to cut their losses and leave California. None the less, superb posters remain of the phantom gigs, sadly reminding us of how what should have been the Pink Floyd's moment of triumph turned into one of epic defeat. The band did however stop in New York to play the Cheetah Club in New York City on 12 November. They flew home to England, with Waters arguing for hours with Andrew King about Syd's bizarre behaviour.

Alas, the Machine wasn't to be satiated, and insanity or not, Barrett was compelled to appear in Rotterdam, Holland, for a 13 November appearance at the incongruously titled Hippy-Happy Fair Club. Tapes of the show survive, the only other known complete recording of a Syd-era gig. The set list for the forty-four-minute show included 'Reaction In G', 'Pow R. Toc H.', 'Scream Thy Last Scream', 'Set The Controls For The Heart Of The Sun' and a ragged, incredibly loud 'Interstellar Overdrive'. Syd apparently didn't sing any lyrics until about halfway through the performance.

Astonishingly, bookings made months before then forced a plainly exhausted Barrett and co. to embark on a gruelling British package-tour of one-nighters supporting the Jimi Hendrix Experience. In less than forty-five minutes, Amen Corner, the Nice, Heir Apparent and Outer Limits ran through their brief sets, before the Pink Floyd played a seventeen-minute set. UFO habitués the Move were billed above the Floyd, with a thirty-minute set, followed by the Jimi Hendrix Experience closing with forty minutes. The package tour débuted on 14 November at The Alchemical Wedding at the Royal Albert Hall.

In an interview in 1970, Syd Barrett seemed to be blissfully unaware of the chaos he'd occasioned on their American tour. 'There's no gloom or depression for me. It's been very exciting, especially when I went to America for two weeks before the split-up. Then we came back and played at the Albert Hall and it was very much a crescendo and I felt very good.'[78] One aspect of a severe mental breakdown, perhaps, is that a divorce from reality becomes complete. Those in Barrett's circle weren't terribly cognizant of the implications of him losing his grip. With the lack of knowledge that still pervades the way mentally ill people are viewed in society, Barrett wasn't given the help he so desperately needed.

Melody Maker reviewed the concert, 'The Pink Floyd threatened to walk out on the tour during the afternoon when it was said they couldn't use their own gear and a cinema screen behind the stage, as it would block the view for fans seated in the rear. In the end difficulties were resolved, the Floyd went on and the fans' view was blocked. The Floyd gave one of their colourful and deafening displays of musical pyrotechnics, and indeed all the groups were painfully loud, with all the agony increased by the horror of the Albert's acoustics.'

The package tour involved playing a gig or more a night while travelling throughout the British Isles. Roger Waters remembers it simply as 'a real nightmare'. 'The only one we ever did,' said Nick Mason. 'A seventeen-minute set limit which was terrific because we were pretty frazzled at the time, towards the end of the Syd Barrett period. What was great was that we actually met some other musicians. We'd led a pretty solitary life as a band until then and suddenly we were hanging out with Hendrix. It was an opportunity to wallow in a bit of all-musos-together. I think it was the last big tour of that time. After that everyone wanted to go out on their own with just a support act.'[79]

'I toured with Hendrix, you know,' recalled Syd Barrett. 'Lindsay and I used to sit on the back of the bus, with him up front; he would film us. But we never spoke really. It was . . . very polite. He was better than people really knew. But very self-conscious about his consciousness. He'd lock himself in the dressing-room with a TV and wouldn't let anyone in. Hendrix was a perfect guitarist. And that's all I wanted to do as a kid. Play a guitar properly and jump around. But too many people got in the way. It's always been too slow for me. Playing. The pace of things. I mean, I'm a fast sprinter. The trouble was, after playing in the group for a few months, I couldn't reach that point.'[80]

During the tour Barrett would either not show up, refuse to play when he did, or stand on-stage in mute terror. More than once he vanished, leaving the others to fend for themselves as best they could. Dave O'List, the guitarist of the Nice and formerly of mod band the Action, stepped in to cover for Barrett on a couple of dates during the tour. On one occasion Barrett apparently tried to board a train for London before Jenner caught up with him. A growing schism in the band and in its immediate circle was becoming all too apparent. Jenner and King dismissed Wynne-Wilson halfway through the tour, citing the high cost of his salary. John Marsh took over as lights man, receiving a wage rather than a percentage as Wynne-Wilson had done. He and Susie were more than happy to leave the sinking ship; they were the ones who spent the most time with Syd, and watching him burn up before their eyes was saddening.

'It was heartbreaking, really,' says Wynne-Wilson. After a long pause, he adds, 'and quite frightening to see the deterioration. It wasn't that other people weren't deteriorating. [Floyd roadie] Pip Carter was a junkie and used to get into terrible states that were hard to believe, and also used to bring people around that were in terrible states. So it's not as if there weren't people falling apart. But it was heartbreaking with Syd because he had been so vital and so light. He walked in a very light way, he had a very particular walk, with heels raised . . . But it was heartbreaking to see him getting into such a state. And it's frightening in those situations where there's nothing you can do to assist in any way.' Jenny Gordon says, 'Syd just always had this wonderful bounce to his walk, very light, and that was nice. A bouncy walk, springing up on the ball of his foot.'

Barrett began to take on the look of a Romantic poet in the slightly tubercular mode of Shelley, combined with a soldier who had returned from the wars with shell-shock. There was one last brief happy interlude, when Syd, Susie and Peter and went to visit poet Neil Oram in his country cottage. Syd, in comfortable unpressured surroundings reminiscent of Earlham Street, with the same friendly faces, was able to shake loose the catatonia and relax. His smile returned as they sat around a hearth fire in the ancient cottage, seated on the floor as autumnal evening fell. But Syd's smile masked a growing fear and uncertainty. He was unhappy.[81]

Peter Whitehead told *Record Collector*, 'The music would have held together and been successful if Syd had not simply gone on a twenty-four-hour trip everyday. And that's what finally blew it. All the talent and originality, the best improvising, psychedelic thing, went with Syd, and the rest of them carried on with their less interesting mainstream, metaphysical science fiction music.' The other band members began actively looking for someone to replace Syd on-stage full-time. Jeff Beck was approached, but turned them down. David Gilmour, Syd's old childhood friend, whom the other Floyds knew from the various gigs they'd played with Joker's Wild supporting, seemed the next logical choice.

On 18 November the Pink Floyd's oft-delayed third single was finally released – 'Apples And Oranges/Paintbox'. Barrett told the press, 'It's unlike anything we've ever done before. It's a new sound. Got a lot of guitar in it. It's a happy song, and it's got a touch of Christmas. It's about a girl who I just saw walking around town, in Richmond. The "apple and oranges" bit is the refrain in the middle.' Sadly, the single was a marked chart failure. Syd Barrett was asked how he felt about it, 'Couldn't care less. All we can do is make records which we like. If the kids don't, then they won't buy it. The kids dig the Beatles and Mick Jagger not so much because of their music, but because they always do what they want to do and to hell with everyone else. The kids know this.'[82] He'd come full circle; he simply didn't care any more. Barrett added, referring to the record business, 'All middle men are bad.'[83]

The failure of the third single, coupled with Barrett's erratic behaviour on-stage, didn't auger well for the band or its finances. Gig promoters became increasingly reluctant to book them and money began to dry up along with bookings. Jenner said, 'The way we ran things was so haphazard. At one time we had the Floyd, Andrew and me, June Bolan, two roadies and two lights people all on salary, and we didn't keep any sort of control over expenditure. Ludicrous amounts were spent on ridiculous things, and the money scene got very unstable because of the reputation the band had gained for being unreliable.'[84]

The Pink Floyd recorded another *Top Gear* session at BBC's Maida Vale Studio, London, on 20 December. On 'Vegetable Man', the band depart significantly from the studio version, making it much more a R&B rave-up. Nick Mason hammers the drums as Syd sings about his nylon socks. The mood fluctuates rapid, with tempo changes galore, dissolving into garbled voices. The black humour of this track becomes apparent with the campy chorus, a take-off of the *Batman* theme which harks back to their R&B days at Highgate. A great Barrett guitar solo effortlessly leads into the self-deprecatory middle eight bars, 'I've been looking all over the place. . .'

On 'Scream Thy Last Scream', Barrett's guitar work is solid, proof that his Muse hadn't fully deserted him yet; his sense of timing steady. This version is one of Barrett's most compelling performances, difficult listening to be sure, but it's a shame that it hasn't been heard widely. On 'Pow R. Toc H.' Rick Wright turns in a bluesy jazz piano solo, giving an idea of the future Floyd's emerging sound. Ragged, forceful guitar lines from Barrett with a clear phrase quote taken from the Butterfield Blues Band's 'East/West'. On 'Jugband Blues' a chorus of kazoos are substituted for the Salvation Army brass of the studio version. Wright leans in with an organ barrage, Waters striking sonar blips on his Rickenbacker bass, and an extended coda with staccato drumming from Mason. A farewell coda from Barrett, with organ and background vocals courtesy of Wright. It's a wonderful session, and one that raises significant doubts about Barrett's 'madness'. In this relaxed setting, Barrett simply shines.

The Christmas On Earth Revisited spectacular at the Kensington Olympia, on 22 December, with the Jimi Hendrix Experience, the Move, the Animals, Tomorrow and the Soft Machine, was to be Syd Barrett's last major appearance with the Pink Floyd.

What a meteoric year it had been, one where the Pink Floyd had been catapulted to fame and Syd Barrett, at age twenty-one, became a star. The star that had shone so brightly had now imploded and was turning into a black hole, literally siphoning off energy from everyone else around him in the midst of his own creativity's death throes. By now, the vast oceanic solos were beginning to dissolve into repeated notes, dissolving like a Binson echo refrain. It was as if the vortex of the black hole was drawing in the very flourishes and themes which powered his flights. Barrett was caught in a bind, his persona of 'Syd Barrett' threatening to subsume Roger Barrett. The schism would have to come sooner or later, with one sacrificed in favour of the other.

His musical thesis was the dismantling of harmony, the search for melody, for the perfect note, for the lost chord. The freeing of music from rhythm, metre, lyrics, in short, any subjective measure used to determine quality. The purest expression of feeling, unfettered by thought. The victory of the subconscious over the conscious. Dispensing with tonal modalities, chord scales (which gave Coltrane's most extreme music some structure), everything; Barrett wanted to jettison the lot. Syd, in a sense, meant to go all the way. And in a sense he accomplished it, like Kurtz reaching the end of the river in Conrad's *Heart Of Darkness.*

The antithesis of Syd's improvisational thesis was the tight structure of his 'closed' songs, with verse-chorus-verse structures. The synthesis was a progression of the jazz improvisation, a statement of thesis, a free-form exploration, a restatement of thesis, elucidation. Acid aided this synthesis, but was it crap or genius? Maybe it was both.

Syd's free-form music seemed to embody what author James Gleick, in his book *Chaos*, called 'the taste for randomness and complexity, for jagged edges and sudden leaps'.[85] Syd's pursuit of an idealised creative chaos eventually lost sight of the order underlying those chaotic flights. He embraced free-form but lost touch with the form that enables one to pursue the former effectively. His internal logic would progress from 'order masquerading as randomness'[86] to its inverse, randomness masquerading as order, as the ragged epic sprawl of 'Interstellar Overdrive' descended into incoherence. There is a streak of turbulence that pervades 'Interstellar Overdrive' that would drag Syd's guitar technique into the throes of chaos. One of the saddest signs of Syd's unravelling technique was his growing difficulty in adhering to steady tempo. The patterns of his rhythm became skewed. Like jazz pianist Bud Powell's late recordings, made after Largactyl and mental illness had taken their toll, time signatures are all over the map, before the beat, after the beat, sometimes tantalizingly dead on it, but one fears out of accident rather than design. Mike Watkinson and Pete Anderson succinctly note, 'Syd had finally brought his free-form ideas to a logical if unsatisfactory conclusion.'[87] In the aftermath of the disastrous Olympia gig, where Syd stood at the edge of the stage, staring in horror into the void, Roger Waters rang up Nigel Gordon and asked him to get hold of Dave Gilmour. Gilmour was now back from his ill-fated jaunt around France with the Flowers, and had been observing the Pink Floyd's performances during the end of 1967 with a critical eye. 'They were a piece of crap,' he said. 'Syd was thrashing about on his guitar terribly and everyone was thinking it was wonderful.'[88] Gilmour told the German *Stern* magazine, 'People were full of drugs, and they went along with everything. A full hour of guitar feedback, no problem, they loved that. I loved the first album, but I thought the gigs were pretty interminable. It was too anarchic. I was all for musicking things up a bit. I definitely considered myself a superior musician and I remember thinking that I could knock them into some sort of shape.[89] The band just before Syd departed had got into a totally impossible situation. No one wanted to book them. After the success of the summer of 1967 the band sank like a stone; the gigs they were doing at the time were all empty because they were so bad.'[90]

Rick Wright said, 'The band was an improvising group in the beginning. A lot of rubbish came out of it but a lot of good too. A lot of that was obviously to do with Syd, that was the way he worked. Then things got a lot more structured when Dave joined. He was a fine guitarist, but he wasn't really comfortable with all that wild psychedelic stuff.'[91]

Indeed, Gilmour disowned the Pink Floyd's more overtly psychedelic early music; perhaps he was never fully comprehending of its instinctive chaos. The blues basis of Jimi Hendrix's music, which Gilmour had spent an entire year playing cover versions of in France with the Flowers, provided him with outlines on which to draw from. Not to slight Gilmour's exceptional sense of the perfect solo (a soupçon of notes perfectly placed, notably on the solo in 'Time') but his style is far more technical and analytical than Syd's. A brilliant musician, but not an innovator.

Duggie Fields said, 'Syd went more than slightly bonkers; it must have been very difficult for him. The pressures on Syd must have upset him very much, the kind of pressure where it takes off very fast, which Pink Floyd did, certainly in terms of the way people behaved towards them. I used to be speechless at the number of people who would invade our flat, and how they would behave towards anyone who was in the group; especially girls. I'd never seen anything like it. Some of the girls were stunning, and they would literally throw themselves at Syd. He was the most attractive one; Syd was a very physically attractive person, I think he had problems with that.'[92]

Jenny Fabian was one of those girls who was fascinated by Syd. She kept company briefly with him during 1967, and recalls, 'Syd was so beautiful. His violet eyes. I only sort of lay beside him, nothing more could be accomplished. Then he had a breakdown and was gone. He hardly spoke. He would just tolerate me because I was so overpowered, so in awe that I didn't really speak either . . . I knew Syd was wonderful because he wrote such wonderful songs.'[93]

Syd was displaying the classic symptoms of schizophrenia, though whether he was schizophrenic is wide open to interpretation. The very use of terms like 'schizophrenia' should be seen as an attempt to define the indefinable. A blanket term like that does little to explain the unusual circumstances Barrett was in. Sudden fame, ingestion of drugs, an unstable homelife and a profound identity crisis, personality conflicts with his peers, and unreasonable demands made on him all conspired to aggravate whatever underlying disposition to madness Barrett may have had. In the strictly literal clinical definitions used by mental health 'professionals', Syd Barrett was schizophrenic. His catatonic episodes, loosening of associations in speech, aberrant behaviour, sudden violence, extreme range of moods, impaired facial expressions (or 'affect') and paranoia all fit the description. However, sanity isn't something that can be tallied up on a scorecard. As R. D. Laing would posit, Barrett's dilemma mirrors the insanity of the situation he was in. The pressure was on him, the pressure to write the music and lyrics, perform live to hostile audiences, sing, play guitar, be interviewed by witless journalists, have his photo snapped, be ordered to write commercial songs; in short, he was compelled to be 'Syd Barrett' and the first taste of success had a profoundly bitter aftertaste. Was Syd that crazy? What would you or I have done in his position?

Like an errant moon orbiting a planet in an ellipse, as Syd broke away, his mind swung in ellipses around reality, each orbit took him farther and farther out. It was as if his mind went out of phase, crisscrossing patterns cancelling each other out. Thought patterns, stripped of structure, became frustrating, with ideas and theories analysed to the point of paralysis, like an algebraic equation that never breaks down into prime numbers. Stripped of the logical criteria of analysis, ideas became ever more vague and abstract, until that very vagueness and abstraction was substituted for logic and analysis. Catatonia would alternate with exaggerated motion. The oscillations began to quicken, as the impending eclipse disrupted Syd's inner orbits. Waving his arms in the air, casting spectral shadows, as if signalling his imminent breakdown, he was calling for help. The once dazzling psychedelic wash of colours gave way to murky darkness as the stage act became reality. Standing stock still on the edge of the stage, Barrett's fantasy of the Scarecrow, if anything, seems prophetic, as if Syd foresaw his inevitable progression to catatonia with chilling clarity.

A mental breakdown is perhaps experientially akin to being submerged slightly under water, reaction time is slowed, and though there is an awareness of what is happening on the surface, perceptions are muddled and unclear. Barrett's breakdown could be seen as a self-protective psychic exile from extreme environmental stress, a severe distress that precipitates, complicates and facilitates a breakdown. One who is in the throes of a breakdown believes their delusions to be fact, and how can fact be considered suspect? The breakdown of traditional walls dividing fantasy and reality, the conscious and the subconscious, are aided by the reckless consumption of drugs; 'break on through to the other side' indeed. LSD exaggerates everything, including stress, especially for a creative mind in formative stages and in the absence of a foundation, framework or structure. Peter Jenner said, 'Syd was extraordinarily creative and what happened was catastrophic: a total burnt-out case. All his talent just came out in a flood in two years and then it was burnt out.'[94]

David Gilmour mused on whether Syd was the victim of excess acid ingestion, 'Well, that's what people say. I don't actually hold with that theory myself. I've said it before, but I always imagine that that would have happened anyway to him at some other point, and maybe the pressures of being a rock'n'roll star and things like acid and stuff I suppose acted as catalysts. I think it's more that he couldn't handle success on that level than it has to do with drugs really. And to do with his past life, his father dying and all that stuff which happened shortly before he was fifteen.[95] In my opinion, it would have happened anyway. It was a deep-rooted thing. But I'll say the psychedelic experience might well have acted as a catalyst. Still, I just don't think he could deal with the vision of success and all the things that went with it.'[96]

On 10 January 1968, the television series *Tomorrow's World* screened a presentation on Mike Leonard's light machines. The Pink Floyd were on hand to play an instrumental backing as Leonard demonstrated his various machines and technique. The camera catches Syd staring up with haunted eyes. Leonard remembers the change in Barrett, and says, 'The Pink Floyd found it more difficult to accommodate the fact that he wasn't "there", or wasn't in the mood to play. And in the end they had to drop him.'

Barrett, Lindsay, their two cats and Rick Wright all moved into a flat in Richmond Hill owned by Andrew King's father. It was a last-ditch attempt to get Barrett away from the hangers-on and parasites who seemed to dog his every step. The arrival of Jock and Sue Kingsford, two old Cambridge friends who had previously lived at Earlham and Cromwell didn't bode well for a stable home life. Some referred to them as 'Mad Jock and Mad Sue', but Duggie Fields says, 'Jock and Sue didn't necessarily strike me as madder than anyone else. I knew people who got committed, and Jock and Sue wouldn't have been people I would have put up for commitment myself. They were quite fun in their way. They lived in Cromwell, and had lived in Earlham before. Then they lived with Syd in Richmond. I never went to that flat.'

David Gilmour was asked to join Pink Floyd on 6 January. Duggie Fields says, 'Dave Gilmour was working at Quorum in Chelsea, a design partnership between Alice Pollack and Ossie Clark.' Gilmour promptly quit his day job driving a delivery truck for Quorum, went home to Cambridge and celebrated by buying the most expensive guitar in a local music instruments shop, much to the astonishment of the sales staff.

On 8 and 9 January, the five-member Pink Floyd began rehearsals and the next two days returned to EMI for the first time in months. Nick Mason said, 'So we were teaching Dave the numbers with the idea that we were going to be a five-piece. But Syd came in with some new material. The song went, "Have you got it yet?" and he kept changing it so that no one could learn it.' Roger Waters said, 'It was a real act of mad genius. The interesting thing about it was that I didn't suss it out at all. I stood there for about an hour while he was singing "Have you got it yet?" trying to explain that he was changing it all the time so I couldn't follow it. He'd sing "Have you got it yet?" and I'd sing "No, no!" Terrific!'[97]

'Syd turned into a very strange person,' said Waters. 'Whether he was sick in any way or not isn't for us to say in these days of dispute about the nature of madness. All I know is that he was murder to live and work with . . . When he was still in the band in the later stages, we got to the point where any one of us was likely to tear his throat out at any minute because he was so impossible.' 'We staggered on,' said Nick Mason, 'thinking to ourselves that we couldn't manage without Syd, so we put up with what can only be described as a maniac.

We didn't choose to use those words, but I think he was. It seemed his whole bent was on frustrating us . . . We definitely reached a stage where all of us were getting very depressed just because it was a terrible mistake to go on trying to do it. He had become completely incapable of working in the group.'[98]

When asked if he had been difficult to work with, Syd Barrett replied somewhat nebulously, 'No, probably my own impatience is the only thing, because it has to be very easy. You can play guitar in your canteen, you know, your hair might be longer, but there's a lot more to playing than travelling around universities and things.'[99] In a 1983 *Penthouse* interview, producer Alan Parsons, who worked both as an engineer on Barrett's solo albums and helped create Pink Floyd's classic *Dark Side Of The Moon*, said, 'Barrett was the victim of harassment from within the group. In a certain way the other Floyds liked to have a "weenie" in their middle. They loved sarcastic remarks, to really embarrass someone. Not everybody can handle that. After Barrett's leaving, Wright was the target. I remember that Wright would make remarks and Waters would laugh at him and shrug.' David Gilmour said, 'I was the new boy. Not only that, I was two years younger than the rest of them, and you know how those playground hierarchies carry over. You never catch up. Roger isn't a generous spirited person. I was constantly dumped on.'[100]

Roger, Nick and Rick went to Egerton Court to visit Storm Thorgerson. The conversation around the kitchen table turned to what to do with Syd. Waters hoped that Thorgerson, who had been relatively close to Barrett, could shed some light on Syd's aberrant behaviour. During the course of their conversation, it became clear that the band did not want to get rid of Barrett, but it was beginning to seem like the only option. Waters said, 'The thing got to a point where we had to say to him that he should leave because we respected him as a writer, but his live performances were useless because he was working out so many things none of us understood. He would de-tune his guitar and strum the loose strings. We used to come off-stage bleeding because we had hits things in frustration.'[101]

John Marsh said, 'At that point it had become apparent that it was no longer a viable proposition. So he went in a fairly bloody kind of coup. Personality problems and differences within the band virtually meant that Syd was elbowed out. It was all very tragic: one week he was playing and the next it's Dave Gilmour. Syd started off on a long downward slide.'[102]

'The band got me in to be a front person, to cover Syd's parts,' said Gilmour. 'I suspect, at the time, to eke out our career a little bit longer. So I learnt to sing all Syd's parts and all his guitar parts more or less. My guitar style and Syd's weren't even close, so it was very difficult for me to know what to do and it took me a while to settle in . . . I'd known Syd since I was fourteen, it was hard dealing with replacing one of my close friends. And having to see one of my close friends no longer functioning as a normal human being.'[103]

*

On 12 January, at Aston University, the Pink Floyd played their first five-member gig with Gilmour. Jenner and King made an official announcement of Gilmour's addition, stating, 'The Pink Floyd wish to explore new instruments and add further experimental dimensions to its sound.'

A version of 'Interstellar Overdrive', from the soundtrack of Anthony Stern's 1968 film *The Committee*, shows Gilmour doing a credible Barrett imitation. He starts with a Dick Dale rhythmic attack, as Wright plays the organ with all the stops out, creating a noise-laden wash. The Keith Rowe 'seagull' sound-effects also figure, showing how closely Gilmour was emulating Barrett's style. On a bootleg of their 25 February 1968 gig at the Piper Club, Rome, Italy, the post-Syd Pink Floyd play a remarkable version of 'Interstellar Overdrive' that largely dispenses with the song's famous riff in favour of a lengthy exploration of the song's more atmospheric improvisation. Any fool who claims that the post-Syd Floyd owes nothing to Barrett's experiments should listen to this version. Barrett had clearly marked out a path for the others to follow.

David Gilmour said, 'It was fairly obvious that I was brought in to take over from him, at least on-stage . . . It was impossible to gauge his feelings about it. I don't think Syd had opinions as such.[104] The first plan was that I would join and make it a five-piece so it would make it easier so that Syd could still be strange but the band would still function. And then the next idea was that Syd would stay home and do writing and be the Brian Wilson elusive character that didn't actually perform with us, and the third plan was the he would do nothing at all. And it quickly changed round, and it was just . . . it was obviously impossible to carry on working that way so we basically ditched Syd, stopped picking him up for gigs.[105] That was it, nothing planned.'[106]

Roger Waters said, 'What happened with Syd was that we were being managed by Andrew King and Peter Jenner of Blackhill Enterprises, for whom I still have a very soft spot. When Syd flipped I had this theory that we could go on with Syd still being a member of the group if he could become Brian Wilson and simply be a back-room boy. But Syd had other ideas: he wanted to get in two sax-players and a girl singer. To which we resolutely said no! But Peter and Andrew both thought it couldn't happen without Syd and stuck with him.'[107]

The five-man Floyd played on 13 January at Weston-Super-Mare, and on 15 and 16 January they rehearsed once more, in preparation for another session at Abbey Road.

Roger Waters said, 'Syd had a great plan to expand the group, get in two other geezers, some freaks that he'd met somewhere or other. One of them played the banjo and the other played the saxophone. We weren't into that at all and it was obvious that the crunch had finally come.'[108] Accounts differ, some say it was a banjo and sax player, or a sax player and female back-up singers, but it had a biting irony to it; Dick Parry, Cambridge saxophonist, and Clare Torry and Doris Troy, female singers, would help give Pink Floyd's 1973 *Dark Side Of The Moon* a majestic sweep beyond the band's four-man trad-rock format. It gave that album a genuine jazz and R&B flavour, something that Syd had always loved. Here, Syd was, as ever, simply ahead of his time. In retrospect a lot of his ideas don't seem that strange, but, rather, prescient and advanced. There are bootleg recordings that purportedly date from a session with the banjo and sax player. Barrett strums out a menacing rhythmic guitar backing as the banjo and sax player break into a dance-hall shuffle. The juxtaposition is quite brilliant, and foreshadows some of the work Barrett was to explore on his solo albums, reflecting his deep affection for the dance music of the thirties.

On 18 January, the Pink Floyd were at Abbey Road, where the band worked on 'Let There Be More Light' and untitled rhythm tracks, both on four-track. Whether Barrett was present is unclear. Rumours allude to him sitting blankly in the reception at Abbey Road, guitar in hand but not actually attending the session.

The next day the band played at Lewes, Sussex, and the day following at Hastings in Sussex. On 26 January, en route to a gig at Southampton University Syd wasn't picked up, effectively ending his tenure in the band he'd founded. David Gilmour said, 'We did five gigs with both Syd and I in the band together. Syd seemed to cheer up a little bit when I was there. I guess it took some pressure off of him. I learnt up the parts like the record, and sometimes Syd sang a bit and sometimes he didn't. But it became very obvious that it wasn't going to continue for a very long time like that.

'We were going to a gig in Southampton. We had an enormous ancient old Bentley and Roger would go round and pick up everyone to go to the gig, and he'd picked all of us up, and Syd was the last one to pick up, in Richmond on the way out of London, and someone said, "Shall we pick up Syd?", and someone else said, "Oh, let's not". And that was it. Just one of those things, it was inevitable.'

Rick Wright said, 'We ended up living together in a flat in Richmond in early 1968. The five-man band idea really wasn't working out, but we couldn't bring ourselves to tell him.[109] We were all very close to him, it was very difficult because we had decided by this point that what we wanted was Syd to become rather like a Brian Wilson, and stay at home and write, because we knew it was impossible, he couldn't perform on-stage. So I had to say things like, "Syd, I'm going out to get some cigarettes" and then go off and do a gig and come back the next day. And it was awful, a terrible time. Eventually, of course, he understood what was happening.'[110]

'We had a big and final meeting at Edbrooke Road one day,' said Roger Waters, 'which came down to me and Syd sitting in a room talking together, and I'd worked out what I thought was the only way we could carry on together, which was for him to still be a member of the group, still earn his fair share of the money, but Syd not come to gigs at all, become a sort of Brian Wilson figure it you like, write songs and come to recording sessions and, by the end of the afternoon I thought I'd convinced him that it was a good idea and he'd agreed, but it didn't really mean very much because he was likely to change his mind totally about anything in an hour. He then went home and I went to see Peter and Andrew and said that this was the end, if this didn't work then we were off, and I asked them to leave it alone for a bit, for all kinds of reasons, the main one being that they didn't see things the same way that I saw it. But they went round to see him and laid various numbers on him, so that was it. We never saw them again except at meetings to dissolve the partnership. We had to sort out who owned what, but that was the end, that day.'[111]

Nick Mason said, 'Jenner and King felt, and I think with some justification, that Syd was the talent they'd discovered and that if we didn't want to work with Syd, well, that was the way it would go. Which for most outsiders, would have seemed a sensible decision to make.'[112] Peter Jenner said, 'If you told me that without Syd they were going to be the biggest working band in the world . . . with Syd I could've believed it, but without Syd, where was it going to come from? Nobody else could write very well; Rick could do a bit of a tune, and Roger could knock off a couple of words if necessary under pressure. But [Waters] wrote only because Syd wrote and we encouraged everybody to . . . Rick wrote before Roger.'[113]

'You could talk to Roger about all kinds of things,' Peter Jenner said. 'Roger was argumentative, the one in the group I was least friendly with, but had most respect for as a businessman. He was this giant ego striding across the landscape. He was the one who had the courage to drive Syd out, because he realised that as long as Syd was in the band they couldn't keep it together. The chaos factor was too great. Roger looked up to Syd and he always felt very guilty about the fact that he'd blown out his mate.'[114]

'Corporal Clegg', recorded in five sessions between 31 January and 13 February, may very well have been the very last track to feature any contribution from Barrett. The song, written by Waters, sounds so crude an approximation of the Barrettonian songwriting style as to constitute a parody; as if all the cliché elements of Barrett's style were combined to create a nightmarish song. Stylistically, it's a virtual re-write of 'Scream Thy Last Scream'. The idea for the song's kazoo break came from the BBC rendition of 'Jugband Blues', when the Floyd had to forsake the song's original Salvation Army band in favour of something simpler. 'Corporal Clegg' introduces a sinister chorus of Brecht-Weill-influenced voices that would pervade such future Pink Floyd musical sequences as the Trial portion of 1979's *The Wall*. Waters was forging a new menagerie of characters to populate Pink Floyd's songs. Syd's black and green scarecrow, Lucifer Sam the cat, the benign gnome and 'mouse called Gerald' would be supplanted over the years with Waters' corrosive worms, pigs, hapless sheep and dogs.

Rick Wright said, 'I cringe at some of my songs, such as "Remember A Day". We were pretty amateurish at the time, but I don't think it was just my stuff that doesn't sound so good now. Something like "Corporal Clegg", which was one of Roger's songs, is just as bad. Syd was the songwriter and then we came in and had to take over the song writing, and it was a lot of responsibility to assume. We could never write like Syd, we never had the imagination to come out with the kind of lyrics he did.'[115]

Though it's unclear now, John Marsh maintains that Barrett might have played one final gig on 16 February at ICI Fibres Club, Pontypool. It marked one of the saddest and strangest episodes in his decline. Dr Sam Hutt, the physician of the Underground recalls Syd being given a bottle of Mandrax, a powerful drug available at the time. 'Syd appeared on-stage with this jar of Brylcreem, having crushed the Mandies into little pieces, mixing them up with the Brylcreem and putting this mixture of Brylcreem and broken Mandy tablets all over his hair, so that when he went out on stage the heat of the lights melted the Brylcreem and it all started to drip down his face with these bits of Mandrax.'[116]

John Marsh recalls, 'What was happening was that Syd for some reason had decided to get into Brylcreem, and thirty seconds before the band go on-stage Syd decides to Brylcreem his hair. And at the moment he's about to apply the substance someone says "Come on, let's go", so what does Barrett do? He upends the jar of Brylcreem on his head and because it's hot the whole shooting match slips out on to his head and he walks out on-stage with a glistening half-pound of Brylcreem on his head. And through the set under the stage lighting and the heat it gradually melts and Syd ends up at the end of the set looking like a gutted candle, except he doesn't know it and he can't see it.'[117]

'I don't know about the Mandrax part of it,' said David Gilmour. 'He did have a thing about Brylcreem at one time. Yes, he did go fairly mad. He did go mad or whatever you want to call it.'[118] 'Syd emptied a can of Brylcreem on his head because he said he didn't like his curly hair,' said Nick Mason.'[119]

What must have gone through Syd's mind at that moment? Was this a statement, a cry for help, or just a caprice? Certainly drugs open up the realms for such behaviour; indeed, it wouldn't be such a stretch if you were stoned. Just eccentric. But that is the realms one visits when in a drugged haze. Perhaps Barrett bubbling out the words through a mask of Brylcreem, indecipherable under the hot stage lights, was a nightmarish cry for help. At, best one can only infer what processes were at work in Syd's mind, and speculating on these processes is tantamount to trying to discern the nature of an object by watching its shadows dance along a wall. Similarly, the study of the etiology of insanity is forever bound to be a fault-ridden science of inferences and assumptions. One of the tragic consequences of mental breakdown is that the inner devastation may be all but invisible to others. 'Pull yourself together!' is a common refrain as the first signs of the breakdown are made manifest. In place of empathy and care, mentally ill people are often at the receiving end of incomprehension and often hostility from others. In addition, the mentally ill, who need most the care and concern of others, are the most likely to prematurely exhaust that care and concern with their erratic behaviour, petulance and aberrant extremes of moods.

On 18 February, David Gilmour was officially announced as a full member of Pink Floyd. Nick Mason said, 'I'm not someone who likes being out of control in any way. Not many people would like the sensation of being on a runaway bus with a drunk at the wheel. You're quite cross at the same time as being frightened. Then, after Syd, Dave was the difference between light and dark. He was absolutely into form and shape and he introduced that into the wilder numbers we'd created. We became far less difficult to enjoy, I think. And that made it more fun to play because you want to entertain, get some rapport going rather than antagonise. To annoy the audience beyond all reason isn't my idea of a good night out.'[120]

Syd Barrett said of the split with the band, 'I don't know that there was really much conflict, except that perhaps the way we started to play wasn't as impressive as it was to us, even, wasn't as full of impact as it might've been. I mean, it was done very well, rather than considerably exciting . . . It wasn't really a war. I suppose it was really just a matter of being a little offhand about things. We didn't feel there was one thing which was going to make the decision at the minute.'[121]

As the realisation of his ouster began to sink in, Barrett became resentful of Gilmour. David Gilmour said, 'I remember one terrible night when Syd came and stood in front of the stage. He stared at me all night long. Horrible!'[122]

The improvisatory ethic of the Pink Floyd was to remain their source of ideas, but increasingly the improvisations would be relegated to rehearsals for live performances and, ultimately, completely in the studio, with the recordings becoming steadily more ordered and less spontaneous, drawing from the highlights of the improvisations. Gilmour would bring with him a different sense of atmospherics, his Fender Stratocaster bringing a liquid tone to Water's lyrics. Barrett said, 'When we parted I had written everything for the group. My leaving sort of evened things out within the group.'[123] Roger Waters said, 'I had no idea that I would ever really write songs, and in the early years, I didn't have to because Syd was writing all the material and it was only after he stopped writing that the rest of us had to start trying to do it. I'd always been told, at school anyway, that I was absolutely bloody hopeless at everything, so I had no real confidence about any of it.'[124]

Waters assumed leadership of the Floyd, 'It was straight after we had split up with Syd. I'm sure you would get arguments about that from the "other boys", but I simply took responsibility, largely because no one else seemed to want to do it, and that is graphically illustrated by the fact that I started to write most of the material from then on. I'm perfectly happy being a leader. In fact, I know I can be an oppressive personality because I bubble with ideas and schemes, and in a way it was easier for the others simply to go along with me.'[125] He developed an arrogance to belie his insecurity. He had to; the conch shell was in his hands, and he had to make himself heard.

Peter Jenner commented on the trademark Dave Gilmour slide and echo guitar style, 'That's Syd. On-stage Syd used to play with slide and a bunch of echo boxes.'[126] David Gilmour said, 'The facts of the matter are that I was using an echo box years before Syd was. I also used slide. I also taught Syd quite a lot about guitar. I mean, people saying that I pinched his style when our backgrounds are so similar . . . That kind of thing's bound to get my back up. I don't want it to go into print saying that I taught Syd Barrett everything he knows because it's patently untrue, but there are one or two things in Syd's style that I know came from me.'[127]

Nothing in Gilmour's 1965 single with Joker's Wild suggests he was thinking along remotely the same lines as Barrett regarding slide and echo. Barrett was the first to realise the potential of the Binson echo unit, and explored the echo side of the 'slide/echo' technique much further than Gilmour did. Gilmour conversely was more adept at slide guitar, having a better grounded sense of R&B. Gilmour's lovely Fender slide is still an element in the modern day Pink Floyd's sound, one of many reasons why the band draws up to 90,000 people per show. They are both brilliant guitarists, springing from the same parties and amateur gigs in Cambridge, when as teenagers they sat around endlessly copying R&B riffs from Stax or from the blues. Their respective styles, from similar origins bifurcated into two equally interesting tangents. Gilmour's epic solo in 'Time' is a masterpiece of understated virtuosity, in the same way that Barrett's pioneering 'glissando guitar' continues to inform guitarists today.

David Gilmour said, 'To be honest, [I was] trying to sound a bit like Syd. But the numbers that they were doing were still Syd's, mostly. Consequently there was a kind of fixed thing in your head of how they had been played previously, and that makes it very much harder for you to strike out on your own.'[128] Rick Wright said, 'Dave was much more of a straight blues guitarist than Syd, of course. And very good. That changed the direction. Although he did try to reproduce Syd's style live; in fact, it was a lot of fun playing "Astronomy Domine" on the 1994 tour because Dave was trying to play it the way Syd would have done.'[129]

On 2 March, Blackhill Enterprises was dissolved and Pink Floyd parted way with their managers, Peter Jenner continuing as Syd's manager.

Rick Wright said, 'Peter Jenner and Andrew King thought Syd and I were the musical brains of the group, and that we should form a breakaway band, to try and hold Syd together . . . And believe me, I would have left with him like a shot if I had thought Syd could do it.'[130]

'Andrew and I have always been very well taken care of by the Floyd ever since,' said Peter Jenner. 'We originally had a six-way partnership, which they have never queried. They're incredibly honourable. The Floyd's yearly royalty cheques have kept the wolf from the door on many occasions.'[131]

On 6 April, Syd Barrett officially left the Pink Floyd. In May, with Jenner as producer, Syd began his solo career. 'I only did a couple of sessions,' recalls Peter Jenner of his and Syd's studio sessions during spring 1968. 'It was reasonably together in a fairly wacky way, at least there were songs and things.'[132] EMI was to file complaints of Syd's chaotic behaviour during the sessions, which allegedly left a trail of damaged equipment in his wake. On the 6th, Jenner supervised as Barrett recorded demos of 'Swan Lee' and 'Late Night'.

On the 14th, Barrett recorded a backing track for 'Golden Hair' as well as 'Lanky (Part One)' and 'Ramadhan', which Malcolm Jones, who was later to produce Barrett recalled as, 'very long and rambling' percussion instrumentals. Engineer Peter Bown's announcement on the tape of 'Lanky (Part One)' is, rather wearily, 'Five minutes of drums!' It wasn't very good! 'Ramadhan' lasted for almost twenty minutes, and in its unfinished state was also pretty boring. Syd too wasn't satisfied with it and overdubbed several conga drums in random improvisation.[133] 'Lanky' and 'Ramadhan' were Syd's last stabs at trying to free music from any rules; he would attempt it just one more time, and ironically, it would be his final attempt at music making. On Cleopatra Records' compilation of 'space rock' music, *Space Daze*, Syd's instrumental 'Lanky' seems to fit far better in the context of others such as Hawkwind than as a stand-alone piece.

Barrett and Jenner returned to Abbey Road on 28 May to add overdubs to new versions of 'Swan Lee' and 'Late Night'. 'Swan Lee' features Barrett emulating the guitar work of the Shadows' Hank Marvin, whose trademark treble and echo-laden tone was such an influence on a generation of sixties British guitarists. The guitar work also hints at the Ventures surf guitar and Duane Eddy's twang, achieved by tuning the guitar down an octave.

On 7 June, Peter Jenner kicked off another session with the optimistic intro, 'This is "Clowns And Jugglers", *and it's take one!*' But after take after wearying take, his enthusiasm began to sound forced. 'I had underestimated the difficulty of working with him,' said Jenner. EMI noted with growing displeasure what they felt were uncontrolled sessions, and the number of broken microphones and 'general disorder'. It wasn't only carelessness, but Syd's style of overloading amplifiers and microphones to get the right feedback destroyed a lot of equipment throughout his career. Despite a few more attempts to add overdubs, the sessions were abandoned, and Barrett wouldn't return to the studio until April of 1969. Waters said, 'They did four tracks in all, all of which were an elbow except for one, and Peter finally gave up.'[134]

Blackhill Enterprises' parting gesture for the Floyd was to organise an epochal free concert in London's Hyde Park on 29 June to mark the release of *A Saucerful Of Secrets*, their second album. Many people, John Peel included, remember this as the best concert they ever attended. The album featured only one songwriting contribution from Barrett, his poignant 'Jugband Blues'. His guitar work shows up on Rick Wright's 'Remember A Day', with beautiful glissando ascensions and descensions; on 'Set The Controls For The Heart Of The Sun', with deeply atmospheric and echo-laden guitar deep in the mix; and perhaps on 'Corporal Clegg', with ragged chords and sharp trebly notes. David Gilmour said, 'Syd's on three or four other tracks on the album, including "Remember A Day" and "Jugband Blues". He's also on a tiny bit of "Set The Controls For The Heart Of The Sun". I think I'm on "Set The Controls" as well.[135] We used "Jugband Blues" for no ulterior motive, it was just a good song.'[136]

Barrett said, 'I mean, we did split up, and there was a lot of trouble. I don't think the Pink Floyd had any trouble, but I had an awful scene, probably self-inflicted, having a Mini and going all over England and things.'[137]

He took off in his Mini to seek out some solace, some relief. It wasn't enough though, as the events of the previous year had left an indelible mark on his psyche. According to Mike Watkinson and Pete Anderson, Barrett ended up back in Cambridge, where he entered a sanatorium. It was to be the first of several visits. Sitting in a room, staring out of the window at the gusty winds of autumn sweeping leaves along the quiet streets of Cambridge, Syd was utterly shattered.

He was twenty-two years old.

Andrew King said, 'You'd occasionally see brief flashes of that wonderful imagination, echoes of that extremely pleasant lad who had written "See Emily Play" and "Arnold Layne". But you got the sense that he was trying to battle his way through the most enormous barrier to say two coherent words. Eventually I think he just stopped trying. It was too difficult and painful for him. It was terribly sad to see, and none of us will forget what happened. He was isolated beyond anyone's help. Utterly alone.'[138]

---

1 *Shades Of Pink*, interviews with Charlie Kendall, Source. 1984
2 *Mojo*, May 1994
3 *Shades Of Pink* interviews with Charlie Kendall, Source. 1984
4 *Melody Maker*, 5 August 1967
5 Fabian, Jenny & Byrne, Johnny. *Groupie*. 1970,
6 *ZigZag*, July 1973
7 *Melody Maker*, 12 August 1967
8 *NME*, 5 August 1967
9 *NME*, 13 April 1974
10 *Mojo*, May 1994
11 Unedited transcripts of interviews with June Bolan. Greene, Jonathan. *Days In The Life: Voices From The English Underground, 1961-1971*. Minerva, 1988
12 *Mojo*, May 1994
13 Jonathan Greene. *Days In The Life: Voices From The English Underground, 1961-1971*. Minerva, 1988

14 Ibid.
15 Giovanni Dadomo interview with Syd Barrett, 1970
16 August 1996, by Mark Blake
17 Schaffner, Nicholas. *Saucerful Of Secrets*. Delta, 1991
18 Q, November 1992
19 *Melody Maker*, 5 December 1970
20 Macdonald, Bruno, editor. *Pink Floyd: Through The Eyes Of...* Sidgwick & Jackson, London, 1996
21 Schaffner, Nicholas. *Saucerful Of Secrets*. Delta, 1991
22 Schaffner, Nicholas. *The British Invasion*. McGraw-Hill, 1982
23 *The Pink Floyd Story*: Six-part documentary broadcast on Capital radio, London. December 1976-January 1977
24 Macdonald, Bruno, editor. *Pink Floyd: Through The Eyes Of...* Sidgwick & Jackson, London, 1996
25 Ibid
26 Barrett Interview with Michael Watts, *Melody Maker*, 27 March 1971
27 Jonathan Greene. *Days In The Life: Voices From The English Underground, 1961-1971*. Minerva, 1988
28 *Melody Maker*, 9 December 1967
29 *Melody Maker*, 31 January 1970
30 *NME*, 13 April 1974
31 *Disc & Music Echo*, 8 August 1970
32 Jones, Cliff. *Echoes: The Stories Behind Every Pink Floyd Song*. Omnibus Press, 1996
33 Ibid.
34 Schaffner, Nicholas. *Saucerful Of Secrets*. Delta, 1991
35 Ibid.
36 Schaffner, Nicholas. *Saucerful Of Secrets*. Delta, 1991
37 Jonathan Greene. *Days In The Life: Voices From The English Underground, 1961-1971*. Minerva, 1988
38 MTV interviews with Pink Floyd, 1992
39 Schaffner, Nicholas. *Saucerful Of Secrets*. Delta, 1991
40 Jonathan Greene. *Days In The Life: Voices From The English Underground, 1961-1971*. Minerva, 1988
41 'Syd Barrett Careening Through Life'. Kris DiLorenzo, Trouser Press, February 1978
42 Ibid.
43 August 1996, by Mark Blake
44 *Rolling Stone*, December 1971
45 Barrett Interview with Michael Watts, *Melody Maker*, 27 March 1971
46 Ibid.
47 Jonathan Greene. *Days In The Life: Voices From The English Underground, 1961-1971*. Minerva, 1988
48 'Syd Barrett Careening Through Life'. Kris DiLorenzo, Trouser Press, February 1978
49 *NME*, 13 April 1974
50 Ibid.
51 Ibid.
52 Ibid.
53 *NME*, 7 October 1967
54 *Melody Maker*, 7 October 1967
55 *NME*, 7 October 1967
56 *Go*, 4 August 1967
57 *Mojo*, May 1994
58 Schaffner, Nicholas. *Saucerful Of Secrets*. Delta, 1991
59 *NME*, 13 April 1974
60 *Mojo*, May 1994
61 Jones, Cliff. *Echoes: The Stories Behind Every Pink Floyd Song*. Omnibus Press, 1996
62 *Melody Maker*, 8 December 1967
63 *NME*, 13 April 1974
64 *Record Mirror*, 8 July 1967
65 *ZigZag*, July 1973
66 Miles & Mabbett, Andy. *Pink Floyd: The Visual Documentary*. Omnibus Press, London 1994
67 Ibid.
68 Jonathan Greene. *Days In The Life: Voices from the English* Underground, *1961-1971*. Minerva, 1988

69 Schaffner, Nicholas. *Saucerful Of Secrets*. Delta, 1991

70 Miles & Mabbett, Andy. *Pink Floyd: The Visual Documentary*. Omnibus Press, London 1994

71 '*The Pink Floyd Story*': Six-part documentary broadcast on Capital radio, London. December 1976-January 1977

72 Jonathan Greene. *Days In The Life: Voices from the English* Underground, *1961-1971*. Minerva, 1988

73 *Mojo*, May 1994

74 'Syd Barrett Careening Through Life'. Kris DiLorenzo, *Trouser Press*, February 1978

75 Ibid.

76 *Dancing In The Streets*, BBC series, 1996

77 '*The Pink Floyd Story*': Six-part documentary broadcast on Capital radio, London. December 1976-January 1977

78 *Melody Maker*, 31 January 1970

79 *Mojo*, July 1995

80 *Rolling Stone*, December 1971

81 Schaffner, Nicholas. *Saucerful Of Secrets*. Delta, 1991

82 *Melody Maker*, 8 December 1967

83 Ibid.

84 *ZigZag*, July 1973

85 Gleick, James, *Chaos*, Sphere, 1987

86 Ibid.

87 Watkinson, Mike & Anderson, Pete. *Crazy Diamond: Syd Barrett & The Dawn Of Pink Floyd*. Omnibus Press, 1993

88 *Musician*, November 1992

89 *Mojo*, May 1994

90 *NME*, 11 January 1975

91 Interview with Rick Wright by Kevin Whitlock

92 'Syd Barrett Careening Through Life'. Kris DiLorenzo, *Trouser Press*, February 1978

93 Unedited transcripts of interviews with Jenny Fabian. Greene, Jonathan. *Days In The Life: Voices from the English Underground, 1961-1971*. Minerva, 1988

94 Jonathan Greene. *Days In The Life: Voices from the English Underground, 1961-1971*. Minerva, 1988

95 *Sounds*, May 1983

96 *Musician*, November 1992

97 *ZigZag*, July 1973

98 Ibid.

99 Barrett Interview with Michael Watts, *Melody Maker*, 27 March 1971

100 *Mojo*, May 1994

101 Miles & Mabbett, Andy. *Pink Floyd: The Visual Documentary*. Omnibus Press, London 1994

102 Jonathan Greene. *Days In The Life: Voices from the English Underground, 1961-1971*. Minerva, 1988

103 *Omnibus* special on Pink Floyd, 1994

104 *NME*, 13 April 1974

105 'Shades of Pink', interviews with Charlie Kendall, Source. 1984

106 *Mojo*, July 1995

107 Roger Waters Interview with Chris Salewicz, June 1987

108 *ZigZag*, July 1973

109 *Mojo*, May 1994

110 *Omnibus* special on Pink Floyd, 1994

111 *ZigZag*, July 1973

112 *Omnibus* special on Pink Floyd, 1994

113 *Opel*, Syd Barrett fanzine #8

114 *Mojo*, May 1994

115 Interview with Rick Wright, August 1996, by Mark Blake

116 Jonathan Greene. *Days In The Life: Voices from the English Underground, 1961-1971*. Minerva, 1988

117 Unedited transcripts of interviews with John Marsh. Greene, Jonathan. *Days In The Life: Voices from the English Underground, 1961-1971*. Minerva, 1988

118 *Sounds*, May 1983

119 *Mojo*, May 1994

120 *Mojo*, July 1995

121 Barrett Interview with Michael Watts, *Melody Maker*, 27 March 1971

122 *Melody Maker*, 19 May 1973

123 *Terrapin*, 7 1975

124 'Shades of Pink', interviews with Charlie Kendall, Source. 1984
125 Roger Waters Interview with Chris Salewicz, June 1987
126 *NME*, 13 April 1974
127 *NME* 11 January 1975
128 Schaffner, Nicholas. *Saucerful Of Secrets*. Delta, 1991
129 *Mojo*, July 1995
130 *Mojo*, May 1994
131 Ibid.
132 *The Amazing Pudding*, # 57
133 Jones, Malcolm. *The Making Of The Madcap Laughs*. Orange Sunshine Press, 1986
134 *ZigZag*, July 1973
135 *Guitar World*, 1993
136 *NME*, 13 April 1974
137 Barrett Interview with Michael Watts, *Melody Maker*, 27 March 1971
138 Jones, Cliff. *Echoes: The Stories Behind Every Pink Floyd Song*. Omnibus Press, 1996

Stage Five: Thunder Within The Earth (January 1968-January 1970)

'Thunder within the earth:
The image of THE TURNING POINT.
Thus the kings of antiquity closed the passes
At the time of solstice.
And the ruler
Did not travel through the provinces.'

Chapter 24: Fu/Return – The Turning Point
The I-Ching or Book Of Changes

'I had just come back to London from visiting America with Gilly, a girl who Syd started going out with,' says Duggie Fields. 'Syd and I were hanging out and spent a lot of time together. We had lived together at Cromwell, but mostly one was part of a group sitting around, or part of different groupings. We were just part of a group but hadn't spent that much time together before, just the two of us.' In short order, Syd and Duggie decided to get a flat together and Fields found a comfortable two-bedroom flat near Earl's Court Square. 'I got the flat with Syd right after Christmas 1968.' Fields would be Barrett's flat-mate during the recording of Syd's two solo albums, *The Madcap Laughs*(1969) and *Barrett* (1970).

Dave Gilmour was living in Old Brompton Road, across from their flat. 'You could almost see David Gilmour's flat from our window. Syd and Dave still saw each other. I can't remember Syd articulating any resentment towards Dave for replacing him in the band. Certainly Syd's two solo albums would never have happened without Dave, and Dave must have made a great effort to get those together. Dave's flatmate would come around and visit quite a lot, and we would go over there to visit quite regularly, sometimes several times a week. Jerry Shirley [drummer on Syd's solo work] lived right down the road. There were always people visiting here too.'

Barrett's post-Floyd 'lost weekend' was ending. Since 1968 he had been inactive, recovering as best he could from the traumas of his life as Syd Barrett. On 27 March, he went down to Oxford Street's 100 Club to see the Soft Machine play. In the two years since they had shared bills with the Pink Floyd at UFO, the Soft Machine, Hugh Hopper (bass), Robert Wyatt (drums), Mike Ratledge (organ) and Kevin Ayers (guitar), had developed considerably. Their tour of the US with Hendrix had forced them to become much tighter, refining their remarkable psychedelic jazz to the point where they were widely respected for their skill as musicians. Barrett was plainly delighted with what he saw, so much so that he felt compelled for the first time in a year to have a second go at making a solo album.

Robert Wyatt said, 'I didn't really know Syd at all, that session came about because we were playing at the 100 Club. Syd just happened to come along and see the gig, and in his very, very oblique way said, "Would you like to come along and record?"[1] The Soft Machine, minus guitarist Kevin Ayers, agreed to back Syd on some tracks. The next day Barrett called EMI's studio booking office to ask if he could go back into the studios and start recording again.

The request was referred to Malcolm Jones, the twenty-four-year-old head of Harvest, EMI's new alternative label, home to Pink Floyd among others. Jones had joined EMI just before the failed Jenner-produced Barrett sessions of a year before. Syd was in luck, Jones was understanding and accommodating, and also a fan. In 1982, he privately published his account of the ensuing Barrett sessions, a valuable document in the study of Barrett's music. 'It had occurred to me on several occasions to ask what had become of Syd's own solo career. Dark references were made to "broken microphones in the studios and general disorder" by EMI management, and this had resulted in a period when, if not actually banned, Syd's presence at Abbey Road wasn't particularly encouraged. None of Peter Jenner's recordings of Syd had been releasable, and no one in EMI's A&R department had gone out of their way to encourage Syd back.'[2] Jones rang Syd back the very next day.

Barrett seemed eager to return to the studio. Many of the songs which would grace his first solo album, *The Madcap Laughs*, had actually been written long before. 'Golden Hair' was perhaps his first-ever song, dating from when he was around sixteen, living in Cambridge and beginning to experiment with music. He set his music to the poem of the same name by James Joyce. Several other songs had been written during Barrett's creative songwriting peak during his stay at Earlham Street in 1966, as well as at Cromwell Road.

'I think Syd was in good shape when he made *The Madcap Laughs*,' states Peter Jenner. 'He was still writing good songs, probably in the same state as he was during "Jugband Blues".'[3]

Barrett's solo albums are alternately derided as either trash or lauded as works of genius; they are both. The detritus of a fogged mind litters them, but the beguiling images, ideas and music affirm Barrett's peculiar genius. *The*

Madcap Laughs and its successor *Barrett* were alternately wonderful and disturbing aural paintings. Barrett's lyrics are often rendered muddled and abstract to the point of being confusing, but then he'll turn and astonish with a lyric that evokes potent, poetic images. Parts of both albums are stunning, with songs that are among Barrett's best – the good-natured humour of 'Here I Go', with its echoes of English dance hall music of the thirties and forties, or the clever, mathematical metre of 'Octopus', one of Barrett's best-loved songs. But there were intimations of an enveloping darkness on the horizon as well. The unhinged schizophrenic logic which made Barrett sing in stream of consciousness rants, like someone spinning a ball of yarn that spools out all over the place, was all too apparent.

In the thirty-five-odd songs he attempted during the following year, flashes of the familiar old Syd would appear sporadically, intermittently illuminating all the tracks with the transcendent beauty that was his trademark, along with the erratic singing and playing that would lead others to dismiss him. The two albums and various out-takes are as essential listening as is *The Piper At The Gates Of Dawn*, yet are harder to understand or appreciate; brilliant and erratic in equal measure.

Barrett's voice comes through unsteadily, his sense of timing uneven. In a sense, LSD's time and space distorting effects had become permanent. His sense of timing had become skewed to the point that the other musicians struggled to play along with him. In particular, the drummers who accompanied him on these albums seemed at a loss as how to best follow the odd time signatures. Syd would skip freely over increasingly bizarre chord changes and tempos, often frustrating even himself. DiLorenzo noted, 'Barrett's rhythms were usually unpredictable; one never knew what process in Syd's brain dictated when to speed up or slow down the pace.' At times Barrett is unable to maintain either rhythm nor melody.

There was a slow diminution of coherence and fluidity in his guitar playing, regressing in technical finesse to his 'Lucy Leave' level. As compositions the songs are superb and when the ensemble playing is coherent they shine on a par with his best Floyd work. The gradual diminution of his major talent is deeply sad, but even as Syd struggles for the right note, tone, feel, riff or lyric, his talent is in evidence throughout.

Reservations aside though, *The Madcap Laughs* and *Barrett* are beautiful albums, with so many lyrical and musical twists and surprises that the listener is constantly drawn in. Truly music for the late nights of the soul.

In her superb essay 'The Madcap Loved: The Love Songs Of Syd Barrett' (published on the Internet only), Elisa Roney goes track by track through *The Madcap Laughs*, explaining it accurately as a song cycle about the ins and outs of love. She notes that eight of the twelve songs deal directly with differing aspects of love, while the others allude to love or its attendant joys and fears.

The *NME*'s Nick Kent characterised the albums as 'essays in distance', which is an apt summary. Barrett beguiles and beckons, yet with a palpable air of detachment from the proceedings. He fades in and out, like the Cheshire Cat; now you see him, now you don't. At times Syd seems in control, close up, whimsical. At other times he seems to be lost in the firestorm of his own arcane contemplations, and the songs take a ragged, paranoid edge. The songs are strewn with metaphors for his own inner chaos: 'When I live I die', 'a broken pier on a wavy sea' or 'inside me I feel alone and unreal'. In his confusion Barrett is all too aware of what is happening, and his sighs of exasperation after false starts reflect this.

The solo albums portray a tremendous talent struggling with an incapacitating mental illness. On some tracks, as if dictating over the phone, taking care to ensure his enunciation is correct, but with little corresponding feeling, Syd sings his lyrics in that detached, emotionless voice so peculiar to schizophrenia. At his worst he sounds like he is reading a shopping list, a dull flat monotone stripped of emotional nuances and subtleties. Kris DiLorenzo noted, 'There are painful moments when his voice cracks or careens out of control reaching for notes he once could sing; he shouts the higher notes, not believing he can make them. His acoustic guitar playing is mainly a rhythmic strumming full of arbitrary and often clever tempo shifts and reversals, punctuated with extreme dramatic bursts and tenuous pianissimo.'[4]

Malcolm Jones checked with his superiors and got the thumbs up for sessions on *The Madcap Laughs* to begin. 'Syd seemed very together in contrast to all the rumours circulating at the time,'[5] said Jones. Syd outlined his new compositions: 'Opel', 'Terrapin', a song about an Indian maiden a la Pocahontas called 'Swan Lee', and 'Clowns And Jugglers'. Also included was 'Golden Hair', the James Joyce poem Barrett had put to music when he was sixteen. Jones was enthusiastic: 'It all sounded too good for words!' Jones and Barrett agreed to work with the basic tracks laid down the year before during the failed Jenner sessions as well.

The brass at EMI had only one stipulation, that Barrett have a competent producer who would direct him. They were anxious to avoid the disorder of the Jenner sessions the year before. Jones began searching for a producer; Norman Smith and Jenner turned down the offer in light of other commitments. Later, Jones realised Joe Boyd might have been a good choice, but didn't think of it at the time. 'I talked it over with Syd, his response was stark and simple – "You do it." Syd knew I was a musician of sorts, and saw me as his ally at EMI. I probably was a logical choice to him.'[6]

This concluded, Jones, who also lived in Earl's Court Square, went over to Syd's flat to hear tapes of the previous year's sessions. Barrett played his tapes of Jenner's rough versions of 'Swan Lee', 'Ramadhan', 'Lanky (Parts One and Two)' and 'Golden Hair'. Barrett was especially keen to finish 'Golden Hair'. 'Late Night' was slated to be remade. 'Ramadhan' were twenty tedious minutes of overdubbed conga drums, and ragged improvised guitar, and neither Syd nor Jones were particularly enthused with it. Having gone through the Jenner session tapes, Barrett pulled out his acoustic guitar and presented his new songs. Jones's favourite was 'Opel', in waltz tempo and dirge-like; 'an extremely haunting song; very stark and poignant'. 'Clowns and Jugglers' met with similar approval. Syd played Jones a few bars of 'Terrapin' which he was still working on. Although 'Love You' didn't strike Jones's fancy, 'Syd was pretty keen on it, largely because it was up-tempo. I left Syd's flat totally elated, determined next day to book studio time immediately and to get started.'[7]

The first session was on 10 April at EMI's Studio Three. Barrett was familiar with Studio Three from *The Piper At The Gates Of Dawn* days, which had a cosy atmosphere. Jones and Barrett sat from 7 p.m. until 12.30 a.m. going through the Jenner session tapes. According to Jones, they overdubbed guitar and vocal tracks on to 'Swan Lee' and worked on ideas for 'Clowns And Jugglers'. Neither version was to be used, but the session served as a chance for Barrett to re-acclimatise himself to the studio, always a slightly intimidating place.

On 11 April, Jones wrote, 'Syd was in a great mood and in fine form, a stark contrast to the rumours and stories I'd been fed with. In little over five hours we laid down vocal and guitar tracks for four new songs and two old.' When the mood was right, and in a relaxed and unpressured environment, Barrett would shine, working with dedication and focus. With engineer Peter Mew and Jones at the desk, Barrett sat down on the stool with guitar in hand, arranged his lyric sheets on a stand in front of him, and played 'Opel'. Both Jones and Barrett were particularly keen on the song, and spent a lot of time on it. Syd struggled with it, trying to get the tempo and vocal style just right. 'It took Syd nine runs at it to get a complete take, and even that was not perfect. Nevertheless it had a stark attraction to it, and most of the early takes were merely false starts.'[8] Two entire takes were completed.

'Terrapin', recorded on 11 April in one take, with lead guitar overdubs on 4 May, led Roger Waters to comment, upon hearing it during a *Melody Maker* 'blind date' interview: 'This song makes everything else you have played me look completely sick and silly. I think this is very beautiful. Don't take it off, I'm going to listen to it all the way through. I think that is a great song. In fact all the songs on the album are great. No, some of them are GREAT, in capital letters, and all of them are good. Syd is a genius.'

'Terrapin', taking its title from the street in Cambridge where Syd's beloved sister Rosemary lived while studying, is one of Syd's nature elegies blended with the alternately wistful and melancholy love songs which pervade his solo works. In the vein of 'Scarecrow' or 'Flaming', Syd described a sluggish terrapin's trawl around an Edward Lear seashore. With clever poetic skill, he weaves one lyrical line into another with a totally different image, sometimes overlapping lines: 'Below, the boulders/hiding all the sunlight/is good for us'. The mood, halfway between idyll and torpor, illustrates Barrett's Mandrax-influenced tenure at Earl's Court.

Barrett's genius lies in such wordplay. Taking the puns and double meaning so prevalent in Belloc, Carroll, Grahame and Lear, he colours his songs with multiple meanings, some banal and others revealing. In 'Terrapin', Barrett goes from one tangent to another, taking the listener along. The non-linear flow of logic in his head is laid out plainly for all to hear. His lyrical work reflects the English fascination with words and language, fitting for a country with so many dialects and accents.

The paranoia of 'No Good Trying', recorded on 11 April with subsequent overdubs by the Soft Machine, is alarming; 'It's no good trying to hide your hand, where I can't see, because I understand, that you're different from me'. Why is the heroine of the song hiding her hand? Elisa Roney in her essay on the underlying themes in *The Madcap Laughs*, points out, 'The woman in the song is *real* and not merely an archetype, although she tries to feign "archetypal attitudes" by "holding a sequined fan" or as she's "trying to hold her love where [I] can't see. . ." when he sees how she truly feels about him. She tries to hide herself and her feelings from him'.[9]

The woman stokes Syd's jealousy and paranoia by hiding herself behind the sequined fan, under a 'caterpillar hood', as well as placing her hands where Syd can't see. The images of a lover's hands recur in several songs on the album, a Barrett metaphor for secrets or lies. What comes through strongly is Syd's fear of abandonment coupled with a dread certainty that she is lying or hiding something from him.

'No Good Trying' echoes those intense bad trips where very specific minutiae assumes monumental importance. Very ragged guitar work that skirts the edge of chaos mirrors the disturbing lyrics. The lyric is one of annoyance and paranoia, with Syd's ultimate commentary on an acid trip going out of control: 'Yes, you're spinning around and around in a car with electric lights flashing very fast'. On alternate versions, Barrett sounds weary and a bit vexed, sighing dramatically between takes. He demands, 'I'd like to keep [the guitar] jangly' followed by a sigh of frustration. Barrett plays an extended guitar solo at the end of one alternate version, a take that bubbles like a cauldron, its cross-rhythms churning uneasily, Syd getting lost on rhythmic tangents in an effort to shut out the frustration at hand.

'Late Night', its backing track recorded five months after his last stage performance and sudden exit from the Pink Floyd, is suitably jittery but beautiful. Barrett added vocals and guitar on 11 April. Syd's vocal is grafted with difficulty on to the erratic melody, forcing him to sing it in a clipped monotone that rarely wavers but for his stunning diatonic ascension and descension, as he sings a sadly touching: 'Inside me I feel, alone and unreal, and the way you kiss will always be a very special thing to me'.

Jones noted, 'Syd's guitar playing could, at times, be extremely erratic. He would frequently switch from playing rhythm to lead at double the volume, setting the metres well into the red and requiring a re-take. It was a matter of having too many ideas and wanting to record them all at once.'[10] Barrett had a gift for inferring a see-saw of moods within the same eight bars. On 'Here I Go' he uses a cliché dance hall vamp to establish the mood, starting on F# with 'This is a story. . .' Bouncing up to B, back down to F#, he sings the intro with campy gusto in parody of a dance hall band singer. At the end of the intro his voice descends to the lowest note in his register, before doing one of those patent Barrett (D#/Db/E) plummeting drops, ending on the lowest note in his vocal range, 'A big band is far better than *you*', conveying the girl's condescension. It's one of those subtle Barrett touches, deceptively simple, as he takes the jaunty mood and brings it spiralling down to a note of slightly sour accusation. Then 1, 2, 3, and Syd is off into a jaunty dance hall shuffle.

Joe Boyd says, 'One of the sad things is that I had a tape of Syd playing his music for many years, but no longer have it, and have no idea where it is. The tunes represent to a side of Syd's personality; they were very melodic. If you can, imagine listening to "Arnold Layne" or "Bike" done not by the Pink Floyd but done by a guy with a guitar, in a slightly skiffle or music hall style. Take those melodies out of the context of the group, and you see a guy with wit, a jaunty sense of humour and a great sense of melody and playfulness. That was an aspect of Syd and a side of Syd that I wanted to do more things with. After the Pink Floyd session I even discussed with Peter Jenner doing a solo record with Syd, though nothing came of it. The tape had six songs, including the one we were going to do with the Purple Gang, which was "Here I Go".'

Malcolm Jones said, '"Here I Go" used a music-hall-style chord structure. With its unusual introduction and overall theme, it shows Syd at his relaxed best. He wrote it, I seem to remember, in a matter of minutes. Syd nearly always had his lyrics in front of him on a stand, in case of the occasional lapse of memory. This song was the only one I remember him needing no cue sheet at all. The whole recording was done absolutely "live", with no overdubs at all. Syd changed from playing rhythm to lead guitar at the very end, and the change is noticeable.'[11]

On 23 April, Syd and Jones took the tube up to Abbey Road. Jones noticed that Syd was carrying a small, portable Uher cassette player. 'I'd like to overdub some motorbike noises on to "Ramadhan",' he said, 'I've been out on the back of a friend's bike with the cassette player. They're all ready to put on to the "Ramadhan" four-track.' Jones said, 'When Syd played the cassette of the sound effects, it was terrible! Not only was it poor quality for casual listening, it was certainly no good for professional recording. Syd was quite insistent, so I said nothing more until we got to Abbey Road.' Jones and engineer Peter Mew spent one hour trying to connect Syd's small recorder to the four-track master machine in Studio Three. Their efforts were in vain, and as a restless Syd wandered in and out of the studio, one of the workshop staff had to *make* a connecting lead out of spare parts. Finally, Syd's motorcycle recording was dubbed on to 'Ramadhan's' chaotic drum track. Syd smiled beatifically as the rumble of the motorcycle and the conga drums, beating according to a rhythm all their own, boomed through the control-room speakers. Mew and Jones were appalled at the motorcycle track full of honking horns, long pauses at traffic lights, and recorded so low that the tape hiss threatened to drown out even the erratic drums. Mew and Jones spent another hour making a thirty-second loop of motorcycle noises dubbed from Abbey Road's sound library, by which time, of course, Syd had completely lost interest. 'Ramadhan' wasn't heard from again and remains in the vaults to this day, unheard.[12]

The failure of the 'Ramadhan' session shook Syd's confidence, as the subsequent session of 26 April suggests. The low point of both albums, a severely shaken and irritable Syd, perhaps under the influence of drugs, is clearly at sea during the session. What emerges is his most disturbing song, showing his inner dilemma plainly. 'If It's In You' was recorded in five takes, each successively worse than before. Oddly, the fifth take was included on the finished album. 'Yes, I'm thinking. . .' pleads Syd, his voice going wildly out of pitch. Feeling rushed, he breaks off. Barrett always did bad work when rushed, he always hated to be hurried. Frustrated, he tells Jones, 'Look, you know . . . I'll start again, I'll start again.' Jones says from the control-room, 'Syd, how about tuning the guitar down so . . .' Syd shakes his head, 'No, it's just the fact of going through it. I mean, if we could just cut . . .' Syd starts again, stretching the word 'thinking' from two to eleven syllables, shouted out in a tuneless warble. It's alarming to hear Barrett so completely lose control over his voice. 'It was all going on in his head,' said Jerry Shirley, 'but only little bits of it managed to come out of his mouth . . . Sometimes he'd sing a melody absolutely fine, and the next time round he'd sing a totally different melody, or just go off-key . . . "If It's In You" is a classic example of Syd in the studio. Between that and talking in very obscure abstracts . . . And then the way he sings he goes into that scream . . . But some of his songs are very beautiful. You never knew from one day to the next exactly how it would go.'[13]

On 3 May, Mike Ratledge and Robert Wyatt of the Soft Machine overdubbed various parts on to 'Love You'. Wyatt's drumming fluctuates between the superb and the shambolic, either way giving the tracks a harder rock edge. The Soft Machine could rock, but backing the Madcap was a bit of a departure. Robert Wyatt, the drummer, said, 'I thought the sessions were rehearsals! We'd say "What key is that in, Syd?" and he'd say "Yeah!" Or we'd say "That's funny Syd, there's a bar of two and a half bars and then it seems to slow up and then there's five beats there." And he'd go "Oh really?" And we just sat there with the tape running, trying to work it out, when he stood up and said "Right, thank you very much."'[14] Hugh Hopper said, 'Syd had most of the tracks just put down, the guitar and vocal. He just said "I'd like you to play on these two tracks and do what you can." He didn't even tell us how it went, we just had to listen to it until we had some idea. His music was not very symmetrical, you had to really listen and then it changed suddenly.'[15]

Wyatt said, 'I liked the tunes on *The Madcap Laughs* and the way we did them. We just started to feel our way round them when Syd said "OK, that's it". So the final recording was like a sketch of a painting never completed. Dead punk when you come to think of it.'[16]

Barrett increasingly sought refuge by popping Mandrax tablets. Methaqualone, or 'Mandies' as they were referred to, were a downer with some nasty side effects. They wreaked havoc with Syd's sense of time. 'I had a Mandrax prescription for ten years of my life,' says Duggie Fields, 'and it didn't do that to me. Drugs are a catalyst and how you use them is how you use them, drugs have their incipient qualities, but it's up to you if you get affected, to a degree. No one makes you take them or keep on taking them. Mandrax was eventually banned, but I personally thought it was a very good drug. Certainly, if you are going to take downers, they were a stronger down than most. Dangerous mixed with alcohol, dangerous when taken in excess. I knew someone who wouldn't get out of bed before she had taken a Mandrax. Certainly Syd took Mandies in a way that I wouldn't have taken them. I would take half a tablet at a time, occasionally a whole one. Syd one day took four, which is crazy. That day we couldn't decide whether to take him to hospital or not. I was sitting on him, we were worried that he would vomit and choke, because he was frothing at the mouth when we found him on the floor of the bathroom. He might have smoked some dope as well.'

'No Man's Land', recorded on 17 April with cursory overdubs on 4 May, prefigures the sound of such bands as Sonic Youth or Dinosaur Jr. A wash of distortion unusual for the era's music courses through the composition, giving it a hard edge more reminiscent of the Stooges fuzzed-out distortion epics than any of Syd's other contemporaries. At the end Barrett lapses into several stanzas of barely audible mumbling; an alarmingly correct illustration of the muted dialogue many schizophrenics hear through much of their lives, eternally present and eternally out of range, like a radio that can't be turned off but is too quiet to hear properly. Barrett said, 'Originally the words were meant to be heard clearly, but we went and actually did it. That's how it came out, which wasn't really how I planned it.'[17]

DiLorenzo noted the post-Syd Floyd's continued use of the Barrettonian technique of 'submerged speech and incidental sounds chatter beneath instrumentals'. Pink Floyd would utilise spoken dialogue during instrumental passages on *The Dark Side Of The Moon* or the *musique concrete* babble of televisions in *The Wall*, itself an evocation of Barrett's fondness for television as a tool to drown out his thoughts. 'No Man's Land' is also oddly evocative of AMM's work as well, where they would use a transistor radio to 'source' melody during their improvisations.

Back home, Syd was having a hard time saying no to his many guests. Duggie Fields says, 'Syd would still get all these girls coming round, or people just wanting to hang around. I could let people hang out and carry on working, but I did find it difficult. I could end up in here working, and I had a TV in here at one time and there would be a dozen people watching TV. They would all be stoned and when the television show ended, they would turn to watch me working, because I would be the only activity. That drains your energy. But I never had to lock people out to the same extent that Syd did, I actually managed to work. Whereas Syd wouldn't manage to work. Syd had problems working both on his own and with people around. Once he'd left the Pink Floyd, he had money coming in so he didn't have to think too much about money. It wasn't a lot of money, but he didn't have to get a job or do something. He could say he was a painter, but he didn't have to sell a painting. He didn't even have to finish a painting.'

EMI was beginning to balk at the expense and length of the album sessions. Though Jones denied it, Gilmour alleged that EMI were about to put an end to the sessions. Barrett attended the 30 May Pink Floyd gig at Fairfield Hall in Croydon and collared Gilmour after the show to discuss him taking over production duties on the album. Waters said, 'Syd came and saw Dave and asked him for help, and then Peter Jenner and Andrew King saw EMI and said that the boys were going to help, give us another chance. So EMI said all right and gave us two days, but we had a gig on the second day so we had three sessions, one afternoon and two evenings, and we went in and recorded seven tracks in three sessions. They were fantastic songs.'[18]

Gilmour agreed to help Barrett, having wrapped up the bulk of his work on Pink Floyd's *Ummagumma*. On 12 June, Gilmour, and occasionally Roger Waters, began sessions with Syd to finish *The Madcap Laughs*. David Gilmour said, 'EMI understood Syd's potential at the time. They knew he was very talented and they wanted him to carry on. So they got Malcolm Jones who started recording this album and he spent ages on it. I think it was over six months. Eventually, EMI thought that too much money had been spent and nothing had been achieved. So Syd came and asked if we could help him. We went to EMI and said, "Let us have a crack at finishing it up." And they gave us two days to do it, and one of those days we had a Pink Floyd gig, so we had to leave the studio at four in the afternoon to get on a train and go to the show. But basically, Roger and I sat down with him – after listening to all his songs at home, and said, "Syd, play this one, Syd, play that one." We sat him on a chair with a couple of mikes in front of him and got him to sing the song. On some of them, we just put a little bit of effect on the track with echo and double-tracking. On one or two others, we dubbed a bit of drums and a little bass and organ. But it was like one side of the album was six month's work and we did the other tracks in two and a half days. And the potential of some of those songs . . . they could have really been fantastic.'[19]

With Waters and Gilmour in the control booth, Syd started once more on 'Clowns and Jugglers' (now renamed 'Octopus'), ten takes ensued, and on the 11th all were satisfied, resulting in a shorter, more uptempo version that clipped a verse from the original. The next song 'Dark Globe', recorded in two takes on 12 June, is a deeply poignant acoustic ode to lost love and the chaos of confusion, with Barrett pleading 'Wouldn't you miss me at all?' in a tortured strained voice. The sense is that he is about to be subsumed by the dying of the light. In a scissor-sharp mood change, the next verse finds Syd singing the sad gentle couplet of 'the poppy birds sway', a brief return to faded happy moments of lyricism and melody, but he sounds exhausted. His voice breaks often, revealing the strain. The title appears nowhere in the song, but was plucked from one of Barrett's readings of *Lord Of The Rings* by J.R.R Tolkien. In Chapter IX, The Palantir, there appears: 'The thought of the dark globe seemed to grow stronger as all grew quiet'. An offhand quote, but a striking image of the land of Syd's mysterious musings, a twilight world of earth and thunder, of a dark swirl frozen in a glass marble. The desperate melancholia of the piece, combined with the bareness of the arrangement, echoes John Lennon's similarly tortured confessionals on 1970's *Plastic Ono Band*. The simplicity of the chords suggests the melody dates from Cambridge days, echoing 'Effervescing Elephant's' arrangement. 'Dark Globe' has a definite desolate appeal, embodied in its simplicity and honesty.*

On his solo outings, Syd had shed most of the studio effects that had suffused *The Piper At The Gates Of Dawn*. The Binson is gone, the wide stereo spectrum, reverb and echo, are minimal. Because of the difficulty of recording Syd, or having others record with him, many of the tracks have an appealing dryness, emphasising the bare vocals and guitar tracks, with a minimum of effects or accompaniment. Since no one could guess what would emanate from the erratic tempos and odd-numbered bars of Syd's playing, the recording process was reversed, with rhythm recorded afterwards, overdubbed on to Syd's idiosyncratic time signatures or lack thereof.

'Golden Hair', remade on 12 June in eleven takes, is one of Syd's solo high-water marks, augmented heavily by Gilmour's production. The arrangement is deceptively simple, the production near immaculate; a cymbal is struck softly with mallets and processed with echo to produce a mesmerising atmospheric wash for the song's drone variation on one chord. The leitmotif is Syd's simple repeated three-note melody. Like 'Chapter 24', it's suffused with a meditative Indian air, due in large part to Rick Wright's droning organ. It echoes 'Set The Controls For The Heart Of The Sun', Roger Waters' masterful ambient song. Syd plays a simple melody clearly and coherently, and sings wonderfully. Waves of cymbals mesh with Barrett's acoustic and double-tracked voice. 'Golden Hair' was one of Barrett's earliest songs, written during the time when he,

*REM's Michael Stipe did a lovely solo piano and vocal reading of it in 1989, often playing it live. 'Dark Globe' is echoed in the Southern gothic poignancy of Stipe's own 'Hairshirt' from 1989's *Green*.

Storm, Dave Gale and others would sit at Mill Pond by the riverbank, during spring, near the Silver Street bridge, with their guitars. The words were taken verbatim from James Joyce's 1907 volume of poetry *Chamber Music*, a book found in the Barrett library in Hills Road.

The session of 13 June was the last Syd would have for over a month, as the Floyd had to finish mixing their own *Ummagumma* and depart on a tour, during most of July, of Holland.*

Barrett, frustrated with the delay, decided to join his Cambridge friend Imo Moore on holiday in Spain, staying on the small island of Formantera, off Ibiza, a fashionable hippie resort. Dr Sam Hutt, an Underground habitué and friend of Peter Jenner, accompanied Syd to Spain. Hutt recalls, 'Formantera and Ibiza were certainly part of the hippie trail and a lot of successful drug smugglers bought their homes there. It was, in its way, a paradise. You'd get on a plane and two hours away was a place that was kind of like southern California, and incredibly cheap. You could live for six months, eight months like a king on £100. A good proportion of the average day was spent in making a fire, of keeping your house, getting supplies to eat; learn the sitar for two or three hours; get stoned. It's very arid, but the people are nice and it was a good place to drop out, to be inactive. Taj Mahal and Joni Mitchell were the two famous people you came across.'[20]

Imo Moore recounted to Mike Watkinson and Pete Anderson how Syd seemed oblivious of the strength of the Spanish sun and eventually got severely burned. He also remembers the electric storms that were common in Formantera driving the now hypersensitive Barrett mad. However, Moore mentioned how on at least one occasion Syd snapped out of his torpor and seemed his old self. Imo, Syd and a few friends clambered down to one of the deserted beach coves at sunset, and sat playing guitars and singing.

Barrett said, 'I have been doing lots of things – things interesting for me. I've done a lot of traipsing around. I've been back to Ibiza, Spain. I first went there with Rick, three years ago. It's an interesting place to be. I've written quite a lot too . . . I've been writing in all sorts of funny places.'[21]

There were a lot of people there for their summer holidays, and a large proportion of Underground revellers skylarking on acid. These English hippies in Ibiza, were echoed twenty years on by the English techno rebels who created the rave scene there while on holiday. When Syd and the Chelsea Set dropped acid and went down to play guitars on the beach at Formentera in 1969, or when the ravers tumbled out of Space or Pacha at dawn to sleep on the beach in 1988 or watch the sunset at Café Del Mar on mushrooms in 1997, they were only echoing what Phoenician revellers had done 2,000 years before them in the same spots, washing up on the beach after an all-night bacchanal. The island seems to

*Barrett later commented on *Ummagumma*, 'They've probably done very well. The singing's very good and the drumming is good as well.'

lend itself to hedonistic psychic exploration.

Barrett said, 'I've certainly not been bored and there are still a lot of things to do.'[22] Returning to England refreshed, Barrett and Gilmour sat for hour after hour looking for usable material to round out the album. The mini-suite of 'Long Gone', 'She Took A Long Cold Look' and 'Feel' show Barrett at his most unvarnished, honest and vulnerable. The three songs, sung by Syd accompanying himself on guitar 26 July, reflect not only the final and frenetic day of the sessions, but of the relationship he was lamenting the break-up of. The trio of songs should be seen as aspects of the same theme, love, loss and fear of abandonment.

'Long Gone' could be a rumination on Barrett's own fleeting muse, ever more distant, obscured by the fog of Mandrax and dope. It's a bitter, tortured folk-blues with Syd lamenting the loss of his loved one, who has left him. It reflects what Elisa Roney called 'the underlying bitterness the second side of this album presents, as most of it is about lost love or "love gone wrong"'. "Long Gone" is a song about lost love, quite melancholy. It seems as if she has just left him for her others, and he is left wondering after others who still find favour with him. It seems he can't believe she has left and may still be in some sort of "shock", although she is long gone, probably never to return.'

Roney describes 'She Took A Long Cold Look' as 'a song of break-up. Barrett may have been going through something personally during the [writing of these] songs as the others seem more detached" from his psyche, yet these are more heartfelt and "real". The song itself displays the last remnants of a dying relationship. His girlfriend likes to "see him get down to ground/she doesn't have the time just to be with me", thus she puts him down and gives him "long cold looks" or stares. Barrett also describes himself as a "broken pier on a wavy sea", like a broken man, unable to find refuge anywhere in his life. "Feel", the next song in this song pattern, seems as if Barrett has not only become detached from his proverbial girlfriend, but from everyone else.'[23] In the song Barrett pointedly sings 'I want to go home', his voice anguished.

On 5 August, Dave Gilmour and Roger Waters did two hurried mixing sessions from multi-track to stereo master. In the first morning session, 'Long Gone', 'She Took A Long Cold Look', 'Feel', 'If It's In You' and 'Octopus' were mixed. After a break for lunch, 'Golden Hair', 'Dark Globe' and 'Terrapin' were finished in a three-hour afternoon.

Pink Floyd were on a European tour for most of the month, but on 16 September Gilmour rushed back to finish mixing all of Malcolm Jones's productions on a third and final session. The final remix was all Gilmour's, as he told Nick Kent. The very next morning Gilmour was on a plane to Amsterdam for a live radio performance. On another short break in touring on 6 October, Barrett and Gilmour together edited the album's sequence together.

Malcolm Jones said, 'It had taken over two months to mix, and Syd was a bit pissed off with the delay, as I was.'[24] But the album was finally done, after innumerable delays and false starts. It had taken nearly eighteen months versus five for *The Piper At The Gates Of Dawn*. However, release was delayed yet again, because EMI insisted on an advertising campaign designed to increase demand. Barrett was beyond caring by this point.

Soon after mixing was completed, Jones took over a reel-to-reel copy of the finished album to Syd's flat. 'What I saw gave me quite a start. In anticipation of the photographic session for the sleeve, Syd had painted the bare floorboards of his room orange and purple. Up until then the floor was bare, with Syd's few possessions mostly on the floor; hi-fi, guitar, cushions, books and paintings. The room was much as appears on the original *Madcap* sleeve. Syd was well pleased with his day's work and I must say it made a fine setting for the session due to take place.'[25]

The photo session for the album cover of *The Madcap Laughs* was supervised by Storm Thorgerson, who brought in old Cambridge friend Mick Rock to take the photographs. Rock recalled it as a 'magical session'. Indeed, the images taken that day added to Barrett's slightly ethereal image, a shadowy figure out of time and place in the real world. A creature who existed on the fringes of dream and reality, a mystery in a crepuscular world. Barrett had taken up with a peculiar half-Eskimo girlfriend called Iggy, who greeted Thorgerson and Rock at the door naked. Storm thought it a bit unusual. Without prompting, Iggy joined Syd for the photo sessions, a nice counterpoint to the stark room. Rock fitted his camera with a wide-angle lens, giving the illusion that the room was much larger than it really was.*

David Gale says, 'When Syd moved to Earl's Court, I would see him less often. I'd bump into him striding through the street looking pale, dark and very threatening. If you said hello to him he'd look straight through you. It was quite clear that we had an acid casualty here, which by now wasn't an unfamiliar sight. There were at least three or four others who had put themselves in that kind of place, some committed suicide and some went into analysis.' But Syd was 'one of the first' and certainly the most famous, his breakdown the most public.

Barrett's retreat to his room and into the recesses of his mind, was an exile from the world returning back to womb-like security. When faced with the impossible demands of life as a pop star, he retreated in panic to the only place, barring home in Cambridge, where he was safe, his room, and once there, his mind. But in his room and in his mind, was there any solace? The wheels of his mind spinning fast and aimless, Syd was losing himself in mazes made with his own thoughts, unchecked by reason. His severe introversion had begun, a regression to a simpler state of being, where his fragile sense of self was no

*It is important to note that the room is much, much smaller than it appears in those photos. Duggie Fields, who still lives in the flat, redecorated the room, but it still has a slightly claustrophobic feel. When the author walked into the room, it struck me as nothing so much as an isolation tank. The room had the same feel as the Powis Square basement flat used in the film *Performance*, a timeless limbo pervading the walls and bare light fixtures.

longer under attack.

Gradually, Barrett began to draw away from the unmanageable persona called 'Syd', and in order to preserve himself Barrett regressed step by step, 'treading the backward path'. Cambridge came to represent home, security, a simpler life, unpressured, relaxed, dream-like, quiet. London, and by extension the larger world of the Underground, acid, fame and touring, was a wild wood of panic and pressure, blinding lights and excessive motion. The thrill of adventure, which he had first set out to find in London, had faded. Barrett, the consummate musical adventurer, had always been compelled by the desire to venture forth, press forward into uncharted zones, yet in the back of his mind, he held an idealised picture of an idyllic Cambridge, where his mother awaited him at Hills Road.

Says Fields, 'When he moved in here, there was just the two of us. He had left the Pink Floyd and wasn't very motivated. He had no reason to be particularly. We lived in adjoining rooms, and I did all my work in my room, and sometimes the wall between us was [flimsy]. I knew exactly what was going on that side of the wall, and I presume that Syd knew exactly what was happening on this side. It was strange. I knew he'd be lying in bed doing nothing, and I knew that he'd be lying there thinking that, while he was lying there, he had the potential to do anything in the world. But the minute he got up he limited his potential, and he kept inhibiting himself by that, so he did nothing in the end. And I kind of knew that. I always thought that was a mistake, because I felt "doing" was enjoyable. I don't what it was like for him, because on the other side of the wall there was me, busy "doing". I didn't do a lot, but I just did. Everyone used to hang around getting stoned all the time, and I enjoyed that very much. But then I'd go off into my room and paint. I started getting people having problems with this; "Hey man, why aren't you hanging around with us any more. Have we done something to offend you? Don't you think we're cool any more?" I would just say I was doing my thing, which was painting. I got used to removing myself from other people so that I could work. Syd removed himself from other people to be left alone, not specifically to work. He removed himself from other people because they were always wanting his attention, wanting him to be charming. Which he could play up to, definitely. But then he used to lock himself in his room against people intruding.'

Duggie Fields refers to Syd lying alone in his room, not painting, not talking, not playing. No music, just an eerie silence when he must have wondered, 'What's Syd thinking about for so many hours every day?' A journalist who visited wrote of Syd , 'living quietly in his sparsely furnished London flat among his stereo equipment, piles of paintings and a heap of battered LPs.'[26]

Jenny Fabian, on assignment for *Harpers & Queen*, went to Syd's flat in Earl's Court to interview him. 'I found him again living up the road from Earl's Court in a flat where he had a room. Again he didn't speak much at all. He was sitting in the corner on a mattress and he'd painted every other floorboard alternate colours. He boiled an egg in a kettle and ate it. And he listened over and over again to Beach Boys tapes, which I found distressing. We sat for hours and we may have touched fleetingly. He was still exactly the same, only now he wasn't Syd Barrett the star.'[27] The interview proper didn't come off, largely due to Syd being very quiet, but what she did come away with was a strong feeling, which led her to sit down at her desk and write the following, presented here for the first time unedited and complete, by kind permission of Fabian herself:

'We had been sitting on his mattress for several hours, half the time in silence. Not even the usual continual background of records as an excuse – he needed no excuse to be silent. His thoughts had the numerous dimensions that come as a result of boiling one's one brains in acid, and, no longer contained with his physical head, were like currents in the air. I felt no need to get through to him because he was out the other side and miles away, and it was like he was looking at me through a telescope. He could see someone a million different ways, and I felt myself changing as he went through his different interpretations of me. When he spoke I felt that although he was listening to the conversation, he was also listening to his thoughts at the same time. Each sentence died after he had spoken it, and he found it hard to remember what he said. His voice was soft and gentle, and he smiled a lot to himself. He was slender, and his face was thin and pale. His eyes seemed to merge with the violet circle under them, and had to be haunted. His wild hair and unshaven face made him look even more desperate. But he was too far away to touch.

'The floor of his big room was alternate orange and blue boards which he had painted himself and sometimes found rather disturbing to look at. The curtains were of thin green material, so that the light filtered in to give the room an eerie green glow. His mother had made them, he told me, and he kept them closed all day to make the room feel like a tank. We lay there into the darkness, until he finally turned on the bare orange bulb that hung from the ceiling, giving the room an entirely new dimension. I could hear television coming from the next room but he seemed to have no inclination to go and watch. He was too busy feeding off his brain's output, which would build up into a cream slice effect that he could stand back from and contemplate. This contemplation would give rise to another creation, and so on. He was completely self-indulgent with his thought processes, never trying to control or direct them within any bounds of reason. Reasoning was inconclusive and unnecessary to him, because one reason led to another indefinitely, like infinity. Surely reason should prove an answer, but as there was no answer, there was no reason. And I remembered all the beautiful songs he had written about gnomes and cats and stars and weird fairyland things. Then he looked straight at me, and said: *'Isn't it boring lying here all day thinking of nothing?'**

Fabian says today, 'At Earl's Court, he'd already gone to where he was going.

*Italics author's own.

His mind had gone there, but his body was still functioning in the real world. You couldn't really say that he was two people, but he was gone and he was still living. I don't know what he thought, I thought he was thinking millions of things. And then for him to say that!'

In December 1969, Barrett played guitar and sang on Kevin Ayers' solo track 'Singing A Song In The Morning'. The track was originally called 'Religious Experience', the producer was Peter Jenner, and the session was mixed by Malcolm Jones, who had also produced part of Syd's *Madcap* album. Jones said, 'Peter Jenner produced the original track and it was really rather messy, [but] it was a really good song, a catchy tune . . . here was me saying "hey, this is a great record here but it's a bit messy", and so I rubbed Syd out! . . . we could still put Syd's version on the LP or whatever, it didn't matter. But it was a very good song and Peter Jenner said "Oh, if we're gonna do that let's call it 'Singing A Song In The Morning'", trying to get [DJ] Tony Blackburn to play it on his morning programme.'[28]

Malcolm Jones made exactly one acetate of the version with Barrett's contribution on it before erasing his parts; this acetate, after Jones's death, made its way on to the *Ramadhan* bootleg album.

The version with Syd was never released officially, which is a shame because it features superb duelling guitar work by Barrett and Ayers. Barrett plays an absolutely stunning riff, reminiscent of Jeff Beck. A version, *sans* Syd, was eventually released as a single in 1970. Ayers says, 'Barrett was displeased with his performance on the song.' Today he simply recalls Barrett as 'a most extraordinary person'. Barrett agreed to open for Ayers at a club date in Holland on 3 January 1970 and even to being billed on the poster. He backed out, though, at the last minute.

At long last, in December 1969, Harvest released a Syd Barrett single: 'Octopus', with 'Golden Hair' as the B-side. 'Octopus' is one of the songs on which Barrett's reputation rests, containing some of Barrett's very best lyrical work, each line feeding into the next with an ever more obscure and evocative image. 'Trip to heave and ho, up down, to and fro,' sings Barrett on 'Octopus', echoing the traditional song 'Green Grow The Rushes, Ho!' The song is rife with the most startling and poetic imagery. The middle eight bars are particularly brilliant, perhaps the single most succinct statement of Barrett's magical dualities: 'Isn't it good to be lost in the wood? Isn't it bad, so quiet there, in the wood?' The title of this book is drawn from these words because they seem to best capture the opposing sides of Syd's nature, eternally in contention and providing a startling contrast to each other.

The title of the album itself was drawn from a line in 'Octopus': 'The madcap laughed at the man on the border'. Elisa Roney writes that this line 'may directly relate to the sanity of Barrett himself, or anyone else. The "madcap" who embraces life wholly and completely with joy and reckless abandon is coupled with the more stable, yet stagnated "man on the border" [border of sanity] who is "within the norm", but may be repressing his inner madcap". This is also true of the "madcap" possessing a "man on the border" who keeps him from going totally 'over the edge.' Thus, Barrett may be relating the age-old theory that to create anything, one needs both stability and recklessness, as in the Apollo-Dionysus theory. One of the last lines of the song is "they'll never put me in their bag", which is Barrett's way of saying that "they", the judging general public, will never "pin him down" into a category, and truly, they never have successfully done that.'[29]

Musically, the song is fascinating, rife with suspended notes, and strange chord progressions. Barrett tuned his guitar a half-step down for the version that ended up in the album, further confusing those who try to figure it out. It's difficult but worth the effort.

In the course of a rather oblique interview with Giovanni Dadomo, where Barrett appears disinterested and answers in vague terms, Syd suddenly comes to life when asked about 'Octopus'. From behind a mask of indifference shines through a flash of Barrett's singular genius. One of the few glimpses, in Barrett's own words, into the labyrinth twists and turns of the skewed geometry of his thinking, as he explains, 'I carried that about in my head for about six months before I actually wrote it so maybe that's why it came out so well. The idea was like those number songs like "Green Grow The Rushes, Ho!" where you have, say, twelve lines each related to the next and an overall theme. It's like a fool-proof combination of lyrics, really, and then the chorus comes in and changes the tempo but holds the whole thing together.'[30]

'"Octopus" is a particular example of recording being discussed as something exceptional because it takes an unusual metre,' said Barrett. 'I don't read much but I think I picked up Shakespeare as a book that just happened to be lying there to read. It was meant to be verse.' Using an ever changing panoply of scattered images of an Octopus fairground ride, and Lord Talbot from Shakespeare's *Henry VI Part I*, Barrett weaves a complex song that seems to encapsulate his state of mind over the past two years. 'I like to have really exciting, colourful songs. I can't really sing but I enjoy it and I enjoy writing from experiences. Some are so powerful they are ridiculous.'[31]

'I hadn't noticed,' said Syd, when asked how the single was faring in the charts; it didn't make the charts, although it was an Underground hit in London. 'I don't think it was necessarily a good idea to do a single, but it was done. It's a track off the album. I've spent a long time doing it – since I left the group. But it was done at a reasonable pace.'[32]

In January 1970, *The Madcap Laughs* was released. Syd remarked, 'I liked what came out, only it was released far too long after it was done. I wanted it to be a whole thing that people would listen to all the way through, with everything related and balanced, the tempos and moods offsetting each other, and I hope that's what it sounds like. I've got it at home, but I don't listen to it much now.[33] I always find recording difficult. I can only think in terms of, "well, I'm pleased with forty minutes of sound", but I can't in terms of the music industry. It's only a beginning, I've written a lot more stuff.[34] *The Madcap Laughs* is my particular idea of a record. It's very together. There's a lot of speaking on it, but there's not a very recognisable mood. It's mainly acoustic guitar and there are no instruments at all.'[35]

'Yes, it's quite nice, but I'd be very surprised if it did anything if I were to drop dead. I don't think it would stand to be accepted as my last statement. I want to record my next LP before I go on to anything else, and I'm writing for that at the moment . . . I'm just waiting to see how the records do, what the reactions are, before I decide on anything else . . . I spent a year relaxing,' he said, 'and another getting the LP together. It's been very slow, like looking back over a long time and playing very little. When I went I felt the progress the group could have made. But it made none, none at all, except in the sense that it was continuing. To make my album was a challenge as I didn't have anything to follow.[36] It was only two years ago,' said Barrett of his departure from the Floyd, but as to what happened immediately after, 'It's really difficult to relate. There's much more interesting things happening right now. There's quite a sense of freedom in doing it as well.'[37] Barrett said that getting another band together would be 'the most interesting thing to do now, to see whether it would have been possible to retain the "See Emily Play" sort of things that were there and on maybe two tracks of the first album.'[38]

Barrett in an *NME* interview with Richard Green stated, 'After I left the group I just spent a year resting and getting the album together. I didn't do much else at all, some painting and thinking about getting a band together. I've got a lot of ideas I want to explore later. Making my album was fine because after two years away from the group I didn't have to lead on from anything. I want to discover now if it's possible to continue some of the ideas that came from a couple of tracks on the first album. I've been writing consistently for two years now and I have lots of undeveloped things lying around. I'm still basically like I've always been, sitting round with an acoustic getting it done. I never get worried about my writing.[39] My time has been fairly well spent since leaving. I haven't had a particularly hard time and I was OK for money. I've heard of a few plans for me to do some appearances but there is nothing positive enough to talk about. There are vague ideas about a group as well.'[40]

The songs on *The Madcap Laughs* are prone to jumpy, if fascinating, moods. Barrett often stressed the sense of his songs as 'moods', much in the same manner that Brian Wilson composed short piano segments, or 'feels', as he dubbed them, which he would use to construct his larger compositions. Steve Turner noted, 'His [Barrett's] songs, like paintings, were used essentially to convey a mood. Throughout the interview he spoke of relating to a "mood" when referring to his work.'[41] What these contemporaries shared was a desire to infuse their songs with an emotionally resonant quality, reflecting their state of mind during composition.

Syd Barrett commented on the importance of lyrics. 'Very important. I think it's good if a song has more than one meaning. Maybe that kind of song can reach far more people, that's nice. On the other hand, I like songs that are simple. I liked "Arnold Layne" because to me it was a very clear song.[42] It would be terrific to do much more mood stuff. They're very pure, you know, the words.'[43]

Many of the songs on *The Madcap Laughs* were played on acoustic guitar, often more out of necessity since it was to put backing tracks on them. 'It puts people off their guard,' said Barrett on the mood of the acoustic songs. 'I think that people miss the fact that it's obviously a gentler thing – because it's clever and it's into that more than content. The message might be a bit lost because people find it hard to grasp.'[44]

It's worth noting that the widening extremes of moods he had been experiencing since his breakdown were beginning to level off. The ups and downs are what gives *The Madcap Laughs* a compelling emotional colouration. One aspect of Barrett's vocals on the album is a gradual flattening of his vocal (and by extension emotional) range, though, and on some tracks, one can hear the emotion leaching out of his voice.

Things at home were edging towards the chaotic once more. Iggy had vanished as quickly as she'd come. Rusty and Greta, two casual friends of Barrett's, decided to move in.

Duggie Fields says, 'Rusty and Greta were homeless when they came to stay here. Greta became good friends with Jenny Spires, who was so gorgeous and had been a model. Jenny had a great sense of fun, I thought she was fabulous when I first met her. Jenny became totally out of control with her life. She went off to America, with Greta, and they ended up in a mental home in Texas at one point in the late sixties. In Texas, they thought one was mad anyway because of the way one looked. Jenny wasn't mad, but was just out of control. Greta and Rusty came into Syd's life because of that connection. They were in my life to a degree, but I didn't want them around. Greta did a lot of speed and was quite manic, though with charm. I remember we had problems discouraging them from coming around, and they were homeless. Syd would let them in, and then they were here. How could we get rid of them? There were dramas with them, with them screaming from the street to be let in in the middle of the night. Or Greta OD-ing in the hallway and having to be taken to hospital. They probably brought stimulants for Syd and he took them. But I could have done the same and I did not. I never liked speed, I thought it was a problem. He could have said no.'

After Iggy the Eskimo had faded from the picture, she was replaced by Gayla

Pinion, a Cambridge girl. Fields says, 'Gayla and Syd, I remember the violence because I lived with them. I remember Syd and Gayla having fights in the flat which would have the neighbours threatening to call the police. The police did come on one occasion. I had to physically break up fights between them, and getting hit by both of them in the middle. By the time Gayla was living here, Syd was definitely becoming dysfunctional. We had a conversation where Syd was telling me off because I wasn't famous, and then he told Gayla off because she was a waitress. But then he was referring to himself as a "has-been pop star". That was quite shocking, that he thought of himself as a has-been at age twenty-three. Whether that was a thought of the moment, or a deep thought, I don't know, but it stuck in my mind.

'I knew there was a problem. Syd wouldn't open his curtains, ever. He pinned a second layer on top of the first curtains, so that they couldn't actually be opened. The result of not being able to open the curtains was that he never opened the window, which made the room smell. I would wait for him to unlock the door to go to the bathroom and I would go into the room and open the windows, because the stench really did get overwhelming. It couldn't have been very good for him to live in it, because he must have been getting oxygen starvation! Little things that started as tests, like when we would be sitting talking and he would just flip a lit cigarette across the room. You were supposed to just leave it, it was uncool to go after it. His room would be littered with cigarette ends, and when Gayla brought her dog, dogshit too. It's one thing if you drop a cigarette and put it out, but even then it's not something you normally do.

'He was playing games, using his power, his ego. When Syd was good, he could be the dominant person in the room for his charm. It's easy to remember the negative stories and not someone's magic. And he enjoyed that, he could sit there telling stories and everyone would be loving him. This was abusing his power, whether he was trying to shock or just test to see what reaction he could get. It was also combined with lack of care and concern, childish. Syd was obviously a spoiled child with an adoring mother. No correction. I remember sitting there thinking "I'm not going to pick up that cigarette" but worrying if anything would catch fire. I had to get used to it happening.

'I remember little things like Syd getting in a car and driving the wrong way up the Earl's Court Road, which has always been one-way. It only happened once. Syd had a Mini when he moved in. I wasn't overly paranoid getting in the car with him. He swapped his Mini for Mickey Finn's Pontiac push-button convertible, bright pink. The car featured in the film of Joe Orton's play *Loot*. Mickey had won the car in a raffle. London isn't built for big American cars, and also it was very conspicuous, and we used to look quite conspicuous, the way we dressed. And it wasn't good for paranoia, because when we drove around everyone would look. We were usually stoned, and someone was usually carrying drugs. I was stopped many times in those days by the police for drugs. The car made one paranoid, so I was never happy being in it, despite it being a wonderful car. Then one day I heard Syd had swapped his Mini for it. And there it was sitting outside the flat, and Syd couldn't drive it, he couldn't get it to work. It just sat there and sat there, for months and months decaying, this enormous pink Pontiac. The police eventually left a notice saying they would tow it away as an abandoned car if it wasn't removed. Syd just gave it away to someone he stopped in the street.'

Fields also notes that Barrett's behaviour was becoming plainly disturbing, 'We were going around to see David Gilmour, and Gilly [another girlfriend of Syd's and a close friend of Fields], who was lying on Syd's bed, didn't want to come. And he didn't want to leave her in his bed for whatever reason, so he just picked her up and threw her across the room. I'm sure I said something to him, but nowadays I wouldn't allow someone to do that, no matter who they were.'

On 24 February, Syd, joined by David Gilmour (bass) and Jerry Shirley (drums), did a live radio session for John Peel's *Top Gear* (broadcast 18 May). The trio played 'Terrapin' from *The Madcap Laughs* before launching into four new songs: 'Gigolo Aunt', 'Baby Lemonade', 'Effervescing Elephant', and Rick Wright's 'Two Of A Kind'.

Syd, Dave Gilmour and Jerry Shirley playing 'Terrapin' is the nearest approximation we have of Syd and Dave sitting in an empty classroom during lunch breaks at the Cambridge Tech, playing guitars together and going through 'In The Midnight Hour' or Stones' numbers. On 'Baby Lemonade', Syd's voice briefly recaptures the sweetness of happier days. A competent reading of 'Dominoes' ensues with Barrett and Gilmour exchanging a bit of open-G-tuning Delta blues twang. Gilmour's presence served to balance Barrett's unsteady rhythms, and the *Top Gear* renditions are among Barrett's most coherent solo work. Gilmour really made an effort with him, working with Syd in the studio, live and on the radio.

The Madcap Laughs had sold well, over 6,000 copies in a few months, and reviews had been generally good. Work on the next Barrett album, produced largely by Gilmour with help from Rick Wright, began on 26 February 1970, with work on 'Baby Lemonade' and the largely forgettable throwaway 'Maisie'. 'Maisie' is cursed with a tempo reminiscent of paint drying or honey dripping off a spoon. That cursed Mandrax torpor! Barrett was having a bit of fun with the cliché twelve-bar blues, as he starts laughing halfway through, doing his best imitation of a Grundig tape recorder running on low batteries.

Rick Wright said, 'Doing Syd's record was interesting, but extremely difficult. Dave and Roger did *The Madcap Laughs* and Dave and myself did the second one. But by then it was just trying to help Syd any way we could, rather than worrying about getting the best guitar sound. You could forget about that! It was just going into the studio and trying to get him to sing. However, I think both of Syd's albums are an interesting part of [his] history.'[45]

On the 27th, Malcolm Jones noted, 'Syd and Dave came back to the studio and Syd ran through four songs, as two-track, guitar and vocal demos. "Wolfpack", "Waving My Arms In The Air", "Living Alone" and "Dylan Blues". On the session sheet for the day, David Gilmour is listed as having taken the tape of the four demos home with him.' It hasn't been seen since. 'Living Alone' and 'Dylan Blues' have never been heard, though rumours of bootleg versions circulating have always tantalised collectors. Sadly, if Gilmour, who opposed the release of the 1988 *Opel* out-takes album, has the tape it's unlikely they will ever be heard.

During the sessions, Barrett was interviewed and stated, 'I'm working on the album. There's four tracks in the can already, and it should be out about September. There are no set musicians, just people helping out, like on *The Madcap Laughs*, which gives me far more freedom in what I want to do . . . I feel as if I've got lots of things, much better things to do still, that's why there isn't really a lot to say, I just want to get it all done. There'll be all kinds of things. It just depends what I feel like doing at the time. The important thing is that it will be better than the last.'[46]

It's worth noting that what others considered demos, Barrett considered finished versions. Fifteen tries at making 'Gigolo Aunt' resulted in only three complete versions. Take 7, take 9 (included on 1988's *Opel*) and take 15 appeared on *Barrett*. Gilmour hoped to have Syd play the material long enough to be fully conversant with the changes and lyrics, but Barrett always found this hard. Many more tries at 'Waving My Arms In The Air' only resulted in the initial, spontaneous take being declared 'best'. With Gilmour on bass, Shirley on drums and Richard Wright on organ backing him, Syd struggled gamely and succeeded. The ensemble work is cohesive. One wonders if editing from different takes would have helped matters, though, to cover up abrupt tempo changes or muffled vocals.

David Gilmour said, 'We had basically three alternatives at that point, working with Syd. One, we could actually work with him in the studio, playing along as he put down his tracks, which was almost impossible, though we succeeded on "Gigolo Aunt". The second was laying down some kind of track before and then having him play over it. The third was him putting his basic ideas down with just guitar and vocals and then we'd try and make something out of it all. It was mostly a case of me saying "Well what have you got then, Syd?" and he'd search around and eventually work something out.'[47]

'Gigolo Aunt' is a long, inspired jam that captures the strengths of Syd's solo work. Benefiting from tight bass runs courtesy of Gilmour, and solid drumming, Barrett turns in arguably his best solo guitar work. His trebly Fender scale climbs and raunchy Bayou tone are superb. Here, Barrett sounds as if he is having constructive musical dialogue with his fellow musicians. The organist, presumably Rick Wright, plays soulful arpeggios, adding to the cohesive ensemble work. 'Gigolo Aunt' reflects Syd's strengths at jamming when backed by clear headed and proficient musicians. Gilmour is a superb bassist, rivalling

McCartney in his ability to tell a story with his bass, taking the central note and dancing around it. The overall mood on songs like 'Gigolo Aunt' and the suite that follows ('Waving My Arms in the Air', 'I Never Lied To You', 'Wined and Dined') is one of contentment, if a bit wistful, as if Barrett was ruminating on memories of happier days. These four songs are in stark contrast to *The Madcap Laughs's* sombre, ravaged bleakness or *The Piper at the Gates of Dawn*'s mystical moods. Interestingly, each of the three albums has a suite of three songs a piece that revolve around a specific key; interrelated thematically, harmonically and lyrically. Another example of Barrett's peculiar genius.

Like *The Hobbit* or *Alice In Wonderland*, Barrett's songs contained unexpected shards of poetic truth and insight. When he sang, 'You shouldn't try to be what you can't be' on the 27 February, one-take master for 'Waving My Arms In The Air', one senses he had reached that realisation the hard way. 'You shouldn't try to be what you can't be,' sounds like the moral at the end of one of Belloc's *Cautionary Verses*. The lyric rings out like the crystal bell of devastating truth, hard learned through the harsh rigours of experience. The jauntiness of the delivery, as always, disguises the deeply felt emotion which prompted the lyric. Perhaps it was Syd musing on the artificial trappings of pop stardom.

'Waving My Arms In The Air' segues directly into 'I Never Lied To You', replete with a lovely accompaniment on piano from Rick Wright. Syd navigates chord changes with difficulty but the progressions are supple and agile, as if Barrett is still reaching for the unattainable ideal in his mind.

On 3 April, Barrett returned to rework 'Wolfpack' from the earlier demo. It was a bizarre session. Duggie Fields remembers, 'I went to the studio with Syd and he was so dysfunctional and literally sat there, not knowing what he was doing. Forgot what he was supposed to be singing, was certainly not focused at all.' Alledgedly, the sessions for the *Barrett* album were closed sessions, with Cliff Jones maintaining that Gilmour and the engineers were wary of EMI staffers or other onlookers witnessing Barrett's loss of control.

'Wolfpack' is a jarring, ragged ode to a pack of wolves, with vocals and lyrics that highlight Barrett's disintegration. He howls his vocal with unhinged glee, and turns in some abstract guitar work reminiscent of Captain Beefheart. In a 1971 interview with Mick Rock, Barrett professed it to be his favourite track on *Barrett*.

Duggie Fields noted, 'Syd really didn't have to have that much control before, but when you have to provide your own motivation all the time it is difficult, certainly in terms of writing a song. When it came down to recording there were always problems. He was not at his most together recording *The Madcap Laughs*. He had to be taken there sometimes, and he had to be got. It didn't seem to make any difference whether it was making him happy or unhappy; he'd been through that, the excitement of it, the first time around.'[48]

Syd's moods were becoming increasingly erratic. 'Syd could certainly change, and he was volatile. But I don't think he turned on the charm consciously. He was that naturally, and then he wasn't that any more. Though I lived with a lot of people during that period, Syd was the only one I can remember with people pounding on the door, saying "Syd! Let me in, Syd!" on so many occasions, and with so many people doing that. He obviously had something that made people do that. It wasn't just his looks, because there were lots of other good looking people around. It had to do with him being good looking, definitely, but it also was some quality that he could make manifest as well. But then he could also be so dead, and just not there. I can remember going out with him and just leading him around like he was a child. He wouldn't make any contribution outside of himself at all, and that was not comfortable, said Fields.

'We got this flat because he was pleasurable to be with, but after a while it became a nightmare. And I realised I would rather not be living with this person any more. I don't remember how long this transition took but he didn't have those problems when I first lived with him at Cromwell Road, and he didn't have them when we first got the flat. They developed. Maybe he had symptoms of them which one didn't really register, but then did because I was seeing him every day. He wasn't like that at first, he functioned. Then he became a dysfunctional person. I had other friends who disintegrated, Syd's wasn't the most dramatic disintegration. He wasn't the most visible disintegration. His paranoid outbreaks and confusions weren't as marked as other peoples'.'

On 5 June, Barrett cut three two-track demos: 'Rats', 'Wined And Dined' and 'Birdie Hop'. The demo for 'Birdie Hop' can be heard on the *Opel* album; a humorous throwaway notable only for Barrett's eulogy of Hoppy, capturing Hoppy's light bird-like demeanour in a few stray lines, and for a repeated line, 'I see the flies'. Flies, in the iconography of Barrett's music, can be taken to represent harbingers of death and destruction. In *Opel* flies feed on a carcass, and in 'Birdie Hop', 'I see the flies' closes each verse like an ill omen. One origin for this Barrett metaphor probably lies in the Flies, the proto-punk band that used to dog the Pink Floyd's steps in the Underground. It was they who stood one night at the side of the stage during a Floyd show and screamed 'Sell outs!' at them for the duration of their set. An apt image of doom, those prototypical hippie freaks coming out of the woodwork, urinating on the audience at the 14 Hour Technicolor Dream.

Work followed on 'Rats', a most disturbing song, where Barrett rants: 'If you think you're unloved, then we know about that.' Former Red Hot Chili Pepper's guitarist, John Frusciante, said, 'Unless you've heard "Rats" I can't really explain what it's about. The riff's mainly acoustic, but when he comes in with the vocal, it's wild . . . a real fugitive sound.'[49] Jerry Shirley said, '"Rats" in particular was really odd. That was just a very crazed jam, and Syd had this lyric that he just shouted over the top. It's quite nuts.'[50]

On 6 June, backed by Gilmour and Shirley, Syd played live at the three-day

Extravaganza 70 Music And Fashion Festival at the Olympia, London. Barrett was nervous, he hadn't performed live in nearly two and a half years. He was plagued by chronic indecision right up to the moment they were scheduled to play. 'He was going to do it, he wasn't going to do it, it was on and off, so finally we said "Look, Syd, come on, man, you can do it!"' said Jerry Shirley. The trio went to the Festival and took the stage. Says Shirley, 'We got up, I played drums, Dave played bass and he managed to get through a few songs.'[51] The impromptu band played 'Terrapin', 'Gigolo Aunt', 'Effervescing Elephant' and 'Octopus'.

'Terrapin', in its live version, is plagued with inaudible vocals, both on the tape and in the performance. A voice from the audience is heard to shout 'We can't hear your voice!' on recordings of the concert. It is symbolic that on Syd's solo live performances his voice couldn't be heard. He was having a tremendously hard time trying to make himself understood in day-to-day life as well. On-stage he was often literally shouting to make himself heard, and yet no one could hear him. By the final song 'Octopus' the PA problems are finally solved, and Barrett's voice breaks through, sounding uncannily like that of one of his musical progeny, Robert Smith of the Cure. But it was, as ever, too little too late, and Barrett's tenuous resolve was shaken.

'It got good,' said Shirley, 'and then after about "Octopus" Syd said "Oh great, thanks very much" and walked off! We tried, you know.'[52] Syd stopped so abruptly that Shirley had to do a hurried drum roll to disguise Barrett's sudden exit. This was to be Barrett's only concert during the making of his solo albums, and one of his last before he disappeared into self-imposed exile.

Barrett and Gilmour returned to EMI the next day to record 'Milky Way', which unfortunately wouldn't be heard by the public for sixteen years. 'Milky Way' highlights everything that is great about Syd Barrett; clever wordplay in the lyrics, rife with humour, vocal tricks, stunning melodic twists. But it also sadly shows how things were going wrong. Syd is clearly struggling to keep time, to hit the notes, to infuse the song with feeling. Sadly, Barrett was in a bad way on this day, yet the strength of the song's composition is such that even in the throw-away performance it's compelling. What comes through clearly in the banjo-like strums is the song's dance hall feel, so deeply ingrained in Barrett, probably from exhaustive listening of his mum's old 78s from the thirties.

'Milky Way' is one of Syd's most tuneful melodies, and to hear the bare version included on 1988's *Opel* is heartbreaking. The tune, one that Syd had written long before, perhaps even before arriving in London, clearly displays the tremendous unfulfilled potential of some of these demos. It must have been saddening for Gilmour to sit behind the console, watching his friend sitting on a studio stool trying to remember the songs he'd played so fluently and clearly at Mill Pond or at garden parties in Cambridge not so very long before. In 'Milky Way' Syd sings with a palpable sadness 'seems like a while since I could smile, the way you do'.

*

On 25 July 1967, the English music press announced the imminent arrival of the Pink Floyd's next single, 'Old Woman In A Casket (a.k.a. 'Scream Thy Last Scream')', backed with 'She Was A Millionaire'. The latter song had been featured in early sets dating as far back as the London Free School shows. On 18 April 1967, the Pink Floyd had recorded a studio version and often played it live during 1967, with versions showing up on concert recordings. Now in 1970, retitled 'Millionaire', two attempts to create a backing track for Syd failed, and 'Millionaire' was abandoned before he even added vocals.* The rest of the day was dedicated to laying overdubs on top of the ragged acoustic demo of 'Rats'.

'Dominoes', recorded on 14 July, is perhaps the one solo Barrett track which hints at what Pink Floyd might have sounded like had Barrett stayed with the band. The band struggled through three takes, all of which are available, one on the finished version of *Barrett* and the other two on the revised version of *Opel* released in 1993. 'Dave was with Syd trying to get a lead guitar track,' said Jerry Shirley, 'but Syd couldn't play anything that made sense. In a brainwave, Gilmour turned the tape around and had Syd play guitar to the tracks coming at him backwards. It played back, and the backwards guitar sounded great; the best lead he ever played. The first time out and he didn't put a note wrong.'[53] When Barrett was inspired and his Byzantine mental faculties clicked into place he was fully capable of doing extraordinary things. Barrett could every once in a while lay down a guitar track that was flawless, with perfect tempo and composition. And here, remarkably, even backwards. 'The song just ended after Syd had finished singing,' said David Gilmour, 'and I wanted a gradual fade so I added that section myself.' Gilmour also played drums.

'Dominoes' is actually not much more than a dreary Mandrax shuffle of the kind that sadly pervades some of the work on *Barrett*. Gilmour takes over on drums, doing a leisurely blues shuffle in the style of Nick Mason. Organist Rick Wright leans in with some Ray Manzarek-inspired right-hand fills, reminiscent of the Doors' 'Riders On The Storm'. The song itself is descended from the Turtles' 'Happy Together', both lyrically and musically. An uneasy symbiosis of what Pink Floyd would have sounded like had Syd remained in the band, 'Dominoes' ambles along in that dreary stoned tempo typical of the tail-end of the sixties. The feeling of the song evokes a Sunday afternoon in that last summer of the sixties, at home with newspapers sprawled around the floor, with tea and a joint in hand. It's rather a drag to be quite honest.

'Wined And Dined', recorded on 14 July as well, with Gilmour dubbing all instruments atop Barrett's sinuous lead guitar, is an exquisite song, reportedly written for Gayla Pinion. Syd sings a lovely ode to lost love and late summer garden parties 'not so long ago' in a haunting, plaintive vocal, capturing the

*The lyrics bear the imprimatur of Roger Waters, suggesting it might have been a collaboration. 'Would you like to be one in a million?/Would you like to be one in five?/Would you like to know all the hidden meaning?/Before they tell you you've run out of time.'

atmosphere of England's most exquisite season and using the languorous feeling to suggest love in bloom. Syd adds slide leads of the sort that affirm that he was one of the pre-eminent guitarists of his time, echoing his work on 'Remember A Day'. There are moments when Syd's songs, and especially his voice echo field recordings made of pygmies in the jungles of Zaire, or of a Peruvian Andean Indian girl singing her wedding song a cappella. It has a curious sadness, the feeling of cupping the flickering light of a candle in high winds. June Bolan said, 'Syd was extraordinary. I've only known two extraordinary people, Syd and Marc Bolan. They both had that . . . quality, like a candle that was about to be snuffed out any minute. Really all illumination. An extraordinary, wonderful man.'[54] The very fragility of these voices, lingering in the twilight, emerging from environments of often harsh extremes. 'Only last summer,' laments Syd in 'Wined And Dined', 'It's not so long, long ago.'

Syd's gifts at music came from a deep fount within. He was mercifully unschooled; his gift was cultivated on his own and according to his own strange metre and stylings. His tunings, voicings and phrases are his own, unoccluded by learned technique. This was a gift that could never be compromised by making three-minute commercial pop ditties. The perfect solo isn't measured by how many notes are played or how fast, but in the ephemeral channelling of feeling. It has far more to do with instinct than technical skill. In Barrett's later solo works, minor flaws or fluffed notes don't detract from the beauty of the compositions, conversely they seem to add to them, perhaps because even in his mistakes he comes across as profoundly human and feeling. Music, at its highest expression, is the successful transmission of thought and feeling from player to listener. According to this criteria, Barrett succeeds.

Kris DiLorenzo noted that Barrett's songwriting became more focused on his internal reality during his solo efforts. Indeed, his songwriting shifted in large part not only to internal dilemmas but also the vagaries of failed romance. The more personal tone gives the songs a deeply human feel, part of their enduring appeal. There is no artifice on these songs, as if Syd were trying to re-establish his sense of identity as a person rather than as a rock star. There is an almost mournful tone as he begins to lament the passing of his youthful *joie de vivre*, and his lost loves.

'Effervescing Elephant', finished in nine takes on 14 July, is one of the first, if not the very first, song that Barrett ever wrote. Written when he was sixteen, 'Effervescing Elephant' takes its cues from several short tales in Hilaire Belloc's *Cautionary Verses* and conjures up a menagerie of an elephant 'with tiny ears and great big trunk', 'stupid water bison' and a 'tiger on the prowl'. The twist ending is typically Belloc, whose black humour pervades this wisp of a song, which clocks in at just over a minute. 'Effervescing Elephant' is Barrett's funniest song, with its punchline so evocative of Belloc at his wicked best. It highlights how playful Barrett could be. Surprisingly, it took nine tries to get a master take, illustrating how hard Barrett was finding it to infuse even this most basic of tracks with the requisite feeling.

Syd's songs, like those of the Beatles, have a vivid cast of characters. Mirroring Lennon, Barrett had mined children's literature as well as his past to create an impressive menagerie of beguiling, peculiar beings: 'Arnold Layne', 'Emily', the 'Gnome', the 'Effervescing Elephant', the 'Scarecrow', 'Puddle Town Tom'. Barrett took his cues from Belloc's *Cautionary Verses*, Tolkien's *The Hobbit*, Edward Lear's *Absolute Nonsense*, and others from the myths of Cambridgeshire. From the Fenlands, we have the scarecrows, immobile and beset by elements and animals, an interesting rumination on the nature of catatonia. The elephant, lion and 'stupid water bison' from Belloc. The 'old lady with a daughter . . . scrubbing bottles on all fours', the revolving door of Jenny, Lindsay and Gayla on his solo efforts, and Lucifer Sam, the Siamese cat who prowls at night and evokes Syd's paranoia. Jennifer Gentle, a.k.a. Jenny Spires, turns into a witch. Dan Dare, the valiant space adventurer of Syd's childhood comics. Matilda, the naughty girl who suffered a terrible fate in Belloc's cautionary tale of the same name.

The atmosphere on songs like 'Love Song', recorded also on 14 July in one take, with minor overdubs on the 17th, reveal the languorous happiness of the lyrics sharply underscored with the sadness of the vocals. Some of the songs were written during Syd's songwriting peak in Earlham Street, and others during his brief idyll with Gayla Pinion in Earl's Court, during the early days of their relationship. Syd's Pink Floyd work is rarely self-referential, with the notable exception of 'Bike'. His solo works, by comparison, are rife with very real accounts of lost love, or of an idyllic time 'not so long ago' when love bloomed. The narrative becomes first-person and intensely personal and specific. The songs were issuing not from his multi-coloured notebooks of songs and ideas, but from his day-to-day existence.

That the mood in the studio on the 14th was tense for Barrett is apparent when he runs through a take of 'Let's Split', which becomes increasingly ragged as he becomes more nervous and less sure of his performance. After breaking off halfway through and starting anew, Syd loses his thread again. He finally breaks off in exasperation and curtly tells Gilmour, 'Hold it, can you? That's all, cheers!' and that's the end of the song. The volume of work recorded on that day though shows what could happen when Syd was working at full capacity and in full possession of his faculties, which happened at irregular intervals. The sheer number of songs attempted on the 14th would suggest Syd had taken speed before the session, or else was tremendously inspired.

'Word Song', a one-take demo made on the 17th, is just a catalogue of alliterations, of what psychiatrists call 'clang associations'; an assemble-your-own Syd Barrett song with words culled from Syd's subconscious. Poems and lyrics are full of 'clang associations'. Creativity, if seen through some eyes, seems like madness. Creativity *can* be a certain form of madness, and ironically, be used in aid of their own destruction. Artists aim for the pinnacle of creative expression in different ways, some paradoxically seek to achieve it through nihilism or derangement. Creativity burns unevenly, but can be made to burn faster with drugs. Is creativity an infinitely renewable resource, or can it finally burn out? Syd's story begs the question . . .

On 14 November 1970, the finished second solo album, eponymously entitled *Barrett*, was released. 'They've got to reach a certain standard,' Syd said of the albums, 'and that's probably reached in *Madcap* once or twice and on the other one only a little – just an echo of that. Neither of them are much more than that.'[55] *Barrett* sold well, approximately 6,000 copies in the first few months, good for an Underground album; remarkably it has also remained continuously in print since it was released.

Syd himself designed the sleeve, which depicted mounted insects, a drawing he made at Camberwell. By accident or design, the rows of insects, on a white background, seem to represent the twelve songs contained within, drawn rather haphazardly but taken together, rather impressive. *Barrett*, on the whole, benefits from better vocal performances by Syd. On songs where his voice was double-tracked, it comes through clear and strong. The more relaxed pace of recording, as well as Gilmour's well-structured production, seems to have helped Barrett. His voice doesn't tremble or break as it often does on *The Madcap Laughs*. However, *Barrett* does suffer from poor sequencing. The first two songs, 'Baby Lemonade' and 'Love Song', fade into the dull mid-tempo shuffle of 'Dominoes', and the album peaks and falls erratically from there, until the beginning of the suite commencing with 'Gigolo Aunt', which is uniformly remarkable, some of Barrett's very best work.

The Madcap Laughs, although less cohesive and more ragged, seemed to capture something essential about Barrett, his spontaneity and off-the-cuff brilliance. *Barrett* by contrast, seems to waver between being too ragged and too polished. Judging by the quality of some of the out-takes, it was surprising that songs like 'Gigolo Aunt' or 'Wined And Dined' came out as well as they did, probably due in large part to Gilmour's patient production. The sparks of mad genius are extinguished after repeated takes, and since Barrett rarely improved with extra takes, *Barrett* partly fails. The spontaneity seen on the many first takes included on the 1993 box set show Barrett in a human, frail mode. Gilmour's objective, perhaps, was to show Barrett in control. The overall tone on *Barrett* is one of greater focus and concentration, as the recording sessions were more regular and well ordered than its predecessor. Barrett benefited from this structure, established by producer David Gilmour, putting down some of his best vocals since the halcyon days of *The Piper At The Gates Of Dawn*. The repeated takes and edits, though, ultimately water down the very madness which fires *The Madcap Laughs*. Also, as DiLorenzo noted, 'It was apparent, however, that this second selection, despite its more intimate framework, captured a talent in the process of disintegration.'[56]

Gilmour said the making of *Barrett* 'was mostly a case of me saying "Well, what have you got then, Syd?" and he'd search around and eventually work something out. We had more time to do *Barrett*, but trying to find a technique of working with Syd was so difficult. You had to pre-record tracks without him, working from one version of the song he had done, and then sit Syd down afterwards and try to get him to play and sing along, with a lot of dropping in. Or you could do it the other way around, where you'd get him to do a performance of it on his own and then try to dub everything else on top of it. The concept of him performing with another bunch of musicians was clearly impossible because he'd change the song every time. He'd never do a song the same twice. I think quite deliberately.[57]

'I don't think anyone can communicate with Syd. I did those albums because I liked the songs, not, as I suppose some might think, because I felt guilty taking his place in the Floyd. I was concerned that he wouldn't fall completely apart.[58] We always felt there was a talent there; it was just a matter of trying to get it out on record so that people would hear it and of course Syd didn't make it any easier for us . . . it was very, very difficult; not really rewarding.[59] It was hell. But you know, we always felt that there was a talent there, it was just a matter of trying to get it out on to record so that people would hear it, and of course Syd didn't make that any easier for us. There were various techniques we had to invent for trying to get the stuff recorded. And I've no idea how Syd felt about it most of the time . . . I've no idea if [the albums] were how he wanted them to be,' says Gilmour.

'But as he didn't offer opinions, we had to take it on to ourselves to decide how it should be, which is quite a normal thing with producers, but it wasn't because we were trying to assert that on him, it's just there wasn't anything coming from him to tell us how he thought it should be.'

Barrett's flattened emotions, and growing indifference, also made it hard to ascertain whether he was pleased with the finished work. 'The only thing he ever said about it was at the end of the second album, when we'd finished,' said Gilmour. 'We were going up the lift in his block of flats in Earls Court, and he turned round to me and he said, Thanks . . . thanks very much." And that's the only expression of approval or disapproval of anything that I got out of him through two albums.'[60]

---

1 Platt, John & Wyatt, Robert. *Wrong Movements*. RAK Publishing. 1994
2 Jones, Malcolm. *The Making Of The Madcap Laughs*. Orange Sunshine Press, 1986
3 *NME*, 13 April 1974
4 'Syd Barrett Careening Through Life'. Kris DiLorenzo, Trouser Press, February 1978
5 Jones, Malcolm. *The Making Of The Madcap Laughs*. Orange Sunshine Press, 1986

6 Ibid.
7 Ibid.
8 Ibid.
9 Roney, Elisa. 'The Madcap Loved: The Love Songs of Syd Barrett', from the Internet
10 Jones, Malcolm. *The Making Of The Madcap Laughs*. Orange Sunshine Press, 1986
11 Ibid.
12 Ibid.
13 'Syd Barrett Careening Through Life'. Kris DiLorenzo, Trouser Press, February 1978
14 Platt, John & Wyatt, Robert. *Wrong Movements*. RAK Publishing. 1994
15 Platt, John & Wyatt, Robert. *Wrong Movements*. RAK Publishing. 1994
16 Macdonald, Bruno, editor. *Pink Floyd: Through The Eyes Of...* Sidgwick & Jackson, London, 1996
17 Giovanni Dadomo interview with Syd Barrett, 1970
18 *ZigZag*, July 1973
19 *Musician*, December 1982
20 Unedited transcripts of interviews with Sam Hutt. Greene, Jonathan. *Days In The Life: Voices From The English Underground, 1961-1971*. Minerva, 1988
21 *Terrapin* 7, 1975
22 *Melody Maker*, 31 January 1970
23 Roney, Elisa. 'The Madcap Loved: The Love Songs of Syd Barrett'
24 Jones, Malcolm. *The Making Of* The Madcap Laughs. Orange Sunshine Press, 1986
25 Ibid.
26 *Terrapin* 7, 1975
27 Unedited transcripts of interviews with Jenny Fabian. Greene, Jonathan. *Days In The Life: Voices From The English Underground, 1961-1971*. Minerva, 1988
28 Interview by Ivor Trueman, *Opel* #8, 1984
29 Roney, Elisa, 'The Madcap Loved: The Love Songs of Syd Barrett', from the Internet
30 Giovanni Dadomo interview with Syd Barrett, 1970
31 *Melody Maker*, 31 January 1970
32 Ibid.
33 Giovanni Dadomo interview with Syd Barrett, 1970
34 *Melody Maker*, 31 January 1970
35 *Terrapin* 7, 1975
36 Ibid.
37 *Beat Instrumental*, 1971
38 *Terrapin* 7, 1975
39 Ibid.
40 *Melody Maker*, 31 January 1970
41 *Beat Instrumental*, 1971
42 Giovanni Dadomo interview with Syd Barrett, 1970
43 *Melody Maker*, 31 January 1971
44 *Beat Instrumental*, 1971
45 Mark Blake interview with Rick Wright, August 1996
46 Giovanni Dadomo interview with Syd Barrett, 1970
47 *NME*, 13 April 1974
48 'Syd Barrett Careening Through Life'. Kris DiLorenzo, Trouser Press, February 1978
49 *The Amazing Pudding*, # 58
50 'Syd Barrett Careening Through Life'. Kris DiLorenzo, Trouser Press, February 1978
51 Ibid.
52 Ibid.
53 *The Amazing Pudding*, # 56
54 Jonathan Greene. *Days In The Life: Voices From The English Underground, 1961-1971*. Minerva, 1988
55 *Beat Instrumental*, 1971
56 'Syd Barrett Careening Through Life'. Kris DiLorenzo, Trouser Press, February 1978
57 *Musician*, December 1982
58 *NME*, 13 April 1974
59 Macdonald, Bruno, editor. *Pink Floyd: Through The Eyes Of...* Sidgwick & Jackson, London, 1996. p. 226
60 *Sounds*, May 1983

Stage Six:
The Return of Ulysses (January 1970-January 1975)

'Turning away from the confusion of external things, turning back to one's inner light, there in the depths of the soul, one sees the Divine, the One. It is indeed only germinal, no more than a beginning . . . to know this One means to know oneself in relation to the cosmic forces. For this One is the ascending force of life in nature and in man.'

Chapter 24: Fu/Return – The Turning Point
The I-Ching or Book Of Changes

'With scoffs, and scorns, and contumelious taunts. In open market-place produced they me, to be a public spectacle to all. Here, said they, is the terror . . . the scarecrow that affrights our children so.'

Lord Talbot. ***Henry VI Part I, Shakespeare***

The end of the sixties brought about great changes in the lives of those who had defined the era. In that wide open decade no boundaries were established, and excess took its toll. The peace and love ethos seemed to have met its demise at the Rolling Stones' violent Altamont concert. As the decade closed, in rapid succession some of the brightest lights of the era died: Jim Morrison, bloated and stiff in a bathtub; Brian Jones, drowned in his swimming pool; Hendrix, choked on his own vomit; Janis Joplin, lifeless and blue from an overdose of heroin – all victims of the very Dionysian excess they embodied. And others too had fallen earlier on: Tara Browne, the Guinness heir and Chelsea *bon vivant*, speeding into the back of a lorry pulling out of a Kensington side-street in his Lotus Elan at 90 mph, high on acid. The doors of perception had been opened by drugs, but what lay beyond no one really knew. For some, the first steps toward a spiritual life or a vague enlightenment; for others, madness or death.

And there was a new kind of victim from the fallout of the era: Arthur Brown, Syd Barrett, Roky Erikson (13th Floor Elevators), Arthur Lee (Love), and Peter Green (Fleetwood Mac) all suffered profound mental distress in the aftermath of the sixties. It was as if they were the living dead, present in body but absent in mind or soul.

Nigel Gordon says, 'When I came back from India everything had changed in London. Everything changed when Brian Jones died, that was when the music died. For me, that was the end. And with the new decade, Jenny and I had changed, become responsible parents by 1970, starting a family. I just knew I had to work, and couldn't have fancy ideas of going to Hollywood.' Duggie Fields states, 'When I came back to London from America, things had changed, and a lot of people had disappeared. There were a lot of drug casualties, and also a disillusion with the realities of life. How were you going to make a living?'

Likewise, the beginning of the seventies marked a period of uncertainty for Barrett; his recorded output complete, he would waver for a few years over whether or not to continue with music. The intensity of Syd's musical vision had reached its apogee (or nadir, if you prefer) with the rant of 'Scream Thy Last Scream'; his best playing was already crystallised on *The Piper At The Gates of Dawn* or had dissolved into the ether at Pink Floyd's countless unrecorded gigs. The tightness, coherency and skill of Barrett's playing all steadily declined after 1967. In the parlance of jazz, he had lost his chops. Syd had, in a sense, already given up the race by 1970. He had long since ceased to push himself relentlessly to produce perfect interpretations of the sound in his head. His ears had become fogged with bad acid and Mandrax, feedback-drenched amps and inner exhaustion. There was a paradox for Syd, because his role in the Floyd had been so prominent, much of the weighty pressure in live performance rested on his weary shoulders; but as a solo artist, without the interplay among the band members, the weight remained on them.

When Syd was in the right state of mind, he could still play brilliantly, but the very striving itself only served to increase his nervousness. With repeated takes he lost his intensity and, subsequently, his interest. Years later, he would ask his ex-band mates why they insisted on hearing constant replays of a song in progress, 'Why? You've already heard it once!' It had to be spontaneous and interesting, but it also had to be easy. When his errant muse couldn't be summoned easily, Syd didn't pursue it further.

During the Pink Floyd's 1970 recording sessions for *Atom Heart Mother*, Syd occasionally dropped into the studio. He watched his former bandmates from the sidelines as they struggled to graft their rhythm track and Ron Geesin's orchestral arrangement together. Barrett could somehow never come to terms with the fact that he had been thrown out of the band he had created.[1]

*

At home at Earl's Court, Barrett was plainly tired of the chaos which seemed to surround him day and night. Duggie Fields says, 'There were some visitors who were parasites, and also some who were confused in their drug use, not even abusing drugs necessarily. Syd wasn't unique in his disintegration. And I can't say it was drug induced, I think the drugs were just a catalyst. Drugs could be very destructive, but Syd didn't get into heroin, for example.'

Eventually Barrett had had enough of the parasites and hangers-on, and decided to retreat to Cambridge with Gayla. By the beginning of 1970 he sought to return to an idyllic Cambridge that perhaps existed mostly in his imagination. He was twenty-four and looking for somewhere to call home.

There were of course those who are more than happy to sit at the table of his slow demise, partaking of the feast and fleeing at first sign of trouble. Where were Syd's many friends when he began to crack? Remarkably few stuck around to see what would happen to him. Even today, people who knew Syd quite well in the sixties, ask, 'Is Syd still alive?' As for the unwanted houseguests, Syd rang Duggie a few days later from Cambridge and told him to ask them to leave. Fields refused but, of course, ended up doing it anyhow. Fields told them, 'Look, Syd wants you out; he's coming back!' They were a bit frightened of him because he did have a violent side.'[2] For the next thirteen years, Barrett would oscillate between London and Cambridge but the returns to London diminished as time went by.

On 1 October 1970, Syd and Gayla became engaged in Cambridge. At their engagement dinner at the Barrett home, Gayla recalled that Barrett stopped eating in the middle of the meal and went upstairs. In the bathroom he took a pair of scissors and calmly cut off all his long hair. He rested the scissors on the sink, paused to look into the mirror, and came back downstairs to take his place at the table. Gayla said, 'And would you believe it, no one batted an eyelid. They just carried on with the meal as if nothing had happened, didn't say a word. I thought, Are they mad or is it me?"'[3] Peter Jenner said, 'I'm tempted to view it as a symbolic gesture; good-bye to being a pop-star.'[4] It was as if Barrett had severed links with his past with a pair of scissors, rejoining the family fold with a symbolic gesture. Barrett said in a 1971 interview, 'Cambridge is very much a place to get adjusted to. I've found it difficult. It was fairly unusual to go back because it's the home place where I used to live and it was pretty boring, so I cut my hair.'[5]

His relationship with Gayla was rife with the fear of abandonment which permeates his solo works, as well as paranoid jealousy stemming from deep-seated insecurity, and the relationship foundered quickly amid violence and recriminations. By obsessively trying to keep Gayla he eventually drove her away. Syd said, 'I've often been in love. The last time it lasted only a few months and at the end of it I almost broke down. Early on, being in love was more of a necessity. Now it's more of an involvement. I'd love to get married and have kids. The trouble is I've forgotten how to love. But I don't worry too much. It is something which occurs to me when I feel a bit blue-jeaned – which I don't always feel.'[6]

Syd moved from his old bedroom at Hills Road down to the cellar, where he could play his guitar undisturbed, his mother pottering away in the garden. After his initial difficulties in getting readjusted to the slow pace of life in Cambridge, he seemed to be settling down. 'I've been at home in Cambridge with my mother. I've been getting used to a family existence, generally. Pretty unexciting. I work down in a cellar.[7] It's quite fun . . . a nice place to live, really, under the ground.'[8] But beneath the surface, there was still that restlessness that fired all his best music. Like a pendulum that had been set in motion years before, it would take a while before its swings would halt and he would be at peace.

Other signs of Syd's withdrawal were ever more apparent and his friends and intimates found him increasingly nebulous and detached. Jerry Shirley said, 'You'd get some sort of sense out of him, and then he'd just laugh at you.'[9] David Gilmour said, 'Various people tried to see him and get him together, and found it beyond their capabilities.'[10]

Barrett had still not fully severed links with his pop past, though, and following the release of *The Madcap Laughs* and *Barrett*, his music publisher Bryan Morrison sent him on a promotional junket to all the music newspapers. Syd was asked questions of varying degrees of intelligence and responded in kind. Inevitably the interviews tend to start out with Barrett answering in relatively coherent sentences and finishing in increasingly vague, monosyllabic replies. As Michael Watts wrote, 'Syd occasionally laughed, seemed agitated or trailed away into silence during our conversation. Anything that seemed uninteresting or irrelevant merely provoked strained and disordered replies.'[11]

The interviews were a rather futile undertaking. Jonathan Greene, author of *Days In The Life*, the definitive history of the underground, was then a reporter for the British edition of *Rolling Stone* magazine. Of his ill-fated attempt to interview Barrett, Greene said, 'He didn't have an album out, and I didn't know why I was doing it'. Greene dropped into the offices of Bryan Morrison to interview Barrett; 'I went into this big white room, and there was Syd, dressed all in white clothes. It was really very sad. Syd spent the whole time looking at the top corner of the room, saying, "Hey, man . . . hey . . . right . . . now look up there, can you see the people on the ceiling?"'[12]

Peter Barnes, publicist at the Bryan Morrison agency who represented him, said that interviewing Syd was fairly ludicrous on the surface: 'You just had to go along with it all. Syd would say something completely incongruous one minute like "It's getting heavy, isn't it?" and you'd just have to say "Yeah, Syd, it's getting heavy", and the conversation would dwell on that for five minutes.' In an acute observation, though, Barnes captured one of the most interesting and puzzling aspects of Barrett's mental distress: his mind was orderly in its chaos. 'Actually, listening to the tape afterwards you could work out that there was some kind of logic there, except that Syd would suddenly be answering a question you'd asked him ten minutes ago while you were off on a different topic completely!'[13] The patterns of Syd's thinking seem the very embodiment of chaos theory, those erratic ellipses which are consistent in their inconsistency, and stable in their instability. Even in this state of mental chaos, perhaps somewhere below the chaos even the most fantastic flights of fancy are undergirded by a non-linear flow of logic.

Barrett's speech patterns, never conventional or particularly linear, became soliloquies of evasion, paranoia, metaphor and irony. They were confusing, as related bits of thought were spoken, but all context omitted. Without being armed with some knowledge, the listener was left to wonder what was implied or suggested. Simply divorced from constants such as linear logic, Syd's interviewers must have felt like they were trying to tune into a distant short-wave radio station, where snatches of dialogue emerge from the haze only to be swallowed back again. Since it was forever tantalisingly out of reach, it acquired an air of mystery, as if words of dramatic import were being conveyed. But there were few clues to help decipher them.

For Syd, there would be occasional moments of blinding clarity, such as when he explained the ideas behind the composition of 'Octopus' or recorded a perfect backwards solo on 'Dominoes'. As he orbited in ever widening ellipses, he would fade in and out of view. The (il)logic of clinically defined schizophrenia lies in the loosening of associations. Being asked a question in an interview might suggest fifteen possible paths to explore in his reply. The average mind would be able to screen out fourteen options and follow one in a coherent way, but perhaps Syd couldn't differentiate between the options and skipped freely from one to the next; a sort of logic baffling to most people.

Somewhere behind Syd's immense confusion, perhaps he saw himself being interviewed from afar and found it quite humorous. The vague answers he provided also served as a protective shield or elaborate smokescreen, because for someone in the throes of paranoia a seemingly innocuous question could carry manifold intimations of threat or danger, whether imagined or real. Paranoia is one of the strangest maladies; all it takes is a seed of doubt to blossom into a tree of uncertainty. Connections are seen where there are none, unrelated events or thoughts seem linked in a sinister, threatening way. The loosening of associations between thoughts is paradoxically matched by paranoia, which sees associations everywhere. It's almost as if the mind, in trying to hold together thought patterns inexorably drifting apart, seeks to link them back together in a most erratic way. An analogy would be trying to arrest the continental drift by constantly building bridges that teeter perilously and then collapse. Barrett was struggling for the right words; if he tried to explain what he was thinking it came out scrambled in the translation to speech. Either way, he wasn't getting through, and the result hardly justified the effort. In 1971, he would grant his last interview.

Jerry Shirley said, 'Sometimes he did it just to put everybody on, sometimes he did it because he was genuinely paranoid about what was happening around him. Like the weather, he changed. For every ten things he said that were off-the-wall and odd, he would say one thing that was completely coherent and right on the ball. He would seem out of touch with what had gone on about just before, then he would suddenly turn around and say, "Jerry, remember the day we went to get a burger down at the Earl's Court Road?", [with] complete recall of something that happened a long time ago. Just coming and going, all the time.'[14]

One of the most frustrating aspects of these on-again, off-again transient bursts of clarity alternating with bouts of confusion, is that eventually one system will prevail, and complete or partial recovery would be as likely as descent into chronic confusion. Others simply spend the rest of their life oscillating between the two extremes. There are a couple of photographs of Syd from this time which capture him stuck between his two worlds, literal and metaphorical: he's captured in a Crombie coat with his Telecaster dangling around his neck like a strange ornament, as if the accoutrements of rock'n'roll had become foreign to him. His eyes, like green beach pools where no tides run any more, reflect only the strange incongruity of a guitar strapped on a increasingly ordinary looking person.

Though Syd continued to write songs, none of them actually seemed to reach completion, 'I always write with guitar. I've got this big room and I just go in and do the work. I like to do the words and music simultaneously, so when I go into the studio I've got the words on one side and my music on the other. I suppose I could do with some practice.' Asked if he still painted, Barrett replied, 'Not much. The guy who lives next door to me paints, and he's doing it well. I don't really feel the need . . . A lot of people want to make films and do photography and things, but I'm quite happy doing what I'm doing.'[15]

He said, 'I don't really buy many records, there's so much around that you don't know what to listen to. All I've got at home is Bo Diddley, some Stones and Beatles stuff and old jazz records. I like Family, they do some nice things.'[16] After suffering the sort of traumas Barrett did, he retreated to what he knew best; Bo Diddley, the Beatles, the Rolling Stones and old jazz records were his favourite listening before he left Cambridge for London, presumably the very same scratched LPs he'd left behind when he moved to London.

'During the past six months there have been some very good things released,' said Syd. 'The best things I've bought are the new Taj Mahal album, Captain Beefheart, and the Band. I don't think any of them have influenced my writing though. I've been writing in all sorts of funny places. I'm just waiting to see how the records do, what the reactions are, before I decide on anything else. My time has been fairly well spent since leaving. When I was with the Floyd the form of music played on-stage was mainly governed by the records. Now I seem to have got back to my previous state of mind.'[17]

'When Syd came to my wedding in 1971,' said Seamus O'Connell, 'he was still good looking, lovable and friendly, though he had started to get a bit strange.'

On 16 February 1971, Barrett did a solo session for BBC's 'Whispering' Bob Harris on Radio 1 in London. A set, comprising 'Terrapin', 'Baby Lemonade', 'Dominoes' and 'Love Song', showed him to still be playing well, save for the occasional marked lapse in tempo, but he seemed to be singing out of obligation rather than any desire to perform.

Steve Turner of *Beat Instrumental* finally caught up with Syd in April 1971 after several months of trying to see him for an interview. Although they had made plans to meet, Barrett simply didn't show. Turner then rang him, but to his astonishment Syd accused him of not turning up and being a timewaster, and slammed the receiver down. Eventually Barrett relented and allowed the interview to be rescheduled, taking the train from Cambridge to meet Turner. He had taken to wearing fashionable glam clothes, with his hair cut like David Bowie's, and a purple satin jacket and stack-heeled boots like Slade. Turner was struck by 'the fear behind his eyes . . . almost as if there was the danger of my discovering more than I should know. His answers to my questions were interesting. He would start off by saying something that related to my question but then begin to free associate and would soon be off in a different direction altogether. Even then much of what he said was highly perceptive, reminiscent of the Dylan *Playboy* interview, for instance, where much of what was said was seen as a joke at the time but proved to be penetratingly true. "Do you see pop as an art form?" I asked. "As much as sitting down is," he replied. He talked excitedly about buying a new guitar.

'During the interview he lights each cigarette from the remnants of the previous one and pivots his eyeballs at an incredible speed as he speaks. "I've just left a train and had to pay an awful taxi ride," he said, slowly tipping his ash into an empty coffee cup. I've come to look for a guitar. I've got a neck in the other room. Quite an exciting morning for me." Something about him makes you think that this may well be right. His talk is slow and unrevealing. The answer given often bears no relation to the question asked. Particular areas of his life he carefully avoids mentioning. In those two years he had returned to his home in Cambridge where he now lives in a cellar. His time is spent listening to records and playing his own music. "I mainly play the guitar," he said. "It's very comfortable playing and it sometimes gets very interesting. I'm writing songs with it as well. You can play it all day through and you're not really saying much."'[18] I asked if he would join me in a taxi where he could be dropped off at the music store, he obviously didn't want that and made an excuse about something else he had to do. But the real reason, I'm sure, was his paranoia. Months later I met him on an underground train, he acknowledged me and remembered the interview, but it's the frightened face I'll always remember.'[19]

Relics, a Pink Floyd collection of singles, out-takes and curios, was released in May 1971, including 'Interstellar Overdrive', 'Bike', and the Barrett-penned singles 'See Emily Play' and 'Arnold Layne'. Strong sales, due to Pink Floyd's growing popularity, ensured a sizeable royalty cheque for Barrett.[20]

In December 1971, the last interview with Barrett, by Mick Rock for *Rolling Stone,* was published. 'Syd doesn't see many people these days. Visiting him is like intruding into a very private world. "I'm disappearing," he said, avoiding most things." He seems very tense, ill at ease. Hollow-cheeked and pale, his eyes reflect a permanent state of shock. He has a ghostly beauty which one normally associates with poets of old. His hair is short now, uncombed, the wavy locks gone. The velvet pants and new green snakeskin boots show some attachment to the way it used to be. "I'm treading the backward path," he smiles. "Mostly, I just waste my time." He walks a lot. "Eight miles a day," he said. "It's bound to show. But I don't know how. I'm sorry I can't speak very coherently," he said, "it's rather difficult to think of anybody being really interested in me. But you know, man, I am totally together. I even think I should be." Occasionally, Syd responds directly to a question. Mostly his answers are fragmented, a stream of consciousness. "I'm full of dust and guitars," he said.

'He still paints. Sometimes crazy jungles of thick blobs. Sometimes simple linear pieces. His favourite is a white semi-circle on a white canvas. In a cellar where he spends much of his time, he sits surrounded by paintings and records, his amps and guitars. He feels safe there, under the ground. Like a character out of one of his own songs. Syd has been known to sit behind locked doors, refusing to see anyone for days at a time. Syd leaves the cellar and goes up to a sedate little room full of pictures of himself with his family. He was a pretty child. English tea, cake and biscuits, arrives. Like many innovators, Barrett seems to have missed the recognition due to him, while others have cleaned up. "I'd like to be rich. I'd like a lot of money to put into my physicals and to buy food for all my friends.

'"I'll show you a book of all my songs before you go. I think it's so exciting. I'm glad you're here." He produces a folder containing all his recorded songs to date, neatly typed, with no music. Most of them stand alone as written pieces. Sometimes simple, lyrical, though never without some touch of irony. Sometimes surreal, images weaving dreamily, echoes of a mindscape that defies traditional analysis. Syd's present favourite is "Wolfpack", a taut threatening, claustrophobic number. Syd thinks people who sing their own songs are boring. He has never recorded anyone else's. He produces a guitar and begins to strum out a new version of "Love You" from *Madcap.* "I worked this out yesterday. I think it's much better. It's my new twelve-string guitar. I'm just getting used to it. I polished it yesterday." It's a Yamaha. He stops and eases it into a regular tuning, shaking his head. "I never felt so close to a guitar as that silver one with mirrors that I used on-stage all the time. I swapped it for the black one, but I've never played it."

'Syd is twenty-five now, and worried about getting old. "I wasn't always this introverted," he said, "I think young people should have a lot of fun. But I never seem to have any." Suddenly he points out the window. "Have you seen the roses? There's a whole lot of colours." Syd said he doesn't take acid anymore, but he doesn't want to talk about it... "There's really nothing to say." He goes into the garden and stretches out on an old wooden seat. "Once you're into something..." he said, looking very puzzled. He stops. "I don't think I'm easy to talk about. I've got a very irregular head. And I'm not anything that you think I am anyway."'[21]

Barrett lying on that bench, staring with all consuming yet blank eyes through the sun dappled leaves of the trees in his mother's garden makes for a vivid, poignant and rather sad picture. Boredom nipped at his heels, and he told an interviewer, 'Living in Cambridge I have to find something to do. I suppose I could've done a job. I haven't been doing any work. I'm not really used to doing quick jobs and then stopping, but I'm sure it would be possible.' Barrett strained for the right words: 'Perhaps it has something to do with what I felt could be better as regards music, as far as my job goes generally, because I did find I needed a job. I wanted to do a job. I never admitted it because I'm a person who doesn't admit it.'[22]

Inactivity bothered Barrett, but not enough to make him give up his hard-won privacy and isolation. He joked, 'The only work I've done the last two years is interviews. I'm very good at it . . . I may seem to get hung-up, that's because I am frustrated work-wise, terribly. The fact is I haven't done anything this year, I've probably been chattering, explaining that away like anything. But the other bit about not working is that you do get to think theoretically.'[23]

Asked about a return to live performance, Barrett admitted that playing again 'would be nice. I used to enjoy it, it was a gas. But so's doing nothing. It's art school laziness, really . . . I've got this Wembley gig and then another thing in summer . . . I'll be getting something together for the Wembley thing and then just see what happens.[24] I've never really proved myself wrong. I really need to prove myself right.'[25]

At this point Barrett still wanted to continue with music: 'I've got some songs in the studio, still. And I've got a couple of tapes. It should be twelve singles, and jolly good singles. I think I shall be able to produce this one myself. I think it was always easier to do that . . . I feel though the record would still be the thing to do. And touring and playing might make that impossible to do . . . I'm afraid I think I'd have to get on with the [musicians]. They'd have to be good musicians. I think they'd be difficult to find. They'd have to be lively.[26] But I can't find anybody. That's the problem. I don't know where they are. I mean, I've got an idea that there must be someone to play with. If I was going to play properly, I should need some really good people.[27] It'd be a groove wouldn't it? I'm still in love with being a pop star really. As a job it's very interesting but very difficult. You can be pure enough to talk about it where you can actually adapt to the grammar of the job. It's exciting. You channel everything into one thing and it becomes the art.'[28]

Barrett commuted regularly between Cambridge and London, doing little of anything and much of nothing, not really out of laziness but more out of utter confusion with what to do as a second act in the theatre of his life. Meanwhile Pink Floyd were moving their career into high gear with the first live performance of a new suite called *Eclipse* at the Dome in Brighton, 20 January 1972. They were beginning to piece together the album that would be their breakthrough to mass popularity, *Dark Side of the Moon.*

That January, Jenny Spires, Syd's ex-girlfriend from the mid-sixties, came to visit him at Hills Road. They had remained on friendly terms, and Spires made efforts to roust Barrett from his lair and get him outside. Spires had married bass player Jack Monck, who was active in local Cambridge rock circles. She took Barrett down to see guitarist Eddie Burns play at the King's College Cellar. During interviews conducted over the previous two years, Barrett had often spoke of getting a band together. As was the case when he saw the Soft Machine in 1969, the sight and sound of live music shocked Barrett out of his complacency.

In *Terrapin* fanzine, Mervyn Hughes reported on the Burns' gig. After Burns' solo spot, the announcement of 'Syd Barrett on guitar' made Hughes sit up. Barrett got up on-stage and jammed with Jack Monck on bass and old UFO crony and ex-Tomorrow drummer Twink, jamming loosely on a few boogie tunes. Hughes reported that Barrett played quite well, mostly staying in the background. Monck said, 'The Cambridge Blues Society booked Eddie Burns and they asked Twink and I to be the backing band, and we had a jam session which Syd played on. He was playing a black Telecaster with white inlays that was very nice.' Hughes talked briefly to Barrett after the gig, and Barrett stated, incorrectly, that it was his first performance since leaving the Floyd. Syd said he was working on songs for a new album, and had come 'to watch some people'. 'He seemed very shy,' wrote Hughes, 'and surprised that I knew anything about him.'

'I was living in a small cottage in Graveley with Jenny Spires and our daughter Jessie,' says bassist Jack Monck. 'I was working at Red House Records, playing in bands in Cambridge, running a club at Fisher House. We had bands that we knew up from London and would have jam sessions. I was playing with Twink and we were involved in running the club and playing in bands. It was through Jenny that I met Syd; she had known him pretty well before. Syd was living at Hills Road with his mum. In the post-Floyd period, he was very withdrawn and couldn't communicate very well. He didn't feel at ease around people.'

'I remember going to his flat in Cambridge and winkling him out to come and meet some people,' says Peter Wynne-Wilson. 'I thought that if there were people around who totally wanted him to be all right that he would be relaxed, but it wasn't like that. He fairly rapidly got jumpy so I took him back home.'

But Barrett had enjoyed playing in the unpressured atmosphere of the King's

College Cellars, and he showed up unexpectedly at another local gig. 'Syd also jammed with us when we were playing at the Corn Exchange when Twink and I played in a last-minute-put-together boogie band, an *ad-hoc* collection of people based around an American singer and guitarist called Bruce, who was in the Allman Brothers tradition, and that was the kind of music we were doing. Once we had Fred Frith and Syd sitting in with us playing guitars. That was all right, because there wasn't any spotlight on Syd, no pressure on him, and a lot of other people on-stage as well.'

Pete Brown joined ex-Cream bassist Jack Bruce for a jazz/poetry performance in Cambridge. 'I got there very late, and there was this insane band on-stage, playing this interesting, weird kind of jazz. Somebody had recognised Jack and handed him a double bass, which he was playing, and there was a guitarist who I vaguely recognised. Then during my set, I said, "I'd like to dedicate this poem to Syd Barrett, because he's here in Cambridge and he's one of the greatest song-writers in the country." At which point, the guitar player from that band, who was sitting in the audience, got up and said, "No I'm not." That was him. And that he could get up and play with Jack Bruce was something.'[29] Brown adds, 'When I heard him play with Jack Bruce in Cambridge, he was playing very well. On a completely different level to what he was doing with the Pink Floyd. They were playing a kind of jazz, with Jack Bruce playing a stand-up bass, and a drummer. It wasn't rock. I certainly remember that, at that gig in Cambridge, his time was very good. It's a shame that he didn't develop further as a musician, because he would have developed into something very interesting.'

Jack Monck says, 'Jenny suggested getting together with Syd and doing some playing. He was a great talent and wasn't doing anything. It seemed like he would have enjoyed some contact with other people. I thought it was a good opportunity for me and could result in something. There was no grand master plan, not on Syd's part and certainly not on mine. It just seemed like a good idea. If anybody did put it together, it was Twink, I don't know what Twink's motivation was, but he probably just thought it seemed a good idea; "Let's do it!" It was a decision we drifted into and everyone around us was saying, "Yes, do it, it would be good!" It was all done on a small Cambridge level. But very quickly we came up against not being able to live up to these expectations.'

Peter Jenner credited Twink as the last person who tried to get Syd together. 'I didn't know him closely for that long,' said Twink, 'but I was in the same space and I could understand exactly where he was at. I thought he was very together. As a friend it was a very warm relationship; no bad vibes at all. We didn't have any crazy scenes.'[30] Within a few weeks of their first pub jam, the trio dubbed themselves Stars. Stars started rehearsing with an eye to playing live, and Barrett seemed enthusiastic to return to the stage.

Practice sessions in Syd's cellar ensued; 'Twink said he reckoned that Syd taped some of the rehearsals down in his mother's cellar,' says Monck, 'but they were primitive. I wouldn't describe the rehearsals as tight, but there wasn't the same pressure as playing a major gig.'

A small-scale gig at the Dandelion coffee bar soon followed, with friends and supporters all around. 'I was really amazed working with him,' said Twink, 'at his actual ability as a guitar player.'[31] Their first proper show as Stars was at an open-air gig in Market Square in Cambridge's town centre. There was no doubt as to who was the focus, and the material was almost totally made up of Barrett compositions, including a few Pink Floyd songs. 'We had a gig on the corner of Petty Curry and Market Square, with a drum kit and some amps,' says Monck. 'In those days having electric bands playing in open-air spaces, especially in the middle of town, was a bit unusual. People weren't as used to it as they are now. There was no stage and we had some power from somewhere. It was our second gig and quite a good one. With Stars, the first gig was the best and after that it was a bit downhill, because we never lived up to expectations.'

In February 1972, Twink arranged with a promoter for Stars to play at the Cambridge Corn Exchange on the 24th, closing for Skin Alley and the MC5. The Corn Exchange gig was hyped around town as a come-back gig of sorts for Syd. The fear of being back in the spotlight only served to unnerve him, adding to the sudden pressure. Not only was this to be a come-back but also a hometown gig, which would be crowded with dozens of people who Syd had known well for ten years or more. He may very well have felt pressured by the expectations of many. And, without a doubt, there would be those who would come out of a morbid curiosity, to see if the Madcap could really pull it off. To add to Barrett's customary stagefright and indecision, Syd decided to go and see his old band perform.

On 17 to 20 February, Pink Floyd played a series of critical gigs at the Rainbow Theatre in Finsbury Park, London, introducing *The Dark Side Of The Moon* to the press. Barrett took the train down to see them. 'I went to a post-Syd Pink Floyd concert in Finsbury Park,' says Mike Leonard, 'quite an important one for them, and I met Syd lurking in the hall. I don't think they'd even invited him, he'd just come on his own. I'd heard he'd overdosed on things, and was fairly freaked out. He looked a bit taut and a bit gaunt . . . He was still Syd, though, and he hadn't put on a lot of weight yet. I thought it must have been strange for a guy who'd been in the group to look at it from the outside.' Pink Floyd's performance of *The Dark Side Of The Moon* was well received by critics and fans alike. What ran through Barrett's mind as he watched them only he knows, but it may very well have influenced his decision to withdraw from music.

Stars rehearsed 'Octopus,' 'Dark Globe,' 'Gigolo Aunt,' 'Baby Lemonade,' 'Waving My Arms In The Air,' 'Lucifer Sam,' and 'See Emily Play'. Syd was visibly nervous during rehearsals. Come the night of the 24th, he anxiously awaited their turn to go on. The Cambridge Corn Exchange wasn't even full. *Terrapin* reporter Robert Chapman wrote the following review: 'The gig was either a disaster or a shining pinnacle of Syd's twilight shellshock, but I'm not going to say which. Syd mostly rambled up and down his Stratocaster searching for tunes that probably weren't there.'

From the first song, a slow version of 'Octopus', the Corn Exchange PA wasn't up to the task and, once again, like his Olympia gig, the vocals were well nigh impossible to decipher. Chapman wrote, 'The only times he spoke were to introduce "Octopus" and to mumble "I don't know what that one was called" after playing "Gigolo Aunt".' Everything that could possibly go wrong did: in addition to Syd's memory blanks, hesitant playing, and the PA sabotaging his vocals, somehow he cut his finger open, bleeding on his Stratocaster as he played. It was an apt symbol. Though 'See Emily Play' had been rehearsed earlier in the day, the tail end of the gig was left to a 'shapeless and ragged' twelve-bar instrumental. Chapman noted that the band, however, played a remarkable version of 'Lucifer Sam'.

'We had a very bad PA system which was mixed badly,' said Twink. 'Syd couldn't hear his vocals. The guitars were completely lost. All Syd could hear were the drums. But we did manage to get across "Lucifer Sam".'[32] There seemed to be a profound feeling of dismay from both the audience and the performers. Ironically, in the audience at this, Barrett's last concert, was Clive Welham, who had played with Syd in his very first band Geoff Mott And The Mottoes ten years before. 'He looked completely at a loss, stumbling and stammering to sing,' remembers Welham sadly. 'The applause from the audience was only in sympathy, because the music was poor quality, like some drunk performing.'[33] It was a frustrating finale for Syd. Roy Hollingsworth wrote a bad review of the gig for the *Melody Maker*, which Syd very much took to heart. 'We just weren't ready for it,' said Twink. 'It was a disastrous gig, the reviews were really bad, and Syd was really hung up about it; so the band folded. He came round to my house and said he didn't want to play any more. He didn't explain; he just left.'[34]

Syd vanished from the public eye again, retreating back to his room. This time the game was over.

'My own personal memory of the Corn Exchange gig was that it was a failure,' says Monck. 'I felt we'd brought a lot of people down and failed on that occasion. It was a high-profile appearance, we were supporting the MC5, and had a lot of people rooting for us and wanting it to be good. You could tell Syd just wasn't interested. He had to front the whole thing, he had the hardest job. He couldn't remember the words, he just didn't want to be there. You could just see him thinking, "What the hell am I doing here? I don't want to be here at all," and not being able to communicate with anybody. It was a real let-down. I never heard of him doing any other gigs after that. That last experience, I would have thought, would have cured him for good. If it was depressing for us, it was even more depressing for him.'

Barrett went back to his cellar to lick his wounds. The experience had upset him, and he may very well have realised the best thing for him to do was to quit music.

In March 1973, Pink Floyd released what would become their best known and largest-selling album, *The Dark Side Of The Moon*; an epic exploration of madness, insanity and mortality. Its stunning breadth and universality of themes made it an instant classic and its appeal has never waned. Also in 1973, David Bowie, now a major star, released *Pin Ups*, an album of sixties' covers of songs which had influenced him. Among them was 'See Emily Play'.

In April, Barrett visited Bryan Morrison, his publisher at Lupus Music, to collect his royalties. His hair had grown out a bit, but he was overweight and looked divorced from his former self. Morrison asked if he had written any new songs, as he was still contractually obligated to Harvest. Barrett indifferently said, 'No', and left.[35]

Peter Barnes said, 'Syd has always had this big phobia about his age. When we would try to get him back into the studio to record he would get very defensive and say, "I'm only twenty-four, I'm still young. I've got time."'[36]

In the absence of any new product, Harvest decided to repackage his solo albums in a double LP package called *Syd Barrett,* with a new sleeve; it was released in 1974 only in the US. Storm Thorgerson and Hipgnosis were commissioned to design the sleeve. Thorgerson went to arrange a photo session with Barrett, who slammed the door in his face. Rather annoyed, Thorgerson none the less designed a superb evocative cover utilising one of Mick Rock's *Madcap Laughs* photo session pictures of Syd sitting cross-legged. The cover also featured a plum, orange and matchbox, the obscure reference to Barrett's first acid trip in Cambridge.

Pink Floyd's *Nice Pair* double LP repackaging of *The Piper At The Gates of Dawn* and *Saucerful Of Secrets*, was issued in December, which meant additional royalties for Barrett.

By December 1973, Barrett had moved into Flat 902 on the ninth floor of the Chelsea Cloisters, off the King's Road in Chelsea. His frequent perambulations around town, walking for hours, through the winding roads of Chelsea or across the Thames River to Battersea and back, would always end at the same terminus. His room, a figurative womb, a burrow underground like Badger's home in *The Wind In The Willows*, was an isle of safety in the midst of the mortal terror of the wild wood outside; London was suddenly full of strangers, the blank faces of friends that would pass him on the street, some of whom he'd known since childhood. Syd would sit in the corner of his regular Earl's Court pub, the Marlborough, staring quietly into space and sipping Guinness.

Barrett spent many, many hours doing very little. His seclusion could be seen as almost monastic save for the lack of discipline or schedule of any sort. He outfitted his flat with a large refrigerator and began eating heavily. 'Watching the telly till all hours,' as Syd sang in 1967's 'Scream Thy Last Scream', seems very prescient indeed, as that was what he largely dedicated himself to at the Chelsea

Cloisters. He would watch telly, occasionally strum his various guitars, listen to LPs on his hi-fi, eat and drink a lot of beer. In two years he put on a great deal of weight. Music was forsaken for food and TV – Barrett filling the void of an inactive life with junk food and the *News At Ten*.

Once in a while Syd would hit the town, probably out of force of habit rather than a strong need to be around people. At an age where one is old enough to reflect, but still young enough to enjoy life, Barrett didn't seem to be capable of either. Duggie Fields ran into him at London's hip nightclub, the Speakeasy, where musicians, groupies and record company executives, DJs and drug dealers would gather to assiduously avoid scrutinising each other. Syd's face registered nothing; 'I wasn't sure he recognised me. I was with some people he'd known for years; we talked for about five minutes, but did he really know who we were? That was when he was starting to get heavy, and he didn't look like the same kind of person at all.'[37]

With his royalties Barrett was able to stay at times, Howard-Hughes-like, in the penthouse suite at the Park Lane Hilton. Jenny Fabian recalled, 'I was told that he lived in the Penthouse Club and was very fat and got a weekly cheque from the Floyd.'[38] John Marsh saw Syd at South Kensington tube station, 'He looked like a picture of the middle-aged Aleister Crowley. Totally bald, about fifteen stone, wearing a Hawaiian shirt and Bermuda shorts.'[39] Hoppy said, 'I did see him once after he'd split from the Floyd and there's only one thing I remember, he was very fat, whereas he had always been thin.'

Myths and rumours abounded in inverse proportion to his activity. Nick Kent wrote a lengthy article on Barrett for the *NME*, published on 13 April 1974. Although informative, the piece perhaps served more than anything to feed the myth-making already springing up around him. Like Roger Waters' subsequent ode 'Shine On You Crazy Diamond', the piece manages to both deride and praise Barrett, unsure of how to remember him. Ultimately, it was easiest to view him as a barmy 'madcap' instead of analysing what had led to his downfall.* Kent's piece, however, was well-researched, relying primarily on first hand accounts.

When an artist visibly declines, their creative output markedly paling before previous work, it's easy to lose sight of the brilliance of their achievements, focusing rather on their dissolution. Why? It makes for better copy; sensation-

*In late 1996, a one-man multi-media performance was staged at London's Institute of Contemporary Arts. The artist in question depicted the life of Syd Barrett using slides, monologues, songs and video. The overall tone was mocking, with the less salient aspects of Barrett's breakdown played for laughs, which rose in a chorus from the back of the hall. Curiously, when the artist performed versions of 'See Emily Play' and ''Golden Hair', they were reverent and beautifully performed, and a dramatisation of an EMI old-school exec strong-arming Syd into writing commercial material was sharp and insightful. But the performance suffered through its contemptuous depiction of Barrett as a pathetic figure more deserving of our derision rather our compassion. At the ICA, opinions differed sharply, Peter Whitehead enjoyed it, but Duggie Fields walked out.

alism sells. Roger Waters said the media 'definitely don't want to know the real Barrett story. There are no facts involved in the Barrett story so they can make up any story they like, and they do. There's a vague basis in fact: Syd was in the band and he did write the material on the first album, 80 per cent of it, but that's all. It's only that one album, and that's what people don't realise. That first album, and one track on the second. That's all; nothing else.'[40] Waters own paranoia was stoked by the seemingly inescapable presence of Syd. 'Because we're very successful we're very vulnerable to attack and Syd is the weapon that is used to attack us. It makes it all a bit spicy, and that's what sells the papers that the people write for. But it's also very easy because none of it's fact, it's all hearsay and none of them know anything, and they all just make it up. Somebody makes it up once and the others believe it.'[41]

Perhaps motivated by the publicity the Kent article had generated, Bryan Morrison and Harvest repeatedly urged Barrett to work on new material. Barrett acquiesced for the last time.

In November 1974, Syd returned to Abbey Road for three days of sessions with Peter Jenner presiding. In recent years, a supposed bootleg from this session began circulating. If it is indeed from the session, it shows Barrett having regressed completely to the early rhythmic guitar stylings of his Shadows and R&B days. The process was abandoned before any vocal tracks were attempted. The box containing the tape had a scribbled inscription from one of the engineers, 'Various bits and pieces – details inside tape box'. Inside were the rough titles Jenner had marked to differentiate them, reflecting the content: 'Echo Stuff', 'John Lee Hooker', 'If You Go, Don't Be Slow', and the evocatively titled 'Chooka-chooka-chug-chug'.[42]

'It was very frustrating and upsetting, and very sad,' said Peter Jenner of the sessions. 'Glimpses of things would come through in the chaos and confusion, a bit of a melody line or lyric. From the doodling of a sick mind, bits of clarity would emerge. In the undergrowth the flowers were still growing, but he could not get at them. He was a great artist, an incredibly creative artist, and it's tragic that the music business may well have a lot to do with doing him in.'[43]

'It was an abortion,' said Peter Barnes more emphatically. 'He just kept overdubbing guitar part on guitar part until it was just a total chaotic mess. He also wouldn't show anyone his lyrics, I fear actually because he hadn't written any.'[44] Layer upon layer of guitar tracks, reflecting Syd's muddled thought patterns; trying to clarify with each layer and only succeeding in confounding himself. This is the soundtrack of mental illness, in a box on a cabinet shelf in a dark, empty room many feet below the ground in one of EMI's tape storage facilities. Hundreds of false starts and mistakes. Syd couldn't match the ideal he had in his mind and, worst of all, he knew it. And knowing you are going wrong inside must be very frustrating; not being able to do anything about it must be doubly so.

Peter Jenner said, 'There was this great thing one of the engineers spotted. Syd would come in to Abbey Road studios and glimpses of tunes would come out, and we'd think "Record that!" and then it would disappear into incoherence again. Then he'd just walk out of the studio. The engineer sussed that if he turned left he came back and if he went right he didn't. This was absolutely uncanny, but it was what happened. There was probably some banal reason, but at the time you thought "Hooooo. . ."'[45]

One-time Tyrannosaurus Rex member Steve 'Peregrine' Took, another sixties casualty, had remained in touch with Syd. In late 1974, Syd purportedly sat in on a topsy-turvy session at Took's house. Took had taken to entitling his songs with the names of the participants. 'Syd's Wine' is alleged to feature Syd on guitar. The song is desperately sad, because there is an intriguing rich melody hidden behind the drug-bound haze, under the layers of nearly impenetrable confusion.

In a bizarre sort of last hurrah for the public persona known as Syd Barrett, 5 June 1975 saw an unusual visitor arrive at Pink Floyd's sessions for 'Shine On You Crazy Diamond' at Abbey Road. The song, the centerpiece of Pink Floyd's 1975 *Wish You Were Here*, was to be Waters' tribute to his childhood friend and former bandmate. *Wish You Were Here* also featured 'Have A Cigar', a bitter indictment of the record business and the sorts of hoop-jumping the Floyd had been obliged to perform when they signed with EMI; and the title track, a lament of loss, alludes to Syd in its 'steel rail' image, borrowed from Barrett's own 'Dark Globe'.

The themes had been brewing in Waters' mind for some time. Related reflections on insanity and the perilous cost of fame were to preoccupy Waters straight through to 1979's *The Wall*. The themes of insanity so prevalent on *The Dark Side Of The Moon*, particularly on 'Eclipse' and 'Brain Damage', was to be expanded into an elegy of the absence of Syd Barrett. And this literal and metaphorical absence of Syd Barrett, was expanded into a theme of universal absence.

'It was very strange,' said Roger Waters on writing the lyrics for 'Shine On You Crazy Diamond'. 'The lyrics were written, and the lyrics are the bit of the song about Syd, the rest of it could be about anything. I don't why I started writing those lyrics about Syd. I think because that phrase of Dave's was an extremely mournful kind of sound and it just . . . I haven't a clue . . . but it was a long time before the *Wish You Were Here* recording sessions when Syd's state could be seen as being symbolic of the general state of the group: very fragmented.'[46]

'The whole album sprang from that one four-note guitar phrase of Dave's in "Shine On You Crazy Diamond",' said Rick Wright. 'We heard it, and went, "That's a really nice phrase." The wine came out, and that led to what I think is our best album, the most colourful, the most feelingful.' The four-note phrase, one of Pink Floyd's most recognisable, evoked Syd Barrett's lead-in guitar phrase on 'Astronomy Domine', played immediately after the introductory build-up. It was the perfect counterpoint to the melancholy lyrics. The vitriol of many of Waters' lyrics are offset by equally remorseful sentiments. The lyrics to 'Shine On You Crazy Diamond' are by turns clumsy and poignant, laudatory and condescending, reflecting the ambiguity of Waters' feelings about Barrett. Depending on the interpretation, the song can be seen as a message to Syd to get himself back together, or even as an apology. Waters states, 'Syd was seriously cut up by the winds that were wafting in through those early days of rock'n'roll. He was carved by it.'[47]

Of 5 June, Rick Wright said, 'I walked into the studio at Abbey Road, Roger was sitting, mixing at the desk, and I saw this big bald guy sitting on the couch behind. About sixteen stone: huge, bald, fat guy. And I didn't think anything of it. In those days it was quite normal for strangers to wander into our sessions. I thought, "He looks a bit . . . strange." Anyway, so I sat down with Roger at the desk and we worked for about ten minutes, and this guy kept on getting up and brushing his teeth and then sitting, doing really weird things, but keeping quiet. And I said to Roger, "Who is he?" and Roger said, "I don't know," and I said, "Well, I assumed he was a friend of yours," and he said, "No, I don't know who he is." Anyway, it took me a long time, and then suddenly I realised it was Syd, after maybe forty-five minutes. He came in as we were doing the vocals for "Shine On You Crazy Diamond", which was basically about Syd. He just for some incredible reason picked the very day that we were doing a song which was about him. It was a huge shock, because I hadn't seen him for about six years. He kept standing up and brushing his teeth, putting his toothbrush away and sitting down. Then at one point he stood up and said, "Right, when do I put my guitar on?" And of course he didn't have a guitar with him. And we said, "Sorry Syd, the guitar's all done." That's what's so incredibly . . . weird about this guy. And a bit disturbing, as well, particularly when you see a guy and you don't recognise him. And then for him to pick the very day we start putting vocals on a song about him. Very strange.[48] It was a real shock, because I hadn't seen him really since his breakdown when he was very good looking, and here was this huge bloated guy about sixteen stone.'[49]

David Gilmour said, 'This chap walked in and no one recognised him and we always argued about who spotted him first. I naturally think I did, no one really knows. And there was a point where people were nudging each other saying, "Bloody hell, that's Syd!" and no one recognised him at all.[50] He was very fat and he had a shaved head and shaved eyebrows and no one recognised him at all first off. There was just this strange person walking around the studio, sitting in the control room with us for hours. If anyone else told me this story, I'd find it hard to believe, that you could sit there with someone in a small room for hours, with a close friend of yours for years and years, and not recognise him. And I guarantee, no one in the band recognised him. Eventually, I had sussed it. And even knowing, you couldn't recognise him. He came two or three days and then he didn't come any more.'[51]

Jerry Shirley said, 'They were putting the finishing touches on *Wish You*

Were Here. Earlier that day Dave Gilmour had gotten married and they had to work that night, so EMI had this round-table dinner in the canteen for them. Across the table from me was this overweight Hare-Krishna-looking chap. I thought maybe it was just someone who somebody knows. I looked at Dave and he smiled; then I realised it was Syd. The guy had to weigh close to 200 pounds and had no hair on his head. It was a bit of a shock, but after a minute I plucked up enough courage to say hello. I introduced my wife and I don't know; I think he just laughed. I asked him what he was doing lately. "Oh, you know, not much: eating, sleeping. I get up, eat, go for a walk, sleep."'[52]

Andrew King, the Pink Floyd's ex-manager was also on hand that evening, and recognised Barrett. He was plainly shocked to see Barrett in such a sorry state; walking up to him he exclaimed, 'Good God, it's Syd! How did you get like that?' Barrett, in one of his classic rejoinders, responded, 'I've got a very large fridge in the kitchen and I've been eating a lot of pork chops.'

Roger Waters said, 'When he came to the *Wish You Were Here* sessions, ironic in itself, to see this great, fat, bald, mad person, the first day he came I was in fucking tears . . . Shine On You Crazy Diamond" was not really about Syd, he's just a symbol for all the extremes of absence some people have to indulge in because the only way they can cope with how fucking sad modern life is to withdraw completely. And I found that terribly sad. . .'[53] The band played the track back several times, looking for minute flaws in the vocal tracks. Barrett reportedly said, 'Why bother? You've heard it once already.'[54] When Waters played Barrett his tribute to him, the subject of the song didn't seem to register with Syd. 'When the song ended Roger Waters turned to Syd and said, Well, Syd what do you think of that?"' recalled Jerry Shirley. 'Syd said, Sounds a bit old." I believe Syd just got up and split not too long after that. After two years of nobody seeing him, of all the days for him to appear out of nowhere!'[55]

'It couldn't have happened without him,' Waters told French magazine *Rock et Folk*, 'but on the other hand it couldn't have gone on with him. I wanted Shine On You Crazy Diamond" to get as close as possible to what I felt . . . that sort of indefinable, inevitable melancholy about the disappearance of Syd. Because he's left, withdrawn so far away that, as far as we're concerned, he's no longer there. Syd wore out his welcome with random precision.'

The romantic image of insanity is so far removed from its banal, dull reality. Madness is a sad, grim business. Loss of control is hardly romantic. Instead of bringing a release from reality it becomes a more complex trap. The overwhelming overload of sensation rendered Barrett's reflective capacities paralysed. The insight and heightened perception of his genius was squandered in the mire of mental illness. Roger Barrett walked out of the studios, down the steps, across the gravel driveway, past the guards at the gate and down Abbey Road for the last time, shopping bag in hand. He walked to the tube station, descended below and returned home to Cambridge, leaving the illusory apparition known as 'Syd Barrett' behind.*

---

1 Schaeffner, Nicholas. *Saucerful Of Secrets*. Delta. 1991
2 'Syd Barrett Careening Through Life'. Kris DiLorenzo, Trouser Press, February 1978
3 Watkinson, Mike & Anderson, Pete. *Crazy Diamond: Syd Barrett And The Dawn Of Pink Floyd*. Omnibus Press, 1993. p. 102
4 *NME*, 13 April 1974
5 Rock, Mick. *A Photographic Record*, Century 22 Limited, 1995
6 *Beat Instrumental*, 1971
7 *Melody Maker*, 31 January 1971
8 *Beat Instrumental*, 1971
9 'Syd Barrett Careening Through Life'. Kris DiLorenzo, *Trouser Press*, February 1978
10 *Melody Maker*, 19 May 1973
11 *Melody Maker*, 31 January 1970
12 Schaffner, Nicholas. *Saucerful Of Secrets*. Delta, 1991
13 *NME*, 13 April 1974
14 'Syd Barrett Careening Through Life'. Kris DiLorenzo, *Trouser Press*, February 1978
15 Giovanni Dadomo interview with Syd Barrett, 1970
16 Ibid.
17 Miles & Mabbett, Andy. *Pink Floyd: The Visual Documentary*. Omnibus Press, London 1994
18 *Terrapin* 4, 1975
19 *Beat Instrumental*, 1971
20 Watkinson, Mike & Anderson, Pete. *Crazy Diamond: Syd Barrett And The Dawn Of Pink Floyd*. Omnibus Press, 1993
21 *Rolling Stone*, December 1971
22 *Melody Maker*, 31 January 1971
23 *Rolling Stone*, December 1971
24 Giovanni Dadomo interview with Syd Barrett, 1970
25 *Melody Maker*, 31 January 1971
26 *Ibid.*
27 *Rolling Stone*, December 1971
28 *Beat Instrumental*, 1971
29 Schaffner, Nicholas. *Saucerful Of Secrets*. Delta, 1991
30 'Syd Barrett Careening Through Life'. Kris DiLorenzo, *Trouser Press*, February 1978
31 'Syd Barrett Careening Through Life'. Kris DiLorenzo, *Trouser Press*, February 1978
32 Miles & Mabbett, Andy. *Pink Floyd: The Visual Documentary*. Omnibus Press, London 1994
33 Schaffner, Nicholas. *Saucerful Of Secrets*. Delta, 1991
34 *NME*, 13 April 1974
35 'Syd Barrett Careening Through Life'. Kris DiLorenzo, *Trouser Press*, February 1978
36 *NME*, 13 April 1974
37 'Syd Barrett Careening Through Life'. Kris DiLorenzo, *Trouser Press*, February 1978
38 Greene, Jonathan. *Days In The Life: Voices From The English Underground, 1961-1971*. Minerva, 1988
39 Ibid.
40 '*The Pink Floyd Story*': Six-part documentary broadcast on Capital radio, London. December 1976-

*Barrett's sister Rosemary, in an interview published in Luca Ferrari's *A Fish Out Of Water*, had a different view of her brother's EMI visit on 5 June. She said that Syd was actually joking, and that everything from the white outfit to the shaved head and eyebrows was actually meant in jest. Judging by Barrett's humorous comments on that day, the theory is plausible. Maybe the madcap laughs at all of us, especially at authors who write wordy books about him!

January 1977
41 Ibid.
42 Macdonald, Bruno, editor. *Pink Floyd: Through The Eyes Of...* Sidgwick & Jackson, London, 1996
43 Schaffner, Nicholas. *Saucerful Of Secrets*. Delta, 1991
44 *NME*, 13 April 1974
45 Unedited transcripts of interviews with Peter Jenner. Greene, Jonathan. *Days In The Life: Voices From The English Underground, 1961-1971*. Minerva, 1988
46 '*The Pink Floyd Story*': Six-part documentary broadcast on Capital radio, London. December 1976-January 1977.
47 *The Amazing Pudding*, # 58
48 'Shades of Pink,' interviews with Charlie Kendall, Source. 1984
49 *Omnibus* special on Pink Floyd, 1994
50 Ibid.
51 *Musician*, November 1982
52 'Syd Barrett Careening Through Life'. Kris DiLorenzo, *Trouser Press*, February 1978
53 '*The Pink Floyd Story*': Six-part documentary broadcast on Capital radio, London. December 1976-January 1977
54 Schaffner, Nicholas. *Saucerful Of Secrets*. Delta, 1991
55 'Syd Barrett Careening Through Life'. Kris DiLorenzo, *Trouser Press*, February 1978

Stage Seven: 'And the Seventh Brings Return . . .' (February 1975 to the present day)

'Walking in the midst of others, one returns alone, and so follows the right way. The idea of a turning point arises from the fact that after the dark lines have pushed all of the light line upward and out of the hexagram, another light enters the hexagram from below. The time of darkness is past. The winter solstice brings the victory of light. After a time of decay comes the turning point. The powerful light that has been banished returns. There is movement but it is not brought about by force . . . the movement is natural, arising spontaneously.'

Chapter 24: Fu/Return – The Turning Point
The I Ching or Book Of Changes

Great interest arose about Barrett, ironically much of it after he had ceased recording and retreated into exile. One of the mysterious attractions of the Barrett story lies in the fact that he withdrew from the world. He has become a mythical figure because his withdrawal was complete, reminiscent of Arthur Rimbaud renouncing poetry to become a gun-runner in Ethiopia. For better or for worse, Syd is seen as a romantic figure, his 'madness' an element of his myth.

But David Gilmour for one has no illusions about Barrett. 'It's sad that these people think he's such a wonderful subject, that he's a living legend when, in fact, there is this poor sad man who can't deal with life or himself,' said Gilmour. 'He's got uncontrollable things in him that he can't deal with and people think it's a marvellous, wonderful, romantic thing. It's just a sad, sad thing, a very nice and talented person who's just disintegrated. Syd's story is a sad story romanticised by people who don't know anything about it. They've made it fashionable but it's just not that way.'[1]

'I mentioned the Syd Barrett Appreciation Society to Syd once,' said Peter Barnes. 'He just said it was OK, you know. He wasn't interested in any of it. It's ironic. I suppose, he's much bigger now as the silent cult-figure doing nothing than he was when he was functioning.'[2] Roger Waters, certainly one of the greatest Syd enthusiasts himself, however saw no harm in it. 'If your hobby is to be interested in . . . whether Syd did this or did that, or what colour shoes he wore on 18 March 1967 or whatever, who am I to say that's obsessive? Some people collect stamps! It's better than watching TV, in my view. Being a Syd Barrett fan seems to me to be a perfectly legitimate and reasonable way of spending your spare time. He was a very interesting man. He wrote some fantastic songs. There's a body of work; unfortunately it's complete. There won't be any more, I don't think.'[3]

Syd's various nieces and nephews would sometimes visit their grandmother at Hills Road. One of them was Ian Barrett. 'When I was growing up I never really knew him at all, as whenever we visited the house we would visit my grandmother, and he would stay in his room and we'd hardly ever see him. All I knew was that he wasn't very well and liked to be alone. I had no concept that he might be famous for quite some time and never knew any details about what he might have gone through until I was a teenager, really.'[4]

Barrett stopped playing music, and took up painting again. In 1971, he had remarked, 'I'm a painter, I was trained as a painter . . . I seem to have spent a little less time painting than I might've done . . . you know, it might have been a tremendous release getting absorbed in painting. Anyway, I've been sitting about and writing . . . I think of me being a painter eventually.'[5] Barrett was in a process of returning to his former self, before he had left Cambridge, before he had taken acid, really.

Pink Floyd, on the other hand, ascended to mass stardom, playing stadia in America accompanied by an ever-expanding light show and assortment of special effects and props. Their music changed in focus as well: 'We stopped trying to make overtly "spacey" music and trip people out in that way in the sixties,' said David Gilmour. 'But that image hangs on and we can't seem to get shot of it.'[6] Like the albatross round the damned sailor's neck in Coleridge's epic poem 'The Rime Of The Ancient Mariner', the Pink Floyd were dogged by their reputation as a 'drug band'. By the mid-seventies, the Floyd themselves were tired of this image. 'We don't want people to be stoned out of their minds all the time when they go to hear us,' said Roger Waters. 'We'd like to induce an experience without drugs. Anyone is free to have that kind of experience.'[7]

As Pink Floyd were finishing up sessions for the 1977 *Animals* album, a young malcontent named John Lydon walked down the King's Road wearing a T-shirt with the Pink Floyd logo on it. Above it he had scrawled in black marker, 'I HATE'. Soon after, under the aegis of Malcolm McLaren, he was rechristened Johnny Rotten and was shouting out taut three-minute rants against Queen, country and the hippie excesses of the previous years. Punk was born, drawing from such disparate sources as the Stooges, the Flies, the New York Dolls and the Ramones, not forgetting bands like the Creation or Syd's Floyd. Rick Wright said, 'I thought punk was good because it bought me back to the UFO Club days. At last I thought there was something that had come along and was really pushing the boundaries. Unfortunately, I didn't like the music, but I liked the whole movement and people like Malcolm McLaren and Vivienne Westwood. I was quite flattered when the Floyd were criticised by some of the punk bands [laughs], but it didn't bother me.'[8]

In summer 1977, Barrett was back living at the Chelsea Cloisters, and Gayla Pinion, his one-time fiancée, paid him a brief visit. Though Syd was in good spirits, she felt oppressed by the dingy state of the flat; its darkness and stale smell of complacency, and fled while Syd fixing up some tea in the kitchen. He must have emerged with the cups of tea and staring at the open door wonder what he'd done wrong.[9]

Writer Kris DiLorenzo in 1978 wrote a lengthy analysis of Barrett's life and times in American magazine *Trouser Press*. It's the best piece written on Barrett and well worth seeking out. DiLorenzo seemed to be the first writer to articulate what makes Barrett's music so compelling. Publicist Bryan Morrison told DiLorenzo, 'Syd had psychiatric problems and was actually in a sanatorium. He doesn't have any involvement with anything or anybody. He is a recluse, with about twenty-five guitars around him. I see him very rarely. I mean, I know where he is, but he doesn't want to be bothered; he just sits there on his own, watching television all day and getting fat. That's what he does.'[10]

Susie Wynne-Wilson took Barrett to see the Master Charan Singh Ji at a Sant Mat meeting in Cambridge in the late seventies, in what Nicholas Schaffner referred to as an attempt to repair the damage done by Barrett's rejection ten years previously. Jenny Gordon says that she understood Barrett attended two meetings, sitting quietly in the aisle. Unfortunately, he was recognised by a fan and promptly fled.[11]

On 30 November 1979, Pink Floyd released *The Wall*, a double album with the bulk of music and lyrics written by Roger Waters. The album consisted of roughly three movements, all interwoven to form a compelling, if bleak, masterpiece. The first movement is part elegy for Roger Waters' father , Eric Fletcher Waters, whose senseless death at the beach-head in Anzio shaped much of Waters' world view, and part melancholy meditation of his unhappy schooling and loneliness as a child. Full orchestrations are contrasted with plaintive acoustic songs detailing the alienation and sadness Waters felt both from his father's death and his childhood. The second movement is a caustic rock analysis of the bitter travails of fame and success, as Pink Floyd, the archetypal rock star retreats into isolation and madness. Waters combined his own experiences, and vignettes from other rock performers' lives, such as Roy Harper [a popular seventies folk-rocker; he sang vocals on 'Have A Cigar' on *Wish You Were*

Here], with a harrowing depiction of Syd Barrett's own downfall. In the third movement, Waters constructs a mini-opera in the style of composer Kurt Weill's and poet/writer Bertolt Brecht's *The Threepenny Opera* to explore the links between rock'n'roll and fascism. The band performed a series of monumental shows where an enormous wall, each brick symbolising the fictional character Pink's growing alienation, frustration and despair, was constructed across the stage, obscuring the band. It was the high mark of Waters' theatrical ambitions, which he had been building on since those far-off days of the Games Fof May concert in May 1967. In 1982, a film adaptation of the work was released, with Bob Geldof.

June Bolan said, 'I was absolutely shell-shocked; it was so close to Syd I couldn't bear it. When Pink was looking in that bathroom mirror and shaving himself, I just had tears, and was sitting rigid in the cinema, because it was ever so close to home; I could feel for Syd totally.'[12]

Roger Waters said, '"Comfortably Numb" is actually about the kind of living death condition that a lot of people find themselves in when life seems unreal to them and they can't work out why. I remember having a fever when I was a child and characterising the recurrent feeling of numbness . . . it's not numbness exactly. The thing about that delirium is that you can't put your finger on it . . . you can't describe the feeling using words. It's a feeling that I think you get when you're going crazy, probably: that everything suddenly is wrong. "My hands felt like two balloons": that doesn't adequately describe the feeling of everything being too big or too small or too . . . something. Everything is wrong . . . For Syd, it must have felt very like that . . . Apart from the tangible, explainable manifestations of schizophrenia, like hearing voices and all that stuff . . . there's the discomfort of everything not being right. It must be almost beyond bearing. . .'[13]

Peter Jenner, among others, wasn't as impressed with the breadth of *The Wall*, 'I really don't want to hear about him and his whinging on about how his Dad died and his guilt feelings about Syd. He's just done that over and over again.'[14]

During the early eighties, Mike Watkinson and Pete Anderson tell us in *Crazy Diamond*, Barrett spent time in a sanatorium in Essex. His nephew Ian said, 'I remember going to visit Rog in some sort of rehabilitation home out in the country and going for a walk with him through some woods, but I didn't have any idea what he might be in there for. All I remember is that the house looked quite scary.'[15]

By the summer of 1982, Barrett was doing well enough to return to London for a final brief stay at the Chelsea Cloisters. Watkinson and Anderson noted that Barrett had lost his excess weight after an operation for a stomach ulcer, and had grown his hair long again, albeit a bit balding on the top. However, this was his last oscillation between London and Cambridge, and he only stayed a few weeks before returning home to Cambridge. He was home to stay.[16]

In 1983, two French reporters from *Actuel* magazine set out to find the legendary Madcap. All they found at the Chealsea Cloisters, their first stop, was a bag of laundry Barrett had left behind. Contriving to return it to Barrett in an effort to meet him, they went to Hills Road and rang the bell. A very plain man in his mid-thirties opened the door, dressed unassumingly in jumper and jeans, hair short-cropped and thinning. Only the penetrating eyes hinted that this man had once been anything more than a suburban burgher. Barrett thanked them for the laundry, but seemed to get noticeably jumpy when he realised the reporters knew who he was. They told Barrett that his friends in London missed him and wished him well, for which he thanked them. With his mother calling him from the garden to come meet her friends, Barrett made his excuses and bade the reporters goodbye, politely but firmly shutting the door. Barrett would sometimes be spotted around town, going to the market or to buy art supplies. Most locals wouldn't have even known who he was, and if they did, they knew better than to pester him.

In 1988 *Opel,* an album's worth of out-takes and unreleased Syd solo tracks was issued. David Gilmour said, 'I've listened to *Opel* and there's nothing on there that really illuminates very much or gives very much to anyone. I didn't approve of it, personally, but it's not my choice.'[17]

Roger Waters said in 1992, 'I haven't seen Syd for ten years . . . more than ten years probably. I don't know what went wrong with Syd because I'm not an expert on schizophrenia. Syd was extraordinarily charming and attractive and alive and talented, but whatever happened to him, happened to him.'[18] Waters would tire of having Syd Barrett brought up in every interview he did. His own view of Barrett always seemed to oscillate between disdain and admiration, emotional involvement and distance. He said in 1975, 'I'm very sad about Syd, I wasn't for years. For years I suppose he was a threat because of all that bollocks written about him and us. Of course he was very important and the band would never have fucking started without him because he was writing all the material. It couldn't have happened without him but on the other hand it could not have gone on with him. He may or may not be important in rock'n'roll anthology terms but he's certainly not nearly as important as people say in terms of Pink Floyd. So I think I was threatened by him.'[19]

David Gilmour noted his contact with Syd during the eighties was limited to a 'bit of checking on whether his money was getting to him properly. I asked Rose, his sister, whether I could go and see him. But she didn't think it was a good idea, because things that remind him of that period of his past tend to depress him. If he sees me or other people from that period, he gets depressed for a couple of weeks. It's not really worth it.[20] I know people who have seen him recently. He's quite reasonable, I understand.[21] I'm in second-hand contact with his relatives in Cambridge, who give me reports on how he's doing from time to time. He's not mentally OK, but he gets by. He manages, he lives, he takes his clothes to the Laundromat to get them cleaned. I'm actually very tempted to visit him. He was a wonderful talent and friend.'[22]

Rick Wright said, 'We don't see him, because apparently if he's ever reminded of Pink Floyd and when he was in it, he goes into a depression for weeks on end. His mother asked us to stay away a few years ago. Apparently, most of the time he's quite happy, or was, but our faces can trigger off a lapse. Would it have always happened or was it because of a huge overdose of acid? Who knows? I suspect it was a bit of both. All I know is one week he was fine and a week later he turned up again and was completely different. It's just a terrible tragedy.'[23]

The *News Of The World* sent a reporter to track down Barrett. In an article that encapsulates the very worst of the interest in the 'Syd Barrett myth', the reporter noted that Barrett, photographed taking out his rubbish, 'looked like a dirty tramp'.

An EP of Barrett's *Peel Session* was also released. Clive Selwood of Strange Fruit Records said, 'It was difficult to find Syd, but once I'd found his brother, who handles his business, that was fine . . . We also had to have the approval, as we always do, of the other musicians involved. We had to track down Jerry Shirley, who was then working with the new version of Badfinger in the States, and also ask Dave Gilmour. I understand that Syd himself is alive and quite well, has a happy life, spends a lot of time working in the garden and has a decent income from his songwriting royalties. So he's probably got a better life than any of us!'[24]

His nephew Ian said, 'While it would be wonderful if Roger was able to cope with family events and parties, he doesn't enjoy socialising and finds it very disturbing to be around large groups of people. Saying that, he has visited my previous home in Luton several times; just for the day; and in the early eighties he visited us for Christmas which was lovely. I received an electronic game that you can play tunes on as a gift and I have a vivid memory of sitting with him on the sofa and teaching him how to play little tunes and games on the toy! Unfortunately no primitive renditions of "See Emily Play" were forthcoming that afternoon.'[25]

On 27 October 1988, Syd's brother-in-law, Paul Breen, was interviewed by BBC Radio One. Breen stated that Roger Barrett pursued 'a very ordinary sort of life-style. He doesn't play any musical instruments any more. He's not interested in writing music. He's started to develop an interest, yet again, in painting, which was originally his main interest back in the early sixties.' As for the sixties, 'I think it's part of his life which he prefers to forget now. He had some bad experiences, and, thankfully, has come through all the worst of these, and is now able, fortunately, to lead a normal life in Cambridge. There's a level of contentment now which he probably hasn't felt since before he got involved in music, in fact. He is developing new interests and particularly his painting, which has progressed as the years go by.'

Ian Barrett said, 'Over the past few years I and the rest of my family have felt on meeting him that he is definitely starting to find a sense of contentment that has eluded him since his breakdown. He is happy to just potter about at home; watching TV and doing a bit of painting or reading. Having a conversation with Roger isn't the same as one with most people as he does have quite a strange and fragmented way of speaking; so everyday things come out sounding quite abstract; but it all has its own internal logic and it's just his way of expressing himself. If people still want to think that Roger is this wild lunatic he was supposed to be in the sixties (even though I'm sure much of this was complete invention) then they are welcome to; but I feel that this is a disservice to his contribution to music and him as a human being, and is also a very lazy way to view the situation. What really makes me sick about the media attention of Roger's career is the way he is written off as a madman – a rock genius who was just such a crazed madcap that there is no need to worry about the extent of pain and anguish he went through in the years directly after the band became successful. Without going into details, I don't think people are prepared to understand the true extent of Roger's breakdown or the pressures he was put under.'[26]

On 30 September 1991 Roger Barrett's mother Winifred died at home, aged eighty-six. Roger was, in all likelihood, deeply saddened, but perhaps could rationalise his mother's death as being in the normal course of life, whereas his father's death had been unexpected and a major trauma. Ian Barrett said, 'Roger has lived alone since his mother, my grandmother, died a few years ago.'[27] He left Hills Road for a small house in suburban Cambridge.

Rick Wright said, 'Just listen to Syd's songs, the imagination he had. If he hadn't had this complete breakdown, he could easily be one of the greatest songwriters today. I think it's one of the saddest stories in rock'n'roll, what happened to Syd. He was brilliant, and such a nice guy.[28] I do think about him, I think about when we started, and I have a fantasy, I would love for Syd to walk in my room and say, "I'm ready to play in the band again."'[29] In 1995, Wright commented, 'Now we have become a lot more professional and we don't take risks like we used to. Today we could put a show on, pretend we were there and not be and probably no one would know. For me, one day I'd like to go full circle.[30] I'm still very aware of what we were doing back in the late sixties. We were very experimental and, because we were, we were playing a lot of bad things too; I mean, not good music. On the other hand, I sometimes miss that. What we do is very good, but it's not pushing boundaries as much as we used to.'[31] It's strange to think how far the Pink Floyd have travelled from their experimental early days at the Spontaneous Underground and All Saints' Hall.

Rick Wright said, 'The late sixties was a purely experimental time in the band's history. But it was a learning process. By the seventies we'd consolidated ourselves and we knew what we could do: what we could write, what we could play. *Dark Side Of The Moon* and *Wish You Were Here* was a very enjoyable time.[32] Nick Mason said, 'Syd was a major talent as a songwriter and maybe could have been as a musician. He hasn't done anything for years. And consequently, people who don't entirely achieve all their potential become even more legendary.'[33]

Roger Waters said in 1987, 'I last saw him about ten years ago. But my mother still lives in Cambridge and I get to hear about him from time to time. He's not doing very much at all.[34] He was a visionary, he was an extraordinary musician, he started Pink Floyd . . . well, Syd and I started the band together but if he hadn't been there, nothing would have happened. I'd be working for an architect . . . I might be my own boss by now, I probably would, but I wouldn't be doing the work that I'm doing, I don't think. He was the key that unlocked the door to rock'n'roll for me.'[35]

On his solo *Radio KAOS* tour, Roger Waters screened the old 'Arnold Layne' film clip during the intermission, at the end of which he would tell the audience, 'The great Syd Barrett, lest we forget'. Waters also confessed to singing Barrett's 'Bike' and 'Dark Globe' in the bath. Waters said, 'What was so stunning about Syd's songs was, through the whimsy and the crazy juxtaposition of ideas and words, there was a very powerful grasp of humanity. They were quintessentially human songs and that is what I've always attempted to aspire to. In that sense, I feel a strong connection to him.'[36]

During their 1994 tour, Pink Floyd opened their shows with Barrett's 'Astronomy Domine'. Gilmour told *Guitar World*, 'It wasn't a conscious decision to pay homage to Syd. We've probably paid homage to him quite enough [laughs]. We basically just wanted to widen the spectrum a little . . . find something we haven't done before. "Astronomy Domine" just struck us as being a very good opening number. It's fun to go back and do that.' Gilmour adds, 'It needed a bit of dusting, I don't think we'd played it since 1968.'[37] It was a thrill to hear the band perform the song live, Gilmour playing the leads with a decidedly more bluesy, fluid feel. A comparison between the original and the live track on *Pulse* is a telling commentary on both the similarities and differences in their respective styles Nick Mason said, '"Astronomy Domine" was chosen as a tribute to Syd, who continues to be an inspiration to us.'[38]

Gilmour said, 'Syd was fantastic, a great guy, but the Pink Floyd he was in was a completely different band to the one that came afterwards. If people say we weren't the same after Syd left, fair enough. The first album was English whimsy at its best, with large slices of psychedelia thrown in, but it bears very little resemblance to anything we've tried to do since.[39] The importance of Syd in the modern-day Floyd is vastly over-emphasised. I don't think it's nearly as important a thing as people seem to think. However, he was a fantastic talent.[40] In the beginning the songs were all Syd's and they were brilliant. No one disputes that. But I don't think the actual sound of the whole band stems from Syd. It stems just as much from Rick.'[41]

While the Pink Floyd's later music, post-Syd, is often discussed as being diametrically opposed to their earlier Barrett-led experimental wanderings, it isn't necessarily true. To this day, when Mason, Gilmour and Wright convene on Gilmour's Astoria houseboat studio, long jams ensue, which are gleaned for material to use in more structured songs. Actual elements of Barrett's 'sound' may not be present in the later Pink Floyd's work, but the spirit is there; and that the band feel compelled to deny Barrett's influence is unfortunate. On Pink Floyd's 'The Division Bell', Gilmour and co-writer Polly Samson paid tribute to both Waters and Barrett on the track 'Poles Apart', lamenting the breakdown of communication that is a theme throughout the album.

David Gilmour said, 'I don't know, maybe if he was left to his own devices, he might just get it together. But it's a tragedy, a great tragedy because the guy was an innovator. One of the three or four greats along with Dylan. I know though that something is wrong because Syd isn't happy, and that really is the criteria, isn't it? But then it's all part of being a legend in your own lifetime.[42] Syd was one of the great rock'n'roll tragedies. He was one of the most talented people and could have given a fantastic amount. He really could write songs and if he had stayed right, could have beaten Ray Davies at his own game.'[43]

Roger Waters said, 'Replacing Syd as leader of the Pink Floyd was OK. But Syd as a writer was a one-off. I could never aspire to Syd's crazed insights and perceptions. In fact for a long time I wouldn't have dreamt of claiming any insights whatsoever. I'll always credit Syd with the connection he made between his personal unconscious and the collective group unconscious. It's taken me fifteen years to get anywhere near there. But what enabled Syd to see things in the way he did? It's like why is an artist an artist? Artists simply do feel and see things in a different way to other people. In a way it's a blessing, but it can also be a terrible curse. There's a great deal of satisfaction to be earned from it but often it's also a terrible burden. Even though he was clearly out of control when he was making his two solo albums, some of the work is staggeringly evocative. Dave Gilmour and I worked with him on *The Madcap Laughs*, there was a backlog of material he'd written before he flipped. It's the humanity of it all that's so impressive. It's about deeply felt values and beliefs. Maybe that's what *Dark Side Of The Moon* was aspiring to. A similar feeling.[44] I dreamt about him only last night. It was in the open and he was still gone, but I sat down and talked to him and it felt good. He was still saying things I wasn't in a position to understand, but I was supporting him and he was accepting it. We were both happy.'[45]

'He seems reasonably content,' said Mason, 'but he's certainly not able to function really and he can't be put back to work. There's a million people out there who would love to see Syd do another album, come back and all that. I just think that it's quite beyond him.'[46] Or, more likely, Barrett is beyond it.

Jenny Fabian said, 'I prefer to remember him as this white, thin, violet-eyed nutter who didn't speak much and who wrote wonderful songs. I knew the others but they were absolutely nothing at all compared to him. His words and his music were the Pink Floyd and I've never been interested in them since. Nothing ever reached the heights of that first album which was mad and mysterious – like him.'[47]

The lines of 'Scarecrow' seem prescient now: 'But now he's resigned to his fate, 'cos life's not unkind, he doesn't mind.' When asked in a 1971 interview if people still remembered him, Barrett simply replied, 'Yes, I should think so.'[48]

Space, ultimately, is silence. A complete void, a vacuum devoid of sound. Syd's music was subsumed by this silence, so absolute that his hands were stilled, with only the odd aftershock animating his eyes and ears. Something severed Barrett's mooring, and the apparition known as Syd Barrett was lost in a starless atmosphere. Syd's playing, frozen like prehistoric insects fossilised in amber, leaps out at the listener thirty years on. It's a very pure distillation of an intensely creative individual who lost his mastery; 'So strange and beautiful and new' laments Kenneth Grahame's Mole, and the sentiment is all too true when listening to these frozen ideas. The sheer fervour with which Syd's musical explorations are carried forth bring to mind Vaslav Nijinksy's diaries, written during the feverish twilight months as he descended into irrevocable madness, silence and incoherence. 'I want to finish this book before I die,' wrote Nijinsky, in frantic scrawl, speaking not of physical death but that of his formidable, sensitive and unschooled mind. A similar urgency suffuses such Syd Barrett songs as 'No Good Trying', where he stated unequivocally, 'When I live I die'. Like Arthur Rimbaud or Nijinsky, Barrett absolved himself of what he had become.

Fame, acid, the uneven seesaw between his art and music and EMI's commerce, all conspired to send a streak of turbulence through Syd's mind. Augmented by tremendous doses of LSD, this growing turbulence left Syd plainly shaken. The pressures of sudden fame, intense drug abuse, his artistic conflict with commercialism, his desire to surpass himself at every gig, was too much for Syd at twenty-one; he never recovered. It was no joke, it was terror to those who couldn't weather the downside of sudden adulation.*

Roger Barrett had to detach himself from his past traumas, discarding the identity of 'Syd' on the road home. After he had withdrawn to the sanctuary of the old house in Cambridge, he refused to discuss his past any more. 'The past isn't something Rog ever talks about,' said his nephew Ian. It's all too easy to romanticise Barrett's leap into the unknown, while not seeing how whatever he found in the unknown left him bereft of his sanity, leaving him a shadow of his former self.

David Gale said, 'Syd went out to lunch and never came back, he's taken the

*To this day, Scott Walker, a contemporary of Syd's, suffers from the trauma of his own fame in the mid sixties, when he was physically injured repeatedly by overzealous fans who screamed relentlessly and tore at his hair and clothing, sometimes leaving him badly bruised. He prefers to live apart from the bizarre machinations of fame as well.

longest lunch of any of us. And is still out there. In theory, Syd should even now be reclaimable. People have tried and he's always shunned it. It's quite possible that LSD taken in massive, repeated doses does something that produces schizophrenia-like symptoms. It's possible that something gets permanently rewired. I don't know if it could be called brain damage, or what we should understand by that term, does it mean that the cells in the brain are actually destroyed, or does it mean that the neurochemistry has been personally altered for so long that it can no longer find its correct levels any more. Clearly, whatever is happening in Syd's brain, whether it has to do with serotonin levels, or, in a more Freudian reading, he was confronted with contents of his own subconscious that he found he couldn't face, we will never know.

'I haven't seen him in decades, all I've heard are rumours. There's a bald, tubby man living not uncomfortably financially because of his royalties. The Floyd are quite careful to ensure that he gets the right money. He was definitely a sixties casualty, and the sun went in, really, and never ever came out again. From being a sunny, delightful young guy to a dark, troubled, brooding, potentially violent casualty. Whether or not you would call it schizophrenia is highly debatable. Laing contended that schizophrenia was a process that should be encouraged to unravel in its fullness, and it was a healing process. If you did the right thing to the right kind of people, had enough time and sympathy, they could actually take a person through the process and back again.'

There are those who endlessly pine for Syd Barrett to return to music, but there is no sense in him doing this. Syd freaks idly wait for their Piper at the Gates of Dawn to come back. In April 1992, Atlantic Records allegedly offered Barrett £75,000 to record his poetry, acoustic strumming or basically anything he had in mind. In their high-minded beneficence, Atlantic even gave him the chance to record in his living-room with musicians of their choosing.[49] There are parallels with the story of Brian Wilson, who was endlessly resuscitated throughout the seventies and eighties to little effect. On several occasions, advertisements were taken out in the music press by his label Capitol announcing the 'return' of Brian Wilson, when Wilson was plainly incapable of performing or writing at anything close to his mid-sixties peak. Eventually, all the well intentioned desire for Barrett to return to music reveals itself as the parasitism it truly is. There is still money to made off of the ghost of what was once Syd Barrett. He remains a commodity.

Ian Barrett said, 'I always think it's amazing that there is still such a huge interest in Roger's works after all this time, and I never fail to be amazed at the strange stories people tell me about what they've heard he's been up to all these years. The reality is that Rog is a lot happier now than he has been for a hell of a long time and while not as stable and sociable as most people might seem, he's found a peace he's not had for a long time, if ever.'[50]

The humane thing would be to leave Barrett alone; anyone who understands his story would rather have Roger Keith Barrett potter happily away in the Cambridge garden of the home he moved to after the death of his mother than be dragged bodily back into the limelight for another ill-starred go on-stage. Barrett was eaten, body soul and mind, by the machine and wisely chooses to remain far from its nefarious workings. To be stalked by photographers and Syd-freaks must be an enormous trial to Roger Barrett. His connection with the apparition known as 'Syd' is, by now, tenuous at best.

Ian Barrett, one of the handful of people to have seen him in the past years, said, 'The past isn't something Rog ever discusses. Roger does have a little record player, but he's only got a few records and tapes and they're mainly of classical concerts. He really isn't very interested in music any more. He does have an acoustic guitar which I assume he strums to himself, but I've never heard him play it. Rog doesn't care one little bit about the past and is so removed now from the glamour and excitement of the showbiz world he once longed for, that I'm sure it confuses him that anyone else would care so much that he sung a few songs and played a bit of guitar in the sixties.'[51]

'The one thing I'd really like to say to people wanting to visit Roger and see how he is, is please DON'T!!!' pleaded Ian. 'I know many fans are genuinely very caring and are interested in his well-being; but he really doesn't enjoy having people knock on his door virtually every day wanting to wish him well. PLEASE leave him in peace to get on with his life happily. I can reassure anyone concerned that he really is happy and content, and he'd be more so if he didn't have to awkwardly meet fans hanging outside the house and nervously knocking on his door. To this end I'd appreciate it if anyone reading this who knows his [new] address would refrain from publicising it further. Please don't tell people where he lives. Surely everyone has the right to a bit of privacy and peace and quiet? If Roger was still involved in the music business then he would be more fair game for a lack of privacy; but as it is, he hasn't made a record for over *twenty* years! Please show him some consideration and leave him in peace. I know that Roger is touched by all the concern of his fans but he'd be much happier if you simply let him get on with his life undisturbed.[52]

'He simply isn't interested in going back over a time in his life that precipitated his breakdown and retreat from society. The whole Floyd time is so long ago that he simply wants to be left in peace to get on with his painting and reading.'[53] Ian noted that Roger paints often, 'He likes to explore different kinds of painting; and I've seen various different styles of work. Lately he's been very interested in geometric patterns and repeated shapes; the kind of things you might see on tiles or in weaving. I've seen abstracts in oils, naturalistic watercolours, wood-block work. I haven't talked in depth about painting with him; so I couldn't give you any detailed information about what he's trying to achieve. In the last few years he's been writing a book, purely for his own enjoyment; about the history of art, tracing its development through history. I haven't read it, and before you ask I very much doubt he would ever want it published;

but he's used a word processor to put it together; and I assume it's brought him a lot of pleasure.'[54]

Those sixties voyagers who were spiritually inclined forsook the false spirituality of LSD for a drug-free pursuit of consciousness expansion.

Nigel and Jenny Gordon went to Dera, and, like Paul Charrier before them, were irrevocably changed. They follow the Path of the Enlightened masters to this day, and it has brought them a sense of inner peace and well-being that acid simply couldn't provide.

Hoppy said, 'I went to AMM's Eddie Prevost's fiftieth birthday party at the October Gallery, and the soprano sax player, Evan Parker, played for fifteen minutes without a break. Fifteen minutes of continuous sound, like water falling. And that, with Eddie, was amazing. I walked around with a bunch of flowers, giving them to everyone.'

Fortunately, the spark that illuminates a remarkable person can never be crushed. Today Hoppy remains involved in the Underground. He and a friend who is wheelchair-bound frequently go out to clubs, where Hoppy's chum does graceful movements on the dancefloor to drums'n'bass, or gabba or whatever is on the sound system. 'If you are dancing to some music and like it, it doesn't matter what it is. It may turn out to be techno or trance, but it depends on what my body tells me when I'm dancing. The DJs have it together and if it's the music that I like, then it's fine.'

Jenny Gordon recalls the sixties, 'Those times were happy, because there was a lot of love between us all. If it hadn't been for that . . . There were jealousies and all sorts of things, but actually there was a lot of love. Recently a lot of us met up again at David Gilmour's fiftieth birthday party and there was a tremendous love and warmth between us. I remember that time very fondly, and don't regret it. It was wild and I don't think we were very moral, but it was great. And there was that tremendous love between us, a great camaraderie. And love always wins through. It was quite wild, but it was good, yes. Risky business, lucky to survive it. A lot of people didn't make it.

'There was Johnny Johnson, who completely lost it. He jumped out of the window, twice. The first time, he became crippled, and the second time he killed himself. Then there was Pip Carter, Imo's friend, he was murdered. Pip Carter was a heroin user and was in a Turkish jail for two years. Ponji Scofield, who came from a very academic family in Cambridge, threw himself in front of a tube train. And there was Julian Puck, who just recently died; he became manic-depressive and alcoholic, and stumbled across the road and was killed . . . William Pryor became a junkie very early on, in 1964, when he was still at university, so he was a bit out of it. Pete Downing also, who became a bit of a tramp, in and out of prison. Like Syd, I would see him wandering the streets of Cambridge. So there were a lot of casualties.'

Ian Barrett said, 'I have no idea what Rog's views on drugs are now; but I don't really think it takes too much imagination to work out what his viewpoint might be after all he went through because of them.'[55]

Jenny said, 'I've seen Syd a lot in the last two years, though not recently because he's been ill. He's just very ordinary and middle-aged now. I did try to speak to him once at the gardening centre, and I just said, "Syd, it's Jenny!" and he just sort of said, "Oh yes . . . yeah, yeah." I used to see him nearly every week in the town or in the supermarket. I'd find that I was standing next to him without even realising it. But there was that barrier there and I couldn't speak to him. I felt so loving towards him but he just doesn't want to be loved. But that's just the way he wants to be.'

Nigel Gordon said, 'Syd clearly is schizophrenic now. You can't take substances like LSD and turn someone into a schizophrenic. My assumption is that Syd would have become schizophrenic anyway. These strong chemicals coupled with fame and fortune speeded it up. Maybe he could have gotten through his whole life without it.'

Pete Brown said, 'Syd was one of the spearheads, and main inspirational figures of the sixties so-called psychedelic movement, for good reasons and bad reasons. He was undoubtedly one of the two or three people who widened the range of English lyric writing. He made it possible for English people to write about being English, briefly. Potentially, the more I think about it, he could have been a terrific musician as well. But that was cut short by his self-disabling process. I have a strong image of him as also being a terrific performer, he was incredibly charismatic on-stage. He became a hero very fast, because he was moving into uncharted territory. And he was going in there without much equipment. Going into the jungle without a sun hat. It was very interesting. It was an awful shame to have such a bad aftermath, and that it had to be linked to stupid drugs. I feel quite strongly that with drugs there was a certain amount of conspiracy, if you like. People regarded certain aspects of the Underground as a threat and made sure that the Underground got the drugs it did so that it would fall apart. Had he remained more together, Syd would have turned into a very interesting musician. Apart from the fact that he could write and came up with great lyrics, and was set to become a full-fledge British eccentric hero, Syd would have been a player. If he'd looked after himself, he would have become a very good musician.'

'I don't know if he was schizophrenic,' Mike Leonard said, 'or whether it was too many drugs, and they drilled a hole in his brain. I did see a film once on TV, and they'd really done it to denigrate him. It was sad, they portrayed him as the fifth Beatle, fallen by the wayside, struggling about. They visited his house and you saw this strange shadowy figure who'd put on a lot of weight, and he looked out through the door and popped back in again. It was unpleasant. This programme dwelled on his mental problems. It would be better if he was just left to live his life. I did see these odd shots of him, and it was quite startling to see this rather sprite little gnomish face suddenly in this great big frame, as you get with people who are in mental trouble. They suddenly look like somebody else. If I think back, I have a softer spot and more empathy for Syd. His personality I can still feel thirty years later. If he came around the corner I could just imagine how we would be. It's sad really, Syd has acquired a mythical image now, partly due to the fact that one wonders what he would have done had he remained for twenty or thirty years in music, what kinds of things he could have produced.'

Peter Whitehead said, 'Syd was the most important icon of the sixties. He was destroyed in the way that we all assumed we might be destroyed. He was the young god who was sacrificed for all of us.'[56] Jenny Fabian said, 'Syd was a young god of that era. Without dying, something in him went, but it seemed to be for all of us. Syd symbolised the time, and the look, and the music. He was the symbol of that time. People who liked the Pink Floyd also listened to Dylan. Dylan said it for all of us at that time. I don't know what it was about Syd, maybe it was because we did lose him. He was like James Dean, except that he's still there which makes it even more poignant. It's more poignant that he's still alive. Like Hendrix, who did things with a guitar that no one else could do, Syd stands the test of time, even if the recordings weren't that good. I'd want to have *The Piper At The Gates Of Dawn* in my collection today, and two or three Beatles LPs, but there is a whole other mishmash of stuff from the sixties that I wouldn't want to have.'

The sixties unfettered air of experimentation was a mixed bag. With no conception of limits, radical experiments were realised. The downside of following Aleister Crowley's infamous edict 'Do what thou wilt shall be the whole of the law' was a terrifying fall-out of some of the brightest minds of the psychedelic Underground, banished to a realm of purest Stygian darkness. The world of fantasy was tinged with dangers, real or imagined. There were curious macabre twists to this world of childlike whimsy.

Peter Wynne-Wilson said, 'There were a lot of psychological risks with acid, which is part of the interest and excitement that it seemed to generate. It wasn't just a panacea. If you didn't get your head in the right space, you would certainly have trouble.'

'I'm interested in today's culture,' said Jenny Fabian. 'The sixties obviously had to happen, it brought about the change. The kids have taken over. They worry that they can't get the kids to vote or interested in issues, but think about how many kids would vote for the government that would legalise cannabis. But you can't say it, can you? I don't think the straight people realise how many kids take drugs now, or the quantity.'

Peter Wynne-Wilson adds, 'I think we're probably due for a movement of some kind.' Duggie Fields laments the passing of the "vibe" that powered the sixties, 'I don't see it around now particularly. I keep thinking, "Well, maybe it's something to do with one's age." And occasionally, I do meet people who echo that day nowadays, but not very often. I know a girl who is a real beauty, and so much like the girls we used to hang out with then. She has taken an enormous amount of acid, and she has that same feel as those girls who took a lot of acid then. There was a general optimism among young people then that there isn't now. Nobody these days would write a song like "The Times They Are A-Changin'". That song was a big cultural echo for a lot of people.'

The times have changed, but they have also remained the same. There will always be innocents dreaming of changing the world; there will always be a select few in the crowd who are light years ahead, thinking of innovations. Strange echoes of the sixties reverberate to this day, with periodic flare-ups of psychedelic culture: the rave scene, New Age travellers and the poll tax riots. In the end, human nature remains the constant, a see-saw of cynicism and idealism. The concrete and the abstract. The left and the right brains. There will always be a world to change, for the world remains constantly changing but always the same. The revolution the hippies spoke about happens every day; it isn't behind barricades or in the streets, it's inside of us.

Barrett's search transcended the vagaries of acid, music or the psychedelic era. In essence, unleashing a storm of echo-laden guitar thunderbolts on-stage at UFO, he was an explorer of unknown territory, as much as Burroughs, Magellan or Coltrane. As author Ted Morgan once memorably stated of William S. Burroughs, 'He had to cross the border and come back, while knowing that it is not always possible to come back'. Barrett the explorer opened up new realms, but it was up to the more mundane journeymen to deplete the ground he had broken. His themes, whether intentional or implied, were of madness, mystery, transcendence, space, travel, whimsy, of the nebulous other world he had found. Syd Barrett broke through; he remains there.

Ian Barrett said, 'I may be biased; but I love all the early Pink Floyd stuff; but I get kind of bored by a lot of the later Floyd music. It's really nothing personal, it's just not really my kind of music. I've always been into psychedelia a lot more than the later more mellow records. Listening to Roger's music, especially his solo albums is a strange experience that I can't really explain. Basically, while my ears hear Roger singing, my mind feels that it's someone else from the Roger I go and visit. You must realise that I wasn't even born when the records were made and it doesn't really feel like it's the same person. When I listen to his songs there is a lot more psychic baggage I have to carry around than most people would have when listening; and while for many people it's easy to block out the real pain the songs put across, and convince themselves the songs are just the funny ramblings of a "rock nutter". I'm afraid I can't do that. . .'[57]

By degrees, from 1968 on, Barrett had dispensed with the accoutrements of pop stardom one by one. The King's Road velvet trousers, Gohills boots, the satin shirts, the Hendrix-style perm all fell by the wayside. His long hair was shorn, the eyeliner removed, the guitars given away. And there was method to the madness, as the persona of 'Syd' was jettisoned in favour of Rog Barrett, Cambridge painter of still lives, a quiet reclusive and fairly ordinary man who did his shopping, bought his paints and brushes and cycled around town largely unnoticed. It took Roger ten years to return to the life he'd left behind for the bright lights of the big city that Jimmy Reed had once sung about.

It was here in Cambridge, back home, that he was to find what his brother-in-law Paul Breen termed 'a level of contentment that had eluded him'. There is no reason to pity Rog Barrett, he has finally returned, through various stages, to the life he left behind, and staged a true 'comeback'. He is today free to pursue his own style of life, and if ever he picks up a guitar, paintbrush or pen, it's purely for his own enjoyment. In the place of music, Roger Barrett returned to what he first loved, painting, and, later, writing. As if to emphasise the transitory nature of his art, he destroys his paintings after he finishes them.

I sit on the concrete embankment of the River Cam, in the Coe Fen, the grass at my feet, 100 metres from that ochre bridge where I saw the undulating underwater grass. The late autumnal light coats the grass and trees with the thick air that precedes the descent into long unforgiving winter. The sun sets quickly as we approach November; by five it will be dark. Spring and summer are gone. The sun drops beyond that bridge in degrees, quickening and hastening the long moonlit night ahead. I stand up and walk back over the rickety wooden boards of the bridge, looking once more into the dark water. The grass, mystic symbolic embodiment of all those young reeds that sprang from the mud, marsh and water of Cambridge so long ago. The water is surprisingly deep, the grass reeds are dying slowly, assuming their place in the spoke of the wheel of generations, driven by nature, the seasons' implacable restlessness for forward momentum.

In time there will be another spring, ripening all living things. Will there be another Syd Barrett? Of course, and maybe this book will spare that soul some madness as they make their way into the wild wood, into the world.

It's dark now and that chill dread wind from the north begins to pick up in gusts. The sun drops down past the horizon with alacrity. There's no one around, anywhere. The leaves in the tall trees are blown off, one by one. Darkness falls, 'the land in silence stands'. I feel the Fens at my back, and something stirs there, I feel it. Something in the water, in those endless currents pulsing in darkness.

I turn to walk back to the dim lights of town, and as I step off the creaking boards of the bridge I hear someone laugh right behind me. Just a mischievous, slightly embarrassed laugh. I turn and look back, thinking it's one of my friends who are waiting back at the Anchor pub on the other side of Mill Pond, sneaking up behind to play a joke on me. There isn't anyone there. Was it just the wind, which is picking up now through the tall trees above, or just my mind playing tricks on me?

Like the Piper at the Gates of Dawn, who appears at daybreak for an instant only, it's just beyond my reach. I remember the Piper in Kenneth Grahame's *The*

Wind In The Willows, whose lilting pipes of Pan echo across the pasture land bordering the riverbank, the epochal riverbank. The Piper will be there at dawn, I'm sure, to herald the new day, but I won't be there. I'll be back in London, and after that far, far away from the fabled banks on Mill Pond, where the enigma of Syd Barrett remains, untouched.

I turn and head back to the town, and think of his alter-ego Roger Barrett, sitting in his home not far away. Does he stand at the window watching the moon casting its pale luminescent light over the trees? Does he stare blankly into the TV, listen blankly to the evening news, with the parched voice intoning the day's bad news? Does he sit on the floor, drinking a cup of tea and listen to his classical LPs, the music quietly humming out of an old stylus? Does he cry, does he laugh? Is he happy? Most Syd Barrett fans ask themselves these questions, The enigma of someone who withdrew completely leaves so many unanswered questions.

I'll never know, but as I reach the edge of town and emerge from the mystic Fens eerie oblique dark majesty, I feel the ghost of Syd out there, that madcap 'angel-headed hipster' who bared his soul to the woods and lost it. Syd Barrett was the Piper at the Gates of Dawn, that far-off lysergic dawn of 1967, when it seemed the consciousness-expanding quest engendered by LSD would change the world. And Syd, like Pan with his pipes, was providing the soundtrack: 'Isn't it good to be lost in the woods? Isn't it bad, so quiet there in the woods.'

One day Syd Barrett got lost in the woods and never came back. Roger Barrett came back instead, leaving his invented alter ego out there somewhere. The ghost of Syd Barrett remains there, and also in his magical, mysterious songs. But Roger Barrett found his way home. 'All movement is accomplished in six stages, and the seventh brings return,' says the *I-Ching*.

Today Roger Keith Barrett continues to live in Cambridge, in self-imposed exile and isolation. His mother Winifred having died, his family cares for him. He collects coins and listens only to classical and jazz music. Every once in a while a man can be spotted walking the streets of Cambridge; he's in his early fifties, bald on top, a bit stocky. With paint flecks on his jeans, and hands in his coat, he's indistinguishable in the crowds who do their shopping in the town centre. The only thing which makes him stand out are those eyes, which still retain a shadow of preternatural luminescence. It's the man once known as Syd, and in his head, as he walks, perhaps he hears the distant echoes of the thunder that was his music and smiles at how he passed it all by.

---

1 *Musician*, November 1982
2 *NME*, 13 April 1974
3 *The Amazing Pudding*, # 57
4 Ian Barrett interview with Rob Peets
5 *Melody Maker*, 31 January 1971
6 *Musician*, November 1982
7 *The Amazing Pudding*, # 58
8 August 1996, by Mark Blake
9 Watkinson, Mike & Anderson, Pete. *Crazy Diamond: Syd Barrett And The Dawn Of Pink Floyd.* Omnibus Press, 1993
10 'Syd Barrett Careening Through Life'. Kris DiLorenzo, *Trouser Press*, February 1978
11 Schaffner, Nicholas. *Saucerful Of Secrets*. Delta, 1991
12 Ibid.
13 *The Amazing Pudding*, # 58
14 Macdonald, Bruno, editor. *Pink Floyd: Through The Eyes Of . . .* Sidgwick & Jackson, London, 1996
15 Ian Barrett interview with Rob Peets
16 Watkinson, Mike & Anderson, Pete. *Crazy Diamond: Syd Barrett And The Dawn Of Pink Floyd.* Omnibus Press, 1993
17 *The Amazing Pudding*, # 56
18 November 1992
19 '*The 0ink Floyd Story*': Six-part documentary broadcast on Capital radio, London. December 1976-January 1977
20 Schaffner, Nicholas. *Saucerful Of Secrets*. Delta, 1991
21 *Sounds*, May 1983
22 *Interview*, 1994
23 Mark Blake interview with Rick Wright, August 1996
24 *The Amazing Pudding*, # 57
25 Ian Barrett interview with Rob Peets
26 Ibid.
27 Ibid.
28 *The Amazing Pudding*, # 6
29 *Omnibus* special on Pink Floyd, 1994
30 *Mojo*, July 1995
31 Radio One, *Saturday Live*, 15 October 1994
32 Mark Blake interview with Rick Wright, August 1996
33 'Shades of Pink,' interviews with Charlie Kendall, Source. 1984
34 Roger Waters Interview with Chris Salewicz, June 1987
35 *The Amazing Pudding*, # 57
36 *Rolling Stone*, 19 November 1987
37 *Interview*, 1994
38 Miles & Mabbett, Andy. *Pink Floyd: The Visual Documentary*. Omnibus Press, London 1994
39 *NME*, 9 July 1988
40 MTV interviews with Pink Floyd, 1992
41 *NME*, 11 January 1975
42 *NME*, 13 April 1974
43 *Melody Maker*, 19 May 1973
44 Roger Waters Interview with Chris Salewicz, June 1987
45 *Observer*, 12 July 1987
46 *Musician*, 1988
47 Greene, Jonathan. *Days In The Life: Voices From The English Underground, 1961-1971*. Minerva, 1988
48 *Melody Maker*, 31 January 1971
49 Watkinson, Mike & Anderson, Pete. *Crazy Diamond: Syd Barrett And The Dawn Of Pink Floyd.* Omnibus Press, 1993
50 Ian Barrett interview with Rob Peets
51 Ibid.
52 Ibid.
53 Ibid.

54 Ibid.
55 Ibid.
56 *Harpers & Queen*, November 1996
57 Ian Barrett interview with Rob Peets

Discography

by Vernon Fitch of the Pink Floyd Archives

The following is a discography of original Syd Barrett releases in the United Kingdom (U.K.) and the United States (U.S.), plus other international releases of interest. All entries are vinyl releases unless noted otherwise. Reissues and release variations are not covered here. For complete listings with pictures, see 'The Pink Floyd Discographies Page' on the Internet at:
http://ourworld.compuserve.com/homepages/PFArchives/DiscTOC.htm

U.K. RELEASES

Pink Floyd Singles:

'Arnold Layne'/'Candy And A Currant Bun', Columbia Records, DB 8156, 11 March 1967 (promo* dated 10 March 1967)
'See Emily Play'/'The Scarecrow', Columbia Records, DB 8214, 16 June 1967 (promo dated 27 July 1967)
'Apples And Oranges'/'Paint Box', Columbia Records, DB 8310, 18 November 1967 (promo dated 17 November 1967)

* Note: promo releases were issued with picture sleeves.

Solo Singles:

'Octopus'/'Golden Hair', Harvest Records, HAR 5009, 2 December 1969

Pink Floyd Albums:

The Piper at the Gates of Dawn, Columbia Records mono issue (with different mixes), SX 6157, 5 August 1967
The Piper at the Gates of Dawn, Columbia Records stereo issue, SCX 6157, 5 August 1967
Side 1: 'Astronomy Domine', 'Lucifer Sam', 'Matilda Mother', 'Flaming', 'Pow R. Toc H.', 'Take Up Thy Stethoscope and Walk'.
Side 2: 'Interstellar Overdrive', 'The Gnome', 'Chapter 24', 'The Scarecrow, 'Bike'.
The Piper at the Gates of Dawn, (1994 stereo remaster)
The Piper at the Gates of Dawn, (1997 mono remaster), EMI, 7243.8.59857.13, 18 August 1997.
A Saucerful of Secrets, Columbia Records mono issue (with different mixes), SX 6258, 29 August 1968**
A Saucerful of Secrets, Columbia Records stereo issue, SCX 6258, 29 August 1968**

** Note: Syd Barrett appears on only a few songs on *A Saucerful of Secrets*, including 'Jugband Blues', 'Remember a Day' and 'Set the Controls for the Heart of the Sun'.

A Nice Pair, EMI Harvest, SHDW 403 (UK), SABB 11257 (US), 1974 – a double album comprising *Piper at the Gates of Dawn* and *Saucerful of Secrets*.
Pink Floyd: London '66-'67, See for Miles Records, Sep. 1995 Contains 'Interstellar Overdrive' and 'Nick's Boogie' from the Whitehead session.

Solo Albums

The Madcap Laughs, Harvest Records, SHVL 765, January 1970
Side 1: 'Terrapin', 'No Good Trying', 'Love You', 'No Man's Land', 'Dark Globe', 'Here I Go'.
Side 2: 'Octopus', 'Golden Hair', 'Long Gone', 'She Took a Long Cold Look', 'Feel', 'If It's In You', 'Late Night'.

Barrett, Harvest Records, SHSP 4007, November 1970
Side 1: 'Baby Lemonade', 'Love Song', 'Dominoes', 'It Is Obvious', 'Rats', 'Maisie'.
Side 2: 'Gigolo Aunt', 'Waving My Arms in the Air', 'I Never Lied to You', 'Wined and Dined', 'Wolfpack,' 'Effervescing Elephant'.

Opel, Harvest Records, SHSP 4126, 17 October 1988
Side 1: 'Opel', 'Clowns And Jugglers', 'Octopus', 'Rats', 'Golden Hair' (vocal), 'Dolly Rocker', 'Word Song', 'Wined and Dined'.

Side 2: 'Swan Lee', 'Silas Lang', 'Birdie Hop', 'Let's Split', 'Lanky' (part 1), 'Wouldn't You Miss Me', 'Dark Globe', 'Milky Way', 'Golden Hair' (instrumental).

The Peel Sessions, Strange Fruit Records, SFPS043, a 1987 release of Syd's recordings made for *The John Peel Show* on Radio 1 on February 24, 1970
Side 1: 'Terrapin', 'Gigolo Aunt'.
Side 2: 'Baby Lemonade', 'Effervescing Elephant', 'Two of a Kind'.

Syd Barrett – Crazy Diamond, 3-CD set, Harvest Records, Syd Box 1, 0777 7 81412 2 8, issued in a box with a booklet, each disc includes out-takes added on to the end of the original album release, 26 April 1993
Disc 1: 'Terrapin', 'No Good Trying', 'Love You', 'No Man's Land', 'Dark Globe', 'Here I Go', 'Octopus', 'Golden Hair', 'Long Gone', 'She Took a Long Cold Look', 'Feel', 'If It's In You', 'Late Night', plus out-takes of: 'Octopus', 'It's No Good Trying', 'Love You', 'She Took a Long Cold Look at Me', 'Golden Hair'.
Disc 2: 'Baby Lemonade', 'Love Song', 'Dominoes', 'It Is Obvious', 'Rats', 'Maisie', 'Gigolo Aunt', 'Waving My Arms in the Air', 'I Never Lied to You', 'Wined and Dined', 'Wolfpack', 'Effervescing Elephant', plus out-takes of: 'Baby Lemonade', 'Waving My Arms in the Air', 'I Never Lied to You', 'Love Song', 'Dominoes', 'It is Obvious'.
Disc 3: 'Opel', 'Clowns and Jugglers', 'Rats', 'Golden Hair', 'Dolly Rocker', 'Word Song', 'Wined and Dined', 'Swan Lee', 'Silas Lang', 'Birdie Hop', 'Let's Split', 'Lanky' (part 1), 'Wouldn't You Miss Me', 'Dark Globe', 'Milky Way', 'Golden Hair' (instrumental), plus out-takes of: 'Gigolo Aunt', 'It is Obvious', 'Clowns And Jugglers', 'Late Night', 'Effervescing Elephant'.

Tonite Let's All Make Love in London, Instant Records, INLP 002, 1968 Soundtrack to the movie of the same name that features segments of 'Interstellar Overdrive' plus 'Nick's Boogie' (re-released in 1992, by See for Miles Ltd.)

U.S. RELEASES

Pink Floyd Singles:

'Arnold Layne'/'Candy And A Current Bun', Tower Records, Tower 333 (promo issued in 1967 with a title sleeve)
'See Emily Play'/'The Scarecrow', Tower Records, Tower 356, (originally issued 25 September, 1967 with a picture sleeve, reissued a year later with a promo title sleeve)
'Flaming'/'The Gnome', Tower Records, Tower 378, an unusual 1968 U.S.-only issue of unique mono mixes of the songs reputedly done by Syd Barrett

7-inch EPs:

'Crazy Diamond' EP ('Terrapin', 'Octopus', 'Baby Lemonade', 'Effervescing Elephant'), Capitol Records, NR 7243 8 58186 7, a limited edition EP released only in the U.S. in 1993 on pink vinyl with a picture sleeve

12-inch EPs:

'Wouldn't You Miss Me' ('Dark Globe', 'Wouldn't You Miss Me', 'Dark Globe'), Capitol Records promo only release, SPRO-79606, released only in the U.S

Pink Floyd Albums:

The Piper at the Gates of Dawn, Tower Records mono issue, T 5093
The Piper at the Gates of Dawn, Tower Records stereo issue, ST 5093 3 Tower Records altered the songs on *The Piper at the Gates of Dawn* from the original British release by including the single 'See Emily Play', and dropping the songs 'Astronomy Domine', 'Flaming' and 'Bike' from the record. The song order on the U.S. release is:
Side 1: 'See Emily Play', 'Pow R. Toc H.', 'Take Up Thy Stethoscope and Walk', 'Lucifer Sam', 'Matilda Mother'.
Side 2: 'The Scarecrow', 'The Gnome', 'Chapter 24', 'Interstellar Overdrive'.

A Saucerful of Secrets, Tower Records mono issue, T 5131
A Saucerful of Secrets, Tower Records stereo issue, ST 5131

Solo Albums:

The Madcap Laughs/Barrett, Harvest Records, SABB-11314, 1974
A double album release of Syd's two albums with a unique gatefold cover (this is the original release of these two albums in the United States as *The Madcap Laughs* and *Barrett* were never released in the U.S. as single albums)

OTHER INTERNATIONAL RELEASES OF INTEREST

Albums:

The Piper at the Gates of Dawn, Japan, Odeon Records, OP-8229
Issued on red vinyl, the Japanese release of *The Piper at the Gates of Dawn* includes the same songs as are on the original British release of the album plus an extra song, 'See Emily Play', added to the end of side 2

The Piper at the Gates of Dawn, Italy, Columbia Records, 3C 062-04292
This album was not released in Italy until 1971 and was issued with a different cover that shows a picture of Pink Floyd with David Gilmour

A Saucerful of Secrets, Japan, Odeon Records, OP-8743
Issued on red vinyl

A Nice Pair, Canada, SABB-11257
The Canadian issue of *A Nice Pair* includes a version of 'Jugband Blues' with a different mix

The Madcap Laughs, Japan, Odeon Records, OP-8927
Issued on red vinyl

Barrett, Japan, Odeon Records, OP-80173
Issued on red vinyl

Singles:

'Arnold Layne', 'Candy And A Currant Bun', 'Interstellar Overdrive', France, Columbia Records, ESRF 1857
An EP released only in France that includes a unique version of 'Interstellar Overdrive' recorded at one of the first recording sessions, issued with a picture sleeve of the band (this EP was also reissued in France as a limited edition in 1987)

'Arnold Layne'/'Candy And A Currant Bun', this single was issued with a picture/title sleeve in Denmark, Holland, Germany, Sweden, the United Kingdom and the United States

'See Emily Play', 'The Scarecrow', 'Arnold Layne', 'Candy And A Currant Bun', Spain, Columbia Records, EPL 14377
An EP released only in Spain with a unique picture sleeve of the band

'See Emily Play'/'The Scarecrow', this single was issued with a picture sleeve in Brazil, Denmark, France, Germany, Italy, Japan, Holland, Sweden, the United Kingdom and the United States

'Apples and Oranges'/'Paint Box', this single was issued with a picture sleeve in France, Germany, Holland, Sweden and the United Kingdom

'Octopus'/'Golden Hair', France, Harvest Records, 2C 006-04435
The only release of this single with a picture sleeve (of an octopus)

67-69, Poland, Polpress 005
A set of five playable picture postcards that were issued in Poland that featured the songs: 'See Emily Play', 'Apples & Oranges', 'It Would Be So Nice', 'Paint Box, and 'Julia Dream'

VIDEODISCS

Tonite! Let's All Make Love in London, Japan, VAP laser videodisc, VPLU-70626, released in Japan 8 December 1996
The soundtrack of this movie included 'Interstellar Overdrive'

The Pink Floyd – London 1966-67, Japan, BMG laser disc, BVLP 124

A film by Peter Whitehead that shows an early Pink Floyd recording session, in its entirety with complete versions of 'Interstellar Overdrive' and 'Nick's Boogie'. Interspliced is footage of the Pink Floyd at UFO and the 14-Hour Technicolour Dream.

ROIO (RECORDS OF INDETERMINATE ORIGIN)

Listing compiled by Scott Frank

Albums:

Vegetable Man, Where Are You? SB 1167
Format: LP
Date: 1967-1970

Cover: The cover has a bizarre drawing by Robyn Hitchcock on the front, with a rare b/w photo of Syd in his garden on the rear

Tracks:

Side One:
1. 'Vegetable Man' – Autumn 1967
* 2. 'What a Shame Mary Jane' – The Beatles, 15 April 1967
3. 'Swan Lee' (backing track) – Autumn 1967
* 4. 'Milky Way' (take 5) – 7 June 1970
5. 'Instrumental 1' – Autumn 1967
* 6. 'Words' (take 1) – 17 July 1970
* 7. 'Birdy Hop' (take 1) – 5 June 1970

Side Two:
* 1. 'Opel' (take 9) – 11 April 1969
2. 'Clowns and Jugglers 1-3'
2.1 'False Start' – 12 June 1969
2.2 'Middle Bit' – 12 June 1969
* 2.3 'Complete Song' (take 1) – 20 July 1968
3. 'Long Gone' – 12 June 1969
4. 'Dark Globe' (falsetto voices) (take 1) – 26 July 1969
5. 'Instrumental 2' – Autumn 1967
6. 'Singing a Song In the Morning' (with Kevin Ayers)
7. 'Vegetable Man' – Autumn 1967

* – Later officially released

Lucy Leave & Other Rarities, DIYE 16
Format: CD

Tracks:

*1. 'Gigolo Aunt' (Peel Session) – 24 February 1970
*2. 'Terrapin'
*3. 'Baby Lemonade'
*4. 'Effervescing Elephant'
*5. 'Two of a Kind'
*6. 'Nick's Boogie' (TLAMLIL soundtrack) – 14/15 January 1967
*7. 'Interstellar Overdrive'
*8. 'Interstellar Overdrive'
*9. 'Interstellar Overdrive'
*10. 'Interstellar Overdrive'
11. 'Lucy Leave' – Oct/Nov 1965
12. 'King Bee'
13. 'Dominoes' (Sounds Of The Seventies) – February 1971
* 14. 'Milky Way' (take 5) – 7 June 1970
15. 'Instrumental 1' – Autumn 1967

* 16. 'Word Song' (take 1) – 17 July 1970
* 17. 'Birdie Hop' (take 1) – 5 June 1970
18. 'Long Gone' – 12 June 1969
19. 'Dark Globe' (falsetto voices) (take 1) – 26 July 1969
20. 'Instrumental 2' Autumn 1967

* – Officially released
Magnesium Proverbs (Night Tripper Productions)

Format: CD
Misc.: Gold CD
Produced: Made In Germany

Tracks:

1. 'Lucy Leave' – Oct/Nov 1965
2. 'King Bee'
3. 'See Emily Play' (acetate) – 21 May 1967
* 4. 'Arnold Layne' – 27 February 1967
* 5. 'Candy And A Currant Bun'
* 6. 'Flaming' (slightly different mix) – June 1967
7. 'Pow R. Toc H.' (*Look Of The Week* TV broadcast) – 14 May 1967
8. 'Astronomy Domine'
9. 'Interstellar Overdrive' (UFO Club, London, England) – 20 January 1967
10. 'Reaction In G' (Cosmopolitan Ballroom, Carlisle, England) – 23 July 1967
11. 'Stoned Alone' (Star Club, Copenhagen, Denmark) – 11 September 1967
12. 'Vegetable Man' – Autumn 1967
13. 'Scream Thy Last Scream' – 7 August 1967
* 14. 'Apples And Oranges' – Oct/Nov 1967
15. 'Baby Lemonade' (Sounds Of The Seventies) – February 1971
16. 'Dominoes'
17. 'Love Song'
18. 'Terrapin' (Extravaganza 70, Olympia, London, England) – 6 June 1970
19. 'Gigolo Aunt'
20. 'Effervescing Elephant'
21. 'Octopus'
22. 'Clowns And Jugglers'
22.1 'False Start' – 12 June 1969
22.2 'Middle Bit' – 12 June 1969
* 22.3 'Complete Song' (take 1) – 20 July 1968
23. 'Mystery Bits' (part of The Wall backwards)
* 24. 'Jugband Blues' (mono) – Autumn 1967

Total length: 73:48

* – Officially released
Ramadhan, *Syd Barrett And The Dawn Of Pink Floyd* (9865-4JHG, No Man's Land Production)

Format: CD
Misc.: Studio out-takes
Produced: EEC; CD
Matrix: "MADCAP SB0003 BENELUX'"/"(95356105)"

Cover: INSERT: Folded; Front has been adapted from the cover art of the book *Crazy Diamond*, stretched in horizontal and with 'Ramadhan' in place of 'Crazy Diamond'. The subtitle 'Syd Barrett & the Dawn of Pink Floyd' has been retained. Rear has a reproduction of a Syd Barrett Appreciation Society membership card. Inside has familiar b/w photo of Syd resplendent in tie-dye T-shirt, track list/source info, and a tiny reproduction of a UFO Club ticket for 13 January 1967. TRAY LINER: Yellow field with false colour photo of Syd 'wearing' a floral bouquet(?) and basic track listing. CD: Picture disc screen-printed with photo of Syd.

Tracks:

1. 'Love You' (fast version) (take 2) – 11 April 1969
2. 'Love You' (slow version) (take 5) – 11 April 1969
3. 'Long Gone' – 12 June 1969
4. 'Ramadhan' – 14 May 1968
* 5. 'Octopus' (take 1) – 20 July 1968
6. 'Clowns and Jugglers' (Middle Bit) – 12 June 1969
7. 'Instrumental 1' – November 1974
8. 'Dark Globe' (falsetto voices) (take 1) – 26 July 1969
9. 'Singing a Song In the Morning' (with Kevin Ayers)
10. 'Intro/Matilda Mother' (UFO Club, London, England) – 20 January 1967
11. 'Interstellar Overdrive'
12. 'Interview' (*Look of the Week* TV broadcast) – 14 May 1967
13. 'Instrumental 1' – Autumn1967
14. 'Interstellar Overdrive' (CBC Interview) – 1967
15. 'Arnold Layne' (acetate) – 27 February 1967
16. 'Candy And A Currant Bun' (acetate)
*17. 'Interstellar Overdrive' (edited version of the PATGOD track)
18. 'Don't Ask Me' (Joker's Wild 7″ single) – 1966
19. 'Why Do Fools Fall In Love'
20. 'Interstellar Overdrive' (San Francisco soundtrack) – 31 October1966

* – Officially released

Psychedelic Games For May (snap-01)

Format: LP

Cover: front: white top with band name and title in pink wavy letters, lower portion is black & pink photo of band taken circa 1966/67 (left to right: Mason, Barrett, Waters, Wright) rear: pale pink & white background is a picture of Syd, band name and title in pink wavy letters along left, track list in black text in centre, description of each track in small black text to the right. Also available as a Picture LP.

Side 1:
1. 'Lucy Leave' – Oct/Nov 1965
2. 'King Bee'
3. 'See Emily Play' (acetate) – 21 May 1967
*4. 'Arnold Layne' – 27 February 1967
*5. 'Candy And A Currant Bun'
*6. 'Flaming' (slightly different mix) – June 1967
7. 'Pow R. Toc H.' (*Look Of The Week* TV broadcast) – 14 May 1967

Side 2:
1. 'Astronomy Domine' (*Look Of The Week* TV broadcast) – 14 May 1967
2. 'Interstellar Overdrive' (UFO Club, London, England) – 20 January 1967
3. 'Reaction In G' (Cosmopolitan Ballroom, Carlisle, England) – 23 July 1967
4. 'Stoned Alone' (Star Club, Copenhagen, Denmark) – 11 September 1967
5. 'Vegetable Man' – Autumn 1967
6. 'Scream Thy Last Scream' – 7 August 1967

* – Officially released

Sessionography

The primary source for the Floyd sessions listing is the EMI tape library records, which Malcolm Jones analysed in 1983 for his book *The Making of* The Madcap Laughs. Jones also had access to Nick Mason's list of gigs and studio dates, which likewise provide valuable information. *The Madcap Laughs* and *Barrett* sessions listing are a compilation of various sources, including those listed in Jones' book, in the *Crazy Diamond* box set and through my own research, correcting a few errors and adding information here and there.

As Jones notes, for the Pink Floyd tapes listed below, 'when a title appears several times on 4 track tapes [it] is most likely a continuation of the same recording, representing later overdubs onto the same original take. For example: tape numbers 63934 and 63951 both relate to the session dated 11 April 1967. 4 and 8 track tapes are shown generally as 4T and 8T. Without this a tape can be assumed to be stereo, or rarely, in the Pink Floyd's case, mono. Tape numbers with no 4T suffix are stereo or mono mixdowns. Generally speaking, the dates noted are the dates of the actual session.'

About 90% of the time the tape library records reflect the dates of the sessions. There are however notable exceptions. Both the first single and its B-Side, 'Arnold Layne/Candy and A Currant Bun' as well as 'See Emily Play' were recorded at Sound Techniques Studios in Chelsea. 'See Emily Play' was recorded on 21 April 1967. Jones consulted Nick Mason's personal records which confirmed this date.

Apparently, some of the tapes for sessions during August-October 1967, recorded at DeLane Lea and Sound Techniques, were not filed into the EMI tape library until May 1968. It is not conclusively known whether Syd Barrett played on tracks such as the fabled 'In The Beechwoods' (see below) or even when they date from exactly.

The Pink Floyd: 1965-1968

Syd Barrett: Lead vocals, electric and acoustic guitar, Binson echo unit, sound effects
Roger Waters: Bass, background vocals, sound effects
Rick Wright: Farfisa and Hammond organs, piano, Binson, background vocals, cello
Nick Mason: Drums and percussion, sound effects

October 1965

'Lucy Leave'
'King Bee' (by Slim Harpo)

Note: The recording dates of the first two are widely disputed. A recording date of October 1965 is claimed, as well as 31 October 1966. In terms of the fluency of playing and choice of R&B cover, I would venture to say October 1965 is the correct date.

31 October 1966

'Interstellar Overdrive'
'Let's Roll Again'
'Silas Lane'
'Stoned Alone'
Recorded at: Thompson Private Recording Company, Hemel Hempstead
The latter two songs have never been released, but they were both Barrett originals, and 'Silas Lane' may have been an early version of 'Arnold Layne'.

(9 January Rehearsal)

11/12 January 1967

'Interstellar Overdrive' 16.46
'Nick's Boogie' 11.50
Recorded at: Sound Techniques Studios, Old Church Street, Chelsea, London

(22 January rehearsal)

23/25 January
Sound Techniques Studios, Old Church Street, Chelsea, London

(26 January rehearsal)

29 January
Sound Techniques Studios, Old Church Street, Chelsea, London

(30 January Rehearsal)

31 January
Sound Techniques Studios, Old Church Street, Chelsea, London

1 February
Sound Techniques Studios, Old Church Street, Chelsea

(8 February Rehearsal)

21/22 February

'Matilda Mother' 63417 (4 Track)

23 February

'Matilda Mother' 63409 (mono mixdown)
Recorded at: EMI Abbey Road Studios, St. John's Wood, London (confirmed by Nick Mason's personal recollection, via Malcolm Jones)
(26 February Rehearsal)

27 February

'Candy And A Currant Bun'
'Arnold Layne' (2 takes) 7XCA 27877
'Chapter 24' 63428 (4 Track)
'Interstellar Overdrive' 63429 (4 Track)
Recorded at: Sound Techniques Studios, Old Church Street, Chelsea, London

1 March

'Chapter 24' 63424 (overdubs)
Sound Techniques Studios, Old Church Street, Chelsea, London

15 March

'Chapter 24' 63667 (4 Track)
'Interstellar Overdrive' (short version)
Note: This version forms the first layer of the finished song, with a second track overdubbed over it.
The Beatles visitation. Paul and George come into Studio Two to visit, Pink Floyd are taken into Studio One.

16 March

'Flame' 63669 (4 Track)
'Interstellar Overdrive' (short version)

20 March

'Take Up Thy Stethoscope' 63673 (4 Track)
'The Gnome'

20 March

'Take Up Thy Stethoscope' 63676 (4 Track)
'The Scarecrow'
'Pow R. Toc H.'

21 March

'Pow R. Toc H.' 67678 (4 Track)

22 March

'Interstellar Overdrive'

27 March (tapes filed 29 March)

'The Gnome' 63692

'Pow R. Toc H.'
'The Scarecrow'
'Take Up Thy Stethoscope and Walk'

3 April
Monday, Monday radio show

'Arnold Layne'
'Candy And A Currant Bun.'

Live session broadcast from BBC Playhouse Theatre, London

11 April

'Astronomy Domine' 63934 (4 Track)
'Astronomy Domine' 63935 (4 Track)
'Percy the Ratcatcher' 63951 (4 Track)

17 April

'Astronomy Domine' 63952

18 April

'Astronomy Domine' 63953

18 April

'She Was a Millionaire' 63954 (4 Track)
'Lucifer Sam'

18 April

'Lucifer Sam' 63955 (4 Track)
Cross-fades of 'Interstellar Overdrive' and 'The Bike Song'

Note: The liner notes to Pink Floyd's *Relics* album state that Rick Wright's 'Remember a Day' was recorded on 9 May, but there is no corresponding session listed.

12 May

Pink Floyd's 'Games For May' concert at the Queen Elizabeth Hall, South Bank, London, was recorded by the BBC

18 May
Sound Techniques Studios

21 May

'The Bike Song' 64402 (4 Track)
'See Emily Play' 7XCA 30214

Sound Techniques Studios

1 June

'Lucifer Sam' 64571
'The Bike Song'

5 June

'Chapter 24' 63956

7 June

'Matilda Mother' 64532 (4 Track)
'Chapter 24'
'Flaming'

27 June

'Flaming' 65057 (4 Track)

29 June

'The Bike Song' 65094
'Flaming'
'Matilda Mother'
'Wondering and Dreaming' (most likely 'Matilda's Mother')
'Sunshine'
'Lucifer Sam'

Note: 'Sunshine' is either an alternate version of 'Matilda Mother', or a basic track for Rick Wright's 'Remember A Day'.

3 July

'The Bike Song' 63956 (same reel as 5 June 1967)

5 July

'Astronomy Domine' 64109
'Lucifer Sam'

18 July
(LP master)

Side One:
'Astronomy Domine'
'Lucifer Sam'
'Matilda Mother'
'Pow R. Toc H.'
'Take Up Thy Stethoscope'
'Flaming'. 65106

Side Two:
'Interstellar Overdrive'
'The Gnome'
'Chapter 24'
'The Scarecrow'
'Bike' 64925

28 July
Saturday Club radio session, BBC Playhouse Theatre, London
(cancelled)

5 August

The Piper at the Gates of Dawn released

7-8 August

'Scream Thy Last Scream' 65464 (4 Track)
'Set The Controls For The Heart Of The Sun'
Note: Gilmour overdubs added on 23 and 26 April 1968.

15-6 August
Sound Techniques Studios, Old Church Street, Chelsea, London

5-6 September
Sound Techniques Studios, Old Church Street, Chelsea, London

25 Sept
Top Gear radio session

'The Gnome'
'Scarecrow'
'Set the Controls for the Heart of the Sun'
'Matilda Mother'
'Reaction in G'
'Flaming'
'Apples and Oranges'

Recorded at BBC Playhouse Theatre, London

Broadcast 1 Oct 1967, except 'Apples and Oranges', broadcast 5 November 1967

5-6 October
Sound Techniques Studios, Old Church Street, Chelsea, London

October 9-12

Abbey Road

'Scream Thy Last Scream'
'Vegetable Man'

20-21 October
De Lane Lea studios

24 October 1967

'Jugband Blues' (mono)
'Remember A Day' (mono)

Abbey Road

Note: Welcome to the black hole of Syd-era Pink Floyd research. Pink Floyd departed for the United States and their ill-fated tour on 29 October. No further sessions were held until the beginning of 1968. Tapes from the Sound Techniques and De Lane Lea studio sessions listed above were delivered to EMI on the following dates.

30 October 1967

'Apples and Oranges' 66462 (4 Track)
'Apples and Oranges' 66463 (4 Track)

1 November

'Apples and Oranges' (not master) 66464
'Paintbox' 7XC[A] 30454
'Apples and Oranges' (note 3) 7XCA 30453
'Untitled' 66409 (4 Track)
'Untitled' 66461 (4 Track)
'Apples and Oranges'

2 November

'Untitled' 66460 (4 Track)
'Paintbox' 66563 (4 Track)

15 November

'Apples and Oranges' 66771 (stereo)
'Paintbox'

Note: The single, 'Apples and Oranges' backed with 'Paintbox', was issued on 18 November 1967. In addition to these delivered tapes, we have the mystery of several tapes logged into the EMI tape files on 5, 6 and 9 May 1968. These tapes were on ½ inch tape, a format EMI did not use, which indicates they were made at Sound Techniques Studio or De Lane Lea between 7 August and 21 October 1967, before the band departed for the U.S.

Logged into EMI tape files on 5 May 1968

'In The Beechwoods' 68409 (4 Track)
'Untitled'
'Vegetable Man'
'Instrumental' 68410 (4 Track)
'In The Beechwoods'

Logged into EMI tape files on 6 May 1968 (Curiously, the day Barrett began solo sessions at EMI)

'Untitled' 68411 (4 Track)

Logged into EMI tape files on 9 May 1968

'Remember A Day' 68412 (4 Track) ½ inch

'Remember A Day' 68413 4T ½ inch
'Jugband Blues'
'Vegetable Man'
'Remember A Day' 68414 (4 Track) ½ inch
'Jugband Blues' 68415 (4 Track) ½ inch
'John Latham' 68416 (4 Track) ½ inch
'Remember A Day' (mono re-mix) not used
Jugband Blues' (used for mono LP) 68417
'Remember A Day' (reject mono mix) 68418
'Remember A Day' (mono LP mix)
'Jugband Blues' (stereo mix)
'Remember A Day' (stereo LP mix)

Note: 'Instrumental', 'Untitled', 'John Latham' and 'In The Beechwoods' might be unreleased Syd Barrett/Pink Floyd tracks, but this is merely hypothesis. They might be the mythic Barrett-led sessions that included a banjo and sax player, purported tapes of which have circulated for years.

20 December
Top Gear radio session

'Vegetable Man'
'Scream Thy Last Scream'
'Jugband Blues'
'Pow R. Toc H.'

Recorded at BBC Maida Vale Studios, London. Broadcast 31 December 1967

(6, and 8-9 January 1968 rehearsals)

10-11 January 1968
EMI rehearsals or sessions

Note: Presumably the infamous 'Have You Got It Yet?' rehearsals with Gilmour

18 January (presumably Barrett's final session)

'Let There Be More Light' 67242 (4 Track)
Rhythm tracks 67243 (4 Track) (possibly 'Have You Got It Yet?')

24/25 January

'The Most Boring Song I've Ever Heard Bar Two' (aka 'See Saw') 67378 (4 Track)

29 June

A Saucerful Of Secrets released

(Source: Jones, Malcolm. *The Making of* The Madcap Laughs, Orange Sunshine Press, 1983)

Solo: 6 May 1968 – 9 October 1969

The Madcap Laughs sessions

Produced by: Peter Jenner, Malcolm Jones, David Gilmour and Roger Waters engineers: Jeff Jarratt, Pete Mew, Mike Sheady, Phil McDonald, and Tony Clark

Musicians:
Syd Barrett: Vocals, lead and rhythm acoustic and electric guitar
David Gilmour: Bass, second organ, rhythm guitar
Jerry Shirley: Drums and percussion
Rick Wright: Organ and piano
John 'Willie' Wilson: bass
Mike Ratledge: keyboards
Robert Wyatt: drums
Hugh Hopper: bass

Producer: Peter Jenner

6 May

'Silas Lang'

'Swan Lee' (1st version unreleased)
'Late Night' (erased)

14 May

'Ramadhan' (unreleased)
'Lanky' (part 1) Released on *Opel*
'Lanky' (part 2) (unreleased)
'Golden Hair' (instrumental backing track only) Released on *Opel*

21 May

'Late Night' (take 2)
'Swan Lee' (overdubs)

28 May

'Golden Hair' (overdubs) (unreleased)
'Swan Lee' Released on Opel with overdubs on 8 June 1968 and 25 April 1969
'Ramadhan' (overdubs) (unreleased)

8 June

'Swan Lee' (overdubs)

20 June

'Swan Lee' (overdubs)
'Late Night' (backing track only) not 28 May as previously stated. Released on *Opel*
'Golden Hair' (overdubs) (unreleased)

20 July

'Clowns And Jugglers' (this session produced by Syd alone) Released on *Opel* with overdubs on 3 May 1969

Producer: Malcolm Jones

10 April 1969
7 pm - 12:30 am session

'Swan Lee' (guitar and vocal overdubs) (unreleased)
'Clowns And Jugglers' (overdubs) (unreleased

11 April

'Opel' Released on *Opel* (take 9)
'Love You' (fast vocal/electric guitar version) Released on *The Madcap Laughs* re-issue
'Love You' (slow vocal/electric guitar version)
'Love You' (take 4) Released on *The Madcap Laughs* with overdubs 3 May 1969
'It's No Good Trying' (take 5) Released as bonus track on *The Madcap Laughs*
'Terrapin' Released on *The Madcap Laughs* with overdubs on 4 May 1969
'Late Night' (overdubbed slide guitar and vocals on 28 May 1968 version) Released on *The Madcap Laughs*
'Golden Hair' (two unreleased versions, the first featuring more prominent guitar and the second with harmony vocal)

17 April

'No Man's Land' (take 5) Released on *The Madcap Laughs* (overdubs 4 May 1969)
'Here I Go' (take 5) Released on *The Madcap Laughs* (with Jerry Shirley: drums, and John 'Willie' Wilson: bass).

23 April

'Ramadhan' (overdubs) (unreleased)
'Motorbike effects' (unreleased)

25 April 1969 (Syd produced session)

'Love You' Released on *The Madcap Laughs* (with overdubs)

Syd Barrett supervised the transfer of original 4 track masters to 8 track tape for later overdubs. Malcolm Jones noted the titles transferred as 'an indication as to the songs that Syd was planning to continue with.'

'It's No Good Trying'; 'Terrapin'; 'Opel'; 'Clowns And Jugglers', 'Love You', 'Golden Hair'; 'Late Night'; 'Swan Lee'; 'Love You' (with overdubs)

26 April

'If It's In You' (take 5) Released on *The Madcap Laughs*

3 May (Soft Machine session)

'Love You' (overdubs) Released on *The Madcap Laughs*

'No Good Trying' (overdubs) Released on *The Madcap Laughs*
(Soft Machine overdubs on 11 April guitar/vocal version)

'Clowns And Jugglers' Released on *Opel*
(Soft Machine overdubs on 20 July 1968 Jenner version)

Mike Ratledge: keyboards
Robert Wyatt: drums
Hugh Hopper: bass
The Soft Machine minus Kevin Ayers: overdubbed backings

4 May

'No Good Trying' (overdubs) Released on *The Madcap Laughs*
(further overdubs on the 11 April version)

'Terrapin' (overdubs) Released on *The Madcap Laughs*
(overdubs on the 11 April version)

No Man's Land (overdubs) Released on *The Madcap Laughs*
(overdubs on the 17 April version)

Produced: David Gilmour (with Roger Waters)

12 June (Gilmour and Barrett session)

'Octopus' (take 11, Barrett: guitar/vocal) Released on *The Madcap Laughs*

Barrett: overdubbed electric guitar
Gilmour: bass
Jerry Shirley: drums

'Golden Hair' (take 11) (Barrett/James Joyce) (Barrett guitar/vocal) Released on *The Madcap Laughs*
'Octopus' (take 2) Released as bonus track on *The Madcap Laughs*
'Dark Globe' (take 1) Released on *Opel*
'Long Gone' (unreleased)
'Dark Globe' version 2 (unreleased)
'Golden Hair' (take 6) Released on *Opel* (Instrumental backing track)

13 June

Octopus (overdubs) Released on *The Madcap Laughs*

26 July

'She Took A Long Cold Look' (take 5) Released on *The Madcap Laughs*
'Long Gone' (take 1) Released on *The Madcap Laughs*
'Wouldn't You Miss Me' (incorrect announcement for 'Dark Globe' re-make, version 3) (unreleased)
'She Took A Long Cold Look' (take 4) Released as bonus track on *The Madcap Laughs*
'Feel' (take 1) Released on *The Madcap Laughs*
'If It's In You' (take 5) Released on *The Madcap Laughs*
Stereo mixdown of four Track tapes

5 August

In a morning session, David Gilmour and Roger Waters mix: 'Long Gone', 'She Took A Long Cold Look', 'Feel', 'If It's In You' and 'Octopus'

Afternoon session (three hours): 'Golden Hair', 'Dark Globe' and 'Terrapin'

16 September (Gilmour only)

'No Good Trying', 'Love You', 'No Man's Land', 'Here I Go', 'Late Night

6 October

Splicing and sequencing session by Gilmour and Barrett

24 February 1970
Top Gear radio session BBC broadcast 18 May

David Gilmour: bass
Jerry Shirley: drums

'Gigolo Aunt'
'Two of A Kind'
'Effervescing Elephant'
'Baby Lemonade'

Maida Vale 4 Studios, London

Barrett sessions
Produced by David Gilmour (with input from Rick Wright)

Musicians:
Syd Barrett: vocals, lead and rhythm guitar
David Gilmour: bass, second organ, rhythm and 12-string guitar, drums
Jerry Shirley: drums and percussion
Rick Wright: organ and piano
Vic Saywell: tuba

26 February

'Baby Lemonade' (take 1) Released on *Barrett* (12 String Guitar: David Gilmour)
'Maisie' (take 2) Released on *Barrett*
'Baby Lemonade' (take 1) (guitar and double track vocals only)

February 27

Four stereo demos: (all unreleased)
'Wolfpack'
'Waving My Arms In The Air'
'Living Alone'
'Dylan Blues'

Note: Malcolm Jones points out: 'David Gilmour is credited, on the recording sheet, as having taken the tape with him at the end of the session.'

'Gigolo Aunt' (take 15) Released on *Barrett* (Second Organ: David Gilmour; Percussion: Jerry Shirley and John 'Willie' Wilson)

'Waving My Arms In The Air' (take 1) Released on *Barrett*
'I Never Lied To You' (take 1) Released on *Barrett*
'Waving My Arms In The Air' (take 1) Released as bonus track on *Barrett* (guitar and vocals only)
'I Never Lied To You' (take 1) Released as bonus track on *Barrett* (guitar and vocals only)
'Gigolo Aunt' (take 9) Released on *Opel*

1 April
Rough mixes of work in progress

3 April

'Wolfpack' (take 2) Released on *Barrett*

5 June

'Rats' (Two-track Demo) Released on *Opel*
'Wined And Dined' (Two-track Demo) Released on *Opel*

'Birdie Hop' (Two-track Demo) Released on *Opel*

6 June

Live performance: 'Extravaganza 70' - Music and Fashion Festival, Olympia, London
David Gilmour: bass
Jerry Shirley: drums

'Terrapin'
'Gigolo Aunt'
'Effervescing Elephant'
'Octopus'

7 June

'Millionaire' (backing track only) (unreleased)
'Rats' (guitar and vocals only) Released on *Opel*
'Milky Way' (take 5) Released on *Opel*

14 July

'Love Song' (take 1) Released on *Barrett*
'Dominoes' (take 3) Released on *Barrett* (Drums: David Gilmour)
'Wined And Dined' (take 10) Released on *Barrett* (All Instruments: David Gilmour except Lead Guitar: Syd Barrett)
'Effervescing Elephant' (take 9) Released on *Barrett* (Tuba: Vic Saywell; Arrangement: David Gilmour)
'Love Song' (take 1) Released on *Barrett*
'Dominoes' (take 1) Released as bonus track on *Barrett*
'Dominoes' (take 2) Released as bonus track on *Barrett*
'Dolly Rocker' (take 1) Released on *Opel*
'Let's Split' (take 1) Released on *Opel*
'Effervescing Elephant' (take 2) Released on *Opel*

17 July

'Love Song' Released on *Barrett* (overdubs: July 14 version)
'It Is Obvious' Released on *Barrett* (overdubs: July 17 version) (second organ: David Gilmour)
'It Is Obvious' (take 2) Released as bonus track on *Barrett* (electric guitar and vocal only)
'Word Song' (take 1) Released on *Opel*
'It Is Obvious' (take 3) Released on *Opel* (electric guitar and vocal only)
'It Is Obvious; (take 5) Released on *Opel* (acoustic guitar and vocal only)

20 July

'It Is Obvious' Released on *Barrett* (overdubs: July 17 version) (second organ: David Gilmour)

November 14
Barrett released

16 February 1971
Bob Harris Show radio session

'Terrapin'
'Baby Lemonade'
'Dominoes'
'Love Song'

Studio T1, Kensington House, Shepherd's Bush

February 1972
Rehearsals of Stars were recorded by Barrett in his cellar. Tapes of the Dandelion Coffee Bar gig, the Market Square Gig and, most likely, the Corn Exchange gig are rumoured to exist.

Public Appearances

1953
Roger Barrett appears with his sister Rosemary in a piano recital, his first appearance on stage.

1962
Geoff Mott and the Mottoes played a benefit gig at Cambridge's Union Cellars for the Campaign for Nuclear Disarmament.
Geoff Mott and the Mottoes:
Geof Mott(low): vocals
Syd Barrett: rhythm guitar
Nobby Clarke: lead guitar
Tony Sainty: bass
Clive Welham: drums

1962-3
Barrett plays bass for various Cambridge bands, including the Hollering Blues.

1963
Barrett performs acoustic sessions with Dave Gilmour at 'The Mill', a pub on Mill Lane in Cambridge.

December 1964
Syd Barrett and Bob Close join the Abdabs. The Abdabs had been around since 1962-3, and had been known variously as The T-Set, Sigma 6, The Meggadeaths, The Architectural Abdabs, The Screaming Abdabs. The band had variously been comprised of Roger Waters (lead guitar), Clive Metcalfe (bass), Richard Wright (piano/organ), Nick Mason (drums), Juliette Gale (vocals) and Keith Noble (vocals). The Abdabs (with vocalist Chris Dennis) play a dance at the Regent Street Polytechnic and Beat City Club on Oxford Street.

2 January 1965
Syd performs with Those Without, in Cambridge - an impromptu band put together during Syd's school holiday, photographed on this date.

Spring
The Abdabs play at the 'Woodman' pub, Archway Road, Highgate, London. They are joined for a few performances by Mike Leonard, billing themselves Leonard's Lodgers. Waters said, 'We played together occasionally. We'd go out and do £10 gigs and play at people's parties, and we bought some gear and gradually got a bit more involved.' (*Disc & Music Echo*, 8 August 1970)

The Pink Floyd Sound play at the Sound and Light Workshops at the Hornsey College of Art.

August
Barrett and Gilmour busk while on holiday in the South of France. In San Tropez they are arrested.

November
Joker's Wild and The Pink Floyd Sound play at Storm Thorgerson's engagement party in Shelford, near Cambridge.

The Pink Floyd Sound play at Syd's alma mater, the College of Arts & Technology, Cambridge.

December
The Pink Floyd Sound play the Countdown Club, Palace Gate, Knightsbridge, London.

January 1966
The Goings-On Club, Archer Street, London.

30 January
First Spontaneous Underground, Marquee Club (though if The Pink Floyd Sound played on this date is not known).

13 March
The Spontaneous Underground ('TRIP': first definite Pink Floyd appearance)

27 March
The Spontaneous Underground ('Mad Hatter's Tea Party'), Church Hall, Bray, Berkshire.

April
The Spontaneous Underground.

May
The Spontaneous Underground (Jenner and King approach the band).

30 September
All Saints Church Hall, Powis Gardens, London ('London Free School Celebration Dance').

14 October
London Free School, All Saint's Church hall, Powis Gardens, London (8-11 pm).

15 October
Roundhouse, Chalk Farm, London (*International Times* launch)

21 October
All Saint's Hall.

23 October
All Saint's Hall.

25 October
All Saint's Hall.

29 October
All Saint's Hall.

4 November
All Saint's Hall.

5 November
Wilton Hall, Bletchley, Buckinghamshire.
Five Acre Nudist Colony, Watford.

8 November
All Saint's Hall.

11 November.
All Saint's Hall.

15 November.
All Saint's Hall.

18 November.
Hornsey Art College, London ('Philadelic Music for Simian Hominids').

19 November
Canterbury Technical College, Canterbury, Kent.

22 November
All Saint's Hall.

29 November
All Saint's Hall.

3 December
Roundhouse ('Psychedelia vs. Ian Smith, benefit in aid of Zimbabwe').

9 December
Marquee Club, 90 Wardour Street, Soho, London.

12 December
Royal Albert Hall, Oxfam, London ('You're Joking?' charity concert)

22 December
Marquee Club.

23 December
Blarney pub basement, 31 Tottenham Court Road, London. ('UFO Presents Night Tripper') and Roundhouse all-nighter. First appearance of Pink Floyd at UFO.

29 December
Marquee Club (with Syn)

30 December
UFO.

31 December
Roundhouse ('New Year's Eve All Night Rave').

1 January 1967
Marquee Club.

5 January
Marquee Club ('7:30-11pm with Eyes of Blue').

6 January
7:30 pm Seymour Hall, London, ('Freakout Ethel').
1:00 am UFO

8 January
Upper Cut, Forest Gate, London.

13 January
UFO ('The Return of the Dreaded UFO' with 'the monstrous Pink Floyd'. 'Gape at the film *Marilyn Monroe*, thrill to the Giant Sun Trolley, gasp at the horrible crawling slides!').

14 January
Reading University, Reading, Berkshire.

16 January
Institute of Contemporary Arts, Dover Street, London.

17 January
Commonwealth Institute, Kensington High Street, London ('Music in Colour' 8pm).

19 January
Marquee Club.

20 January
UFO (with 'Spectral Audio Olfactory')
('Interstellar Overdrive' filmed for 7 March *Scene at 6:30* Underground special *It's So Far Out, It's Straight Down!*)

21 January
Birdcage, Portsmouth, Hampshire.

27 January
UFO (with films by Dave Brown)

28 January
Essex University, Colchester, Essex.

2 February
Cadenna's, Guildford, Surrey.

3 February
Queen's Hall, Leeds, Yorkshire.

9 February
Addington Hotel, Croydon, Surrey.

10 February
Leicester, Leicestershire.

11 February
Sussex University, Brighton, Sussex

16 February
Guildhall, Southampton, Hampshire.

17 February
The Dorothy Ballroom, Cambridge.

18 February
California Ballroom, Dunstable, Bedfordshire.

20 February
Adelphi Ballroom, West Bromwich.

24 February
Ricky Tick Club, Windsor, Berkshire.
UFO ('The Return of the Invisible Pink Floyd').

25 February
Ricky-Tick Club, Hounslow, Middlesex.

28 February
Blaises Club, London.

1 March
Eel Pie Island, Richmond, Surrey.

2 March
Worthing, Sussex.

3 March
St. Albans, Hertfordshire.
UFO

4 March
The Polytechnic, Regent Street, London. ('Poly Rag Ball' – benefit for War on Want and Cancer Research).

5 March
Saville Theater, Shaftesbury Avenue, London.

6 March
The Rave television show, with The Move, Granada TV, Manchester.

7 March
Malvern, Worcestershire.

9 March
Marquee Club (7:30-11pm with The Thoughts).

10 March
UFO (advance screening of the Pink Floyd's film clip for 'Arnold Layne'; *See the Pink Floyd go pop!*).

11 March
Technical College, Canterbury, Kent.

12 March
Agincourt Ballroom, Camberley, Surrey.

16 March
Middle Earth, London.

17 March
Kingston Technical College, Kingston-Upon-Thames, Surrey.

18 March
Enfield College, Middlesex.

23 March
Rotherham, Yorkshire.
Doncaster, Yorkshire.

24 March
Ricky-Tick Club, Hounslow, Middlesex.

25 March
Ricky-Tick Club, Thames Hotel, Windsor, Berkshire.

26 March
Bognor Regis, Sussex.

28 March
Chinese R & B Jazz Club, Bristol Corn Exchange, Bristol, Somerset ('Easter Rave').

29 March
Eel Pie Island, Richmond, Surrey.

30 March
Ross-on-Wye, Herefordshire.

1 April
Birdcage, Portsmouth, Hampshire (EMI press reception at Manchester Square's EMI House).

3 April
Playhouse Theatre, Northumberland Avenue, London (BBC *Monday, Monday* live broadcast).

6 April
City Hall, Salisbury, Wiltshire.

7 April
Floral Hall, Belfast, Ireland.

8 April
Rhodes Centre, Bishops Stortford, Hertfordshire.
Roundhouse ('All night light show continuum' 10-dawn).

9 April
Britannia Club, Nottingham, Nottinghamshire.

10 April
Bath Pavilion, Bath, Somerset.

13 April
Railway Hotel, Tilbury, Essex.

14 April
Club a Go Go, Newcastle, Staffordshire.

15 April
The West Pier, Brighton, Sussex ('Brighton Festival').

16 April
Bethnal Green, London.

19 April
Bromley, Kent.

20 April
Barnstable, Devon.

21 April
Starlite, Greenford, Middlesex.
UFO ('Life is a Dream').

22 April
Rugby, Warwickshire.

23 April
Starlight Ballroom, High Street, Crawley, Sussex.

24 April
The Feathers Club, Ealing Broadway, London.

25 April
Oxford, Oxfordshire.

28 April
Stockport, Cheshire.

29 April
Appearance on *Fan Club* television show, The Netherlands.
Alexandra Palace, London ('14 Hour Technicolor Dream, *International Times* Free Speech benefit' – dawn gig).

30 April
Huddersfield, Yorkshire.

3 May
Ainsdale, Southport, Lancashire.

5 May
UFO (with Soft Machine and Crazy World of Arthur Brown).
Note: Press adverts bill Pink Floyd but they may not have played.

4 May
Coventry, Warwickshire.

6 May
Kitson Hall, Leeds, Yorkshire.

7 May
Sheffield, Yorkshire.

12 May
South Bank Queen Elizabeth Hall, London ('Games for May').
13 Hinkley, Leicestershire.

14 May
Look of the Week (alias *Late Night Up*) BBC 2, London.

19 May
Club a Go Go, Newcastle, Staffordshire.

20 May
Southport, Lancashire.

21 May
Brighton, Sussex.

23 May
Town Hall, High Wycombe, Buckinghamshire ('A Psychedelic Experience in Technicolor').

24 May
Bromley, Kent.

25 May
Abergavenny, Wales.

26 May
Blackpool, Lancashire.

27 May
Nantwich, Cheshire.

29 May
Tulip Bulb Auction Hall, Spalding, Lincolnshire.
('Barbeque '67' with Jimi Hendrix, The Move, Cream).

2 June
UFO ('All-nite intermedia: My watch stops, my radio is silent... but what do I care...at UFO?').

9 June
Hull, Yorkshire.
UFO

10 June
Lowestoft, Suffolk.

11 June
The Immage, Terneuzen, The Netherlands
Concertgebouw, Vlissingen, The Netherlands.

13 June
Blue Opera Club, The Feathers, Ealing Broadway, London.

16 June
Tiles Club, Oxford Street, London.

17 June
Margate, Kent.

18 June
Brands Hatch, Kent.

20 June
Oxford Summer Ball, Oxfordshire.

21 June
Bolton, Lancashire.

22 June
Bradford, Yorkshire.

23 June
Derby, Derbyshire.

24 June
Bedford, Bedfordshire.

26 June
Warwick University, Coventry, Warwickshire.

28 June
Eel Pie Island, Richmond, Surrey.

1 July
The Swan, Yardley, Birmingham.

2 July
The Civic Hall, Birmingham.

3 July
Bath, Somerset.

5 July
Eel Pie Island, Richmond, Surrey.

6 July
First appearance on *Top of the Pops*, BBC1 TV, London.

7 July
Portsmouth, Hampshire.
UFO.

8 July
Pathe News TV screening of *Scarecrow* promo film.
and Memorial Hall, Northwich, Cheshire.

9 July
Roundhouse (filmed by BBC-2 TV).

15 July
The Cricket Meadow, Stowmarket, Suffolk ('The Stowmarket Carnival Pop Show').

16 July
Redcar, Yorkshire.

17 July
Come Here Often? TV Show, ITV, Rediffusion Studios, London (16 June footage).

18 July
Isle of Man.

19 July
The Floral Hall, Gorleston, Great Yarmouth, Norfolk (filmed by BBC-2 TV)

20 July
Second appearance on *Top of the Pops*, BBC1 TV (filmed previously).
The Red Shoes, Elgin, Grampian, Scotland.

21 July
Nairn, Highland, Scotland.

22 July
Aberdeen, Grampian, Scotland.

23 July
Cosmopolitan Ballroom, Carlisle, Cumbria, Scotland (pirate Radio Carlisle broadcast).

24 July
Wellington Club, East Dereham, Norfolk.

27 July
Third appearance on *Top of the Pops*, BBC1 TV.

28 July
'Saturday Club' radio session at BBC Playhouse Theatre, London (cancelled). UFO.

29 July
Wellington Club, East Dereham, Norfolk.
Alexandra Palace, London ('International Love-In').

31 July
Torquay, Devon.

11 August
'The 7th National Jazz & Blues Festival' Windsor, Berkshire. (cancelled).

21 August
Speakeasy, London.

22 August
Olympia Exhibition Hall, Kensington.

1 September
UFO at the Roundhouse ('RIA Festival-benefit for Release').

2 September
UFO at the Roundhouse ('RIA Festival-benefit for Release').

10 September
Boom Dancing Center, Arhus, Denmark.

11 September
Star Club, Copenhagen, Denmark.

12 September
Star Club, Copenhagen, Denmark.

13 September
Star Club, Copenhagen, Denmark (recorded).

14 September
Gyllene Cirklem ('Golden Circle'), Stockholm, Sweden.

15 September
Starlight Ballroom, Belfast, Ireland.

16 September
Flamingo, Ballymena, Ireland.

17 September
Arcadia Ballroom, Cork, Ireland

21 September
The Pier, Worthing, Sussex.

22 September
Tiles Club, London (7:30pm-12am).
UFO, Roundhouse.

23 September
Corn Exchange, Chelmsford, Essex.

25 September
Playhouse Theatre, Northumberland Avenue (BBC *Top Gear* show recording date - broadcast 5 November).

27 September
5th Dimension, Leicester, Leicestershire 28
Skyline Club, Hull, Yorkshire.

30 September
Imperial Club, Nelson, Lancashire.

1 October
Sunday At The Saville, Saville Theatre, London.

5 October
Top Rank, Brighton, Sussex.

7 October
Victoria Rooms, Bristol, Somerset.

12 October
Oude Ahoy Hallen, Rotterdam, The Netherlands ('Hippy Happy Fair').

13 October
The Pavilion, Weymouth, Dorset.

14 October
Caesar's Palace, Dunstable, Bedfordshire.

16 October
The Pavilion, Bath, Somerset.

22 October
York, Yorkshire.

28 October
Dunelm House, Durham University Students' Centre, Durham University, Durham City.

First Tour of the United States

26-28 October
The Fillmore, San Francisco, California, (with Lee Michaels and Clearlight) (most likely cancelled).

30 October
Fillmore West, San Francisco, California (KPFA Benefit).

31 October
Pacific West High School, San Jose, California.

2 November
2 Fillmore West, San Francisco, California (with Janis Joplin and Richie Havens).

3 November
Winterland, San Francisco, California (with Janis

Joplin and Richie Havens).

4 November
Winterland, San Francisco, California (with Janis Joplin and Richie Havens).

5 November
The Pat Boone Show, Los Angeles, California.
The Cheetah Club, Santa Monica, California.

6 November
American Bandstand, ABC-TV, Hollywood, California.

9 November
Winterland, San Francisco, California (with Procul Harum and H.P. Lovecraft) (Most likely cancelled).

12 November
The Cheetah Club, New York.

13 November
Oude-Ahoy Hallen, Rotterdam, The Netherlands ('The Hippy Happy Fair') (recorded).

The Jimi Hendrix Experience tour with Pink Floyd, Move, Amen Corner, Nice, Eire Apparent and the Outer Limits

14 November
Royal Albert Hall, London ('The Alchemical Wedding').

15 November
Winter Gardens, Bournemouth, Hampshire (two shows).

17 November
City Hall, Sheffield, Yorkshire (two shows).

18 November
Empire Theatre, Liverpool, Lancashire (two shows).

19 November
Coventry Theatre, Nottingham, Nottinghamshire (two shows).

22 November
Guildhall, Portsmouth, Hampshire (two shows).

23 November
Sophia Gardens Pavilion, Cardiff, Glamorgan, Wales (two shows).

24 November
Colston Hall, Bristol, Somerset (two shows).

25 November
Opera House, Blackpool, Lancashire (two shows).

26 November
Palace Theatre, Manchester (two shows).

27 November
Whitla Hall, Queens College, Belfast, Ulster, Ireland (two shows) ('Festival of Arts').

1 December
Town Hall, Chatham, Kent (two shows).

2 December
The Dome, Brighton, Sussex (two shows).

3 December
Theatre Royal, Nottingham, Nottinghamshire (two shows).

4 December
City Hall, Newcastle-Upon-Tyne, Northumberland (two shows).

5 December
Green's Playhouse, Glasgow, Scotland (two shows) (last show of Hendrix tour).

9 December
Middle Earth Club, London.

13 December
Flamingo Club, Redruth, Cornwall.

14 December
Pavilion, Bournemouth, Hampshire.

15 December
Middle Earth Club, London.

16 December
Ritz Ballroom, Birmingham.

20 December
Maida Vale Studio 4, London (BBC *Top Gear* show recording date).

21 December
Speakeasy, London.

22 December
Grand and National Halls, Kensington Olympia, London ('Christmas on Earth Revisited').

12 January 1968
Aston University, Aston Clinton, Bucks (with David Gilmour now on rhythm guitar).

13 January
Winter Gardens Pavilion, Weston-Super-Mare, Avon ('Saturday Dance Date').

19 January
Lewes, Sussex.

20 January
Hastings, Sussex (Syd Barrett's final performance with the Pink Floyd).

Post-Syd Pink Floyd

26 January
Southampton, Hampshire (Barrett not picked up)

27 January
Leicester, Leicestershire

7 February
Mary Hopkins TV Show, Paris, France.

10 February
Nelson, Lancashire.

16 February
ICI Fibres Club, Pontypool, Monmouthshire.

On 18 February Gilmour announced as full member of Pink Floyd. On 2 March Blackhills Enterprises dissolved. On 6 April Syd Barrett officially leaves the band. On 6 May Barrett begins solo sessions at Abbey Road.

24 February 1970
Maida Vale 4 Studios, London (BBC *Top Gear* show recording date with David Gilmour, Jerry Shirley and Alan Styles).

6 June
The Olympia, London ('Music and Fashion Festival' with David Gilmour and Jerry Shirley).

16 February 1971
Studio T1, Transcription Service, Kensington House, Shepherd's Bush (BBC1 Radio - 'Whispering' Bob Harris Show recording date).

1972

2 January 1972

Kings College Cellar, Cambridge. Syd jams with Eddie Burns (guitar), Twink (drums) and Jack Monck (bass)

February
Corn Exchange, Cambridge. Syd joined Twink and Jack Monck in an impromptu jam with American singer and guitarist Bruce. A subsequent jam featured Syd, Twink, and Jack Monck backing Fred Frith.

Locale unknown. Syd plays guitar, backing Jack Bruce on stand-up bass and an unknown drummer at a jazz poetry gig with poet Pete Brown in attendance.

Dandelion Coffee Bar, Cambridge. Stars perform informally.

Market Square, Cambridge. Stars play an open-air gig.

24 February

Corn Exchange, Cambridge. Stars open for MC5 and Skin Alley. Syd's final performance.

(Sources: Miles & Mabbett, Vernon Fitch and the Pink Floyd Archives, Jon Rosenberg, Gerhard den Hollander, Malcolm Jones, Watkinson & Anderson, Nicholas Schaffner, Jack Monck, Pete Brown, and personal research of period newspapers in the National Sound Archive, Kensington, London)

Bibliography

Syd Barrett - A Fish Out of Water, Luca Ferrari and Annie Marie Roulin (Sonic Book 2, 1996, Italy)
Italian, with faulty English translation. Syd Barrett's life story, accompanied by photos, an interview with Barrett's sisters Rosemary Breen and Annie Marie Roulin, pictures of Syd's artwork, a good listing of Barrett-related resources and a discography. Includes a semi-legal 3″ CD with 31 October, 1966 versions of 'Lucy Leave' and Slim Harpo's 'King Bee'.

Syd Barrett - Crazy Diamond - Syd Barrett & the Dawn of Pink Floyd, Mike Watkinson and Pete Anderson (Omnibus Press, 1991)
An essential Barrett biography that covers Syd's Cambridge childhood and teenage years in greater detail than any other book. Provides a good introductory overview to Barrett's life and times with many interesting interviews, plus photos and discography.

Syd Barrett - The Making of The Madcap Laughs, Malcolm Jones (Orange Sunshine Press)
Malcolm Jones' exceptional account of the making of *The Madcap Laughs*, with detailed accounts of his period in the producer's chair. Also includes extensive session and tour listings. Privately issued and difficult to find, but well worth seeking.

Syd Barrett - Tatuato Sul Muro - L'Enigma di Syd Barrett, Luca Ferrari (Italian Rockbooks, 1986)
An Italian biography of Barrett, including some lyrics. An English translation *Where is the Madcap Called Syd Barrett?* (1994) is also available.

The British Invasion, Nicholas Schaffner (McGraw-Hill, 1982)
Schaffner, the late author of the definitive Pink Floyd biography, *A Saucerful of Secrets*, chronicles the British Beat boom from an American perspective. An exhaustive account with much period data and a section on Syd's Pink Floyd.

The Complete Guide to the Music of Pink Floyd, Andy Mabbett (Omnibus Press, 1995)
A small book with useful details on each Pink Floyd song.

The Dark Stuff - Selected Writings on Rock Music 1972-1993, Nick Kent (Penguin Books, 1994)
Includes Kent's classic Barrett article from 13 April 1974 *NME*, 'The Cracked Ballad of Syd Barrett'.

Days in the Life: Voices from the English Underground, 1961-1971, Jonathon Greene (Pimlico, 1997)
The definitive study of the English Undergound. The book is comprised of interviews with dozens of the people who made the sixties what it was, a profound turning point in society. Finding this book by chance in a Singapore Airport book shop, reading and re-reading it, spurred me on to come to England and write this biography on Syd Barrett, as well as meet many of the fascinating people profiled in this superb book.

Echoes - The Stories Behind Every Pink Floyd Song, Cliff Jones (Omnibus Press, 1996)
Though containing errors, an important study of every Pink Floyd song. Includes many interesting insights into the studio techniques used to make *The Piper at the Gates of Dawn.* Notable for its objective account of Barrett's story, and a solid analysis of his time in the band, with fascinating insights from Jenner and King among others.

Gong Dreaming - Soft Machine 66-69, Daevid Allen (GAS, 1994)
Daevid Allen of the Soft Machine, and later Gong, provides an interesting look into the zeitgeist of the sixties. Of particular interest is his account of the '14-Hour Technicolor Dream' and the Pink Floyd's performance there.

Groupie, Jenny Fabian with Johnny Byrne (Omnibus Press, 1997)
Originally published in 1970 and just reprinted, *Groupie* is Jenny Fabian's autobiographical account of her days as consort to the famous, as well as her myriad adventures underground. A vivid narrative highlights the fact that Fabian remains a sharp-witted writer with often startling insights. The chapter on 'Satin Odyssey' (alias Pink Floyd) and the disintegration of 'Ben' (alias Syd) is essential reading for any Barrett enthusiast.

Kaleidoscope Eyes - Psychedelic Rock From the '60s to the '90s, Jim DeRogatis (Citadel Press, 1996)
A noble attempt to trace the myriad paths of psychedelia from its inception to modern times. DeRogatis skilfully takes us from UFO, 'Strawberry Fields Forever', The Thirteenth Floor Elevators all the way to Flaming Lips, My Bloody Valentine and The Cocteau Twins.

Learning to Fly, Chris Welch (Castle Communications, 1994)

Despite errors and a singularly hideous layout, Chris Welch, formerly of the *Melody Maker*, provides interesting glimpses into his interviews with Syd Barrett and first-hand accounts of UFO (Welch was the first mainstream journalist to report on UFO), and of Pink Floyd at the Marquee in 1966, via the recollections of Tony Banks (ex-Yes).

Oceans of Sound, David Toop (Serpent's Tail, 1995)
A superb study of ambient (in the broadest sense) music. From Debussy's encounter with Balinese 'gamelan' in 1889 to AMM, Pink Floyd and modern day composers such as Goldie and Kevin Shields, this is a remarkable history of the sort of music Barrett's quieter excursions hinted at.

A Photographic Record 1969-1980, Mick Rock (Century 22 Limited, 1995) Photographer Mick Rock's photo-journal features photographs from the famous *The Madcap Laughs* session as well as his 1971 *Rolling Stone* profile of Syd in Cambridge.

Pink Floyd, Rick Sanders (Futura Publications,1976)
Despite Sanders' anti-Barrett bias, this out-of-print book contains a few interesting sidelong glimpses at Barrett's period in the band.

Pink Floyd: The Visual Documentary, Miles and Andy Mabbett (Omnibus Press, 1994)
A classic Pink Floyd book, Miles and Mabbett trace the development of Pink Floyd day by day from 1965 to 1994. Many photos of Barrett and Pink Floyd that cannot be found elsewhere, as well as a comprehensive discography and essential tour dates information. A must-have.

Revolution in the Head - The Beatles Records and the Sixties, Ian MacDonald (Pimlico, 1995)
A fascinating study of the Beatles' songs, track by track. Contains a handful of references to Pink Floyd, but more noted for its superb evocation of the sixties as well as its in-depth analysis of the Beatles' music and influences. A model for all music writers and self-proclaimed 'pop historians'.

The Madcap Laughs: The Mick Rock Photo Sessions, Mick Rock (UFO Books)
Mick Rock's photo session for *The Madcap Laughs*. Dozens of photos from that session at Barrett and Fields' Earl's Court Square flat that Rock himself described as 'magical'.

Saucerful of Secrets - the Pink Floyd Odyssey, Nicholas Schaffner (Harmony, 1991)
The definitive Pink Floyd biography. The first half deals with Pink Floyd through 1968 and has a plethora of facts about Syd Barrett. A comprehensive overview of the band. Essential.

Space Daze - The History and Mystery of Electronic Ambient Space Rock, Dave Thompson (Cleopatra, 1994)
Traces the development of Space Rock, and addresses Barrett's leading role in defining its parameters (or absence thereof).

Through the Eyes of . . . The Band, its Fans, Friends and Foes, Bruno MacDonald, ed. (Sidgwick and Jackson, 1996)
Compendium of articles written on Pink Floyd over the past 30 years. Also contains a song-by-song breakdown with relevant quotes from the band and associates.

Wish You Were Here *Songbook* (VF 4022, 1975)
Contains a revealing interview with Roger Waters by Nicholas Schaffner.

Wrong Movements – A Robert Wyatt History, Michael King (SAF Publishing Ltd., 1994)
Robert Wyatt of The Soft Machine, and his life and times. Includes passages on *The Madcap Laughs* sessions.

The I-Ching or Book Of Changes, Wilhelm R., ed and Baynes C. F., trans (Princeton University Press, 1967)

Articles

The Amazing Pudding, #46-50
Mabbett & MacDonald's Pink Floyd fanzine, sadly out of print.

Beat Instrumental, October 1967
'Guitarist of the Month' - Interview with Syd Barrett.

Beat Instrumental, May 1971
Interview with Syd Barrett by Steve Turner.

Circus Magazine, September 1972

'Obscured by Clouds' - Interview with Roger Waters.

Dark Side of the Moon Japanese CD edition liner notes
Interview with Roger Waters by Michael Wale.

Disc & Music Echo, 25 March 1967, 8 April 1967, 22 July 1967, 8 August 1970

Financial Times, May 1967

Go, 4 August 1967

Guitar Player, November 1984
'Pink Floyd and beyond' - Interview with David Gilmour by T. Mulhern.

Guitar World, September 1994
David Gilmour and Tim Renwick interviews by Brad Tolinski.

Harpers & Queen, November 1996
'Peter Whitehead' by Jenny Fabian.

Interview Magazine, July 1994
'The Color Of Floyd' - Interview with David Gilmour by Graham Fuller.

IT (*The International Times*)
IT was the house organ of the psychedelic Underground, and still makes for startling reading 30 years on. A complete collection is available for research at the Victoria and Albert Museum collection in London. Also worth looking for are back copies of *OZ*, the Australian-led satiric journal of the Underground. Copies fetch upwards of £10-30, and contain a stunning graphic layout.

Melody Maker, 14 January 1967

Melody Maker, 5 August 1967
'The Great Pink Floyd Mystery' - Interview with Roger Waters by Chris Welch.

Melody Maker, 12 August 1967

Melody Maker, 9 September 1967

Melody Maker, 9 December 1967
'Hits? The Floyd Couldn't Care Less' - Interview with Syd Barrett, Roger Waters and Peter Jenner by Alan Walsh.

Melody Maker, 5 December 1970

Melody Maker, 27 March 1971
'The Madcap Laughs' - Interview with Syd Barrett by Michael Watts.

Melody Maker, 31 January 1970
Interview with Syd Barrett.

Melody Maker, 19 May 1973

Mojo, May 1994
'The Third Coming' - Interviews with Pink Floyd by Robert Sandall.

Mojo, July 1995
'The 30 Year Technicolor Dream' - Interviews with Pink Floyd by Phil Sutcliffe.

Mojo, June 1996
'Syd Barrett' article by Cliff Jones.

Musician, December 1982
Pink Floyd' - Interview with David Gilmour by David Fricke.

Musician, August 1988
'Repent, Pink Floyd idolators! British hordes invade American heartland' - Interviews with Pink Floyd by Nicholas Schaffner.

Musician, May 1992
Interview with Roger Waters.

Musician, August 1992
'Careful With That Axe' - Interview with David Gilmour by Matt Resnicoff.

Musician, December 1992
'Roger and Me – The Other Side of the Pink Floyd Story' - Interview with Roger Waters by Matt Resnicoff.

NME, 5 August 1967
'Pink Floyd Flake Out'

NME, 7 October 1967

NME, 13 April 1974
'The Cracked Ballad of Syd Barrett' by Nick Kent. An essential article and the cornerstone of the Barrett myth.

NME, 23 November 1974

NME, 11 January 1975

NME, 9 July 1988
Interview with Pink Floyd.

Penthouse, September 1988
Interview with Roger Waters.

Q Magazine, November 1992
'Who the hell does Roger Waters think he is?' - Interview with Tom Hibbert.

Q Magazine, December 1992
'Daily Departures from Reality' - Interview with Storm Thorgerson.

Record Collector,1993
Interview with Peter Whitehead by Mark Paytress.

Record Mirror, 8 July 1967

Rock Compact Disc Magazine, September 1992
Interview with David Gilmour by Matt Resnicoff.

Rolling Stone, December 1971
'The Madcap Who Named Pink Floyd' – Mick Rock's brilliant article on Syd Barrett, whom he visited in Cambridge in late 1971 to conduct what became Barrett's last major interview.

Rolling Stone, June 1987
Interview with Roger Waters by Chris Salewicz.

Rolling Stone, August 1996
Interview with Rick Wright by Mark Blake.

Rolling Stone, 19 November 1987
Interviews with Roger Waters, David Gilmour and Nick Mason.

San Francisco Examiner , 4 December 1966
'Making the Rounds of Way-Out London' by Kenneth Rexroth.

Sounds, 17 August 1974

Sounds, May 1983
'The rise of Pink Floyd and the decline of Syd Barrett' – Interview with David Gilmour by David Sinclair.

Sunday Times, 30 October 1966
Interviews with Roger Waters and Andrew King.

Terrapin, (fanzine of the 'Syd Barrett Appreciation Society') #9/10, July 1974. Previously unpublished Giovanni Dadomo interview with Syd Barrett from 1970.

Terrapin, #17, 1975
Contains an interview with Syd Barrett.

Trouser Press, February 1978
'Syd Barrett Careening Through Life' by Kris DiLorenzo. Arguably the best article written on Syd Barrett. A detailed analysis written with due respect and authorative research and interviews.

ZigZag, July 1973
'Any Colour You Like' – Interview with Roger Waters and Nick Mason. Essential interview with the Pink Floyd rhythm section, who talk extensively about the origins of the band and Barrett's tenure in it.

Internet Sources

'Hashish Fudge: Soma and the Wootton Report' by Steve Abrams.

The Echoes FAQ (Frequently Asked Questions)
The guidebook of the Internet Pink Floyd 'Echoes' mailing list. Detailed and useful, updated periodically. To get the 5 parts of the FAQ, send e-mail to: echoserv@fawnya.tcs.com, and write the following, lowercase and left-justified:
send echoes.faq.3.0 echoes
send echoes.faq.3.1 echoes
send echoes.faq.3.2 echoes
send echoes.faq.3.3 echoes
send echoes.faq.3.4 echoes quit

Ian Barrett interview with Rob Peets
Rob Peet's 'Set the Controls' web site is a superb site, with interviews, discography, photos, articles and rich graphics designed by Peets. (http://www.mtnlake.com/~robp/syd1.html)

'The Madcap Loved' by Elisa Roney
An analysis of the themes of love (lost and regained) on *The Madcap Laughs*.

Television Sources

Danish television interviews with Nick Mason and David Gilmour, 1992

Dancing in the Streets, BBC series, 1996
BBC's history of rock included an episode on psychedelia, with an interview with Roger Waters, talking about the band's early days and the ill-fated American tour. Contains the only commercially available footage of the Pink Floyd on *American Bandstand*, with Syd Barrett staring penetratingly into the camera.

MTV News at Nite, 24 November 1992
Interviews with David Gilmour and Roger Waters.

Omnibus special on Pink Floyd, 1994
Contains many interviews with band members and key sixties players.

Radio Sources

Candian Broadcasting Company, February 1967
Interview with Pink Floyd (primarily Syd Barrett and Roger Waters) and Peter Jenner.

The Pink Floyd Story, Capital Radio, London 17 December 1976-January 1977
Six-part documentary series.

Shades of Pink, from *The Source* radio show, 1984
Interviews with Pink Floyd by Charlie Kendall.

Influences

Literary:

Belloc, Hilaire, *Cautionary Verses*
The opening story 'Matilda' provided 'Matilda Mother' with both title and original lyrics. Other Belloc characters appear in Barrett songs such as 'Effervescing Elephant'. A marked Barrett influence.

Carroll, Lewis, *Alice's Adventures Underground* and *Through The Looking Glass*
A key early influence on Barrett's thought, with its emphasis on surrealism and its alternately playful and phantasmagoric characters and scenarios.

Grahame, Kenneth, *The Wind in the Willows*
The title of the Pink Floyd's *The Piper at the Gates of Dawn* is drawn from a chapter in this book. Perhaps the very touchstone to understanding the intricacies of Barrett's work. The characters, the duality between the frightening Wild Wood and the idyllic river, and the lush language Grahame utilises are all key Barrett influences. A must-read for all Barrett enthusiasts.

Lear, Edward, *Complete Nonsense*
Mirrors the more playful side of Barrett's compositions, and was influential in its dense, rich abstractions of language. The bending of words for effect and rhythm that is found throughout Barrett's oeuvre is inspired by these limericks.

Lewis, C.S., *The Narnia Chronicles*
With its wardrobe as a portal into another world, Lewis' seven books helped point the way for such Barrett songs as 'Flaming' and 'Scarecrow'. The underlying currents of fear evoked by the White Witch and her dominion are something Barrett seized upon at once, and his songs echo the mysteries of Lewis' dark woods.

Joyce, James, *Chamber Music*
'Golden Hair', a poem contained in this book, is used nearly verbatim as the lyrics for Barrett's 1969 song of the same name.

Shakespeare, William, *Henry VI*
The character of the Talbot is name-checked in 'Octopus' and may have inspired some of its lyrical content.

Tolkein, J.R.R., *The Lord of the Rings* and *The Hobbit*
A seminal Barrett influence, *The Hobbit* directly inspired the writing of Barrett's 'The Gnome', with its 'no-name grimble gromble'. Barrett's song 'Dark Globe' draws its title from a page of the *Lord of the Rings*, and the deeply engrossing world of sorcerers, gnomes, goblins and trolls depicted by Tolkein was a Barrett favourite throughout his youth.

Milne, A.A., *Winnie the Pooh*
A children's classic with its panoply of innocuous characters such as Christopher Robin, Eeyore and Pooh.

Chaucer, Geoffrey, *The Canterbury Tales*
Like *Henry the VI*, may have inspired some of the lyrical content or format of 'Octopus', as Barrett implied in an interview. Certainly, as with Shakespeare, he read the book when younger.

Musical:

1946-1954

Nursery Rhymes, Children's Songs & Traditional Folk Songs
(With corresponding Barrett songs they may have influenced)

'Sing A Song of Sixpence': 'Matilda Mother', 'Bike'
'Oranges and Lemons': 'Apples and Oranges'
'Twinkle Twinkle Little Star': 'Interstellar Overdrive'
Brahm's 'Lullaby': 'Flaming'
'London Bridge is Falling Down': 'See Emily Play'
'Green Grow the Rushes, Ho!': 'Octopus', 'Clowns And Jugglers'

Dancehall 78's from the 1930s.

These albums, probably his mother's, would prove influential in Barrett's development of uptempo songs such as 'The Gnome', 'Love You', and particularly 'Here I Go', which is a direct tribute/parody of songs from that era. Popular artists of the time included Billy Cotton, George Formby, Jack Hylton and his Orchestra, Henry Hall and Louis Terry and his Gaumont-British Symphony. They are vastly entertaining records worth remembering.

Gilbert & Sullivan operettas.

The final vocal coda in 'Bike', as well as Barrett and Rick Wright's harmonies on *Piper at the Gates of Dawn*, suggest Barrett had both knowledge and appreciation of the works of Gilbert & Sullivan, such as *The Pirates of Penzance.*

1954-56

Lonnie Donegan 'Rock Island Line' (1954)
Lonnie Donegan's adaptation of American folk singer Leadbelly's song sparked the fad for skiffle, the first teen craze in Britain. Though Barrett was bit young, his elder brother formed part of a skiffle band, and Barrett was exposed to the music.

1957-59

Bill Haley 'Rock Around the Clock' (1956 - arrived in UK 1957)
With its inclusion in the film *Blackboard Jungle*, Britain's teenagers lost their collective minds upon hearing this song, causing riots in cinemas. The Teds, the UK's first notable youth subculture were particularly galvanised by early rock and roll.

Buddy Holly 'That'll Be The Day' (1958)
Barrett and friends use to 'jam' to Buddy Holly songs in the late 1950s. Chuck Berry and Little Richard were also Barrett favourites, including Richard's 'Tutti Frutti' and Berry's 'Maybellene'.

Bo Diddley *Bo Diddley* (1958) *Have Guitar Will Travel* (1959)
A key Barrett influence, and one who provided much of his basic inspiration between 1960-66. Diddley's distinctive rhythms form the bedrock of Barrett's playing, and Diddley's songs remained in Pink Floyd's repertoire until late 1966. Diddley's Telecaster staccato riffs were adopted by Barrett and altered significantly.

1960-62

Ventures 'Walk, Don't Run' (1960)
Barrett's 'Matilda Mother' adapts the central riff of this guitarist's favourite. The Ventures were also influential for the heavy echo on the guitars used in their instrumentals.

Jimmy Smith 'Back at the Chicken Shack' (1960)
Storm Thorgerson stated that jazz/R&B organist Jimmy Smith was a favourite among their group of friends, Barrett included, during the early 1960s.

Shadows 'Apache' b/w 'Quatermaster's Stores' (single 1960)
'The Shadows to the Fore' (EP 1961)
The Shadows (1961)
Barrett and Gilmour both endlessly practiced Shadows instrumentals. They both owe a debt to Hank Marvin's guitar style, particularly his use of echo. Traces of Marvin's style can be found in Barrett songs such as 'Swan Lee', as well on his final 1974 recording session, where he reverted to basic Marvin-style riffs.

Yusef Lateef 'Eastern Sounds' (1961)
Barrett probably heard this in 1965 at Mike Leonard's Highgate house, where there is a copy in the library. Lateef's jazz and world music blend perhaps influenced Barrett in his use of Eastern modal tonalities.

Jimmy Reed 'Bright Lights, Big City' (1961)
Barrett performed this song while with The Mottoes.

Booker T. and the MG's 'Green Onions' (1962)
Barrett cited guitarist Steve Cropper as an early influence, and Cropper's distinctive, clean Telecaster riffs

and leads inform Barrett's playing throughout his career.

The Beatles 'Love Me Do' (1962)
Barrett was the first to catch onto the Beatles among his friends in Cambridge. John Lennon was Barrett's favourite Beatle.

Bob Dylan *Bob Dylan* (1962)
Barrett and Gilmour both attended Dylan's first major show in Britain. Dylan provided a song-writing model, with his extended and alternately hyper-realistic and surrealistic narratives.

John Coltrane *Coltrane* (1962)
Barrett named the cat in Leonard's Highgate house 'Tunji', after a track that appears on this Coltrane album. Coltrane's groundbreaking use of stacked chords and 'sheets of sound' soloing was a Barrett inspiration.

Classical works by Leos Janacek, Olivier Messiaen and Bela Bartok, 'Das Rheingold' by Wagner, and others.
These were various LP's that Peter Whitehead played when Barrett and friends were practicing in the next room at Peter Mitchells' house (1962). Certain passages in 'Interstellar Overdrive' and other extended instrumentals would suggest Barrett had more than cursory knowledge of classical music, particularly of Wagner and his epic flourishes and *sturm und drang*. Barrett's father performed in a local symphony and was a classical music enthusiast, implying there were many classical albums at hand at 183, Hills Road.

1963-64

Bob Dylan *Freewheelin' Bob Dylan* (1963), *Times They Are A-Changin'* (1964), *Another Side of Bob Dylan* (1964)

The Beatles *With the Beatles* (1963), *Hard Day's Night* (1964), *Beatles For Sale* (1964)

Davy Graham 'The Thamesiders and Davy Graham' EP (1963)
Contains 'She Moves Through the Fair', a traditional English song which Graham played with Indian overtones, vastly influential on acoustic guitarists of the era.
Folk, Blues and Beyond (1964)
A stunning blend of folk, jazz, blues, Moroccan traditional music and Indian ragas

The Kinks 'You Really Got Me' (1964), 'All Day and All of the Night' (1964)
Notable for their advanced use of distortion and Dave Davies' crunching fuzz box riffs.

The Beatles 'I Feel Fine' (1964)
Notable for its use of feedback in the intro, indicative of the growing experimentalism among British guitarists in the mid-1960s. Barrett always had a keen ear for feedback, distortion and noise, and helped pioneer its use in rock music.

1965

Bob Dylan *Bringing It All Back Home* (March 1965), *Highway 61 Revisited* (August 1965)

The Who 'Anyway, Anyhow, Anywhere' (1965)
A key Barrett influence, with its heavily distorted glissando effects and Morse-code blips in its central 'freak-out' section.

John Coltrane *Om* (1965)
A Barrett favourite while living at Earlham Street in 1966-67, according to Cliff Jones.

Beatles *Help!* (1965), *Rubber Soul* (1965)
Barrett and Gilmour busked around the South of France playing songs from the *Help!* album.

1966

Byrds *5D* (Fifth Dimension)' (1966)
'Eight Miles High' was a pivotal Barrett influence, and its fade-out riff appears in Pink Floyd's 'Candy and a Currant Bun'. 'I Come and Stand at Every Door' probably laid some of the framework for Pink Floyd's 'Flaming'.

The Incredible String Band *The Incredible String Band* (1966)
Influential for its mix of traditional folk and odd instrumentation, as well as Heron and Williamson's vocal stylings.

The Butterfield Blues Band 'East/West' (1966)
Critical in Barrett's development of Pink Floyd's extended improvisations was 'East/West', a 13-minute jazz/blues meld based on Indian raga scales. In a December 1967 BBC session, Barrett clearly plays a Bloomfield lick on 'Pow R. Toc H.'

Rolling Stones *Aftermath* (1966)
A Barrett favourite, this album's faux-Elizabethan 'Lady Jane' and 11-minute blues jam 'Goin' Home' paved the way for *Piper at the Gates of Dawn*'s similar use of 'Interstellar Overdrive' and structured short songs. 'Paint It Black' influenced Barrett's use of gloomy minor chords and menacing vocals.

Yardbirds 'Shapes of Things' (1966)
Jeff Beck's masterful solo, a blend of flamenco, blues, noise and raga, produced arguably Britain's first overtly psychedelic song.

Bob Dylan *Blonde on Blonde* (May 1966)

The Fugs *The Fugs* (1966)
Barrett bought a copy of this album at Miles' Indica bookstore in 1966, and later cited its influence in interviews.

Love *Love* (1966)
Peter Jenner humming Barrett the central riff of Love's cover of Burt Bacharach's 'Little Red Book' led to Barrett's proto-metal riff in 'Interstellar Overdrive'. Arthur Lee's blend of musical moods was also influential.

The Kinks 'Sunny Afternoon' (1966)
Influential on Barrett's more uptempo and playful songs, such as 'The Gnome' and 'Here I Go'.

Frank Zappa & The Mothers of Invention *Freak Out!* (1966)
Barrett cited this album in an interview, stating that he had 'taken quite a lot' from this band as well as the Byrds and Fugs.

The Beatles *Revolver* (1966)

Donovan 'Sunshine Superman' (1966)

Cream 'I Feel Free' (1966)
Notable for the duality of its hard rhythm and poetic lyric.

Luigi Nono *Per Bastiana Tai-Yang Cheng*, Karlheinz Stockhausen *Hymnen*
Barrett may have been exposed to these modern composers during 1966. The more intellectually oriented of the Underground were exposed to works such as these at the Indica Bookstore and in the pages of *IT*.

1967

AMM *AMMusic* (1967)
Recorded in June 1966, AMM's Keith Rowe was arguably Barrett's most important influence of all, opening the door for his experiments and developing techniques which Barrett adapted.

The Rolling Stones *Between the Buttons* (1967)
Peter Jenner earmarked this album as a strong Barrett influence.

'Strawberry Fields Forever' backed with 'Penny Lane' (1967)
'Strawberry Fields Forever' marked the way for Barrett in its revolutionary use of poetic images and superb psychedelic arrangement. It was released just ten days before the sessions for 'Arnold Layne', which bears its influence.

The Kinks 'Waterloo Sunset' (1967)

The Incredible String Band 'The 5000 Spirits Or The Layers Of The Onion' (1967)

Jimi Hendrix Experience *Are You Experienced?* (1967)
Barrett had already been performing 'Interstellar Overdrive' for several months prior to Hendrix's arrival in September 1966. It is probable that Barrett and Hendrix influenced each other equally. Hendrix caught Pink Floyd live at UFO in December 1966 and toured extensively with them in late 1967.

Beatles *Sergeant Pepper's Lonely Heart's Club Band* (1967)

Crazy World of Arthur Brown 'Fire' (1967)

Arthur Brown's sense of showmanship, ominous vocals and his band's rhythmic intensity were likely Pink Floyd influences.

Soft Machine *Soft Machine* (1967)
Contemporaries (and competitors) of Pink Floyd, Soft Machine's jazz/rock improvisations were as influential to Barrett as his work was to them, particularly to Daevid Allen and Kevin Ayers, who both adapted Barrett's glissando technique.

1968-71

Taj Mahal, Ma Rainey, Family, Slade

In interviews during 1970-71, Barrett stated he had been listening to albums by these artists. The blues stylings of Rainey and Mahal come through clearest on the stripped down acoustic blues of 'Long Gone' from *The Madcap Laughs* and the throwaway blues pastiche 'Maisie' from *Barrett*. During 1971 Barrett often went around town dressed in the stacked-heel boots and mullter haircut associated with glam bands like Slade. By that time, though, Barrett was in his musical twilight. It was ironic that Barrett took to dressing in the accoutrements of the glam rockers, who were in a sense Barrett's progeny, both musically and in their fashions.

Index